THE LATER PREHISTORY
OF EASTERN AND SOUTHERN AFRICA

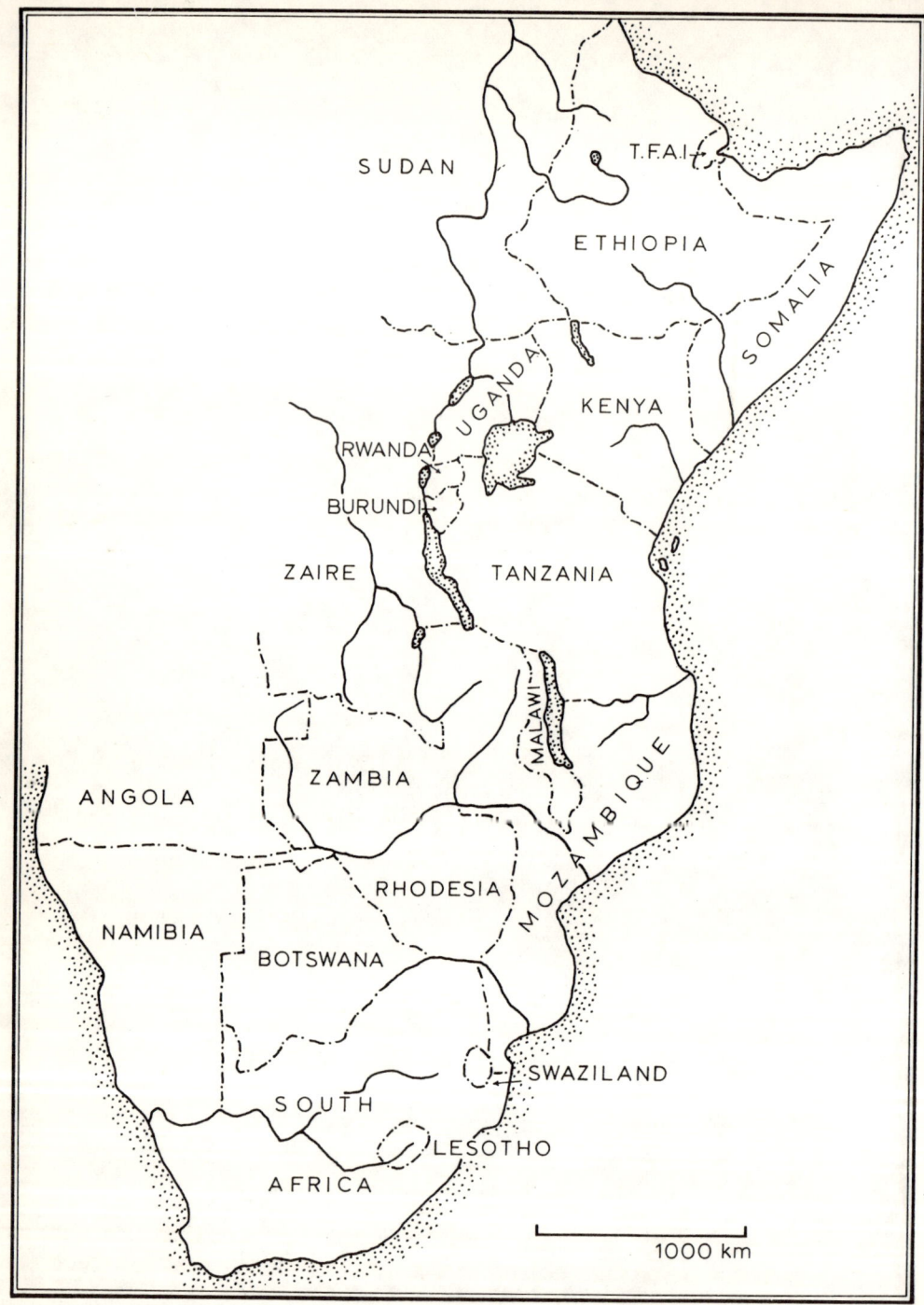

Frontispiece   Eastern and southern Africa, showing the general area discussed in this book

The Later Prehistory
of Eastern and Southern Africa

D. W. PHILLIPSON

Assistant Director, British Institute in Eastern Africa

LONDON
HEINEMANN
IBADAN . NAIROBI . LUSAKA

Heinemann Educational Books Ltd
48 Charles Street, London W1X 8AH
P.M.B. 5205 Ibadan · P.O. Box 45314 Nairobi
P.O. Box 3966 Lusaka

EDINBURGH MELBOURNE TORONTO AUCKLAND KINGSTON
SINGAPORE HONG KONG KUALA LUMPUR NEW DELHI

ISBN 0 435 94750 8 (cased)
        0 435 94751 6 (paper)

Filmset in Monophoto Ehrhardt 10 point
by Northumberland Press Ltd, Gateshead, Tyne and Wear
and printed in Great Britain by Richard Clay (The Chaucer Press) Ltd,
Bungay, Suffolk

Contents

List of Maps and Figures

List of Plates

Preface

To the outsider, the richness of Africa's prehistoric past often comes as a surprise. The Africanist historian, having in recent years disposed of the view that his subject began with the coming of European explorers and colonists, is still hampered by the shallow time-depth of much of his source-material. Conventional historical studies, whether based upon the study of written documents or upon the interpretation of oral traditions, often seem to skate over the surface of the African past. The aim of this book is to summarize our present knowledge of the prehistory of eastern and southern Africa during the last twenty thousand years, up to the time when history takes over. The sources used are primarily archaeological, although considerable use is also made of linguistic and ethnographic data, oral traditions and written records.

The geographical region here covered (Fig. 1) has, of necessity, been defined somewhat arbitrarily. It includes most of the Sudanese Nile valley, the whole of eastern Africa lying to the east of the equatorial forest, the eastern half of the southern savannah, and the whole of the area to the south of the Zambezi–Kuene line. There is no single factor which sets this region apart from the rest of the continent of which it is an integral part: the region has been chosen more on account of the availability of relevant data, and my own familiarity with it. To attempt a synthesis on this level of detail for most other parts of Africa would, at the present time, be premature. I have not hesitated to extend the area considered in connexion with particular topics, where this appeared necessary to achieve a coherent account.

There is often a tendency in studies of African archaeology to regard the more elaborate cultures centred on Meroe, Axum and parts of the East African coast as in some way separate from their less complex neighbours. In this book I have tried to rectify the balance, and to set both literate and preliterate societies in an appropriate perspective. If more space is given to, for example, the Early Iron Age Bantu-speaking communities than to the Kingdom of Axum, it is because of the greater long-term significance of the former to the mainstream of African prehistory.

In an inter-regional study such as this, questions of chronology are of great importance. In this book I have followed the now widespread convention whereby dates in radiocarbon years, or age-estimates based on uncorrected radiocarbon dates, are expressed in years bc or ad. Calendar years are quoted BC or AD.

My understanding of the subject here described is the result of twelve years spent working on prehistoric studies in eastern and southern Africa, first as Secretary/Inspector to the National Monuments Commission of Zambia, and latterly as Assistant Director of the British Institute in Eastern Africa. During this time, in addition to conducting fieldwork and excavations in Zambia, Kenya and Ethiopia, I have travelled to visit sites and museums in many of the countries which lie between Cape Town and Asmara. Consequently, my first debt is to my many friends and colleagues in African prehistoric research who have aided my understanding of numerous problems through discussion, correspondence, conference papers and publications. My wife, Laurel, has been of constant assistance during the writing of this book, and has made many valuable suggestions on the manuscript. The drawings I owe to Mr John Nyakure Ochieng'.

D. W. PHILLIPSON
Nairobi
26 October 1976

I

❧❧❧❧❧❧❧❧❧❧❧❧❧❧❧❧❧❧❧❧❧❧❧❧❧❧❧❧❧❧❧❧❧❧❧❧

Introductory background

The eastern and southern parts of Africa contain an enormously varied range of physical environments – from snow-topped glaciated mountains to papyrus and mangrove swamps, from lush fertile highlands to arid rocky deserts. Few of these environments are not exploited by man, and consequently many and varied are the human cultures which are traditionally practised and which, to an often surprising extent, have so far survived the insidious advance of so-called development. This book is concerned primarily with unravelling the prehistoric past of the peoples of eastern and southern Africa: it is appropriate therefore to begin with a brief outline account of these peoples, their languages, cultures and economies, as they have been seen in recent times against the backcloth of their physical surroundings.

THE PHYSICAL ENVIRONMENT

The greater part of eastern and southern Africa consists of plateau country at between 2000 and 3000 metres above sea level. The coastal plain, which may be regarded as being delineated by the 200-metre contour, is generally remarkably narrow, extending inland usually for less than 50 and often for less than 20 kilometres. In only two areas does the coastal plain reach major dimensions: in southern Somalia and the adjacent part of the north Kenya coast, and in Mozambique south of the Zambezi mouth, where it reaches a maximum width of some 350 kilometres (Fig. 2). The three areas of greatest relief are the Ethiopian highlands, the East African volcanoes and Rift Valley highlands, and the Drakensberg and associated mountain ranges in eastern South Africa and Lesotho. Here, altitudes of over 3000 metres are attained, with Mounts Kilimanjaro and Kenya reaching over 5000 metres above the sea.

The more detailed physical geography is best summarized from north to south. In Ethiopia the rugged highlands are cut off from the rest of the world by precipitous escarpments on all sides except the south-east, where the plateau country around Harar slopes down more gently to the plains of the Ogaden, drained mainly by the tributaries of the Webi Shebelle. In Shoa and Gojjam, in central Ethiopia, are fertile high-altitude grasslands; but to the west these are cruelly bisected by the deep gorges of the Blue Nile and its many tributaries, the waters of which have cut as much as 2000 metres into the plateau, carrying – as they have done for tens of thousands of years – the fertile soil of Ethiopia down to the desert lowlands of the Sudan and Egypt. In northern Ethiopia, beyond the fantastic fastness of the Simien Mountains, the more arid plains of Tigre are similarly rent by the Takazze gorge which leads to the Atbara, another tributary of the Nile.

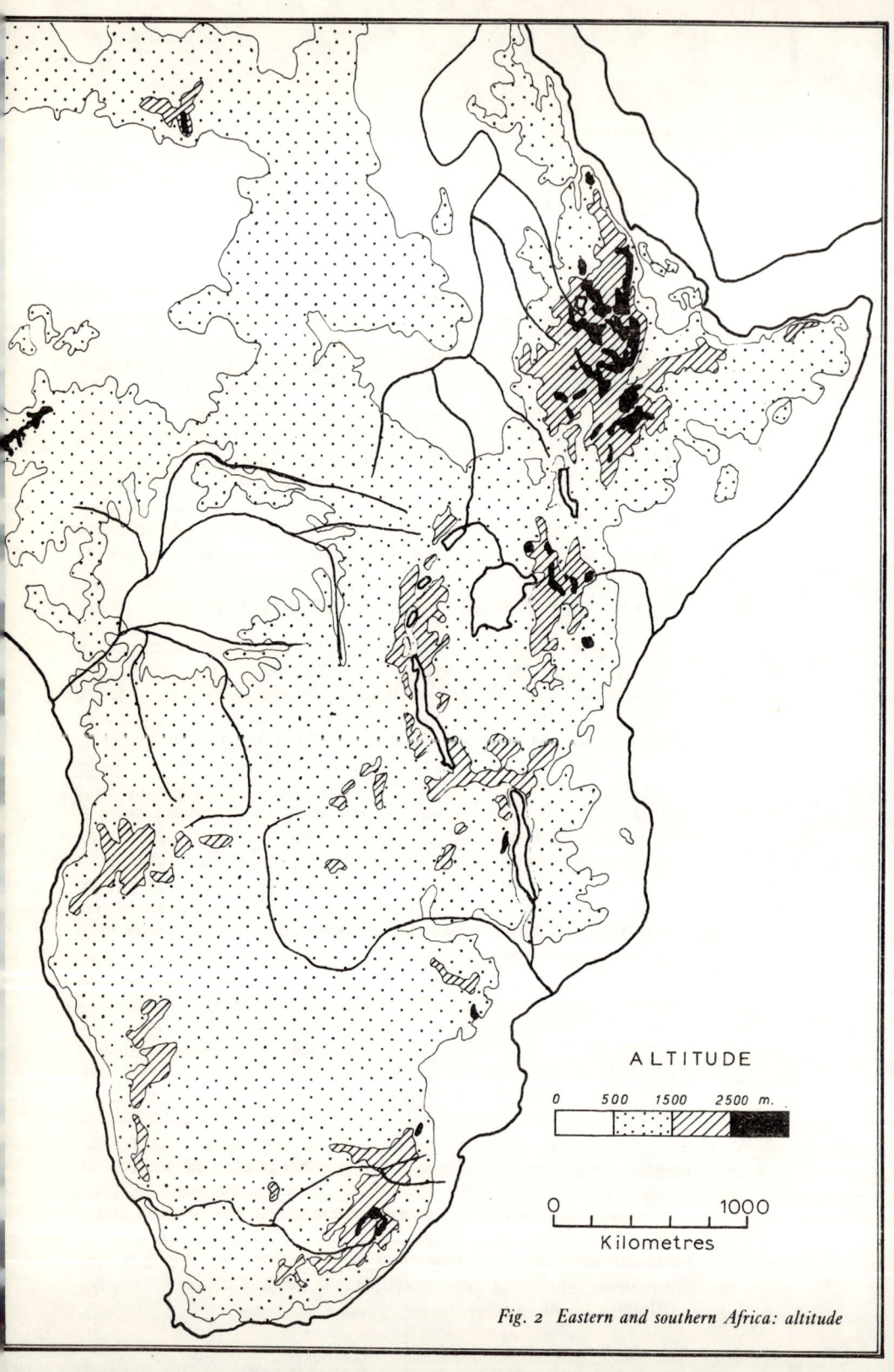

ALTITUDE

0   500   1500   2500 m.

0   1000
Kilometres

Fig. 2 Eastern and southern Africa: altitude

In southern Ethiopia the highlands are divided by an arm of the great Rift Valley, a faulted crack in the earth's surface which stretches from the Sea of Galilee through the length of eastern Africa to the Zambezi. South of Addis Ababa the lake-speckled Rift Valley forms a major region of internal drainage: the streams and rivers of the undulating southern plateau flow either westwards and southwards to the Omo river and Lake Rudolf, or northwards and eastwards to the Awash river which eventually loses itself in the hot arid wastes of the Afar triangle where, in the north, the land drops to below sea level.

On all sides but the north-east, where it borders on the Red Sea, the Ethiopian massif is surrounded by lowlands, most of which are arid. To the west is the Sudan, very much a land of the Nile. Here, the White Nile flows northwards, successively through the well-watered hilly country of Equatoria into the huge papyrus swamp of the Sudd, then through a wide alluvial plain to Khartoum at the confluence of the Blue and the White Niles. North of Khartoum, the river flows through a narrow valley bordered by desert into Nubia and Egypt. To the west of the Nile generally open plains stretch for thousands of kilometres westwards to Lake Chad and beyond: in the north these merge into the Sahara Desert, while southwards they comprise the sahel and sudanic belts, passing into open savannah and tree savannah which itself merges with the equatorial forest of the Congo basin (Fig. 3).

A second area of desert lies to the south of the Ethiopian massif, separating it from the East African highlands in Kenya, Uganda and Tanzania. These arid, low-lying regions merge with the coastal plain of southern Somalia and are in most areas covered with stunted scrub vegetation. In northern Kenya, where this plain is bisected by the Rift Valley, is Lake Rudolf, set in an area much changed by relatively recent volcanism which has left a landscape almost lunar in its desolation.

The highlands of East Africa are intimately connected with the Rift Valley which here divides into two branches. The Western Rift Valley contains a string of lakes: Albert, through the northern end of which the White Nile flows; Edward and Kivu, behind which rise the snow-capped Ruwenzori Mountains marking the eastern edge of the equatorial forest; and, deepest of all, Tanganyika, the bottom of which is several hundreds of metres below sea level. The Eastern Rift Valley bisects the Kenya highlands between the forested Mau and Nyandarua (Aberdare) ranges, passing to the west of the glaciated and snowy mountains Kenya and Kilimanjaro. The dry grassland floor of the rift merges with the Serengeti Plains of northern Tanzania. Between the two arms of the Rift Valley is a slightly dished plain largely covered by the shallow waters of Lake Victoria, source-reservoir of the White Nile. The greater part of Tanzania forms a poorly watered table-land, sloping down from the open Serengeti Plains in the north to the section of the Rift Valley through which the Great Ruaha flows on its way to the Indian Ocean. This river rises in the more mountainous Southern Highlands of Tanzania which stretch between the southern end of Lake Tanganyika and the northern extremity of Lake Nyasa.

Further to the south the relatively monotonous landscape presents a marked contrast with the scenic variety of East Africa. Northern Zambia is a wooded plateau region drained by numerous streams which form the headwaters of the Lualaba and, ultimately, of the Congo. Comparable dry forest continues westwards across the conti-

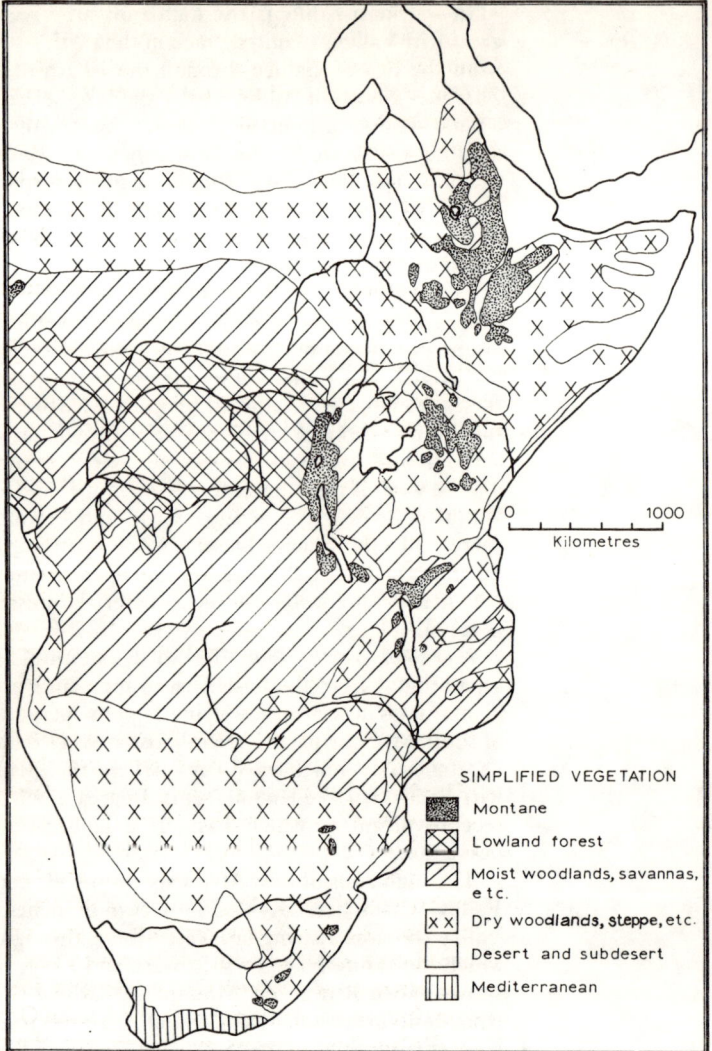

SIMPLIFIED VEGETATION

Montane

Lowland forest

Moist woodlands, savannas, etc.

Dry woodlands, steppe, etc.

Desert and subdesert

Mediterranean

Fig. 3 Simplified vegetation map of eastern and southern Africa

nent into Angola, relieved by occasional lakes and patches of swamp such as Bangweulu, Mweru and the marshes of the upper Lualaba. Most of this country drains to the north and, as the land slopes gently down to the huge wet-forested Congo basin, the vegetation becomes initially more open, forming true savannah broken by the strips of forest which fringe the banks of the northward-flowing Congo tributaries. Eventually, these gallery forests coalesce and merge with the great equatorial forest itself.

The southern part of the dry forest belt lies mainly within the drainage area of the Zambezi, the only really major river which debouches to the eastern coast of Africa. Much of the land through which the upper Zambezi flows consists of a vast flat plain, covering much of western Zambia and south-eastern Angola, which is blanketed by a thick mantle of sand representing an old northerly extension of the Kalahari Desert and now covered for the most part with dense thorn scrub, giving way to more open grassland as the rainfall becomes still less to the south and south-west. Near the centre of this upper Zambezi region, the river flows through the seasonally inundated Barotse Plain, the remains of a formerly permanent lake. Flowing eastwards over the spectacular Victoria Falls, the Zambezi passes through a deep gorge and enters a broader but clearly defined valley where it receives in turn the waters of its major northern tributaries the Kafue and the Luangwa: still further to the east, in the Mozambique lowlands, it is swollen also by the outflow of Lake Nyasa at the southern end of the great Rift Valley.

The southern part of the continent incorporates three major zones: the low, arid west, the highland east and the southerly Cape region. In the west, the dry forest of central Angola gradually gives way to the south, with decreasing altitude, to the northern fringes of Africa's third desert region, that of the south-west, comprising the discontinuous Kalahari, Namib and Karroo thirstlands. Much of southern Angola, north-eastern Namibia and northern Botswana – all open sandy plains with low, stunted vegetation – drains to the internal Okavango basin of northern Botswana, north of the Kalahari proper, where the waters are lost by evaporation. In Namibia the coastal strip receives virtually no rain. Further inland the highlands of Damaraland and Great Namaland provide dry grassland which slopes down to the arid inland plains of southern Botswana and the northern Cape – plains which are bisected by the westward-flowing Orange river bringing the waters of the eastern highlands to the Atlantic Ocean, which it reaches through a deeply cut gorge.

A marked contrast is provided by the eastern half of southern Africa. Between the Zambezi and the Limpopo is the fertile plateau country of Rhodesia, comprising gently rolling plains with their greatest altitude in the Inyanga highlands to the east, and interrupted also in the south-west by the domed granite outcrops of the Matopo Hills. The Limpopo valley is a hot strip of arid lowland connecting the Kalahari region with the plains of southern Mozambique. To the south rise first the grassy highveld of the Transvaal and then the mountains of eastern South Africa which reach their greatest height in the often snow-covered Drakensberg of Lesotho and Natal. The mountains present a steep face to the Indian Ocean seaboard, and the coastal plain here narrows and peters out. To the west, the drop is more gradual and incorporates the undulating grasslands of the Orange Free State. With reduced altitude, the rainfall decreases markedly over the wide plains of the Cape thirstlands and, further south, the stony Karroo Desert. In the extreme south of the continent there is a dramatic change: the Karroo is bordered by an east–west-aligned belt of folded mountains, beyond which is a small area of hilly lowland enjoying a temperate climate and supporting a Mediterranean type of vegetation.

THE PEOPLES

Human populations may be classified in a large number of ways. One of the most obvious, by reference to nationality or membership of a smaller-scale socio-political grouping such as a 'tribe', is of little relevance to our present purpose. The modern nation-states of Africa are of recent origin: their boundaries were fixed in an essentially arbitrary manner by outside interests, with little reference to African realities. In this book there will be frequent mention of the names of modern states, but only as a convenient system of geographical reference. As will be argued below, particularly in chapter VII, membership of the traditional 'tribal' groupings is often in a state of continuous flux, and it is dangerous to project them back far into the past as meaningful historical entities.

The physical characteristics of modern African peoples provide one form of breakdown. It is now realized that the rigid racial classifications proposed by the older schools of African historiography were based upon a misconception of the nature of human variability. Any grouping of individuals, however defined, will encompass a greater or lesser range of physical variation, and these ranges will almost invariably overlap between different groups. A biological classification must therefore be limited to the statement of general trends, and cannot include rigidly defined parameters. An excellent statement along these lines is that provided by Jean Hiernaux (1974), who emphasizes that the description of human biological diversity must be approached statistically, and that major socio-political, linguistic or economic realignments can take place with very little corresponding gene-flow.

Within this framework, several broad biological groupings may tentatively be recognized within the indigenous populations of eastern and southern Africa. In the south-west are the peoples who call themselves Khoi and San – terms which are preferable to the derogatory English equivalents, respectively 'Hottentots' and 'Bushmen'. These yellow-brown-skinned folk are probably the remnants of a formerly more widespread population, now largely replaced by and incorporated into the varied and greatly more numerous Negroid groups, who occupy most of the rest of the continent south of the Sahara and west of the Horn. In the latter areas the African Negroid stock has interbred in varying degrees with related peoples of predominantly North African or Arabian origin, and meaningful differentiation on purely biological grounds is impracticable.

A different means of classification, to which increasing importance is now being attached, is based on language. Here is a criterion which has both historical validity, and also relevance to the individual's sense of identity. The classification of African languages most widely followed today is that of Joseph Greenberg (1963a), which is here summarized in Fig. 4. It provides a useful means of subdividing the Negroid populations and of differentiating them from the peoples of the Horn and the Sahara who show North African and Arabian affinities. Generally, the languages of the latter belong to Greenberg's Afroasiatic super-family which includes the Semitic languages, Berber and the various Cushitic languages of eastern Africa. In much of western Kenya, northern Tanzania, Uganda, the southern Sudan and adjacent areas to the west and north-west, the predominantly Negroid people speak Nilo-Saharan languages, including Nilotic and Central Sudanic, the discontinuous distribution of which suggests that this is an ancient linguistic group, formerly much more extensive before it was partly submerged by the expansion of speakers of other, principally Afroasiatic, languages. Elsewhere, in the parts of sub-Saharan Africa with which this book is concerned, the Negroid people are mostly speakers of Bantu languages. These comprise a grouping of very closely inter-related dialects, evidently of fairly recent dispersal, as will be shown below in chapter VIII. They belong to Greenberg's Niger–Congo family, part of his Congo–Kordofanian super-family

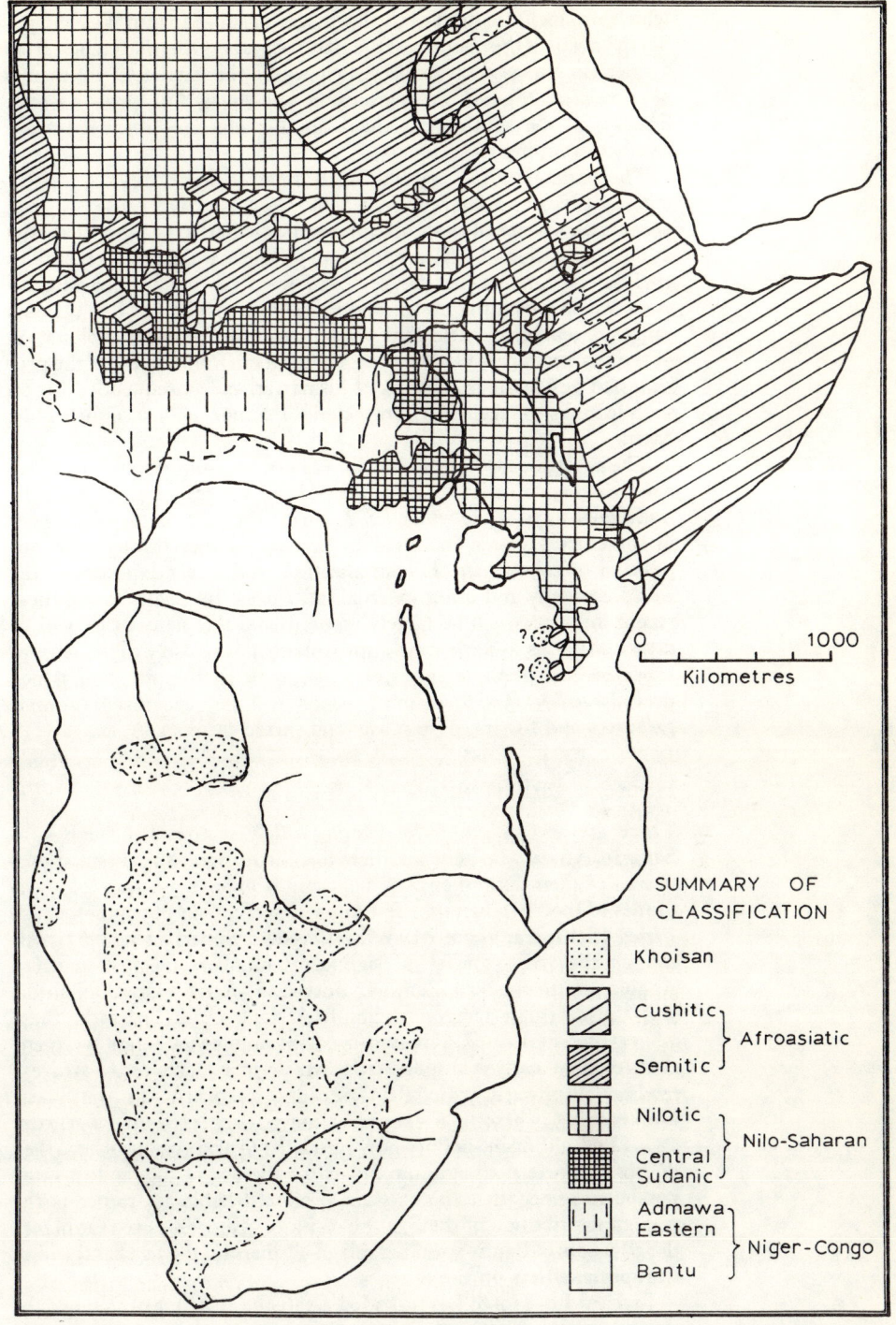

SUMMARY OF
CLASSIFICATION

Khoisan

Cushitic ⎫
          ⎬ Afroasiatic
Semitic ⎭

Nilotic ⎫
         ⎬ Nilo-Saharan
Central ⎭
Sudanic

Admawa ⎫
Eastern ⎬ Niger-Congo
Bantu   ⎭

0 ————————— 1000
Kilometres

Fig. 4 Modern linguistic distributions in eastern and southern Africa (after Greenberg, 1963a)

which also includes most of the languages of sub-Saharan West Africa. To the north of the country of the Bantu-speakers there stretches, from Cameroon almost to Uganda, a belt where the languages are mainly of a related Niger–Congo grouping known as Adamawa–Eastern. Finally, in the south-west, the Khoisan languages form a further distinct grouping of their own.

The evidence of biology and that of linguistics are thus not entirely incompatible; and later in this book we shall have cause to draw upon the evidence of both disciplines, particularly the latter, to assist in the elucidation of African prehistory. The raw data of such studies are, however, somewhat far removed from the main archaeological evidence on which the prehistorian places most reliance. It is on such things as economy, settlement patterns and the means of exploitation of the resources provided by man's natural environment, that the pre-historian builds the framework of his narrative. Consequently, it is on such features of recent African societies that our main account will be based.

The diverse peoples who inhabit eastern and southern Africa today maintain a wide variety of life-styles. Here, we are concerned with the traditional ways of life which have, during the past century (or longer in some areas), been modified to varying degrees through the im-position of colonialism, industrialization, and direct exposure to the world economy and other external influences. In what follows, these recent influences will be largely ignored; and the picture that will be drawn will thus in some ways approximate more closely to the African experience of about eighty years ago than to the situation which prevails today. Three main divisions will be recognized: hunter/gatherers and fishers, pastoralists and mixed-farmers.

Hunters, gatherers and fishers

There are several groups of people widely scattered through sub-Saharan Africa who rely for their livelihood upon the direct muni-ficence of their natural environment and who have not adopted tech-niques of food production. Best known are the San of south-western Africa (Schapera, 1930; M. Wilson, 1969a; Silberbauer, 1965). Al-though they now survive in significant numbers only in southern Angola, south-western Zambia, Botswana, north-eastern Namibia and the northern fringes of South Africa's Cape Province, these yellow-brown-skinned, Khoisan-speaking hunter/gatherers were en-countered by early European travellers over a much wider area ex-tending northwards into Rhodesia and eastwards to the Natal Drakensberg, where their extermination was achieved only a century ago. Thus, although they are now restricted to arid regions where they do not compete with agriculturalists for the use of the land, it must not be imagined that this is their preferred habitat – rather is the present distribution of the San the result of centuries of retreat before the advances of Bantu-speaking mixed-farmers on the one hand and of European settlers on the other.

Richard Lee (1968) has provided a valuable account of !Kung sub-sistence patterns in north-western Botswana, and has demonstrated how, although these people – like other San – are popularly regarded as hunters, they in fact derive the greater part of their nutrition from the collection of wild vegetable foods. Their economic practices, well adapted to their present inhospitable environment, support a nutritional level well above that of many agricultural peoples in surrounding areas. Although some San groups have never adopted metallurgical techniques, most of them now obtain metal tools from their neighbours: only in northern Namibia and, perhaps, southern Angola has the manufacture of stone tools continued (MacCalman and Grobbelaar, 1965). In the central Kalahari the San still continue their nomadic life-style, but in more peripheral areas they now tend to settle for parts of the year and to enter into a client relationship with groups of their Bantu- or Afrikaans-speaking neighbours, continuing a process of assimilation which has continued in much of south-central Africa for many centuries past (Plate I).

Plate I   A settlement of !Kung in the Kalahari (after Gibbs, 1965)

To the north, these processes of assimilation are virtually complete, and only a few scattered remnants of hunting/gathering peoples survive, although their presence in relatively recent times is recalled in many areas in the oral traditions of the Bantu-speakers. Most of these remnant populations, which may in some cases have had Khoi–San connexions, are referred to by their neighbours as Twa – a remarkably widespread term which has frequently absorbed implications of clientship. Until recent times several groups of fishing peoples survived in the marsh areas of Zambia, notably on the Kafue Flats and in the Lukanga and Bangweulu Swamps. These Twa had adopted the Bantu speech of their neighbours but retained a sense of separate identity, due largely to their subsistence which was based almost exclusively upon fishing.

Several distinct hunting/gathering peoples survive in parts of East Africa, although here again their traditional life-style is fast being assimilated into that of their agricultural and pastoral neighbours.

Probably the best known are the Hadza of northern Tanzania (Woodburn, 1968*a*) whose distinctive language is believed by some to be of Khoisan origin: they thus present a marked contrast with their neighbours both in economy and in speech. A second Tanzanian group, the Sandawe, also speak a possibly Khoisan-related language and some of them, until recently, were also hunters and gatherers (Dempwolff, 1916). Several small groups of hunters in Kenya and adjacent parts of southern Somalia speak Cushitic languages: they include the Boni between the lower Tana and the Juba, as well as the Sanye on the Tana river. Their counterparts in more easterly regions of Kenya are the several groups of Dorobo or Okiek (Huntingford, 1929; Blackburn, 1974), who inhabit the forests of the Rift Valley highlands. Despite their reputation as skilled hunters, many Okiek groups in fact rely largely on the collection of wild honey for their food. In most cases the Okiek speak Nilotic languages akin to those of their agricultural neighbours the Kalenjin, but this may be due to recent contact: one outlying group, the Asa of the Serengeti Plain, speak a Cushitic language and retain sharp cultural contrasts with their Maasai neighbours (Fleming, 1969). There has been some debate as to the extent to which the various Dorobo groups represent an anciently distinct population, rather than sections of Kalenjin who have adopted a hunting/gathering existence. There can be little doubt, however, that they are in origin distinct, although much contact and acculturation has taken place.

At the south-eastern corner of Lake Rudolf are small numbers of Elmolo who, until recently, depended for their livelihood almost exclusively on fishing (Dyson and Fuchs, 1937). Today they are gradually obtaining herds of goats, although fishing remains of prime importance. Their settled life-style in semi-permanent villages on the beach or off-shore islands is in marked contrast with the nomadic wanderings of their pastoral neighbours. The Elmolo language differs markedly from those of the pastoralists, but at the time of writing (April 1976) it is still spoken by only eight people (Bernd Heine, personal communication).

Somewhat peripheral to the main subject-area of this book, but nevertheless deserving brief mention, are the Mbuti pygmies of the north-eastern equatorial forest (Turnbull, 1961; 1965). These small-statured people are fully adapted, physically and culturally, to their forest environment. They hunt both with nets and with bows and arrows, the two methods involving different settlement patterns between which there is, however, a constant interchange of population. Most Mbuti are involved in a client relationship with the various agricultural peoples of the forest fringe, whose languages (whether Sudanic, Bantu or Adamawa–Eastern) they now speak.

In the predominantly pastoral areas of southern Ethiopia and north-eastern Uganda are several hunting groups who are much despised by their pastoralist neighbours. Examples are the Ik or Teuso of Uganda (Turnbull, 1972) and the Manjo of south-western Ethiopia (Cerulli, 1956). It is noteworthy that in the regions of sub-Saharan Africa where food-production techniques have been practised for a longer time, relict groups of hunters are virtually unknown. Further to the south we can still witness today the varying stages in the assimilation of the hunters into the societies of their food-producing neighbours.

Pastoralists

Pastoral people, who derive their livelihood almost exclusively from the management of their herds of domestic animals, live today in two major but widely separated zones of Africa. Of these, by far the greater in extent is that which occupies most of the sahel and sudanic belts which stretch across the continent to the south of the Sahara Desert, with an extension into the dry grasslands of East Africa and the Horn. The second zone is in south-western Africa, likewise an area of low rainfall. With few exceptions these pastoralists are traditionally nomadic, although they are increasingly – with outside encouragement – adopting a more settled life-style, wherever environmental conditions will allow (Monod, 1975). Here we are concerned only with the eastern third of the first zone, and with the second.

In the arid coastal plains of the Afar triangle, in Somalia, in the plains of northern Kenya as far to the west as Lake Rudolf, as well as in adjacent parts of southern Ethiopia, pastoralists speaking Cushitic languages form the principal element of the population. They may be divided into the Afar (M. Lucas, 1935) and the Somali (I. M. Lewis, 1961; 1965) in the regions to which they have given their respective names, and the Galla of southern Ethiopia (Huntingford, 1955). In northern Kenya the pastoralists are primarily of Galla and Somali stock with adjunct related groups. They share with the Nilotic-speaking pastoralists, discussed below, a tall, slender physique; but this does not attain the remarkable elongation of body and limb which is present in some Nilotic groups. They herd camels, cattle, donkeys, sheep and goats, all but the last two being used on occasion as pack animals. Among the fully nomadic groups, material possessions are kept to a minimum so that all, including the frames of their dome-shaped huts, may readily be transported on the backs of two or three pack animals. The main foods supplied by the herds are milk and blood obtained by piercing the animal's neck with a special broad-tipped arrow. Animals change hands on a large scale as bride-price and are slaughtered for meat only on special occasions such as a funeral or age-set ceremony.

Pastoralists speaking languages of the Nilotic branch of the Eastern Sudanic sub-family occupy an elongated stretch of territory extending from the west-central Sudan in a general south-easterly direction through the south-eastern Sudan into northern Uganda and Kenya west of Lake Rudolf, then southwards along the line of the eastern Rift Valley to the Serengeti and adjacent plains of northern and central Tanzania. From north to south the principal constituent groups are the Dinka and Nuer (Evans-Pritchard, 1940), the Beir of the south-eastern Sudan (Logan, 1918), and the Jie, Karamojong and Turkana of northern Uganda and Kenya (Gulliver, 1955). Further to the south are the Samburu (Spencer, 1965) and the Maasai (Merker, 1911; Jacobs, 1975).

In the north, the Nilotic-speakers are separated from the Cushitic-speaking pastoralists by the Ethiopian highlands, and it is here that they have developed (or retained) their most characteristic culture. In the south the territories of the two linguistically defined pastoral groups coalesce and a consequent mingling of their cultural traditions has taken place. The bleeding of domestic stock, for example, is practised both by the southern Nilotic-speakers and by the Galla; but it is relatively rare among the Dinka. The latter, however, inhabiting

Plate II Pastoral Galla at a well, northern Kenya

the seasonally inundated Nile plains, supplement their diet with fish, but many Nilotic-speakers further to the south share with the Cushitic-speakers a taboo against eating fish. Likewise, the more southerly Nilotic-speakers and their Cushitic-speaking neighbours employ a common cycling age-set system as well as the practices of circumcision and clitoridectomy. These traits are mentioned here since they provide historical evidence which will be drawn upon in later chapters of this book.

An important feature of pastoralism in the arid regions of East Africa is the digging and maintenance of deep wells such as are wide-spread in the Galla areas of southern Ethiopia and northern Kenya, as well as in Tanzanian Maasailand. These serve as centres for grazing territories and are maintained and operated by communal effort, water being generally passed up in skin buckets hand to hand (Plate II).

The pastoral people of south-western Africa are the Khoi. They are of a comparable physical stock to that of the San, and their languages are likewise related. They inhabited until recently parts of what are now southern Namibia and Botswana as well as extensive adjacent parts of the Cape Province, owning large herds of long-horned cattle and fat-tailed sheep, with lesser numbers of goats. Apart from the Nama of southern Namibia, full-blooded Khoi practising their traditional culture are today virtually extinct, although details of their life-style were recorded by European observers in the eighteenth and nineteenth centuries (Schapera, 1933; M. Wilson, 1969a).

Mixed-farmers

The mixed-farmers – that is, those who rely for their livelihood both upon agriculture and upon the herding of domestic animals – form a very large majority in the population of eastern and southern Africa, both in numbers of individuals and in the variety of their groupings. Here, only representative examples of the mixed-farming economies can be discussed in order to give the reader some idea of their diversity.

In the highlands lying to the west of the Nile in the central Sudan reside several groups of sedentary Negroid farmers, such as the Berti in Darfur and the various Nuba peoples of Kordofan (Holý, 1974; Nadel, 1947). The indigenous languages of this region have been almost completely replaced by Arabic. Among the Berti, bullrush millet is the staple crop; cattle, sheep and goats are herded. Hunting is of minor importance as a source of food. Villages consist of clusters of individual homesteads or compounds. Nuba agriculture is more complex, involving the construction of terraces and the practice of irrigation: millet and sorghum are the staple crops, with maize increasing rapidly in importance from year to year. Cattle and goats are milked, while pigs are kept in some numbers, despite the spread of Islam among most surrounding peoples.

The low-lying plains between the Blue and the White Niles are inhabited by Nilotic-speaking agriculturalists of whom the Shilluk (Pumphrey, 1941) are the most numerous group. Sorghum is the main crop, accompanied by a wide range of other cereals and vegetables: cattle and other domestic animals are herded and the diet is also supplemented by fishing. The Shilluk live in compact villages of conical grass-roofed houses. Closely related Nilotic-speakers are found in Eritrea and in south-western Ethiopia, notably in Wollega.

Most of the inhabitants of the Ethiopian highlands, however, present a marked contrast with those of the lowlands to the west (Shack, 1974). The people of the central and northern regions speak almost exclusively Semitic languages: there are a few isolated groups of Agau who are regarded as the remnants of an earlier Cushitic-speaking population. Ethiopian agriculture is distinguished by the great variety of the crops which are cultivated. In addition to wheat and barley, which will not grow well in most other regions of sub-Saharan Africa, there are two important cereal crops which appear to be of Ethiopian origin: finger millet and teff – the latter is not grown to any appreciable extent anywhere else in the world (Simoons, 1960). Sheep and goats are herded, as are cattle which are used also for drawing ploughs, while both horses and donkeys are important transport animals. Northern Ethiopia has a long history of urban settlement, state centralization and Christianity (Buxton, 1970) which, with the accompanying advances in the field of material culture and technology, will be discussed later in this book.

In south-central Ethiopia, east of the Rift Valley, most of the population retains its Cushitic speech. Here the Sidama peoples, although cultivating the cereals noted above in central Ethiopia, have as their staple crop another local Ethiopian food plant, the banana-like ensete, the stem of which is pounded and made into a sort of flat bread. The undulating land is intensively cultivated, and most people live in scattered homesteads dispersed among the gardens, rather than in villages. Domestic animals are kept but are of minor importance in most areas (e.g. Shack, 1966). Among one ensete-cultivating people, the Semitic-speaking Gurage, south-west of Addis Ababa, hafted obsidian tools are still regularly used, particularly as scrapers and knives for the preparation of skins.

It is now necessary briefly to consider the mixed-farming people of the eastern end of the savannah which borders the northern fringe of the equatorial forest and which falls geographically in the western Equatoria Province of the Sudan, in adjacent portions of Zaïre and the Central African Republic, and in the West Nile Province of Uganda. The Negroid peoples here speak a variety of languages, most of which are classified as Central Sudanic or Adamawa–Eastern. Representative peoples are described by de Calonne-Beaufaict (1921), Schweinfurth (1874) and Evans-Pritchard (1971). They are shifting hoe-cultivators of sorghum and millet, tending the oil-palm also on the forest fringes. Hunting, fishing and gathering are all practised and, where tsetse flies permit, cattle are herded along with sheep and goats. The compact villages traditionally consisted of round, conical-roofed houses; but this style is now being replaced by rectangular, gabled structures through contact with neighbouring Bantu-speaking peoples.

The southernmost representatives of the Cushitic-speakers are a cluster of mixed-farming peoples centred on the Mbulu highlands of north-central Tanzania. The largest group is the Iraqw (Huntingford, 1953). Cereal agriculture and pastoralism are the bases of Iraqw subsistence: cattle are both milked and bled. Settlement is traditionally in scattered homesteads rather than in villages. The typical house-style is the rectangular *tembe*, sometimes semi-subterranean, with a flat earth-covered roof.

A dense area of settlement by Nilotic-speakers extends through the Western Highlands of Kenya to the Winam (Kavirondo) Gulf at the north-eastern corner of Lake Victoria. Among the highland people, known today collectively as Kalenjin, the most populous groups are the Nandi (Hollis, 1909) and Kipsigis (Peristiany, 1939), with the Luo (Northcote, 1907) predominating near the lake. To the west, in northern Uganda, are the related Alur (Southall, 1956) and Lango (Driberg, 1923). In the Kenya highlands intensive agriculture is practised, frequently involving terracing and the construction of irrigation works, some of which (built before the time of European contact) are of considerable complexity. Settlement is generally in dispersed homesteads. In the lowlands, pastoralism is of greater importance. These Nilotic-speaking people have no traditional form of centralized political authority above the neighbourhood level. The Kalenjin have a cycling age-grade system, but this is not found among the Alur or the Luo.

Over the huge expanse of Africa lying to the south of the areas described above, the mixed-farming people are almost exclusively speakers of Bantu-languages. Negroid, Bantu-speaking peoples today occupy, by area, about one third of the continent of Africa: we are here concerned only with those groups who inhabit the regions to the east and south of the equatorial forests. In East Africa the Bantu-speakers traditionally occupy a 'U'-shaped area stretching from the Kenya coastal hinterland and the Eastern Highlands around Mount Kenya, southwards through Tanzania to the south of the Maasai and Iraqw country, and northwards again into Burundi, Rwanda and southern Uganda where they occupy most of the western and northern shores of Lake Victoria.

The Bantu-speakers of the coast and off-shore islands including Zanzibar and Pemba comprise the urbanized Swahili (Prins, 1967) whose elaborate culture has developed in contact with non-African trading peoples of the Indian Ocean, as will be discussed in chapter VII. In contrast, the peoples of the hinterland, such as the Giryama (Prins, 1952; Werner, 1915), have lived in remarkable isolation from these external influences, despite their proximity to the coast. There is evidence that Bantu-speakers may formerly have extended further to the north-east into what is now southern Somalia. Sorghum is traditionally the staple crop, but the American introductions maize and cassava (manioc) are now extensively grown, as are coconuts, bananas and rice on the coast. Sheep and goats are herded, with cattle also in Kenya; but the latter are rare in much of coastal Tanzania. Compact villages are the rule, with rectangular gabled houses, although conical styles are also built. Several groups have cycling age-grades, probably adopted from more northerly Cushitic-speakers. Village headmen are the highest political authority, except among the coast peoples who have traditionally had Sultanates after the Arabian pattern.

In the fertile and relatively well-watered Eastern Highlands of Kenya, among such peoples as the Meru, Gikuyu and Kamba (Middleton, 1953; Kenyatta, 1938; Lindblom, 1916), intensive agriculture supports a dense population, aided by irrigation and the use of animal manure. Maize has now replaced the African cereals as the staple crop in most areas: pulses are also of considerable importance. Domestic animals are extensively herded. The characteristic settlement pattern is one of homesteads dispersed among the fields (Plate III).

In central and western Tanzania, cereal agriculture is the mainstay of the economy; cattle cannot be kept in many areas becase of the presence of tsetse fly (Blohm, 1931–3; Rigby, 1969). Several of those

Plate III Dispersed homesteads, Ukambani, Kenya (by courtesy of Margot Nelson)

peoples who do keep cattle draw fresh blood from them – a practice which they, as several Bantu-speaking groups in Kenya, have presumably adopted from their Nilotic- or Cushitic-speaking neighbours since it is not found further to the south. Compact villages are here the rule: *tembes* (see above, p. 14), rectangular and circular house-styles are all found in different areas.

The Bantu-speaking peoples of Uganda, Rwanda, Burundi and adjacent parts of western Tanzania and Kenya are conveniently labelled the Interlacustrine Bantu. Particularly in Rwanda the population is heterogeneous. The tall, slender Tutsi are often regarded as a people of Nilotic origin who have established themselves in authority (only recently overthrown) over a Bantu-speaking peasantry, the Hutu, whose language has now been adopted by the Tutsi. The Tutsi retain cultural evidence for their Nilotic ancestry in the form of their preference for pastoralism and in the practice of drawing fresh blood from their cattle (d'Hertefelt, 1965). A third, lowest, caste is formed by pygmoid Twa hunters who survive in the mountainois areas of the country. Here, as elsewhere among the Interlacustrine Bantu, particularly in Uganda, elaborate traditional state-systems have developed (Roscoe, 1911). Dispersed homesteads are the usual rural settlement pattern except around the north-east shore of Lake Victoria (Wagner, 1956), and conical houses are the norm. Pastoralism is important throughout the region, while agriculture is based upon the cultivation of cereals, except among the Ganda and some of their neighbours where they have been replaced by bananas.

In considering the Bantu-speaking peoples of more southerly regions, it is convenient to begin with those of Angola, and particularly with the Kongo and related groups who live to the south of the lower reaches of the Congo river (Laman, 1953; 1957). Here, bananas and yams are the staple foods. Domestic animals other than goats are few. This predominantly agricultural economy is a feature of a great belt of territory inhabited almost exclusively by Bantu-speakers and stretching across the continent to the south of the equatorial forests from Angola in the west to northern Malawi and Mozambique in the east. Characteristic peoples include the Bemba (Richards, 1939), Kaonde (Melland, 1923) and Lunda (Baumann, 1935). Much of this land is infested with tsetse fly and cannot support cattle: however, the fly belts continuously shift and the distribution of cattle has altered markedly even within recent times. In many areas the predominantly vegetable diet is supplemented by hunting and fishing. Except in Kongo country cereal crops are more important than yams and bananas: millet and sorghum were the traditional staples but these have gradually been replaced in many areas by crops introduced from the New World, notably maize and cassava. Shifting cultivation in clearings in the dry forest is characteristic (Allan, 1965). In parts of western Zambia and most of Angola the preferred house-type is rectangular with a gabled or pyramidal roof. To the east, conical huts were traditional, but in recent times these have begun to be replaced by rectangular types (Plate IV). In most areas save parts of north-eastern Angola compact villages are the usual settlement pattern. Most peoples have developed centralized state-systems which trace their origins to the Luba and Lunda empires of what is now southern Zaïre (Vansina, 1966).

Plate IV   A village of Bantu-speaking farmers in eastern Zambia

Further to the south the Bantu-speaking people are again cattle-keepers. In the Zambezi valley and to its north are the Ila (Smith and Dale, 1920); the Lozi (Gluckman, 1961) inhabit the seasonally inundated Barotse plain and its environs. Cereal agriculture is still of prime importance as a source of food, however, and cattle are kept primarily as wealth. In some areas, gathering has retained a considerable degree of economic importance (Scudder, 1962). The Lozi form a strongly centralized kingdom with a developed bureaucracy: other groups tend to be acephalous. In southern Angola and northern Namibia the cattle-keeping south-west Bantu incorporate many Khoi–San remnant peoples. The largest Bantu-speaking groups are the Ovimbundu (Hambly, 1934), Ovambo (Lebzelter, 1934) and Herero (Irle, 1906). Animal husbandry increases in importance from north to south, following the decrease in rainfall. Sorghum and millet are now being replaced by maize and cassava as the principal crops. The Herero are traditionally primarily nomadic: elsewhere small compact villages are found.

The Shona of Rhodesia and the Tonga of Mozambique (Kuper, 1955; Junod, 1927) are primarily agriculturalists, with maize as their staple crop, although cattle are kept in most areas. Dispersed compounds with connected cattle kraals are the traditional settlements, with round conical-roofed houses. Building in stone has a long history in this area, as will be shown in chapters VI and VII. Related Bantu-speaking peoples in South Africa and neighbouring parts of Botswana, Swaziland and Lesotho are classed together as the south-eastern Bantu (M. Wilson, 1969b; 1969c; Hammond-Tooke, 1974). The principal groups are the Ndebele (who expanded into south-western Rhodesia during the nineteenth century), the Sotho/Tswana and the Nguni, including the Xhosa, Zulu and Swazi. Strong centralized kingdoms are here established. Pastoralism and agriculture are generally of approximately equal importance, maize being the staple crop. Houses are similar to those of the Shona, but among some peoples – notably the Tswana – large towns with populations of several thousands are traditionally inhabited. Many of these south-eastern Bantu, notably the Xhosa, marking as they do the furthest limit of the expansion of the Bantu-speakers, have a long history of contact and interaction with the Khoi, which may be detected in many aspects of their culture and language.

THE PREHISTORIAN'S APPROACH

The present physical and demographic features of eastern and southern Africa have been summarized in the preceding pages. The main purpose of this book is to inquire how these features have changed over the past twenty thousand years or so, and particularly to use the results of this inquiry in an attempt to elucidate the later prehistory of the peoples who live in the sub-continent today. My emphasis will therefore be on human prehistory. As has been shown, however, man even today has not freed himself from the shackles placed upon him by his natural environment: in fact, many of the most specialized traditional African economies of the present day are based on precise adaptation to particular environmental conditions. Throughout this book I shall therefore attempt to evaluate the extent to which the climate and vegetation of eastern and southern Africa have changed, and the way in which this has influenced the course of human development.

It may not be widely realized how great have been the changes which have taken place in the physical geography and climate of eastern and southern Africa within the past twenty thousand years. For example, it was only about ten millennia ago that the level of the sea rose to its present height following the melting of the ice-sheets of the last glacial period: before that time a coastal plain up to 200 kilometres in width extended out from the line of the present south Cape coast of South Africa. In Kenya, studies of old shore-lines and lake-bed deposits show that Lake Nakuru was 180 metres deeper, holding many hundreds of times the amount of water contained by the modern lake. At the same time, from about 9000 to about 3000 bc, the now arid plain of northern Kenya was a land of lakes, with Lake Rudolf, which today has no outlet, both deeper and more extensive than it is now, and flowing north-westwards into the Nile. Another large lake occupied hundreds of square kilometres of what is now the Chalbi Desert. The Sahara was then fertile grazing country with large lakes and watercourses in areas which are now total desert: the fauna and flora of these regions were thus quite different from those which prevail today. Before about twelve thousand years ago, temperatures in the East African highlands and perhaps elsewhere were between 5° and 8°C. lower than at present, with correspondingly different snow-lines and placement of vegetational zones. No detailed account of the processes of environmental change will be given here. Enough has been said to indicate the scale and variety of the changes which have taken place. It is more appropriate that these processes be described, and the supporting references cited, in the later chapters along with the developments in human life-styles which were, to a considerable extent, reactions to the physical changes in man's natural environment.

The most recent periods of the human past may be studied through reference to written records, which may supply a variety of detailed information on many aspects of previous societies. In much of sub-Saharan Africa, however, the time-depth of the available written records is very shallow. Most of the peoples who inhabited the sub-continent remained at a preliterate stage of development until very recent times – in some cases until the advent of European colonial rule at the end of the last century. Other areas, of course, have a much longer history of literacy: in the Sudan and northern Ethiopia inscriptions have been found which date back to the last millennium bc, although the information which they give us (those of the Meroitic civilization in the Sudan cannot yet be fully understood) is strictly limited. Elsewhere, particularly in the coastal areas, light is thrown on the history of the preliterate peoples by the accounts of visitors. Arabic writers visited the East African coast from the tenth century AD onwards; and Portuguese records from the end of the fifteenth century are also informative.

In many African societies the historical role of written records is at least partly filled by oral traditions whereby accounts of past happenings are passed down verbally from generation to generation (Vansina, 1965; Henige, 1974). It is generally found that oral traditions are most carefully preserved and re-told among peoples who have a strong centralized state-system, whereas in some acephalous societies they are relatively unimportant. The function of traditional history as a support for political authority (by explaining, for example, the origin of the chiefly dynasty and the right of its members to rule) is recognized in several societies by the maintenance of official 'court historians' charged with the task of preserving and transmitting orthodox versions of the oral histories. It is likely that traditions of more recent events will be preserved with greater verisimilitude than those which relate to earlier times, which may eventually acquire mythical qualities. Historians are generally agreed that traditions of more than four or five centuries ago should be interpreted with particular caution, although memories of far earlier events have been preserved in some areas.

Both written and oral histories tend to concentrate on political happenings and on the activities of rulers and other powerful individuals. Only incidentally will they throw light on the everyday life-style and economy of the population as a whole. The picture which they present of the human past is thus essentially one-sided; and these sources need to be used in conjunction with other disciplines if a more balanced view is to be obtained.

It is the archaeologist who is best able to discover information about the human past of the periods before those which are illuminated by written records or by oral tradition. Archaeology as a historical discipline is not, however, restricted in its application to these early periods: it may be employed in the investigation of all sections of the human past, including the most recent.

The archaeologist studies the material remains which past societies have left behind them. These remains include such objects as artefacts (whether tools, utensils, ornaments or the waste products discarded in their processes of manufacture), remains of houses or shelters, paintings or carvings, graves, monuments, or mere domestic refuse such as broken bones thrown out from the kitchen. Through the detailed study of such remains, and particularly of their interrelationships, the archaeologist is able to throw light upon such varied aspects of his site's inhabitants as their technology, architecture, art, religious and funerary practices, diet and culinary methods, clothing and even – perhaps – physical appearance. Since much of this book is concerned with the results of archaeological research, it is not necessary to go into the discipline's methodology in any detail here, for this will become clear through examples in the course of the reader's perusal of the following pages. It must be appreciated, however, that the data provided by archaeology are essentially different from those supplied by the study of oral traditions. The archaeologist investigating the remains of a preliterate society will hardly ever be able to learn the names of individual people; and he will find it very difficult to reconstruct political situations. On the other hand, his interpretation of economy, particularly as regards hunting, agriculture or domestic animals, will be far more complete and reliable than that which the oral historian can obtain. The archaeologist's evidence is often recovered from sealed contexts where it has remained undisturbed since it was abandoned by its ancient makers or users: it has not been subject to the attentions, alterations and revisions (or just straightforward forgetfulness) of the intervening generations.

This last point also serves to distinguish archaeological data and methodology from those of the historical linguist and ethnographer. These specialists are involved in the backwards projection of certain features of modern societies – respectively language and material culture or socio-political institutions. They are thus one stage further removed from the primary subjects of their studies than is the archaeologist. This is not to belittle the contributions which these disciplines can make in illuminating the African past: many of the topics which they illustrate are beyond the reach of archaeology. The linguist, for example, by studying the distribution of modern linguistic forms, can attempt to reconstruct earlier languages and even suggest the areas where they were spoken and the processes by which their descendants have dispersed (Ehret, 1976). Study of these past languages can support hypotheses which illustrate many aspects of culture of their speakers and perhaps demonstrate their contacts or interactions with speakers of different languages. When these linguistic reconstructions can be correlated with a dated archaeological sequence, the prehistorian is on firmer ground.

It is the task of the prehistorian to draw upon the findings of these and other disciplines and to relate them to a composite picture of the human past. As far as eastern and southern Africa is concerned, the availability of data remains extremely uneven, but enough is now known to provide the basis for a coherent narrative, as the following chapters will show.

II

Hunters, gatherers and fishers of the last twenty thousand years BC

When early European travellers at the Cape of Good Hope began to move inland from the limited areas of the colonists' settlement during the eighteenth century, they encountered several San peoples whose technology was still at a premetallurgical stage and the majority of whose tools were made out of stone. Consequently, when pioneer archaeologists at the beginning of the twentieth century began to classify the Stone Age artefacts which they found in South Africa, it is hardly surprising that they designated the most recent of these industries 'Bushman relics' on account of their similarity to those which had, until very shortly previously, been practised by the San (or 'Bushman') people with whom their ancestors had come into contact (Peringuey, 1911).

TERMINOLOGY AND INTERPRETATION

It was formerly believed that all industries of this 'Late Stone Age' type (Fig. 5) were, at least as far as southern Africa was concerned, of comparatively recent date. Indeed, before the advent of radiocarbon dating, it was thought that all these industries fell within the last three or four thousand years (e.g. J. D. Clark, 1959a: 187). The application of radiometric dating techniques has, however, proved that industries of this same general type have a very much greater antiquity in southern Africa and elsewhere in the sub-continent, and that in some areas they may be traced back continuously to some eighteen thousand years ago; while the technological developments which reached their peak in these 'Late Stone Age' industries are of still greater antiquity (Beaumont and Vogel, 1972).

It is largely because of the historical process of the evolution of our archaeological terminology that the concept of a 'Late Stone Age' in sub-Saharan Africa is not yet based on any clear and unambiguous definition. The criteria for its recognition are primarily morphological and technological, being based on the apparent similarity of the chipped stone industries to those of the final stone-tool-using societies of southern Africa.

In most of these industries the technological emphasis is on the production of small parallel-sided flakes and the use of steep backing retouch to produce microlithic implements. We now know that industries of this sort do not all belong to a single finite period of time, but that they developed in some regions of sub-Saharan Africa many millennia before comparable industries become prevalent in other parts of the sub-continent. Indeed, some of these typological features are now known to be present in far older industries, associated with stone-working techniques which have generally been regarded as indicative of earlier phases of the Stone Age. It will be argued below that the production of backed microliths was a response to processes of environmental change which occurred at different times in various areas, even taking place more than once in some parts of southern Africa. It is clear, therefore, that the term 'Late Stone Age' as at present loosely used by archaeologists and historians is incapable of meaningful, accurate definition (Bishop and Clark, 1967: 821–901). The term as currently utilized has, indeed, few implications other than reference to the more recent groupings of stone tool industries in each respective area, and carries an unfortunate mixture of typological and temporal implications.

Many of the pitfalls inherent in the conventional 'Early', 'Middle' and 'Late Stone Age' system can be avoided by using a hierarchy of five modes of lithic technology which has recently been proposed by J. G. D. Clark (1969: 29–31). It avoids the tendency to correlate what are merely industrial phases with finite periods of time; and it also helps to minimize the artificial compartmentalization of what are frequently continuous processes of technological and cultural development. Clark's mode 3 (flake tools produced from prepared cores) correlates in broad terms with all but the latest phases of the 'Middle Stone Age' of the conventional terminology; his mode 4 (punch-struck blades with steep retouch) covers technologies developed in some areas of Africa during the final phases of the 'Middle Stone Age' and also some industries which are conventionally regarded as belonging to the earlier part of the 'Late Stone Age'; while his mode 5 (microlithic components of composite artefacts) falls largely within the 'Late Stone Age' as the term is generally used. These modes, as defined by Clark, appear to form a homotaxial sequence of world-wide applicability. The modes do not form watertight compartments, but it is recognized that elements of the technologies of earlier times may continue alongside more recent innovations. Although Clark's definitions will eventually require further refinement, I have tried to use his taxis in this chapter and in later sections of this book, in the belief that it enables a clearer outline picture to be presented than do the inadequately defined terms of the more conventional nomenclature.

Our knowledge of the succession of stone tool industries in eastern and southern Africa is geographically very unevenly distributed, many substantial areas remaining virtually unexplored by the Stone Age archaeologist. The sequences which have been established are in most areas based primarily upon the excavation of caves and rockshelters (Plates V and VI show typical sites), where conditions of preservation are often superior to those which prevail on open sites. On the other hand, the economic and technological picture which is obtained of the sites' inhabitants may be somewhat one-sided in view of the specialized or limited range of activities which may on occasion have been carried out there. However, rockshelters do have the major advantage to the prehistorian that in such sites occupation will tend to have been concentrated, and prolonged sequences of successive occupations may be discerned such as would but very rarely be located on open sites.

The reader will find that this chapter contains large numbers of summary descriptions of stone tool industries with comparatively little information on their interpretation or on the economic basis of the settlements to which their presence attests. The reason for this is that, despite the frequently enormous numbers of artefacts which are recovered from the majority of sites – particularly those located in caves or rockshelters – we have remarkably little valid information concerning the uses to which these artefacts were actually put by their makers. (Characteristic tool types are illustrated in Fig. 5.) In most cases archaeologists have carried out detailed analyses only of the formally retouched implements which generally represent but a tiny part of the total industry; yet we know, from the few sites where the entire collection has been subjected to microscopic examination for traces of wear due to use, that these retouched implements form only a small proportion of the artefacts which were actually used as tools. Many of the pieces conventionally classified as 'waste flakes' are found to show signs of utilization, and therefore they should be regarded as tools just as much as the formally retouched implements.

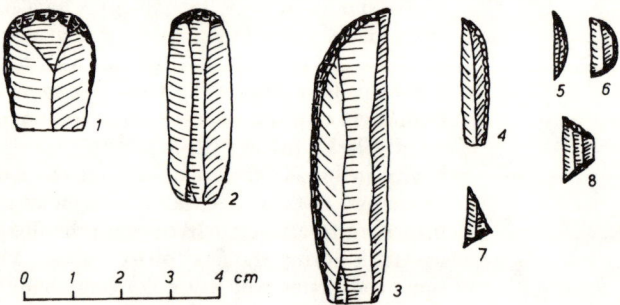

Fig. 5 Types of microlithic (mode 5) stone implements: 1, 2, scrapers; 3, 4, backed blade and bladelet; 5, 6, crescents or lunates; 7, 8, triangular and trapezoidal microliths (after Tixier, 1967)

The most intensive such microscopic examination to have been conducted on a sub-Saharan African stone tool industry is that done on exceptionally well preserved mode 5 material from Chiwemupula on the Zambian Copperbelt (Phillipson and Phillipson, 1970). Here it was found that over seventy per cent of the so-called 'waste flakes' showed signs of utilization, and that among the utilized pieces these 'waste flakes' outnumbered formally retouched tools which bore intentional secondary retouch by a factor of fifteen to one. Analysis of the types of edge-damage sustained by the different artefacts showed that the morphological categories of intentionally retouched tools tended to have been used in mutually distinctive ways, but this conformity was by no means invariable: typologically identical tools could have been used in different ways, and single specimens were evidently often put to more than one use. Identical wear-patterns were found on 'waste' pieces and on intentionally retouched tools. It is thus clear that – at this site at any rate – conventional tool typology can give only a very approximate indication of function, and that analysis restricted to intentionally retouched pieces will cover but a small proportion of the pieces which were actually used as tools. Such analysis can thus be expected to give only a very incomplete picture of the total site activity.

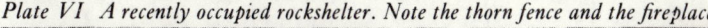

Plate V   An anciently occupied rockshelter in course of excavation

Plate VI   A recently occupied rockshelter. Note the thorn fence and the fireplace

It is clear therefore that our techniques of investigating the sites and industries of the stone-tool users remain extremely rudimentary. Many new techniques of analysis will have to be devised, and many existing collections re-examined, before we can even begin to understand the implications and meaning of the large numbers of stone artefacts which are the remains most frequently encountered on sites of this period.

It is generally accepted that most backed microlithic artefacts were used hafted, and that many of them formed components of composite tools. However, it is only very rarely that specimens have been recovered which clearly illustrate just how they were hafted. Sites in South Africa have yielded a number of hafted specimens, the majority of which appear to be of extremely late date and to be comparable with specimens which have been recorded ethnographically.

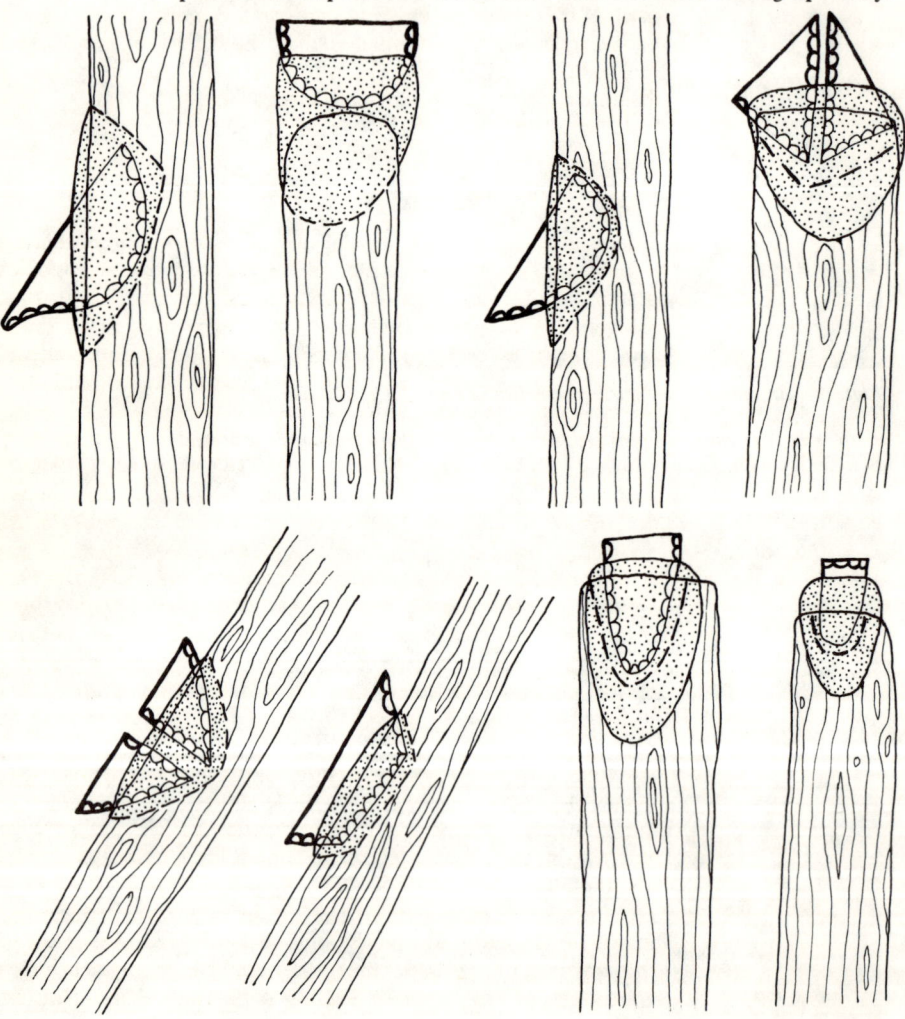

Fig. 6   Reconstructed methods of hafting microlithic tools (after D. W. Phillipson, 1976a)

It is interesting that some specimens from caves in the Cape Province of South Africa consist of hafted flakes which lack intentional secondary retouch (H. J. Deacon, 1966), thus confirming the evidence from Chiwemupula cited above that such artefacts were sometimes used as tools. While several earlier sites in South Africa and elsewhere have yielded specimens which display traces of mastic, it is only from the Makwe rockshelter in eastern Zambia that there has been recovered a substantial collection of microliths retaining mastic in a sufficiently good state of preservation to allow us to draw conclusions concerning the hafting methods employed. Here significant differences could be observed in the manner in which different types of microlith were hafted (D. W. Phillipson, 1976a); specimens are illustrated in Fig. 6. One result of this research has been to support the suggestion that several types of backed microlith could have been used as the points or barbs of arrows.

Such, then, is the methodological framework of our 'Late Stone Age' studies. It is to be hoped that the reader will bear these points in mind while perusing the following sections.

THE ORIGINS OF THE MODE 5 INDUSTRIES

The origins of the mode 5 industries of eastern and southern Africa remain very imperfectly understood. At least in South Africa, the previous millennia – extending back so far perhaps as forty thousand or even fifty thousand years ago – had been marked by the steady development of techniques for producing fine, parallel-sided flakes or blades which were sometimes made into backed microliths (J. D. Clark, 1970: 129, 135; Sampson, 1974: 231–57; Klein, 1974). It is possible, although far from certain, that the mode 5 industries of that region may themselves trace their origins back to such a local mode 3 ancestor. However, no direct continuity between the mode 5 industries of South Africa and these predecessors has yet been demonstrated. Indeed, the sequence between them seems to be interrupted by a completely distinct industrial tradition known as the Oakhurst Complex, which will be discussed in greater detail below. The point to be made is that there is certainly no need now to postulate, as was formerly frequently done, an origin foreign to sub-Saharan Africa for the mode 5 industries of the sub-continent.

In most areas, the makers of the mode 3 industries were hunters of the large gregarious animals, such as zebra and many of the bigger antelope, which are characteristic of plains with a relatively open vegetation. Such conditions would have been widespread in eastern and southern Africa during the relatively cool dry period, known as the 'Mount Kenya Hypothermal', which lasted from about 26,000 to about 12,000 bc (van Zinderen Bakker and Coetzee, 1972). In several areas the later mode 3 industries can be seen to have been developing in the direction of a microlithic technology. However, at present the only part of sub-Saharan Africa where there is evidence for direct continuity of this process leading to a fully microlithic mode 5 industry is in parts of central and eastern Zambia. In the present state of our knowledge it would, of course, be premature to suppose that this area was the only one where such a development took place, or even that it was geographically central to the focus of this development.

The key sites in this area are Leopard's Hill Cave, situated on the plateau some 60 kilometres to the south-east of Lusaka, and Kalemba rockshelter near Chadiza, in the extreme south-east of Zambia (S. F. Miller, 1969a: 301–413); D. W. Phillipson, 1973; 1976a). Of these sites, the present writer's excavations at Kalemba provide the longer sequence of industries and it is possible to see at this site the development of a blade-making technique in a mode 3 context extending back at least as far as 35,000 bc. There are occasional finely-made projectile points in this final mode 3 industry, but by far the most frequent tool-type at this time, and for the next fifteen thousand years, remained a series of crude flake scrapers. Before 22,000 bc we can see the gradual appearance of backing as a technique of retouch for the smaller blades; and by 20,000 bc backed flakes form a significant element in the industries from both Kalemba and Leopard's Hill. A comparable sequence may be present at Kisese II rockshelter south of Kondoa Irangi in central Tanzania, but full details of this have not yet been published by the excavator (Inskeep, 1962b). Here, occasional backed microliths are found associated with numerous scrapers as early as the thirtieth millennium bc.

It is interesting to note that, while these developments of microlithic technology were taking place, the traditional mode 3 tool-types continued to be produced and used at other sites in the same general region (D. W. Phillipson, 1976a). While it is possible that the two technologies were practised by the same populations to produce tools for different – possibly seasonally determined – activities (in other words that the two contemporary industries were what archaeologists would term 'activity variants' of each other) it seems far more probable that they were the work of distinct population groups. Certain sites in Rhodesia, notably Zombepata in the Sipolilo District of Mashonaland and Bambata in the Matopo Hills, have yielded evidence for successive occupation about forty thousand years ago by groups practising a conventional mode 3 technology and by those whose artefacts included a high proportion of parallel-sided blades (Armstrong, 1931; C. K. Cooke, 1971b). There is thus evidence for the early separation of groups who may be assumed to have been ancestral to the makers of the first microlithic mode 5 industries *sensu stricto*. It is to a consideration of the latter that we may now turn.

THE EARLIEST MICROLITHIC INDUSTRIES

The earliest true microlithic industries so far known in sub-Saharan Africa are found in the highland regions of the eastern and central parts of the sub-continent, in a broad belt stretching from Lake Victoria and southern Kenya, through Tanzania and northern Zambia, to the Zambezi. This area and the principal sites are shown in the map, Fig. 7. The most characteristic artefacts (Fig. 8, p. 46) are small pointed backed bladelets and various scrapers: these are sometimes accompanied, especially in Zambia, by smaller numbers of crescent-shaped microliths. In Zambia bored stones are found in industries of this period, but the presence of ground stone axes, while probable, is not firmly demonstrated until more recent times.

This industry has been found at several sites in Zambia, including Kalemba and Leopard's Hill which have already been mentioned; and at several rockshelters further north including Chifubwa Stream in

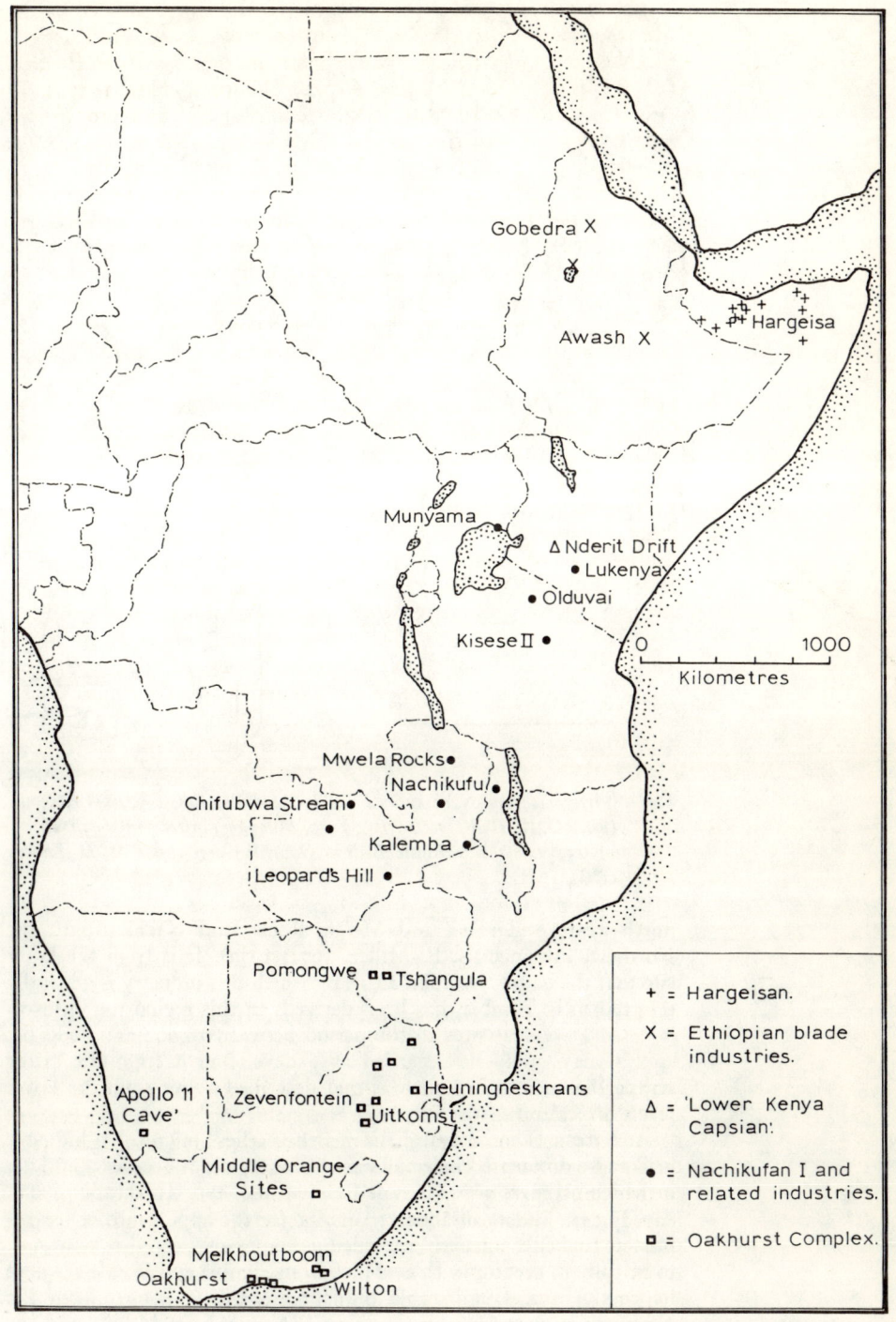

Fig. 7 Distribution of Oakhurst Complex, mode 4 and early mode 5 industries in eastern and southern Africa

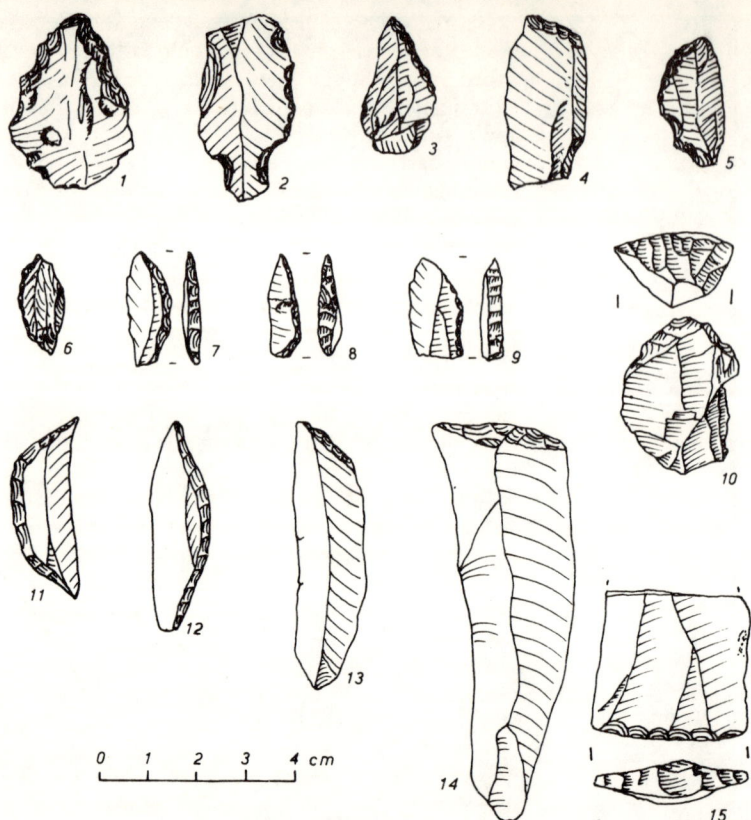

Fig 8 Artefacts from 'Nachikufan I' and related industries: 1–6, from Kalemba (after D. W. Philipson, 1976a); 7–10, Munyama (after van Noten, 1971); 11–15, from the Naisiusiu Beds at Olduvai Gorge (after M. D. Leakey et al., 1972)

north-western Zambia and Mwela Rocks and Nachikufu in the Northern Province (S. F. Miller, 1971; 1973). It is from the latter site that the name 'Nachikufan I', by which this industry is generally referred to in Zambia, has been derived. In this region the industry is dated at several sites to the period between 16,000 and 9000 bc, and it may safely be regarded as a development from the crude scraper-based industry such as that described above from the lower levels of Kalemba.

At Kisese II in central Tanzania the earliest microlithic industry is likewise dominated by small backed flakes, and it overlies a horizon in which scrapers are the most frequent tool-type (Inskeep, 1962b). A radiocarbon date of about 17,000 bc for the appearance of microliths at this site, formerly regarded as impossibly early, is now seen to be fully in keeping with evidence from Zambia and from elsewhere in East Africa. Comparable industries are now known from the Naisiusiu Beds at Olduvai Gorge in Tanzania, from Munyama Cave on Buvuma Island in Lake Victoria, and from Lukenya Hill near Nairobi in southern Kenya (M. D. Leakey et al., 1972; van Noten, 1971; Gramly, 1976). At all of these three sites radiocarbon dates of the sixteenth to the thirteenth millennia bc have been obtained.

No general name has yet been proposed for these early East African mode 5 industries; in each case only brief descriptions have been published and, although their general similarity is apparent, it is not yet clear just how alike they are. Certainly, it would be premature to apply to them the term 'Nachikufan I' by which their Zambian counterparts are generally known. There is, however, a basic family resemblance among all these industries: they are broadly contemporary, typologically similar, and in each case appear to be the first true microlithic mode 5 industry in their respective areas.

At several sites it has been observed that the appearance of a mode 5 technology was accompanied by a change in hunting emphasis, as revealed by the animal bones recovered from the living areas, towards the pursuit of creatures smaller and less gregarious than those which were preferred in earlier times. Such a correlation may be made with the inception of the 'Nachikufan I' industry at Kalemba; and here there is also geological evidence at this time for a return to warmer, wetter conditions towards the end of the 'Mount Kenya Hypothermal' (p. 27, above). It may be surmised that this climatic change, which appears to have been a widespread phenomenon in eastern Africa (van Zinderen Bakker and Coetzee, 1972), resulted in an increased density of vegetational cover in areas which had previously been relatively open plains. As a consequence of this, the gregarious game of the plains would have become less easy to come by: much of it doubtless migrated to more westerly areas where, owing to the lower rainfall, more open conditions continued. The inhabitants of eastern Africa had perforce to adjust their hunting methods to conform with these circumstances: the result was an increased reliance on the bow and microlith-tipped arrow, more effective for hunting the smaller solitary game of the now increasing woodlands than were the larger projectiles which had been used by their predecessors for hunting on the more open plains (D. W. Phillipson, 1976a). It is interesting to note, as will be emphasized later in this chapter, that the commencement of mode 5 technology in other parts of southern Africa, which took place at two different periods in two distinct regions, may in each case be linked with a change to hunting in more densely wooded conditions.

BLADE INDUSTRIES OF NORTH-EASTERN AFRICA

In the more northerly parts of eastern Africa, several areas (Fig. 7) have yielded evidence for industries based on the production of fine large punch-struck blades. Characteristic artefacts from these industries are shown in Fig. 9. These mode 4 industries, in the areas where they occur, invariably pre-date the development of a fully microlithic mode 5 technology.

The best known of these blade industries are the so-called 'Lower Kenya Capsian' in the Eastern Rift Valley areas of Kenya, and the Hargeisan of the northern parts of Somalia. The 'Lower Kenya Capsian' is best represented at the site of Nderit Drift, where it is dated to the eleventh millennium bc (Isaac et al., 1972). Absolute dates for the Hargeisan have not yet been obtained (J. D. Clark, 1954: 218–25). Comparable blade industries have recently been discovered in two separate regions of Ethiopia: in the Awash valley east of Addis Ababa and at Gobedra rockshelter near Axum in Tigre (J. D. Clark, personal

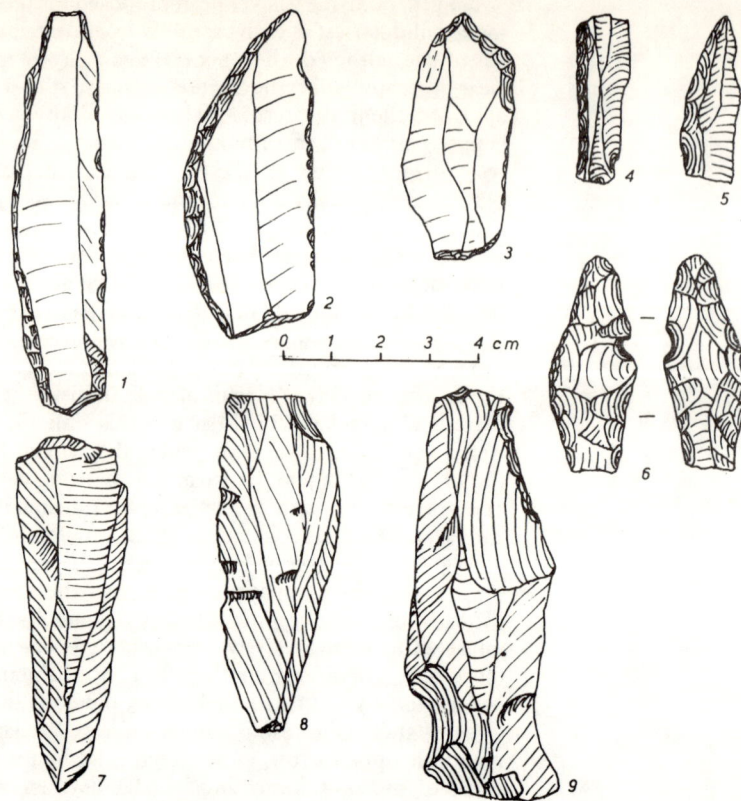

Fig. 9   *Artefacts from the blade industries of north-eastern Africa: 1–3, 'Lower Kenya Capsian' (after L. S. B. Leakey, 1931); 4–6, Hargeisan (after J. D. Clark, 1954); 7–9, from Gobedra (after D. W. Phillipson, 1977a)*

communication; D. W. Phillipson, 1977a). At the latter site the final stage of the blade industry is dated to the eighth millennium bc. The fine punch-struck blades – most frequently, except at Gobedra, of obsidian – sometimes include backed forms, but true microliths do not occur.

So far there has been recovered no convincing evidence that these blade industries were derived from their mode 3 predecessors in their respective areas, and it has frequently been suggested that they were introduced into north-eastern Africa from some foreign source (J. D. Clark, 1970: 162). It should be emphasized that the connexions between the Ethiopian and Somalian industries on the one hand and the 'Lower Kenya Capsian' on the other have not been fully demonstrated. The territory intervening between these two regions (northern Kenya, southern Ethiopia and southern Somalia) is not at all well explored by archaeologists; and even if the Hargeisan and the Ethiopian industries can be shown to be of foreign inspiration, the same does not necessarily hold good for the 'Lower Kenya Capsian'.

Before this question can be answered satisfactorily the following points will have to be investigated. First, the immediate local antecedents of these blade industries will need to be discovered and considered as possible ancestors of the mode 4 industries themselves.

Secondly, more detailed comparisons will have to be made both with the contemporary industries of the Nile valley and with the backed blade industries such as 'Nachikufan I' which have been described in an earlier section. It will be noted that these northern industries are contemporary with the later stages of the 'Nachikufan I' and related industries of the more southerly parts of eastern Africa and of central Africa. It is possible, but unlikely, that the former blade industries will come to be regarded merely as northerly counterparts of the latter, and that their idiosyncratic typology will be found to be due as much to the finer nature of the available raw materials as it is to cultural factors. Should this connexion be substantiated it would be an acceptable hypothesis to suppose that the 'Lower Kenya Capsian' and Hargeisan could trace their origin to these more southerly industries which appear, on our present knowledge, to be their seniors by some five or six thousand years.

THE OAKHURST COMPLEX

It was noted above how there is now a considerable body of evidence that the earliest microlithic mode 5 industries in central and eastern Africa were preceded by crude industries in which large flake scrapers are the most frequently encountered tool-type. We shall now turn to consider a remarkably similar scraper-based industry which was widespread in South Africa, Rhodesia and Namibia. The major sites are shown in the map at Fig. 7. In this area the scraper industries immediately precede the first mode 5 occurrences, but are, interestingly enough, some ten to twelve thousand years later in date than their counterparts further to the north. These southern African large scraper industries of between 12,000 and 8000 bc have been collectively designated the 'Oakhurst Complex' by Garth Sampson (1974: 258–91), the name being derived from the cave on the south Cape coast where industries of this type were first recognized (Goodwin, 1938). (It should be noted that the term 'Oakhurst Complex' has not met with the acceptance of all archaeologists working in southern Africa – e.g. Klein, 1974.) A selection of Oakhurst Complex artefacts is illustrated in Fig. 10.

The ancestry of the Oakhurst Complex remains unclear and, despite our ignorance about its relationship to its chronological predecessors in southern Africa, it has become conventional to regard it as the first stage of the southern African 'Late Stone Age' – even though its connexion with the succeeding microlithic industries of the Wilton Complex is likewise imperfectly understood.

The most northerly certainly identified occurrences of the Oakhurst Complex are at two caves in the Matopo Hills of Rhodesia: Pomongwe and Tshangula (C. K. Cooke, 1963a). At both sites tools of this type overlie a developed mode 3 industry in which techniques of blade-production and backed retouch were developing. Backed implements are, however, completely lacking in the overlying Pomongwan industry which is attributed to the Oakhurst Complex. At both sites the Oakhurst Complex tools occur in a deposit of consolidated ash. It seems possible, therefore, that the sudden appearance and disappearance of this type of industry may here have been due to some transient specialized activity which was not practised in earlier or subsequent times. Such ideas must, however, remain speculative until further studies of the Oakhurst Complex deposits have been con-

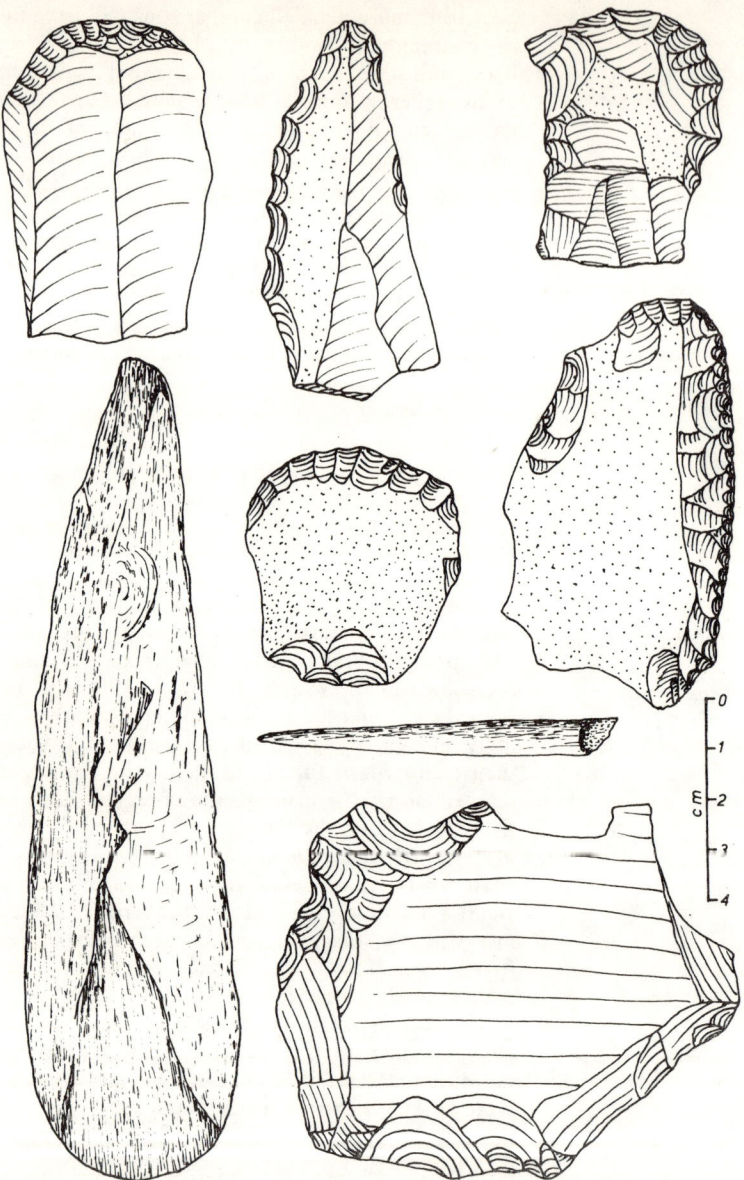

Fig. 10   Artefacts of the Oakhurst Complex (after Sampson, 1974)

ducted, and until more detailed examination of the artefacts themselves has been carried out in an attempt to discover the uses to which
the scrapers were actually put by their makers.

In the middle Orange area a comparable industry, with convex
scrapers on large flakes and virtually no other formalized tool-types,
is found on open sites which have not yet been dated (Sampson,
1967c; 1972). However, it appears to occupy a position in the
sequence comparable to that taken by industries of the Oakhurst Complex elsewhere: it postdates a blade industry of mode 3 type and precedes the introduction of true mode 5 industries into the area. This

scraper industry appears to be directly comparable with those referred to as 'Smithfield A' by J. Goodwin and C. van Riet Lowe (1929).

Further to the south, similar industries occur in the basal deposits of several rockshelters in the eastern and southern Cape, notably Wilton and Melkhoutboom: at the latter site it is dated to the eighth millennium bc (J. Deacon, 1972; H. J. Deacon, 1969; Klein, 1974). Here also, the Oakhurst Complex industries are succeeded by those of a microlithic type to which the Wilton site has given its name. These will be discussed in some detail in a later section of this chapter. It is in this area, too, that the Oakhurst rockshelter itself, after which the complex is named, is situated. This site, near the town of George, was originally excavated by John Goodwin at a time, before the development of radiocarbon dating techniques, when the relatively high antiquity of this industry was not recognized (Goodwin, 1938; see also Schrire, 1962; Sampson, 1974: 263–4).

In the light of the above, it is now possible to reconsider the previously accepted view that the South African 'Late Stone Age' industries fell into two cultural groups, one – dominated by geometric microliths and very small scrapers – being referred to as the 'Wilton', and the other – in which microliths were rare or absent – as the 'Smithfield'. It was at one time felt that these industries were the work of two contemporary but geographically and demographically distinct population groups. It now transpires that this view was mistaken and that the distinction between the two industries is more chronological (H. J. Deacon, 1972).

The industrial succession in the Transvaal remains comparatively poorly known. Industries described as of 'early Late Stone Age' types are associated at sites such as Heuningneskrans in the Lydenburg District with radiocarbon dates as early as the twenty-third millennium bc, but no typological details of these industries have yet been published (Beaumont and Vogel, 1972). It does appear, however, that microlithic industries in this province of South Africa are rare and generally of very late occurrence. It may well be that industries of Oakhurst Complex type will be found to have prevailed in the Transvaal for a somewhat longer period than they did elsewhere. Within this group would be subsumed the industries described as 'early' and 'middle Smithfield' by Revil Mason (1962: 303–10), occurring at such sites as Zevenfontein and Uitkomst respectively. The latter occurrence is dated by radiocarbon to the eighth millennium bc, which is in keeping with the evidence from elsewhere for the date of the Oakhurst Complex. The main 'Smithfield' occupation at Heuningneskrans appears also to be of this same general period.

The evidence from Namibia is concordant with that which we have described from other parts of southern Africa. Here also, microlithic industries are found to be underlain by one in which large flake scrapers are the dominant type. This is at present best known from W. E. Wendt's excavations at the 'Apollo 11 Cave' in the Huns Mountains near the confluence of the Orange and Fish rivers, where the scraper industry is securely dated to between the thirteenth and the eighth millennia bc. The interface with the succeeding microlithic industry is dated to some time in the eighth millennium. At this site, unusually for an Oakhurst Complex deposit, numbers of ostrich eggshell beads and a marine shell pendant were recovered. This horizon of the 'Apollo 11 Cave' is also of importance as having yielded the earliest dated examples of rock painting to have been found at any site in sub-Saharan Africa (Wendt, 1972). These remarkable specimens are discussed in greater detail in a later chapter of this book.

Despite its wide geographical extent, the Oakhurst Complex displays a close homogeneity of its component industries. Throughout its distribution it also has a marked chronological integrity, falling within the period from the twelfth to the eighth millennia bc. Only in the Transvaal are there indications that it may possibly have extended into earlier or later times. Concerning its relationship with its predecessors and successors we remain in almost total ignorance: likewise any interpretation of the functional significance of the flake scrapers, which are almost the only tool type found in Oakhurst Complex deposits, can at present be little more than inspired guesswork.

MICROLITHIC INDUSTRIES
AFTER 8000 bc

In the previous sections we have discussed how industries based upon the production of backed blades came to be established over the greater part of central and eastern Africa by about ten thousand or twelve thousand years ago. By the eighth millennium bc it appears that most of our region, including southern Africa, was inhabited by people producing such artefacts, although in several areas separate groups seem to have continued to practise the earlier mode 3 technology. During the eighth millennium or shortly thereafter regional mode 5 industries – in which the production of geometric microliths played a dominant part – were established over the greater part of the area, and it is probable that this was mainly due to local development from the earlier mode 5 industries of the respective areas which we have already discussed. The principal exception to this, as will be shown below, appears to have been in the regions situated to the south of the Zambezi. It is convenient to discuss these microlithic industries geographically, starting in the north of our region. Sites of this period are exceptionally numerous, and the location of all those mentioned by name in the text is shown in the map at Fig. 11.

In northern Somalia the Hargeisan industries were superseded at an as yet unknown date by microlithic industries described as 'Wilton'. These are best represented at a rockshelter at Mandera near Berbera which was excavated by Desmond Clark. In these Somalia 'Wilton' industries crescents, short end-scrapers and small convex scrapers are the artefacts most frequently encountered. Since some assemblages appear to be typologically intermediate between the Hargeisan and this local 'Wilton', Clark has suggested that the latter may have been derived in Somalia from the former. The 'Wilton' industry of Somalia is to be regarded as one of several basically similar regional industries which are widely distributed in north-eastern Africa. Most of these are, however, known only from undated and poorly documented contexts. Such industries, on which considerable further research is clearly required, include those of Harar Province of Ethiopia, those of the Lake Tana region and also the so-called 'Doian' industries (Fig. 12) of the more southerly and eastern parts of Somalia, which are at present best known from excavations conducted more than thirty years ago by Paulo Graziosi at Gure Makeke

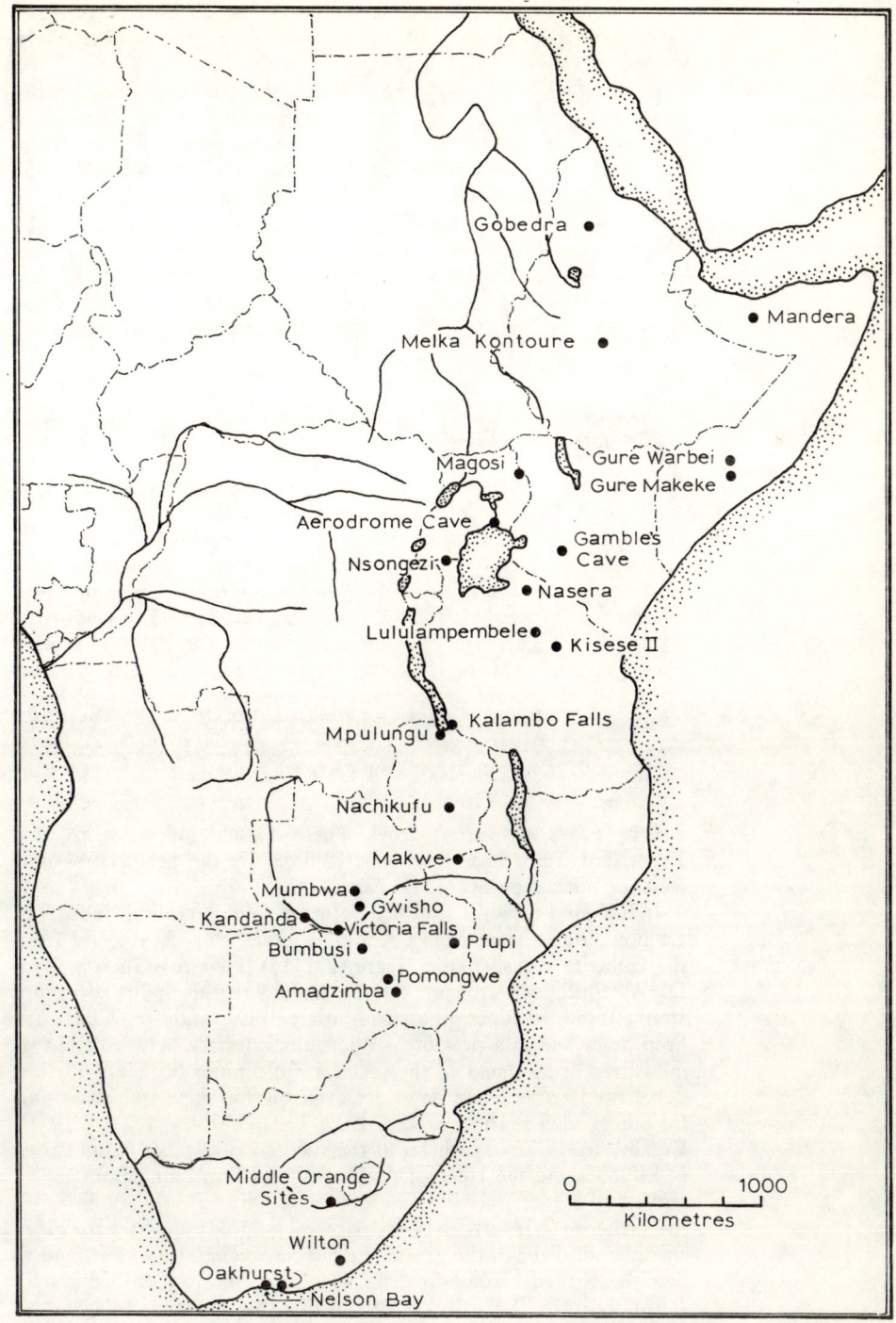

Fig. 11 Principal sites of microlithic industries in eastern and southern Africa

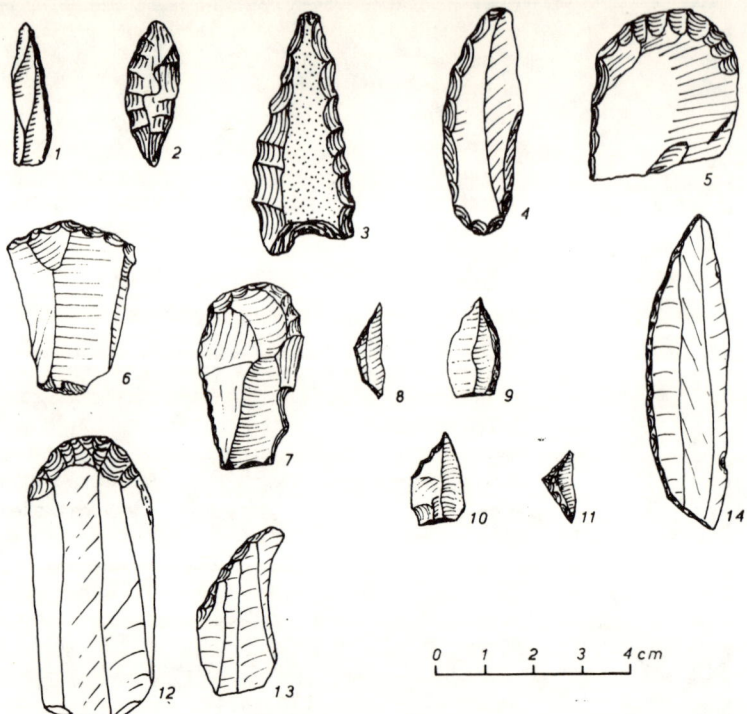

Fig. 12   Artefacts from microlithic industries in eastern Africa: 1–5, Doian (after
J. D. Clark, 1954); 6–11, from Gobedra (after D. W. Phillipson,
1977a); 12–14, 'Upper Kenya Capsian' (after L. S. B. Leakey, 1931)

and by Clark at Gure Warbei. These 'Doian' industries are differentiated from those known as 'Wilton' by the presence of uni-
facial or bifacial points (J. D. Clark, 1954).

In highland Ethiopia stratified occurrences of microlithic industries
are now known from Melka Kontoure near Addis Ababa and from
the Gobedra rockshelter in Tigre (Fig. 12) (Hivernel-Guerre, 1970;
D. W. Phillipson, 1977a). At the latter site this industry occurs
stratigraphically superimposed on a large blade industry which has
been described in a previous section, the interface between the two
industries being dated to the seventh millennium bc. Until further
details and radiocarbon dates are available for these industries and
for others such as those around Lake Tana (Moysey, 1943; L. S. B.
Leakey, 1943), any synthesis of the succession of mode 5 industries
in Ethiopia and the Horn of Africa will lack firm foundations.

Further to the south, in East Africa, microlithic industries are widespread and, through the greater part of this region, they clearly post-
date the backed blade industries which have been described above.
It is only in the Lake Nakuru basin that the transition between the
two industries is at all securely dated. Here, the 'Lower Kenya Capsian', which we have attributed above to the backed blade industrial
tradition, is dated at Nderit Drift to the eleventh millennium bc; while
the beginning of the occupation of Gamble's Cave, which yielded
industries of the microlithic 'Upper Kenya Capsian', has yielded dates

early in the seventh millennium (Sutton, 1972). Although the apparent continuity between the Lower and Upper 'Kenya Capsian' is no doubt to a certain extent due to the effect upon the typology of the locally abundant fine obsidian of which the artefacts are made, there is no reason to believe that the two phases are other than successive manifestations of a single stone-working tradition. It may here be noted that the name 'Kenya Capsian' is derived from a supposed affinity (L. S. B. Leakey, 1952), which is no longer upheld, with a North African industry. The 'Upper Kenya Capsian' at Gamble's Cave (Fig. 12) contains backed blades, crescents, burins and end-scrapers, with ostrich eggshell beads and bone points (L. S. B. Leakey, 1931: 91–171). The economy and significance of this settlement are discussed in greater detail below.

Elsewhere in East Africa comparable microlithic industries occur, as in the upper levels of Magosi in northern Uganda, where the comparatively crude appearance of the microliths when compared with those of the 'Upper Kenya Capsian' may perhaps be explained, at least in part, by reference to the inferior quality of the raw material which was used (G. Cole, 1967). The same is true of the industries which have been attributed to the East African 'Wilton'. The various groups recognized within this complex are not well defined or dated. These industries are found in open sites and rockshelters in southern Kenya and northern Tanzania, and also in shell mounds on the shores of Lake Victoria (L. S. B. Leakey, 1936; Gabel, 1969). The longest sequences, for which it is hoped that detailed descriptions and dating evidence may shortly be forthcoming, are from two sites in northern Tanzania, Kisese II near Kondoa, to the lower levels of which we have already alluded, and Nasera (Apis Rock) in the Ngorongoro Conservation Area (Inskeep, 1962b; L. S. B. Leakey, 1936). The lake-shore shell mounds investigated by Louis Leakey appear to represent a specialized activity variant of the local mode 5 industry; analogous occurrences are found in similar situations on the southern shore of Lake Tanganyika, as at Mpulungu. In these sites stone tools of any sort are remarkably rare. Comparable 'Wilton' industries have been described from further to the west, in Uganda. The most important sites here are Nsongezi rockshelter on the Kagera river west of Lake Victoria, and the Aerodrome Cave at Entebbe (Pearce and Posnansky, 1963; Nelson and Posnansky, 1970; O'Brien, 1939; van Riet Lowe, 1952a: 100).

The mode 5 industries from further south in Tanzania remain poorly known. In the Iramba area Knut Odner (1971a) has excavated a microlithic industry at Lululampembele: the later phases are dated to the second millennium bc, but the age of its earlier stages has not yet been ascertained.

The Zambian sequence of microlithic industries is one of the longest and best known in sub-Saharan Africa. It will be recalled that only here were geometric microliths regularly a major component part of the early backed blade industries, such as those which were being made in the northern and eastern parts of the country between about the seventeenth and the eighth millennia bc. During this period it seems probable that mode 3 industries continued in vogue in the southern and western regions. It has become general to regard the whole succession of local mode 5 industries, which in northern and central Zambia has a duration of some sixteen millennia, as comprising a

'Nachikufan Industrial Complex' (J. D. Clark, 1950a; S. F. Miller, 1973). The direct continuity of the stone-working tradition throughout this period is now open to doubt and the validity of the 'Nachikufan' as a single industrial complex must be regarded as not proven (D. W. Phillipson, 1976a).

In this area the 'Nachikufan I' industry (see above, p. oo) was succeeded around the eighth millennium bc by one described as 'Nachikufan II' in which two phases have been recognized. These phases are clearly related, but consistent dating evidence from several sites indicates that they are successive and more than activity variants. 'Nachikufan IIB' industries continued until early in the third millennium bc. In phase IIA the pointed backed bladelets of 'Nachikufan I' are largely displaced by backed and truncated flakes, in turn yielding pride of place in phase IIB to deep crescents and other geometric microliths. Bored stones and ground stone axes are present in both phases, which each have a more restricted geographical distribution than does 'Nachikufan I' (S. F. Miller, 1973).

In eastern Zambia, the time-span of the later 'Nachikufan' phases is occupied by a distinct industry which has been named after the Makwe rockshelter near Katete (D. W. Phillipson, 1973; 1976a). During the fourth and third millennia bc backed flakes and blades were gradually replaced by crescents and other geometric microliths among which idiosyncratic very deep triangular forms enjoyed a brief vogue. Ground stone axes were frequent, but bored stones – which were present in this area in 'Nachikufan I' times – do not occur in the Makwe Industry, except in its earliest phase. Varied bone points are characteristic, as are beads made of bone or shell. In this area the final stages of the Stone Age sequence are marked by the dominance of crescents to the virtual exclusion of all other implement types (Fig. 13).

The last four millennia bc in northern Zambia are characterized by a variety of microlithic industries, the inter-relationships of which are as yet imperfectly understood. That from Kalambo Falls at the southern end of Lake Tanganyika has been named the Kaposwa Industry (J. D. Clark, 1974: 107–52), but its distinctiveness from the heterogeneous industries attributed to 'Nachikufan III' further to the south is probably to a substantial extent due to the fine-grained mudstone of which the former is made, in contrast with the comparatively coarse quartz raw material of the 'Nachikufan III' (e.g. D. W. Phillipson, 1969).

The distribution of the so-called 'Nachikufan' industries is apparently restricted to the areas of Zambia north and east of the Kafue–Zambezi line. In southern and south-western Zambia the microlithic industries have been conventionally described as 'Wilton'. There is as yet no convincing evidence for the presence of these mode 5 industries in that area prior to the fourth millennium bc. Since several of the contemporary 'Nachikufan III' occurrences have been described as being remarkably similar to those of the 'Wilton', it now seems more reasonable to regard the Zambian 'Wilton' and 'Nachikufan III' industries as regional variants of a common tradition which at this time spread into the more southern and western regions of Zambia – areas which had not previously been occupied by people practising microlithic industries. The comparative scarcity in the south of such tools as bored stones, ground stone axes and concave scrapers may be attributed primarily to the more open environment of these

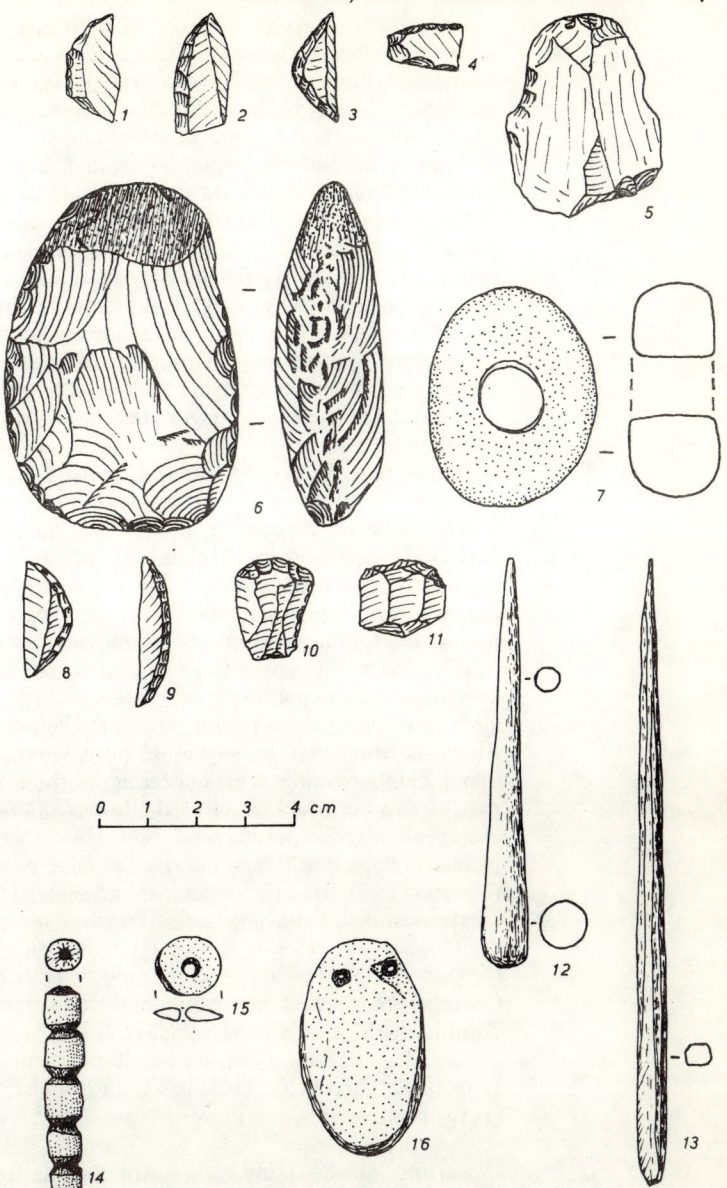

Fig. 13 Artefacts from microlithic industries in southern Africa: 1–7, Makwe industry from eastern Zambia (after D. W. Phillipson, 1976a); 8–16, Matopan from Amadzimba (after Cooke and Robinson, 1954)

southerly regions; but these environmental factors, which were previously regarded as of paramount importance in the distinction between the 'Nachikufan' and 'Wilton' industries, are now seen to be of comparatively minor significance, and the true distinction between the two to be chronological.

The 'Wilton' industries of southern Zambia were first investigated by Desmond Clark (1942; 1950b) at the Mumbwa Cave in the Kafue Valley, and on the banks of the Zambezi upstream of the Victoria

Falls (see also Inskeep, 1959). A clearer and more detailed picture has recently been obtained by Creighton Gabel (1965) and by Brian Fagan and Francis van Noten (1971) at the Gwisho Hotsprings in Lochinvar National Park. Mounds beside the springs have been shown to represent prolonged occupation covering a period of some one and a half millennia beginning around 3000 bc. Crescents, backed flakes, and blades dominate the stone industry, with small convex scrapers being comparatively rare. Organic materials, because of the waterlogged nature of the spring deposits, were comparatively well preserved. Some thirty-five human skeletons were recovered, as were animal bones providing a detailed picture of the hunting-dominated diet of the sites' inhabitants. Grass-lined hollows were probably used for sleeping; and settings of posts are interpreted as the remains of windbreaks. Wooden artefacts include digging sticks, bows, arrowheads and fire-drills. Large numbers of shell beads were also produced at Gwisho.

In the extreme west of Zambia, in the Kalahari Sand country of the upper Zambezi valley, it appears that the microlithic mode 5 industries were introduced at an even later date. Evidence from Kandanda near Katima Mulilo, and other sites further upstream, suggests that a predominantly mode 3 technology continued to be practised until about the middle of the second millennium bc: only then do microlithic implements become common (L. Phillipson, 1976).

Why did mode 5 industries appear in this south-western region only at such a comparatively late date – some thirteen thousand years after their inception in regions only 500 kilometres to the north-east? An explanation may be suggested on environmental grounds. This upper Zambezi valley area, bordering on the Kalahari Desert, is the part of Zambia which receives the lowest rainfall, and the aridity is exacerbated by the porous sandy soil. Here, therefore, the gregarious plains antelope would have survived in large numbers long after their migration away from the better watered areas to the north-east which, I have postulated above (p. 27), took place before 12,000 bc towards the close of the 'Mount Kenya Hypothermal'. It was not until the climatic optimum of about 2700–1300 bc (van Zinderen Bakker and Coetzee, 1972) that environmental conditions in south-western Zambia would have become such as to stimulate the adoption of mode 5 technology. That increased rainfall did occur in this Kalahari area from about 2400 bc onwards has been demonstrated by H. J. Cooke (1975) from research in western Ngamiland.

Turning our attention now to the regions south of the Zambezi, we enter the territory which we have shown above to have been occupied between the twelfth and eighth millennia bc by the practitioners of industries attributed to the Oakhurst Complex. In parts at least of Rhodesia it seems that microlithic mode 5 industries appeared in a fully fledged form at some time during the seventh or eighth millennia bc. Here, as in more southerly regions, it is possible that the mode 5 technology of this time was introduced from north of the Zambezi. It is only from the Matopo Hills near Bulawayo that a detailed dated sequence is available; and here the site most intensively investigated is that of Pomongwe Cave, excavated by C. K. Cooke (1963a). The mode 5 industry of the region was originally known as 'Wilton', but in 1966 the local term 'Matopan' was proposed so as not to presuppose any long-distance correlation with what was, at that time, an inadequately described industry from the eastern Cape. The Matopan industry continued to be practised until well after the arrival of Iron Age peoples in Matabeleland during the first millennium AD; but unfortunately no detailed analyses such as would indicate the extent of typological development during this seven or eight thousand-year period have yet been undertaken. Matopan industries are characterized by large numbers of small convex scrapers; backed microliths are markedly less frequent, and among them backed blades easily outnumber the crescents. At some sites, notably Amadzimba Cave, also in the Matopos, remarkable and varied collections of bone tools (Fig. 13) have been recovered: these include arrow-points, link-shafts, bodkins and eyed needles (Cooke and Robinson, 1954). Ostrich eggshell beads are also a characteristic part of the Matopan assemblages.

There is evidence that the mode 5 industries in other parts of Rhodesia differed in significant respects from those of the Matopan; but these other areas have not yet been investigated in any detail. In the north-west of Rhodesia, material from Bumbusi rockshelter near Wankie is said to share many features with the Zambian 'Wilton' of the Victoria Falls region (J. D. Clark, 1950b). Artefacts excavated by Keith Robinson (1952) from Pfupi and other rockshelters near Marandellas in Mashonaland include bored stones, ground axes and a variety of scraper tools, notably concave types which do not generally occur in the Matopan. It has been pointed out that these industries share certain resemblances with the 'Nachikufan II' material from northern Zambia but, since the Mashonaland finds have not yet been radiocarbon dated nor subjected to quantitative analysis, more detailed comparisons with the more northerly industries cannot yet be made. It is possible that this Mashonaland mode 5 industry may have been established at a date earlier than that of the initial Matopan industries: it will be recalled that there is no evidence for the presence of industries of the Oakhurst Complex further north in Rhodesia than the Matopo Hills.

In our earlier discussion of the Oakhurst Complex it was noted how the South African 'Late Stone Age' was originally regarded as being divisible into two contemporaneous industries, the 'Smithfield' and the 'Wilton'; and we have commented how the most recent research indicates that these industries are better regarded as chronologically rather than geographically and demographically distinguished. In the Transvaal, microlithic industries are sparse and may all be of comparatively recent date (Mason, 1962: 310–30; Schoonraad and Beaumont, 1968). In the middle Orange area also there is no evidence for the presence of microlithic industries before the third millennium (Sampson, 1970: 168–70). In this thirstland region there is, indeed, little evidence for any human occupation during the period 7500 to 2600 bc (J. Deacon, 1974): the appearance of mode 5 industries was therefore broadly contemporary with the corresponding event in south-western Zambia, and may be attributed to the same phase of climatic amelioration.

Further to the south, however, on the south Cape coast, it is apparent that the Oakhurst Complex was replaced by microlithic mode 5 industries during the seventh or eighth millennia bc. This change accompanied a shift in hunting emphasis which closely parallels that recorded in connexion with the inception of the 'Nachikufan I' industry in eastern Zambia some six or eight thousand years earlier. In this southern region the extensive coastal plain on which the large gregarious game had grazed was now flooded by the rise in sea level which followed the end of the last glaciation. Exploitation of marine food-resources partly replaced the plains hunting; and a shift to the hunting of smaller creatures in an environment which probably closely resembled the present is attested both on the coast and in some inland regions (Klein, 1974; H. J. Deacon, 1972).

The Wilton Complex, to which these South African mode 5 industries belong, takes its name from a rockshelter on the farm Wilton not far from Alicedale in the eastern Cape Province. The site was excavated by J. Hewitt as long ago as 1921, but no detailed analysis of the industries recovered was then conducted. Meanwhile, the name 'Wilton' was indiscriminately applied to African microlithic industries from as far afield as Ethiopia and Nigeria, even though these bore only a very general affinity to the material from the type-area. Recently, however (1972), Janette Deacon has re-excavated the Wilton site and has obtained radiocarbon dates for the detailed sequence there. An initial Oakhurst Complex occupation was overlaid by a layer containing a microlithic industry in which small round scrapers were the most common tool type. Backed microliths steadily become more common; and crescents are particularly numerous in a horizon dated to the beginning of the third millennium bc. Thereafter they gradually yield ground to various forms of backed blade. A sequence parallel to the later part of that from Wilton has been described by Garth Sampson (1970; 1972) from the middle Orange area.

Further west along the south Cape coast the microlithic sequence appears to be broadly parallel to that from Wilton. It is known from the upper levels of the Oakhurst rockshelter near George, and also from excavations at Nelson Bay Cave at Plettenberg Bay, where the beginning of the microlithic succession is dated to early in the seventh millennium (Goodwin, 1938; Klein, 1974; see also Keller, 1970; 1973). This recent work by Hilary and Janette Deacon, Ray Inskeep and Richard Klein throws light on the problematical sequence at Matjes River rockshelter where a scraper-based industry overlain by a microlithic one has been known for some years (Louw, 1960; see also Inskeep, 1961). Here, as through the greater part of the southern Cape Province, the Wilton Complex appears to have been succeeded during the first millennium bc by industries in which varied scraper forms again progressively replaced the microliths; these industries are discussed in detail in chapter X. In other parts of southern Africa, however, notably in Lesotho and adjacent parts of the Drakensberg, and in much of Namibia, microlithic industries such as may be attributed to the Wilton Complex continued into more recent times (Carter, 1969; Carter and Vogel, 1974; Wendt, 1972).

The many different methods of analysis and description which have been applied to the mode 5 industries of eastern and southern Africa make it difficult to evaluate their inter-regional similarity and degree of chronological continuity. The effects on artefact typology of the various raw materials employed are also very imperfectly understood. There can indeed be discerned a strong family resemblance between the great majority of the microlithic industries practised throughout eastern and southern Africa from their inception between the seventeenth and eighth millennia bc until the beginning of the Christian era. Such industries are, however, the logical conclusion of processes of typological development which are known to have been under way in several different parts of the sub-continent during the preceding millennia.

The argument for local development of mode 5 technology is strengthened by consideration of the Tshitolian industries of northern Angola and adjacent parts of Zaïre, a detailed description of which falls outside the geographical scope of this book. The stone-working techniques of the Tshitolian are clearly rooted in those of their local mode 3 (Lupemban) predecessors, yet the progress of their evolution quite closely parallels that described here from more eastern regions.

Evidence has been cited above to connect the inception of mode 5 technology with developments in hunting techniques brought about in response to environmental change. In view of this, and of the apparent independent development of techniques of microlith manufacture in Angola, it would be premature to assume, because mode 5 technology seems to have appeared first in the plateau regions of Tanzania and northern Zambia, that the 'Nachikufan I' industries of that region are necessarily directly ancestral to their later counterparts elsewhere. Analysis and comparison far more rigorous than has yet been attempted will be necessary before the spread of microlithic technology through eastern and southern Africa can be fully understood.

THE BEGINNINGS OF PERMANENT SETTLEMENT

In East Africa there is evidence for the establishment, very early in the duration of the microlithic mode 5 industries, of semi-permanent settlements which were based on the exploitation of exceptionally rich environments. These settlement sites are found in the Khartoum area of the Nile valley and, further south, beside Lakes Nakuru, Rudolf and Edward. Comparable sites also occur over an enormous expanse of the southern Sahara and sahel from the Nile westwards to Lake Chad and beyond (see Fig. 14, p. 46) (Sutton, 1974). They are located on the shores of former rivers and lakes; and it is clear that the economic basis of these settlements was the rich fishing which the waters at one time provided.

The period of the high lake levels can be placed between the ninth and the third millennia bc, with a peak level being attained about 7000 bc (Faure, 1966; van Zinderen Bakker, 1972). There is a remarkable concurrence in the fluctuations in the levels of the East African lakes and in those of the southern Sahara (Butzer et al., 1972; Beadle, 1974: 23). Comparable events are attested in the lakes of the Ethiopian Rift Valley at broadly the same time (Grove and Goudie, 1971; Grove, Street and Goudie, 1975). When it is pointed out that the waters of Lake Rudolf at this time stood at eighty metres above their present level, and that the Lake Chad of 9000 years ago was bigger by far than the modern Lake Victoria, the reader will appreciate the extent of the environmental changes which have taken place in these now arid regions.

Beside many of these ancient lakes have been found traces of fishing settlements (e.g. Monod and Mauny, 1957; Huard and Massip, 1964). The stone industries practised at these settlements were diverse, and

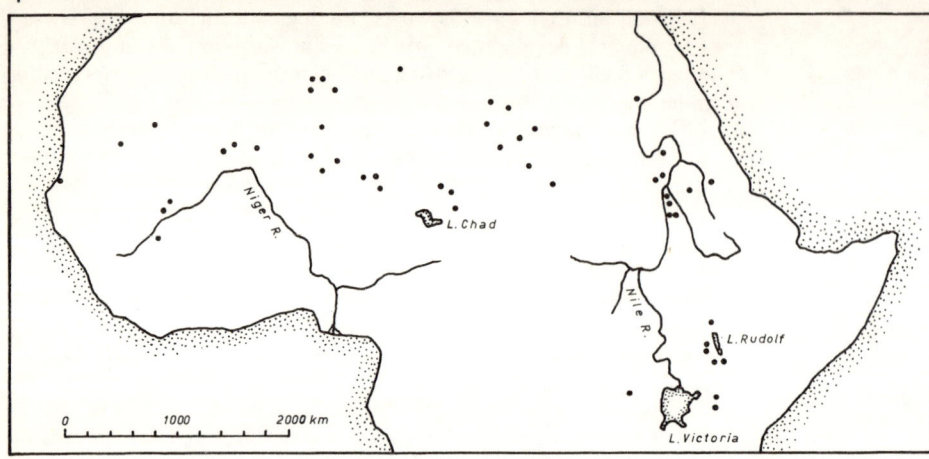

Fig. 14 Distribution of artefacts associated with semi-permanent fishing settlements in the southern Sahara, sahel and eastern Africa (after Sutton,
1974)

they seem clearly to have been rooted in the respective local traditions.
Other aspects of the material culture, notably the bone harpoon-heads
and – in some cases – the pottery, form a typological link between
the widely dispersed sites (Hays, 1974): these similarities are, however,
insufficient to support the hypothesis of a unified widespread 'aquatic
civilization' as proposed by John Sutton (1974).

Although its date is uncertain, it will be convenient to discuss first
the site of the Early Khartoum which was excavated by A. J. Arkell
some thirty years ago (Fig. 15). The riverside site yielded characteristic
microlithic tools including crescents and other geometric types, along
with larger crescent-adzes, long backed blades, and various scrapers.
Grooved and bored stones may have been used as sinkers for fishing
nets. Most remarkable, however, are the bone harpoon-heads, with
a variable number of barbs down one side only, and with grooves
cut around the base for the attachment of the line. It has been shown
that the design of these harpoons was inspired by the naturally barbed
spines of the catfish (D. W. Phillipson, 1977b; see Fig. 16:12). Pottery was found in large quantities, and the most characteristic type
was decorated with multiple horizontal grooved wavy lines, a design
which Arkell was able to show to have been made by using the spines
of catfish as combs. In the later phases of the settlement this 'wavy-line
pottery' was elaborated by the addition of punctate designs made by
jabbing the clay with a blunt bone point. Examples of these artefacts
are illustrated in Fig. 16. The inhabitants of the settlement were
buried within the confines of the site in tightly contracted positions:
the physical anthropology of these people will be discussed in a later
section. It seems that the Early Khartoum site was occupied for a
long period and on at least a semi-permanent basis, for walls of wattle
and sun-dried daub were discovered, and considerable evolution of
the pottery styles took place during the period of occupation. The
material culture indicates that fishing most probably formed the
economic basis for the settlement; and this is substantiated by the
presence of shells of *Ampullaria*, still used as bait by Sudanese fishermen. The animal bones recovered from the site are of exclusively wild

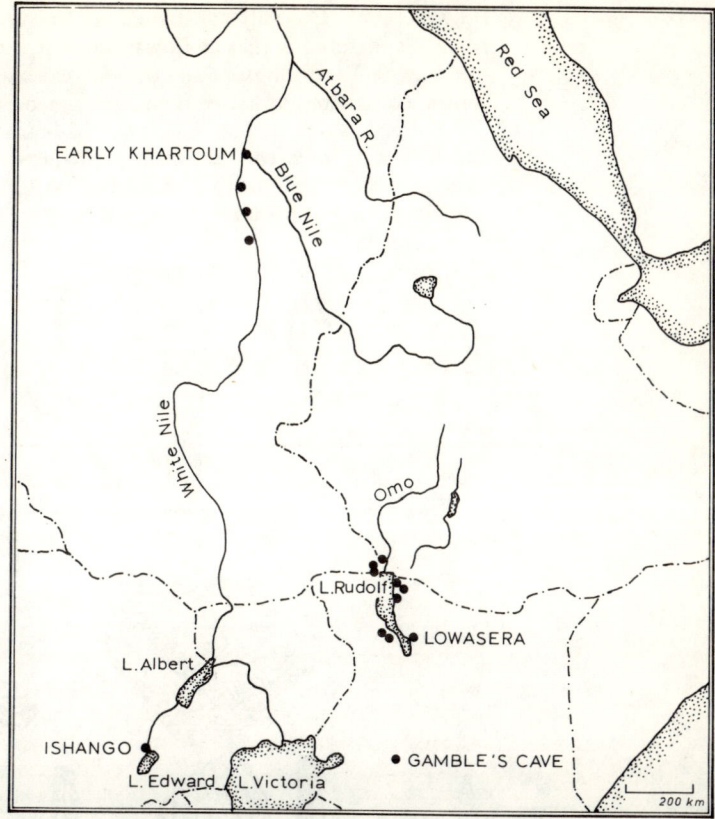

Fig. 15 Distribution of early fishing settlements in eastern Africa

species, indicating that hunting was also important. This fauna includes several swamp species and helps to indicate a climate somewhat wetter than that prevailing today, with the Nile flowing at a level appreciably higher than at present (Arkell, 1949).

The date of the Early Khartoum settlement has been the subject of controversy, in the absence of radiocarbon dates from that site itself. The occurrence of pottery similar to that from Early Khartoum in sites far to the west and north-west which have been dated as early as the sixth millennium bc (Hays, 1975; Posnansky and McIntosh, 1976) suggests that a date of similar magnitude is most probable. This has recently received some confirmation from the discovery, at Nile Valley sites situated both north and south of Khartoum, of barbed harpoon-heads similar to those from the latter site, in contexts dated to the second half of the seventh millennium bc (Wendt, 1966; Adamson, Clark and Williams, 1974).

The 'wavy line' pottery found on these early sites is of particular interest. Arkell (1962) has suggested that may have been an independent invention in sub-Saharan Africa.

Pottery apparently similar to that from Early Khartoum, and bone harpoon heads which show a marked resemblance to those from the latter site, have been reported by Laurence Robbins and others from several sites on the shores of Lake Rudolf in northern Kenya (Arambourg *et al.*, 1943; Whitworth, 1965; Robbins, 1972, 1974; F. H.

Brown, 1975). The only substantial settlement site there which contains this material is that at Lowasera, near the south-east corner of the lake (D. W. Phillipson, 1977*b*), where occupation appears to have continued as late as the third millennium bc. Occurrences of wavy line pottery in this area are dated by radiocarbon to around 6000 bc; and it is now apparent that semi-permanently occupied sites comparable economically to that of Early Khartoum were located along the shores of Lake Rudolf when the waters were 80 metres above their present level.

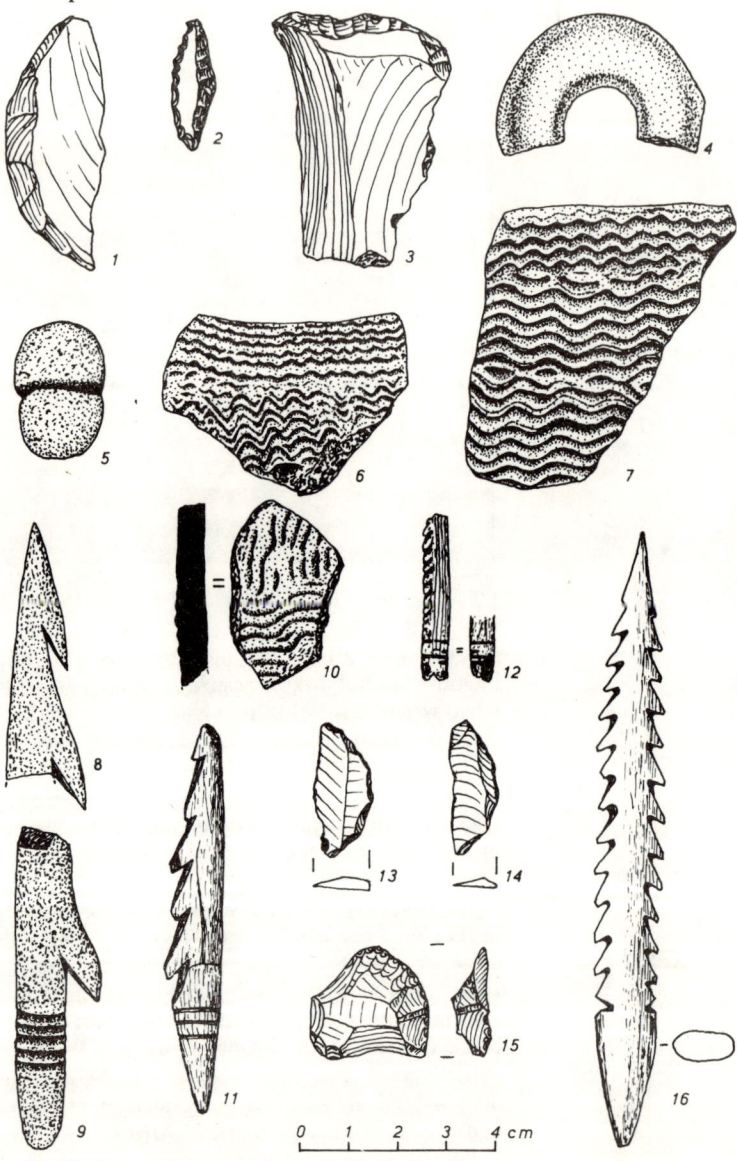

Fig. 16 Artefacts from early fishing settlements in eastern Africa: 1–9, from Early Khartoum (after Arkell, 1949); 10–14, from Lowasera (after D. W. Phillipson, 1977b); 15, 16, from Ishango (after de Heinzelin, 1957)

Further to the south, on the north-western shore of Lake Edward, Jean de Heinzelin (1957) has excavated the Ishango site which has yielded evidence of prolonged prehistoric occupation. The stone industry, or poor quality quartz, is remarkably crude: backed microliths occur in comparatively small numbers but are inexpertly made. Pottery is completely absent. Barbed bone harpoon-heads are again the most characteristic artefact. During the earlier phases of the occupation these were small and barbed on one side only. Later specimens are larger and include examples which are barbed on both sides. The exclusively wild fauna indicates, as at Khartoum, a climate somewhat moister than that which prevails in the Western Rift Valley today. Unfortunately, the date of this site is not firmly fixed, but an age somewhere between the ninth and the fifth millennia bc is generally regarded as probable.

The last of these semi-permanent settlement sites of East Africa which we have to discuss is that at Gamble's Cave, situated 25 kilometres south of Nakuru in the Eastern Rift Valley of Kenya beside a high beach level of the formerly very extensive Lake Nakuru (L. S. B. Leakey, 1931: 91–171). The stone industry from the site is of the type termed 'Upper Kenya Capsian' which we have already discussed. The very high antiquity previously attributed to the 'Upper Kenya Capsian' is not now credited; and radiocarbon dates recently obtained from Gamble's Cave place the beginning of the occupation of that site in the seventh millennium bc. The inhabitants of Gamble's Cave evidently depended for their livelihood on the exploitation of the rich fishing and fowling which the Lake Nakuru basin provided at a time when the water was about 180 metres above the present level (Washbourn-Kamau, 1971). Connexions with the sites discussed above are demonstrated by the occurrence of a single sherd of 'dotted wavy-line' pottery and by a fragment of a uniserial barbed bone harpoon-head (L. S. B. Leakey, 1931: 103 and plate XII; Oakley, 1961). Full details neither of the excavations conducted by Louis Leakey in the 1930s nor of those recently carried out by Glynn Isaac are yet available; and any further discussion of the site and the economy of its inhabitants would be premature.

The eastern African sites discussed in this section, although they have yielded no evidence whatsoever for the presence of cultivated crops or of domesticated animals, nevertheless demonstrate that some of the inhabitants of this region were, from about 6000 bc onwards, taking the first steps towards settled life through the establishment of at least semi-permanent habitation sites in areas where this was permitted by the richness of the natural environment. Desmond Clark (1971b) has argued that similar steps were taken in the Nubian and Upper Egyptian stretches of the Nile valley during these and somewhat earlier times (see also Wendorf, 1968: 1056–7). It is possible to interpret sites such as Gwisho, noted above, as indicating the presence of such settlement patterns, based on intensive food-collecting practices, in even more southerly African latitudes several millennia in advance of demonstrable techniques of food-production. Be that as it may, it is sites such as Ishango and Gamble's Cave, the inhabitants of which had at an early date embarked upon the path towards settled life, which indicate the receptiveness of some of the inhabitants of eastern Africa to the techniques of food production which spread through the region during the last three millennia before Christ.

CONCLUDING OVERVIEW

I have summarized in the preceding sections the industrial successions of the last twenty thousand years BC in eastern and southern Africa, prior to the advent of food production; and it will be apparent that there is a broad similarity in this material culture throughout the area. It is therefore in order to attempt an overall synthesis of the archaeological and other evidence for the economies and general ways of life to which this material culture relates. Much of the detailed evidence on which this summary is based has been noted above, but it should be emphasized that it is very widely scattered through time and space; and a synthesis of the type here attempted must necessarily involve bringing together diverse widely-scattered elements to produce a composite picture which may not represent in detail the conditions prevailing at individual sites.

Economic summary

Thin surface scatters of artefacts, which are often all that remains of open-air settlements lacking some sort of natural focus such as a spring, cave or rockshelter, indicate that settlements of this type were usually transitory. As in earlier times, many of them probably represent briefly occupied encampments established for a single task such as butchering a kill. It is probable that many rockshelters and other sites which appear to show signs of long occupation were in fact repeatedly settled on brief occasions rather than subjected to prolonged periods of continuous habitation. Sites which provided some sort of natural shelter were clearly favoured. Elsewhere, the only artificial shelters which are indicated in the archaeological or rock-painting record are simple semi-circular windbreaks of branches strengthened around the base with settings of stones, and perhaps covered with skins (Fagan and van Noten, 1971; Clark and Walton, 1962; C. K. Cooke, 1970). Comparable structures are also known from far earlier times. Evidence is now beginning to accumulate for the seasonal habitation of sites and exploitations of environments, a factor which would frequently be mirrored in the activities conducted and, consequently, in the typology of the artefacts deposited (Parkington and Poggenpoel, 1971; Parkington, 1972).

The mean sizes of such settlements were markedly smaller than those of later food-producing societies; and they are held to indicate site populations of generally between eight and twenty-five people (J. D. Clark, 1972). Other calculations, based on rock-painting representations, have given broadly comparable results (e.g. Maggs, 1971a). These population figures are within the range of those of recent hunter/gatherer societies in sub-Saharan Africa (Lee, 1968; Silberbauer, 1965).

Investigations conducted throughout the postulated territorial range of a group may be expected eventually to provide a clearer understanding of prehistoric patterns of exploitation than can be obtained through the study of individual sites. Such research, pioneered elsewhere, has but recently been applied to the later prehistory of sub-Saharan Africa (Carter, 1970; Yellen and Harpending, 1972).

The material culture of the various stone-tool-using societies has been described and discussed in detail above. Little recapitulation is necessary. The primary information which can be derived from artefact studies is technological. We have remarkably little reliable data on the actual purpose to which many implement types were put, although logical inferences can often of course be made; and these may sometimes be supported by ethnographic observations. It is clear that many types of microlith were hafted; and study of the hafting methods as outlined above may throw considerable light on their use, as may observation of edge damage and utilization patterns. Such studies are, however, still in their infancy. It is clear from such research, from ethnographic observations and from certain rock paintings, that some microliths were used as arrow-points and barbs (Phillipson and Phillipson, 1970; D. W. Phillipson, 1976a; J. D. Clark, 1959a: 222–4). Various bow-types are depicted in the paintings (e.g. Rudner and Rudner, 1970: Fig. 80); and a fragment of a wooden bow was recovered from a third millennium bc context at Gwisho Hotsprings in southern Zambia (Fagan and van Noten, 1971: 116). Osteological evidence indicates that even the largest animals were successfully killed. Poison was doubtless applied to the arrows, as is done by most recent hunting societies. Pods of one plant, *Swartzia*, used for the production of such a poison, were preserved at Gwisho (*ibid.*: 51). Other stone tools were clearly designed for cutting and scraping purposes such as skinning and butchering, for preparing skin and for working wood and bone.

Other subsistence activities such as fishing and foraging seem rarely to have left their mark on the stone tool assemblages, although microliths used as barbs for fish spears would presumably not be readily distinguishable from those used for arrows. Perishable materials used for nets and traps have not survived in the archaeological record, although such devices are represented in certain rock paintings. It is only when specialized stone artefacts such as net weights or bone artefacts such as barbed harpoon-heads were developed that fishing equipment reflects in the archaeological record the importance which it frequently held.

Gathering of vegetable foods would require little specialist equipment; although digging sticks which could be used for excavating roots and tubers as well as for digging water pits have, as at Gwisho, occasionally been preserved. Some of the bored stones which are widely distributed on sites of this period were used as weights for digging sticks, a practice which is not infrequently depicted in rock paintings as well as having been recorded ethnographically both in southern Africa and in Ethiopia (Schapera, 1930: 141; J. D. Clark, 1944). (Numerous other uses for some bored stone types have been suggested.) This scarcity of specialist equipment for food-gathering, taken with the infrequent preservation of traces of vegetable foods in the archaeological record, has probably resulted in a tendency to underestimate the importance of such foods in the prehistoric diet. This view is supported by the importance which vegetable foods assume in the diet of modern people generally regarded as hunters (e.g. Lee, 1968).

Besides tools and the by-products of their manufacture, the most frequent artefacts encountered on settlement sites are items which may have been used for personal adornment. Bone and shell beads and pendants have a wide distribution; and in some areas, notably eastern Zambia, changing fashions led to an evolution of their styles considerably more rapid than the contemporary changes which have been discerned in the stone tool typology (D. W. Phillipson, 1976a). It is probable that these beads and pendants were not only worn on the body and in the hair but that they were also sewn on to skins and on to clothing. Such is the practice of some peoples who make identical artefacts today. It is also frequently represented in the rock paintings, particularly in southern Africa as at Diana's Vow, Rusape, Rhodesia (Goodall, 1959: plate 5b).

The occurrence of ochre and other colouring matter is noted in many areas from the earliest phases of the mode 5 industries, and has sometimes been recorded from even earlier contexts. This material could have been used for the decoration of clothing or for direct adornment of the body. It does not necessarily relate to the practice of rock painting. The subject of prehistoric rock painting in eastern and southern Africa is discussed in detail in a later chapter of this book. We have noted above certain aspects of the subject-matter of the rock art which throw light upon the interpretation of excavated archaeological material. It may be observed that there is evidence, at least in southern Africa, for the practice of rock painting through the greater part of the duration of the period here considered; but further consideration of the topic would be out of place in this chapter.

Physical anthropology

The indigenous population of eastern and southern Africa is today physically diverse; and a brief description of the various types represented in this part of the sub-continent has been presented in chapter I. The most numerous group is that of the Negroid peoples who form the great majority of the population south of the Equator from southern Kenya to the Cape Province of South Africa. In the extreme south and in south-western Africa are found the remnants of the Khoi–San groups who are known from historical sources to have been formerly more numerous and more widespread than they are today. North of the Equator the picture is more complex, with Negroid or Caucasoid types in the majority in most areas. It is clearly of interest to inquire how much the archaeological record can tell us of the ancestry and inter-relationships of these diverse population elements.

The available data on which any reliance may be placed are disappointingly scanty. Skeletal remains are, of course, almost invariably all that survives of prehistoric populations; and the definable skeletal characteristics even of modern African populations have remained until recent years very imperfectly understood. It is now recognized that the metrical ranges of many individual features display a marked overlap between the different groups; so that the modern types themselves are less clearly differentiated than was formerly thought. Consequently, attributions to particular physical groups of individual or incomplete specimens should be treated with reserve. Statistical analysis of the physical features displayed by groups of skeletons is recognized as the sole means by which valid comparisons and plausible attributions may be obtained. That said, it must at once be admitted that data of this order are simply not yet available for the later prehistoric human remains of eastern and southern Africa, and we must therefore fall back upon such descriptions as are to hand: the resultant conclusions will be correspondingly tentative.

It will be convenient to survey the available material on a geographical basis, from north to south. No accounts of 'Late Stone Age' human remains are yet forthcoming from Ethiopia or Somalia, while a single, poorly preserved, skull from Early Khartoum has been described as showing Negroid features (Derry, 1949). In East Africa proper the published descriptions are more plentiful and the overall picture is correspondingly confused. A number of skeletons, notably those from the 'Upper Kenya Capsian' deposits at Gamble's Cave (L. S. B. Leakey, 1935), have been described as Caucasoid (S. Cole, 1963: 332 ff); they are characterized by narrow skulls (dolichocephaly) and by prominent chins and nasal bones. These features, taken into account with the apparently intrusive nature of the stone industries with which these skeletons are associated, were thought to indicate the former presence in this region of an essentially foreign, non-African, population. However, recent re-examination of this material by Philip Rightmire (1974) has shown that they fall metrically within the range of variation of modern Negroid populations.

It was recognized, however, that this dolichocephalic population did not comprehend all the later prehistoric inhabitants of East Africa. Broadly contemporary with them was a brachycephalic folk represented, for example, at the Homa Bay shell-middens beside Lake Victoria (S. Cole, 1963: 218). The closest affinities of these skeletons were said to be with Khoi–San populations from further south.

It is to the Khoi–San group that the bulk of the relatively numerous human remains found associated with mode 5 stone industries in central and southern Africa have been attributed. Detailed descriptions and comparisons are, however, disappointingly few; and the only closely dated group to have been adequately studied is that of thirty-five poorly preserved individuals from Gwisho Hotsprings (Gabel, 1965; Brothwell, 1971). The Gwisho remains fall clearly within the known range of variation for prehistoric Khoi–San populations. There was considerable sexual dimorphism (a feature which has not been taken adequately into account in connexion with other, smaller, samples of prehistoric skeletal material); but both men and women were appreciably taller than their modern San counterparts. Several 'Late Stone Age' skulls from Central Africa, including most of those from Gwisho, are dolichocephalic; but this characteristic is not so extreme as that encountered in the East African material described above (Wells, 1957). The view that these narrow-headed individuals formed part of a single heterogeneous population receives some support from the fact that the lithic industries with which the Gwisho and other central African remains are associated do not display any of the presumed foreign or intrusive elements formerly recognized in the 'Upper Kenya Capsian'.

Isolated finds from central Africa also display features which fall well within the known range of variation in recent Negroid populations. Such specimens include a series of fragmentary skeletons from Kalemba in eastern Zambia which extends back to about 6000 bc, a skull from Inyanga in Rhodesia and, less certainly, a skull fragment dated to around the sixteenth millennium bc from Lukenya Hill east of Nairobi (de Villiers, 1976; Tobias, 1958; Gramly and Rightmire, 1973). This last specimen may thus be seen as ancestral to the later populations which, as noted above, Rightmire would classify as Negroid.

The prevailing picture of the stone-tool-using populations in southern Africa is broadly comparable to that outlined above for more northerly regions. Despite the relatively large number of human skeletons which have been recovered, the amount of material which is well described and which comes from adequately documented contexts is disappointingly slight. Almost without exception, this material is best regarded as having predominantly Khoi–San affinities (J. D. Clark, 1970; Gabel, 1965).

Such, in broad outline and non-technical terms, is the current inadequate state of our knowledge covering the physical anthropology of the later stone-tool-using populations of eastern and southern Africa. The data are of varying quality, but their overall level of reliability is low. It will be noted that individual 'Late Stone Age' skeletons have been attributed to Khoi–San and Negroid groups, and that these are the dominant population elements found in eastern and southern Africa today. There is also perhaps a tendency for the prehistoric distributions of the respective types to show a pattern comparable with, though more generalized than, that which has prevailed in more recent times, with Khoi–San characters dominant in the south and Negroid ones further to the north. The distribution of specimens to which Negroid characters have been attributed is more general: they are widely but thinly scattered between the Sudan and the Limpopo. This latter feature is in keeping with the evidence that early Negroid populations were dominant in pre-Iron Age times in the sudanic belt south of the Sahara and in West Africa (Chamla, 1968; Brothwell and Shaw, 1971). We may perhaps provisionally postulate a common heterogeneous later prehistoric population through the greater part of eastern and southern Africa in which, as time progressed, groupings occurred more closely approximating to those recognized in modern demography and which gradually assumed their modern ill-defined distributions.

Thus, in terms of both physical and cultural evolution, the later prehistoric hunter/gatherers in eastern and southern Africa may be seen as setting the stage for the early settled food-producing communities which are the main subject of this book. Attention has been drawn to the impracticality of differentiating a distinct 'Late Stone Age' separated either culturally or chronologically in any meaningful manner from its predecessors. Rather, the overall impression which is gained from the archaeological discoveries described in this chapter is one of a series of interlocking local developmental sequences, each firmly rooted in an autochthonous tradition of considerably greater antiquity: inter-regional influences of varying intensity may of course also be discerned. In most areas broadly parallel evolutions led to the development of a basically microlithic technology following a pattern, established in the first place in South Africa far back in Upper Pleistocene times (H. L. J. Deacon, 1976), which was subsequently followed in many other regions. There is, however, no reason to derive all these widespread microlithic industries from a South African source. Indeed, such evidence as we have emphasizes the ability of indigenous technological development to follow broadly parallel courses at different times, resulting sometimes in the presence of contemporaneous industries in neighbouring areas at markedly contrasting stages of technological development. The independence and idiosyncrasies of many of the local successions are such that we can probably discount the possibility of a common ancestor for all the microlithic industries of eastern and southern Africa. Here, migration or even substantial population movement on other than a regional scale seems to have played no great part in the dissemination of mode 5 technology.

Parallel reaction to changing environmental conditions seems to have led to the local development of such technology at several different times as man sought to adapt his hunting methods to more densely wooded situations. In the more northerly regions with which this book is concerned, high water levels in rivers and lakes provided rich fishing grounds which were exploited by people who were thereby enabled to establish semi-permanent settlements. These were the communities which eventually proved receptive to techniques of food-production, as will be described in the following chapter.

III

✂✂✂✂✂✂✂✂✂✂✂✂✂✂✂✂✂✂✂✂✂✂✂✂✂✂✂✂✂✂

The beginnings of food production south of the Sahara

This chapter is concerned primarily with the evidence for the beginnings of food production in eastern Africa. Of all the economic advances which man has achieved during the three or more million years that he has lived in Africa, few have been of greater long-term significance than his adoption of techniques for producing his own food. Such techniques comprise primarily the herding of domestic animals and the cultivation of food crops. It seems probable that, at least so far as sub-Saharan Africa is concerned, pastoralism was adopted somewhat earlier than the advent of agriculture.

THE IMPACT OF FOOD PRODUCTION

Ownership of herds of domestic animals gradually gave man independence from reliance upon the movements and fertility of the migratory game which had formerly been his sole source of meat. Eventually, the pastoralist became able to exercise control over the breeding of his sources of animal protein. Furthermore, he was able to exploit his herds by taking from them milk and blood – foods not available to him from wild animals, and ones which did not require the slaughter of members of his herd. In this way he could feed himself without killing off his stock and thus slowing the rate of increase of his herd.

Agriculture can only be practised in areas where rainfall (or irrigation potential) and soil fertility combine to provide suitable conditions. The regions available for agriculture are thus much more restricted geographically than those where pastoralists may graze their herds. The cultivation of crops secured man's vegetable diet and greatly increased the food yield of a given area of ground. It thus became possible to maintain in permanent or semi-permanent settlements an increased density of population. This in turn provided the basis for important developments in other fields – developments which have been of enormous significance in determining the subsequent history of mankind. It may be useful here to summarize these under two main heads.

The technological developments are perhaps the most obvious. People who are constantly on the move in search of food will have relatively few material possessions other than those which can easily be transported or which can quickly and readily be re-made whenever they are required. For example, among the nomadic pastoralists of northern Kenya today, most families' total possessions can be carried on the backs of two or three pack-animals, be they camels, donkeys or oxen. Even clay pots are usually avoided, in preference for the much lighter wooden vessels, except in those favoured areas where a semi-permanent base can be established. The material culture of nomadic hunters, who do not have pack-animals at their disposal, is generally even lighter and more insubstantial. In a permanent or semi-permanent settlement, however, these restrictions no longer apply. More substantial houses can be built, and more elaborate architectural forms can be developed. For the first time it becomes practicable to make or to accumulate material possessions of a more permanent nature. In the larger settlements which are now viable, society can support specialists – be they scholars, craftsmen or whatever – who are not concerned primarily with the obtaining of food.

Socio-political developments were a natural accompaniment of expansion in the size and economic complexity of settlements. The fact that more people were now able to live together in one place in long-term association with one another necessitated the adoption of modes of behaviour to regulate their now more complex inter-actions. Social or legal sanctions were eventually required to enforce these modes. In due course, it became necessary for man to adopt also increasingly formal conventions regulating, not only the relations between individuals in the comparatively large groups which the economy could now support, but also the relations between different neighbouring groups. In the case of the smaller bands of hunters and gatherers, these had generally been a comparatively simple matter involving mainly territorial delineation, trade in raw materials such as salt and obsidian and the transfer of mates from one group to another, e.g. among the Hadza (Woodburn, 1968b). As larger groups came into much more regular contact with one another, and their exploitation of the land and its resources was on a long-term basis, much more complex social and political institutions were required to regulate human inter-relationships. These developments were the foundations of civilization: indeed, they *are* civilization itself in the original sense of the word.

Here, two points require special emphasis. One is that pastoralism and agriculture are not necessarily inter-related. Nowhere in the world is this more obvious than in eastern Africa. Well over half the total area of Kenya, for example, is today too arid to support a viable agricultural economy, yet almost all of these regions are exploited by pastoral peoples whose entire way of life is geared to the management of their herds. The second point is that, while the settled life so essential to the cultural developments outlined above is generally based upon an agricultural economy, this (at least initially) is not necessarily the case. Later in this chapter an important example from eastern and sudanic Africa will make this point clear.

Attention was drawn in chapter II to the high lake and river levels which prevailed in what is now the southern Sahara and in parts of eastern Africa during the period from the ninth to the third millennia bc, and to the fishing settlements which these waters supported. Research, discussed above (p. 46), has shown that the cultures of these fishing peoples represented a basically similar response to similar environmental conditions, rather than a single uniform culture, for in several areas the roots of their technological traditions may be traced back to a local ancestor. The most important contribution of these fisher-folk to the subsequent history of Africa was not, however, their fishing economy as such, or their invention of pottery, but their settled way of life. The almost exclusively piscatorial existence ceased to be viable, except in a few favoured areas such as the shores of Lake

Rudolf, with the drying up of the rivers and lakes. Almost certainly, however, it was the inhabitants of these semi-permanent riverine and lakeside settlements who first proved receptive to the advent of food-production techniques to sub-Saharan Africa. The reasons for this are not hard to visualize. An adequate, constant, year-round food supply, the realization of which required relatively little expenditure of time and effort, would have enabled the fishers to experiment with secondary economic resources, including those which – like agriculture – required long-term settlement in a single area. Many of the early pastoral societies may also have been settled: there are grounds for regarding nomadic pastoralism as a relatively recent adaptation to deteriorating environmental conditions.

ORIGINS OF FOOD PRODUCTION

It has been widely held that food production in Africa, both pastoralism and agriculture, was derived from the initial development of these techniques in the Near East around 12,000 to 10,000 years ago. While this view is almost certainly broadly correct, it is in need of some revision, for it can now be seen seriously to underestimate the role of indigenous innovation in the inception of food production – particularly agriculture – in Africa south of the Sahara. In the following survey of the beginnings of pastoralism and agriculture in sub-Saharan Africa, I shall be at particular pains to inquire to what extent these can be regarded as indigenous African developments, and how far stimuli or more direct contacts from more distant regions were responsible for their inception.

The Near East

The Near East was almost certainly the centre of dispersal from which knowledge of farming techniques spread through Europe, western Asia, and North Africa (J. G. D. Clark, 1969; Higgs and Jarman, 1972). In this region, notably in the highlands surrounding the basin of the Tigris and the Euphrates, sheep, goats, pigs and cattle were domesticated and wheat and barley were brought under cultivation, all in the period between 9000 and 6000 bc. It is sobering to reflect on the extent to which modern European farming still depends upon domesticates and cultigens which were developed in the Near East so many millennia ago. The picture in sub-Saharan Africa is, however, significantly different from that obtaining in Europe and North Africa. South of the Sahara the main domestic animals which are herded today are ultimately of Near Eastern origin, although local breeding has, of course, produced regionally distinctive types including some strains which – like those cattle immune to trypanosome infection from tsetse flies – are ideally adapted to local conditions (Payne, 1964; Epstein, 1969). On the other hand, most of the traditionally cultivated food crops of sub-Saharan Africa are quite distinct from those of the ancient Near East. Many of them, including the economically important millets and sorghum (which were the staple diets of most agricultural communities in eastern and southern Africa before maize and cassava were introduced from the New World some four hundred years ago), appear to be native to Africa.

Africa

When we consider a list of these indigenous African crops, it is particularly pertinent to attempt to ascertain the areas of the sub-continent where they were first brought under cultivation. This can be done by studying their present distributions and that of their wild prototypes, coupled with consideration of past climatic conditions as well as of archaeological discoveries (Harlan and de Wet, 1973). The map (Fig. 17), based on the research of Jack Harlan (1971), shows the probable homelands of some of the principal local food crops of sub-Saharan Africa. Of the cereals, sorghum appears to have its origin in the broad-leaved savannah stretching from the upper Nile westwards to Lake Chad; fonio in the West African savannah; and the millets (*Pennisetum*) in an elongated belt of dry savanna stretching from Senegal to Darfur – a single exception being finger millet (*Eleusine coracana*) which seems to be of Ethiopian highland origin. Teff (*Eragrostis tef*), the tiny seeds of which are highly nutritious, was also an almost exclusively Ethiopian cereal and has remained so to this day. It is possible, but perhaps not very likely, that some of these cereal crops were originally weeds growing in fields of wheat and barley, from which they eventually took over (Darlington, 1969). The remaining crops fall into two distinct geographical groups. In West Africa are the homelands of groundnuts, guinea rice and of several types of yam (*Dioscorea*). In the Ethiopian highlands are those of the oil-yielding plant noog (*Guizotia abyssinica*), the remarkable banana-like ensete plant (Plate VII, p. 76) and probably coffee. These developments were in marked contrast with the intensive collection of wild cereals noted in the Nile valley of Nubia from some thousands of years earlier (J. D. Clark, 1971*b*; Wendorf, 1968).

The part of the sub-continent which formed the homelands of the indigenous African food crops, particularly those of the cereals, correlates in an interesting manner with the distribution of the stone-tool-using fisher-folk described in the previous chapter. In fact, the areas where these local cereals are thought to have been first brought

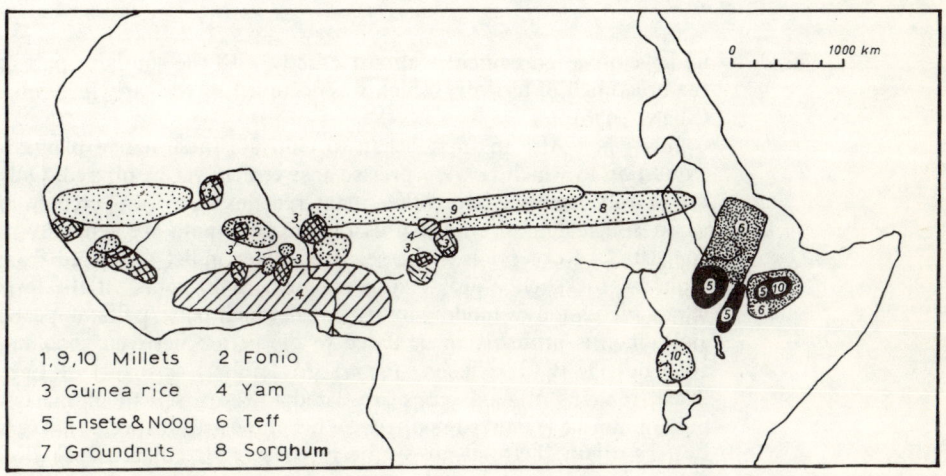

1,9,10 Millets   2 Fonio
3 Guinea rice   4 Yam
5 Ensete & Noog   6 Teff
7 Groundnuts   8 Sorghum

Fig. 17 Probable areas of initial domestication of indigenous African crops (after Harlan, 1971)

Plate VII Ensete (after Bruce, 1790)

under cultivation coincides almost exactly with the southern part of the broad belt of territory which was occupied by the early fishermen (Shaw, 1976).

Just when Africans first began to cultivate these native plants is a question to which no very precise answer may yet be offered. Only very rarely have seeds or other plant remains been recovered from dated archaeological sites in this region; and these are generally of late date. An exception is the seeds of finger millet recovered from Gobedra rockshelter near Axum in northern Ethiopia, at the level in the succession of mode 5 industries at which pottery first appears, and which is probably to be dated to the period between 3000 and 2000 bc (D. W. Phillipson, 1977*a*). At Lalibela cave east of Lake Tana, remains of food crops are dated to the first half of the last millennium bc (Dombrowski, 1970), but these are all species of Near Eastern origin. Teff has not yet been recovered at any archaeological site in its apparent homeland, but does occur, dated to the first millennium bc, at Hajar bin Humeid in South Yemen (van Beek, 1969).

Primary evidence of cultivated crops from the sudanic lowlands is virtually non-existent. Sorghum, for example, is not attested until Iron Age times, when it occurs around the third century ad at Jebel et Tomat in the Blue Nile Province of the Sudan (Clark and Stemler, 1975). However, the general picture which we now possess of changing technologies and settlement patterns across this broad sudanic belt, coupled with archaeological discoveries from further south in both West and eastern Africa, suggests that the third millennium bc may be accepted as a general estimate of the period during which the majority of these African crops were brought under cultivation, both in the sudanic lowlands and in the Ethiopian highlands.

THE SOUTHERN SAHARA AND SUDAN

In order to explain how and why these important economic innovations took place, it is necessary to visualize the population of the southern Sahara and sahel during the fourth and third millennia bc. For thousands of years previously many groups of people had lived a semi-settled existence beside the lakes and rivers of what was then a relatively well-watered region. For their livelihood they depended on the herds of game which roamed these regions and, more especially, on the vast quantities of fish which the waters contained. They had adopted some of the material culture, such as pottery, which goes with a settled life, but their economy and livelihood were very largely – if not entirely – dependent upon the munificence of the natural environment.

Later, some groups probably obtained domestic animals – sheep, goats and cattle – of ultimate Near Eastern origin from contacts to the north, in what is now the Sahara Desert but which then, as the rock paintings (P. E. L. Smith, 1968) so vividly show, was rich grazing country supporting herds not only of domestic animals but also of wild species which now only survive in more southerly, better watered latitudes (Shaw, 1972; Camps, 1974). It is probable that the moister climatic conditions which then prevailed rendered the regions lying to the south of about the eighteenth degree of north latitude liable to infestation by tsetse fly (Mauny, 1967); and indeed the evidence of the rock art does support such a southern frontier for cattle distribution at this time.

An intriguing mystery surrounds the origin of these North African and Saharan cattle. Clearly they spread southwards from north-western Africa, from what is now Algeria: the dated archaeological occurrences of cattle bones allow a neat isochronal map to be drawn which clearly illustrates this spread (Shaw, 1976). The finds in north-western Africa are earlier than any so far recorded in Egypt, where the earliest attestation of domestic cattle, that at the Fayum, is dated to the second half of the fifth millennium (Caton Thompson and Gardner, 1934; Wendorf, Said and Schild, 1970; Mori, 1965: 234–40). Is this because the oldest Egyptian cattle have not yet been discovered, or because the Saharan herds were descended, not from their Near Eastern counterparts, but from the wild short-horned cattle of North Africa itself (Mori, 1964)? Only future research will tell. Whatever their origin, they spread rapidly southwards.

An area which is particularly informative of these processes is Adrar Bous in north-eastern Niger, where the Aïr mountains fall to the Ténéré Desert. Here, a typical fishing settlement, with barbed bone harpoon-heads, mode 5 stone artefacts, and pottery, is dated to the second half of the sixth millennium bc (Faure, Manguin and Nydal, 1963). Later, after a fall in lake level of some 5 metres, which must represent a significant degree of climatic desiccation (Williams, 1971), extensive settlements were occupied by herders of small shorthorn cattle: an almost complete skeleton of the latter has been found and has been dated to about 4000 bc (J. D. Clark, 1971a). The associated 'Ténéré Neolithic' artefacts (Vaufrey and Joubert, 1946; Hugot, 1962) share many characteristics with broadly contemporary material from the middle Nile, to a consideration of which we may now turn.

The most informative site of this period in the Sudanese Nile valley is that of Esh Shaheinab near Khartoum, excavated by A. J. Arkell (1953). The site extends for some 300 metres along a gravel ridge representing an old western bank of the Nile, 50 kilometres north of Omdurman. It appears probable that, at the time of the site's occupation, the Nile was flowing at a level lower than that contemporary with the Early Khartoum settlement described in the previous chapter, but still significantly higher than that of today (Williams and Adamson, 1973). At Esh Shaheinab only one phase of primary occupation was indicated, but there was no trace of structures other than hearths paved with sandstone lumps. On typological grounds it is clear that the material culture of Esh Shaheinab is related to, but later than, that from Early Khartoum: this is confirmed stratigraphically at the site of El Qoz on the southern edge of the modern Khartoum conurbation (Arkell, 1953).

The abundant crescent-shaped microliths and backed blades of Esh Shaheinab are very similar to those from Early Khartoum, as are the bone harpoon-heads, although these now include some which are pierced at the base for the attachment of the line, instead of being notched as were those at the earlier site (Fig. 18). Shell fish-hooks are characteristic of the Esh Shaheinab assemblage, but were unrepresented at Early Khartoum, as were the former site's neatly chipped adzes of rhyolite, some partially ground, and other axe-like implements of ground bone. The pottery shows a continuation of the 'dotted wavy line' style which made its appearance in the later part of the Early Khartoum sequence, but is distinguished from that at the earlier site by being burnished. Black-topped vessels comparable with pre-dynastic Egyptian examples also make their appearance. Beads were made, on the site, from amazonite which was presumably brought from Tibesti over 1700 kilometres away to the west, or from the eastern desert of Egypt.

The abundant bone fragments recovered at Esh Shaheinab are primarily of wild species, including a high proportion of fish. A small type of domestic goat and possibly sheep were recognized (Bate, 1953), but these account for only some two per cent of the faunal remains, suggesting that the economic importance of these domesticates was minimal. The only evidence for vegetable food consisted of nuts of the oil palm (*Elaeis guineensis*), which is also an indicator of a significantly wetter climate since it no longer grows in the Khartoum area. However, at the nearby related but as yet undated site of Kadero, L. Krzyzaniak's excavations have yielded faunal remains of which almost nine tenths are of domestic species, with cattle predominating (Krzyzaniak, 1976).

The date of the occupation of Esh Shaheinab has been for long a subject for controversy. A single radiocarbon determination indicates

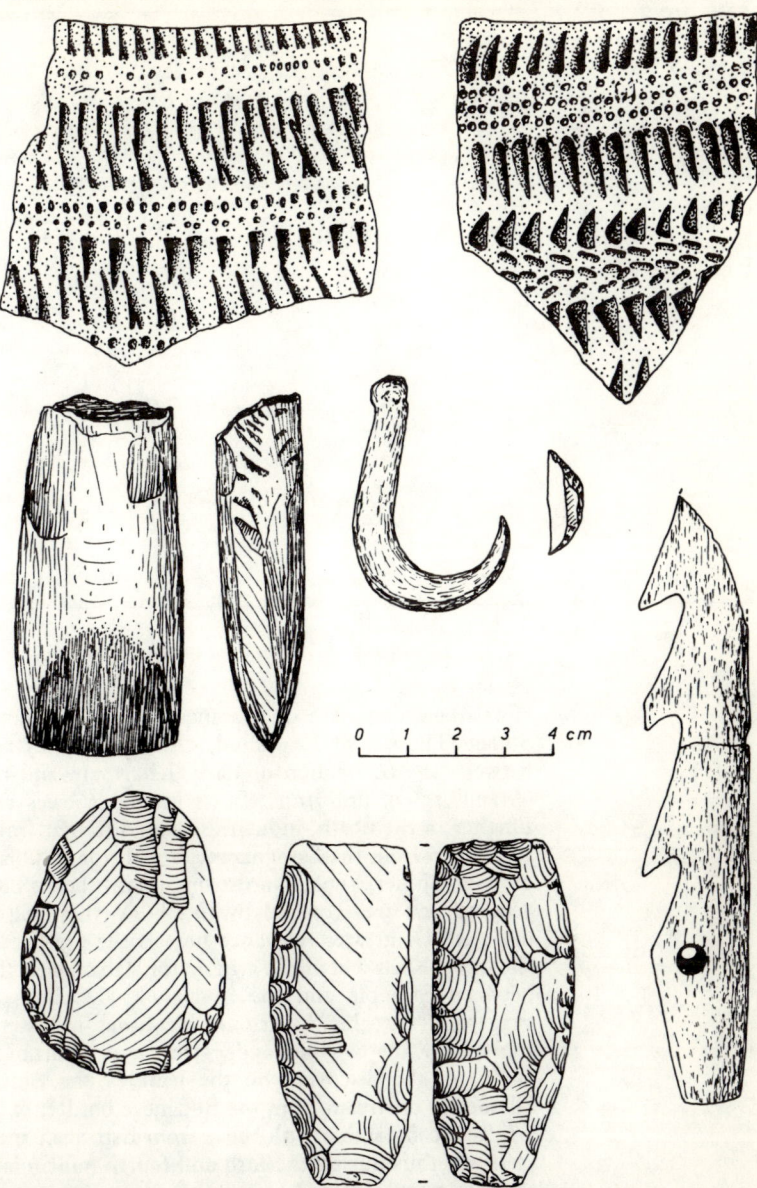

Fig. 18 Artefacts from Esh Shaheinab (after Arkell, 1953)

an age in the second half of the fourth millennium bc, but Arkell
(e.g. 1961: 33; 1972) has argued repeatedly for a considerably greater
antiquity. Recent excavations on closely related sites, the detailed
results of which are not yet published, indicate however that the
original date is unlikely to be seriously in error (e.g. Adamson, Clark
and Williams, 1974).

Sites related to Esh Shaheinab and attributed to a 'Khartoum
Neolithic' industry are located, so far as the valleys of the Nile and
its tributaries are concerned, mainly to the north of Khartoum (Fig.
19), although this picture may be expected to require revision when

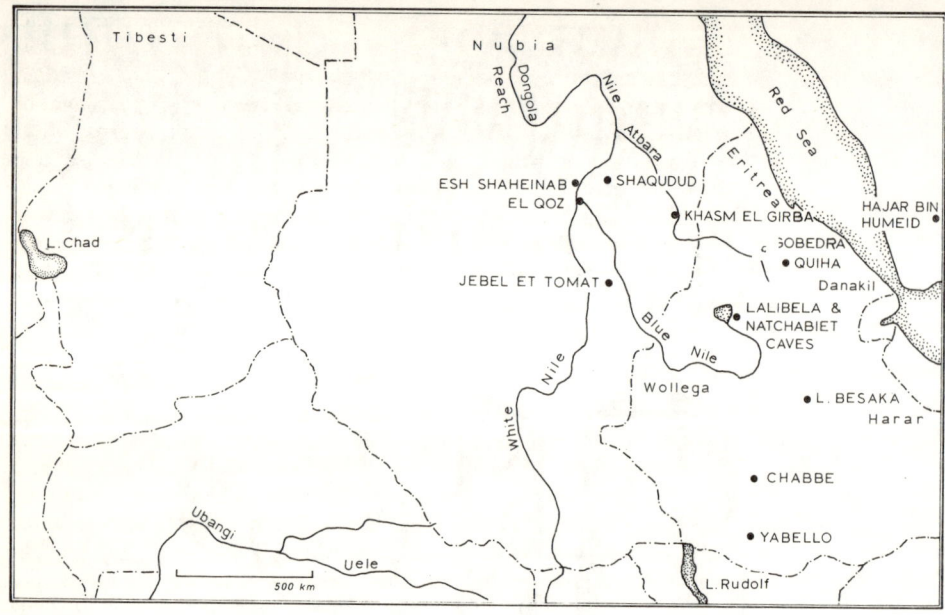

Fig. 19 Location of sites mentioned in chapter III

more archaeological reconnaissance has been conducted in the southern Sudan. The site of Shaqudud (Otto, 1963) may represent a period between the occupation of Early Khartoum and that of Shaheinab (Arkell, 1969): unfortunately its economic basis remains unknown. Further to the north, industries related to that from Esh Shaheinab are known from the Dongola reach and from Nubia (Wendorf, 1968: 1053–4; Shiner, 1968; Nordström, 1972): being outside the general geographical area covered by this book, they will not be discussed in detail. Of greater relevance here is the presence of a comparable site in the Khasm el Girba area on the Atbara near the modern border between Ethiopia and the Sudan (J. D. Clark, 1972). The only suggestion that this 'Khartoum Neolithic' industry may have penetrated the Ethiopian highlands is the vague report by Mansel Spratling (1970) of the discovery on the bank of the Blue Nile, some 150 kilometres upstream from the Sudanese border, of pottery and other artefacts comparable with those from Esh Shaheinab.

It was thus during the fifth and fourth millennia bc that domestic animals were obtained, from the north, by the fisher-folk of the southern Sahara and the middle Nile. Because of the continuing richness of their environment (which was, however, already deteriorating) these early fishers and herders were able to maintain their settled life, thus providing a marked contrast with the nomadic existence which has perforce been adopted by more recent pastoralists in the same region. It is clear that the 'Khartoum Neolithic' is not the exclusively Nile valley phenomenon that was once thought (Arkell and Ucko, 1965), but that it was intimately connected with these parallel developments in the southern Sahara.

Around 3000 bc the deterioration of climate, which had begun many centuries earlier, began to accelerate (Grove and Warren, 1968). Perhaps overgrazing by domestic herds near the waterside settlements was a contributing factor. Be that as it may, major economic changes rapidly took place. Fishing ceased to be a practicable proposition in most areas, and the grazing was inadequate to support the herds. Perhaps it was at this time, if not before, that the intensive exploitation of wild cereals, still used in the area as famine foods, began.

Conditions were doubtless worse further to the north, in what is now the central Sahara and which was then fast becoming desert (Faure, 1966). The earlier inhabitants of that region may be assumed to have cultivated wheat and barley since about the late fifth millennium bc, the date of these crops' first attestation in Egypt (Wendorf, Said and Schild, 1970). They had probably been mixed-farmers on the Near Eastern pattern. As desiccation of the Sahara proceeded, some of these people would have moved southwards, and others eastwards. Wheat and barley were thus introduced to the Ethiopian highlands, where they throve and diversified (Vavilov, 1951). Elsewhere, however, it was found that the climate of the sub-Saharan latitudes was not suitable for the cultivation of wheat and barley, which are temperate zone, winter-rainfall crops. There were, however, abundant local wild cereals, some of which had probably been collected and used as food by the fisher/pastoralists. These were now brought under cultivation in the savannah belt, which was then suited to a settled farming way of life. The advent of agriculture enabled some of the inhabitants of this region to retain their settled life despite the rapid disappearance of fish, following the drying up of the rivers and lakes: others doubtless became nomadic pastoralists. The continuity of the old settlement pattern and, to a certain extent, the old social order, probably explains the apparent speed and completeness with which the mixed-farming economy was adopted. It is, of course, important to realize that pastoralism continued in the Sahara long after the time when agriculture was no longer practicable (Hugot, 1968).

The adoption of a full mixed-farming economy was accompanied by a significant increase in settlement size. Most 'Khartoum Neolithic' and related sites were fairly small, and on them food production, where present, was generally on a very minor scale. By the middle of the third millennium bc, however, much more extensive settlements are attested, particularly in the Nile valley region, such as those at Khasm el Girba on the Atbara which covered almost 100,000 square metres and were evidently repeatedly occupied over a substantial period (J. D. Clark, 1972). These early near-urban communities of the Sudan are discussed at greater length in chapter V.

Thus were both pastoralism and agriculture adopted in sub-Saharan Africa. By 2000 bc or shortly thereafter, many of the descendants of the stone-tool-using fisherfolk were practising a mixed-farming economy in the savannah country which lay between the equatorial forests and the rapidly desiccating Sahara. The advent of food production to this region, together with the southward translation of the climatic zones resulting in a steady narrowing of the savannah belt, can be envisaged as having combined to produce a substantial increase in the human population density, the implications of which will be discussed in subsequent chapters.

ETHIOPIA

It is now appropriate to turn to a more detailed consideration of the early food-producing societies of Ethiopia and the Horn. Ever since the work of N. Vavilov in the 1930's it has been recognized that highland Ethiopia probably played an important part in the early spread of pastoralism and agriculture in sub-Saharan Africa. So far, however, disappointingly little archaeological research has been conducted which throws light on the relevant periods.

The inception of food production in Ethiopia is best viewed as a continuation of processes which affected the middle Nile Valley following the desiccation of the Sahara. In Nubia there is attested a massive influx of pastoralists, known as the 'C group', shortly after the middle of the third millennium BC (Arkell, 1961: 46–54; Trigger, 1976: 49–63). They herded goats, sheep and long-horned cattle, and may or may not have been cultivators of wheat and barley (Steindorff, 1935–7). The affinities of their pottery strongly suggest that they came from the west, from the Sahara. The territory of the 'C group' in the northern Sudan lies outside the geographical scope of this book: they are, however, of relevance because of their apparent connexion with the inhabitants of a group of sites in the Agordat area of Eritrea, at the extreme north-west of the Ethiopian highlands.

These sites appear to be those of four semi-permanent villages: unfortunately they have never been excavated, their remains are known only from surface collections (Arkell, 1954), and it is not clear whether more than one phase of occupation is represented. The collections (Fig. 20) include ground stone maceheads comparable with examples from the Nile valley, and a variety of ground stone axes, some of which – with flared cutting edges or double lugs – are stated on somewhat inconclusive grounds to be derived from metal prototypes. (Not dissimilar double lugged axes have been found as far to the south as Kenya.) There are small stone palettes and dishes, and a variety of stone bracelets, beads, lip-plugs and pendants. The abundant pottery has not been analysed in detail, but includes vessels decorated with applied blobs of clay, and others – on which thickened rims are frequent – decorated with false-relief chevron stamping and with incised or grooved designs. This material strongly suggests an ultimate origin in the southern Sahara, for it may be paralleled in pottery from the area north-east of Lake Chad (e.g. Arkell, 1964; Bailloud, 1969).

Economic evidence from these Agordat sites comprises upper and lower grindstones and a stone figurine of an animal which is compared with representations of domestic cattle found in 'C group' graves in Nubia (Steindorff, 1933–7). Faunal remains, if present at Agordat, do not appear to have been collected. It is plausible to suggest that these sites, with their Nubian and – ultimately – Saharan affinities, may be connected with the introduction of cereal agriculture into the Ethiopian highlands (J. D. Clark, 1967), but clear archaeological evidence for this assertion is not so far available.

Despite recent advances in archaeological research, hypotheses concerning the economic prehistory of Ethiopia still necessitate considerable reliance upon indirect evidence. Frederick Simoons (1965) has argued that, in northern Ethiopia, cereal-plough agriculture may pre-date the arrival of Semitic-speaking peoples during the last millennium BC: it would thus have been practised by the Cushitic-speaking indigenes, although unknown in prehistoric times elsewhere

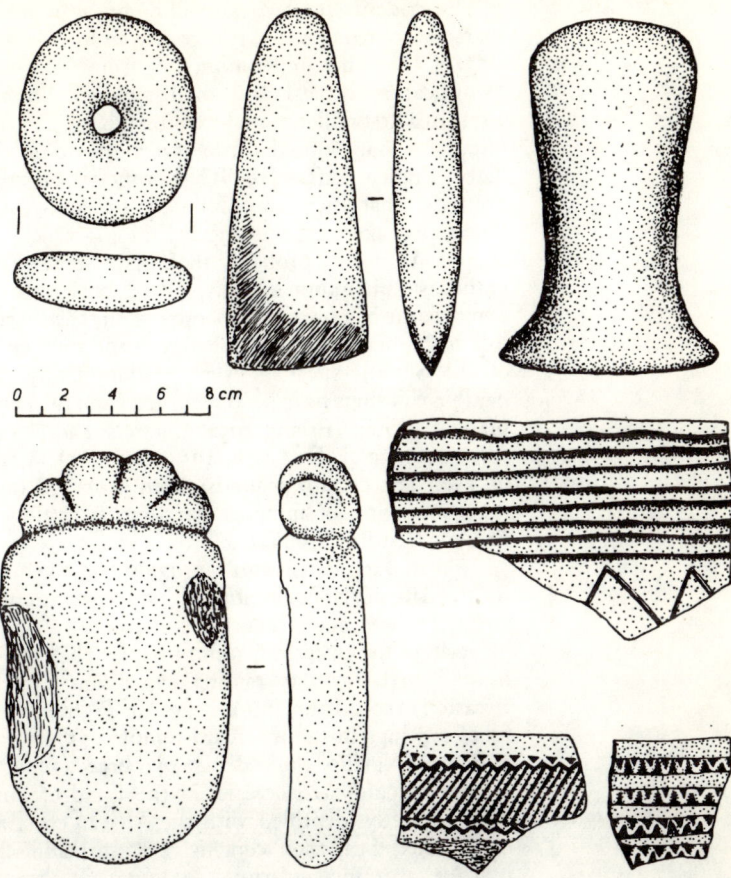

Fig. 20   Artefacts from Agordat (after Arkell, 1954)

in sub-Saharan Africa. This view is supported by linguistic evidence and by the botanical studies, cited above, for the early cultivation of finger millet, teff and sorghum. In the case of finger millet, the present writer's Gobedra excavations (p. 60) now provide archaeological confirmation; while teff, attested in southern Arabia by the first millennium bc (*ibid.*), must presumably have been brought under cultivation in Ethiopia somewhat earlier. There is no archaeological evidence for wheat or barley in this region before the first millennium BC, at Lalibela cave, but the great diversity of the local strains of these crops now cultivated in Ethiopia (Vavilov, 1951; Harlan, 1969) would suggest a considerably greater antiquity, and support the contention, noted above, that they were introduced from the Sahara, *via* the Nile Valley, probably during the third millennium. Simoons (1965) has also suggested that *Ensete edule*, the staple food of the Sidama and some neighbouring peoples, was originally brought under cultivation in southern highland Ethiopia. These proposals would imply a basic economic dichotomy of the Cushitic-speaking inhabitants of Ethiopia during the last two thousand years BC, distinguishing between cereal cultivators in the north and ensete growers in the south. One would expect to find this division reflected in the archaeological record of the period, when this comes to be investigated.

The evidence for early animal domestication in Ethiopia is equally sparse. Archaeologically, it is restricted to a single camel tooth (probably of the third millennium bc) from Gobedra, and inconclusive identifications of cattle and small stock at Lalibela cave (Dombrowski, 1971) in a first millennium bc context. Rock paintings in Eritrea depict humpless long-horned cattle (Graziosi, 1964), but they cannot be dated. Francis Anfray (1968) has proposed, on somewhat inconclusive grounds, that they may antedate the pre-Axumite incursions of Semitic-speakers into northern Ethiopia which, as will be shown in chapter V, below, probably took place somewhat before the middle of the last millennium BC. It is, indeed, noteworthy that these paintings depict cattle of a breed comparable with those herded by the 'C group' folk in Nubia, whereas the herds in the southern Arabian homeland of the Semitic-speakers were predominantly short-horned. Comparable paintings have been recorded from the Danakil lowlands, from Harar Province (Breuil, 1934; Červíček and Braukämper, 1975), and from Somalia (J. D. Clark, 1954: 295–315). A similar date has also, on even less certain grounds, been proposed for these, and for the relief engravings of humpless long-horned cattle at Chabbe in southern Ethiopia (Anfray, 1967a).

Ancient Egyptian records provide two further pieces of evidence for the date of the beginnings of food production in this region. They attest the presence of enormous herds of cattle and sheep in Nubia by early in the third millennium BC, for they were then appropriated by a Fourth Dynasty raiding expedition (Arkell, 1961: 41, citing Breasted, 1906, I: no. 146). Later, in Eighteenth Dynasty times, the relief carvings in the mortuary temple of Queen Hatshepsut at Deir el Bahari (Naville, 1898) depict two breeds of cattle and small stock, as well as cultivated cereals, in the Land of Punt. If this area has been correctly identified with the African coast at the southern end of the Red Sea, then conclusive confirmation is provided for the practice of a mixed-farming economy in this region by 1500 BC. Although an origin for these long-horned cattle east of the Red Sea is not impossible, the apparent Saharan affinities of much of the material culture of this period both in Eritrea (Arkell, 1954) and in Somalia (J. D. Clark, 1954: 277–82) are strongly indicative of an African ancestry. It must be noted that, while the early cattle of Adrar Bous were of short-horned type, those of the slightly earlier Fayum pastoralists in lower Egypt were long-horned (Hays, 1975).

It remains briefly to consider the cultural and technological developments which took place in Ethiopia and the Horn during the period which saw the introduction of food production. In the previous chapter a summary was presented of the archaeological remains of the later prehistoric hunter/gatherers of this region, notably of their mode 5 microlithic industries. In most areas the later industries of this type may be distinguished by the presence of pottery. At Gobedra rockshelter near Axum the appearance of pottery, perhaps about 2500 bc, was accompanied by no significant change in the typology of the associated stone industry (D. W. Phillipson, 1977a), although agriculture (see above, p. 60) was evidently practised at this time also. A comparable pottery-associated microlithic industry is recorded from Quiha near Makalle (J. D. Clark, 1954: 324). It is reasonable to assume a basic continuity of population through this period. The movements from the Nile valley up into the northern Ethiopian highlands, postulated above as responsible for the introduction of cereal agriculture and pastoralism, evidently did not involve sufficient numbers of people to bring about rapid or widespread change among the local population, or to affect in any detectable manner the Cushitic speech of the highlands. Subsequently, late in the first millennium bc, the microlithic industry at Gobedra was replaced by one in which small steep scrapers are the dominant implement type: such artefacts continued to be made into the Christian Axumite period (Puglisi, 1946).

Mention has already been made of the sites excavated by Joanne Dombrowski (1970; 1971) in Begemeder Province, east of Lake Tana. Two caves were examined: in neither case did the occupation prove to extend further back than the first millennium bc. Natchabiet cave showed signs of two successive occupations, of which the earlier appeared to represent several periods of temporary use in which pottery and stone implements, predominantly scrapers, were deposited, apparently during the last few centuries bc. The lower level of the nearby Lalibela cave is dated to a slightly earlier period but yielded comparable artefacts: it is from this deposit that remains of food crops – barley, chickpeas and some unspecified legumes – together with bones which are tentatively identified as of cattle and small stock, were recovered. Unfortunately, the antecedents of these industries remain unknown, so we do not know to what extent they continue the earlier industrial tradition of the area surrounding the headwaters of the Blue Nile. At both Natchabiet and Lalibela the upper occupation levels are attributed to the Iron Age.

Five hundred kilometres to the south-east, in the Afar rift and around Harar, pottery-associated mode 5 stone industries have recently been investigated by Desmond Clark (unpublished). In the former area these industries, dated to about the middle of the second millennium bc, are marked by a proliferation of scrapers; and there are reasons to believe – although primary evidence for this has not so far been recovered – that their development is to be correlated with the introduction of domestic animals. Of particular interest is the discovery, on a site of this period near Lake Besaka, of part of a stone bowl comparable to those found on early pastoralist sites in the Kenyan Rift Valley far to the south. These latter sites will be discussed in detail in chapter IV.

In southern Ethiopia, in the area suggested above as the centre of early ensete cultivation, the study of pre-Iron Age archaeology has hardly begun. Virtually the only artefacts from this region which may be supposed to belong to the time of the early food-producing societies are ground stone hoes or axes, all of which are, unfortunately, surface finds. Mary Leakey (1943) has commented on the similarity between some such ground stone tools from Kenya and those from Wollega and the Tuli Kapi plateau of south-western Ethiopia, but details of the typology, associations and find-spots of the latter material have not been recorded. Material from this area, collected by Azais in 1929–30, has been noted by Gérard Bailloud (1959). The only extant records of the finds (which have themselves been lost) are two letters written by Azais to the then Emperor of Ethiopia (Bailloud, personal communication). The large numbers of chipped or polished stone axes in this apparently closely defined area, which stretches from Beni–Changoul in the north to Lake Rudolf in the south, contrasts markedly with their extreme rarity in other parts of Ethiopia. Azais considered that they were clearly intended for agricultural use. They were found associated with abundant decorated pottery and, in some cases, with metal tools. Although some may belong to the Iron Age, the date of these artefacts remains unknown. It is tempting to believe that future research in this area may throw light on the early cultivators of ensete.

The prehistory of pastoralism in southern Ethiopia remains unknown, even in the extreme south which is today inhabited by the almost exclusively pastoral Boran. Mention has already been made of the long-horned humpless cattle depicted in the undated rock-engravings at Chabbe in the Sidamo. Rock paintings at Yabello represent humped cattle (J. D. Clark, 1945), but are undated and could be very recent (Fig. 21). In the neighbouring Boran areas of northern Kenya, however, there are indications, to be described in later chapters, that pastoralism dates back at least to pre-Iron Age times.

Thus the inception of pastoralism and agriculture south of the Sahara may be regarded as primarily the result of diffusion from what is now the southern Sahara, southwards into the sahel and Sudan, and eastwards to the Ethiopian highlands. The importance which earlier prehistorians have attributed to the Nile valley is not borne out by more recent research. Movements of people undoubtedly took place, but, except perhaps in Nubia, there was no large-scale replacement of whole populations. The roots of the early food-producing communities are with their local predecessors. Even within limited areas some groups doubtless continued in their old way of life long after their neighbours had adopted new economic practices. In all cases the adoption of food-production techniques was a gradual one: hunting and gathering continued to be of economic importance long after the commencement of pastoralism and agriculture, indeed until long after the coming of iron.

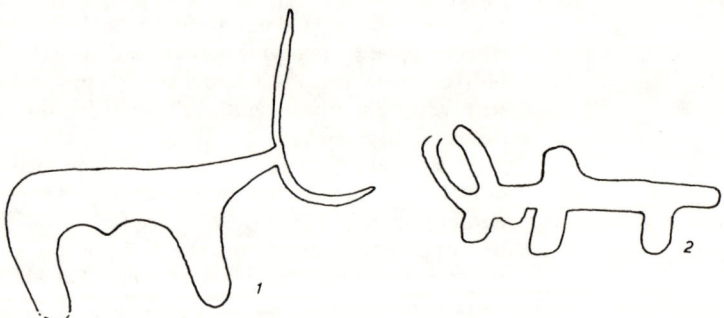

Fig. 21   Cattle depicted in the rock art of southern Ethiopia: 1, carving at Chabbe (after Anfray, 1967a); 2, painting at Yabello (after J. D. Clark, 1945)

IV

꙳꙳꙳꙳꙳꙳꙳꙳꙳꙳꙳꙳꙳꙳꙳꙳꙳꙳꙳꙳꙳꙳꙳꙳꙳꙳꙳꙳꙳꙳

Stone-tool-using pastoralists of East Africa

In contrast with those in areas further to the north, the early food-producing peoples of East Africa are relatively well known from the archaeological investigations which have so far been conducted. In this chapter it will be shown how the stone-tool-using inhabitants of the Eastern Rift Valley and adjacent highlands in southern Kenya and northern Tanzania adopted a pastoral economy rather more than three thousand years ago. An attempt will be made to correlate archaeological evidence with that which has been put forward more tentatively by historical linguists, and it will be argued that the pastoral economy was introduced through relatively small-scale population movement which did little to interrupt the basic continuity of the local succession of mode 5 industries.

THE PRECURSORS OF THE STONE-TOOL-USING PASTORALISTS

In chapter II a description was presented of the East African mode 5 industries and it was emphasized that, during the last few thousand years BC, several distinctive stone working traditions had evolved. It was suggested that the diversity of these industries was due as much to the flaking properties of the varied raw materials that were utilized for tool-manufacture as it was to the presence of separate cultural traditions. A semi-sedentary life-style had been adopted by those people who were able to exploit the rich fishing grounds provided by the high water-levels of lakes such as Rudolf and Nakuru prior to about 3000 bc. We have seen above how analogous conditions in the Nile valley, the southern Sahara, and the sudanic belt supported settled communities which proved receptive to the advent first of pastoralism and then of agriculture as the gradual climatic desiccation brought their previous reliance upon fish to an end. It is pertinent to inquire to what extent a similar model may be employed to illustrate the inception of food production in East Africa.

At North Horr, some 150 kilometres east of Lake Rudolf (Fig. 22), the present writer has investigated settlement sites located beside the north-western shore of the now dry Chalbi Lake. Occupation of the earlier site is attested from at least the middle of the third millennium bc. The chipped stone industry is dominated by backed microliths, scraper forms being noticeably rare. Particular interest attaches to the presence (not necessarily as early as the third millennium, but clearly demonstrable by at least 1500 bc) of thick-walled bowls and platters laboriously hollowed out of solid lava cobbles. Comparable objects are, as we shall see, characteristic of the later settlements of the East African stone-tool-using pastoralists further to the south.

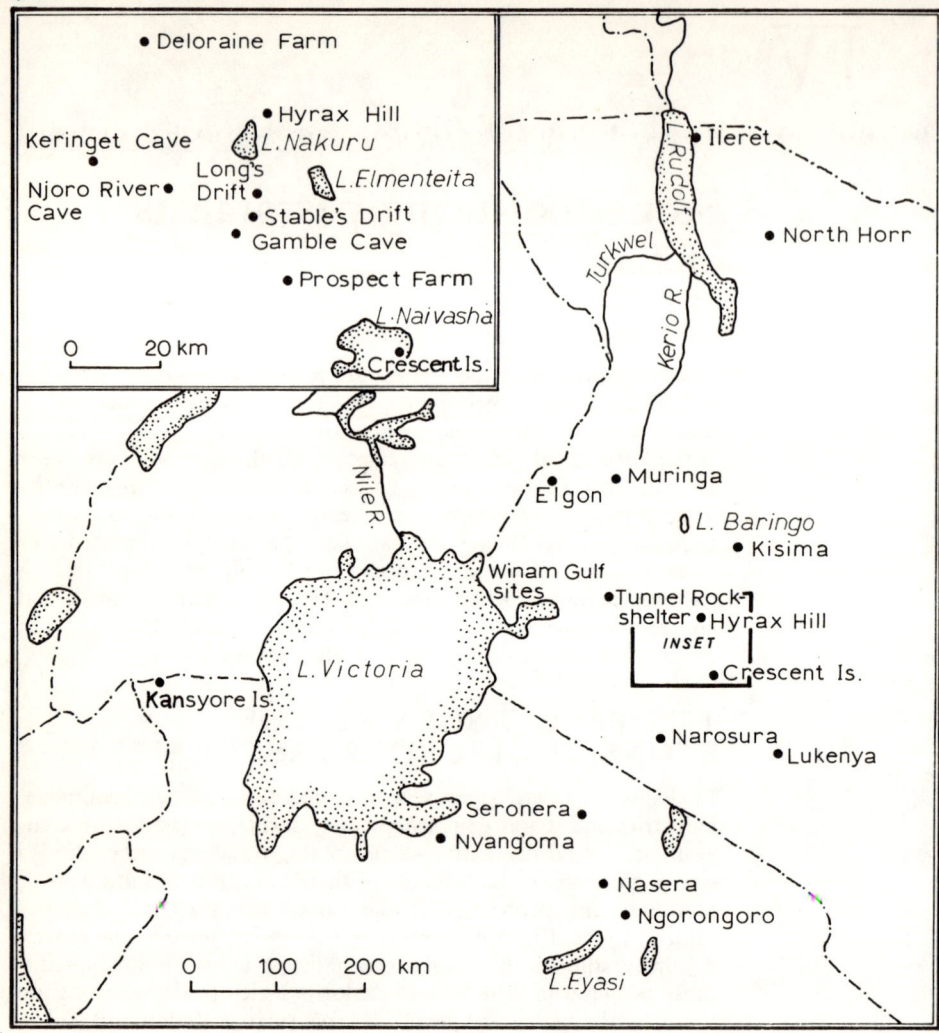

Fig. 22 *Sites of the East African stone-tool-using pastoralists*

They have also been recovered in southern and central Ethiopia
(p. 69, above). Pottery was manufactured throughout the period of
the occupation of the North Horr site. It is possible to see some of
the decorative techniques and motifs of this pottery as descended from
that of the 'wavy line' tradition represented in the Lake Rudolf basin
at the fishing settlements such as Lowasera described above in
chapter II. Other designs represented at North Horr resemble those
found on sherds from pastoral sites of the first millennium bc further
to the south (Fig. 23).

The economic basis of the North Horr settlement is difficult to
ascertain. Bone was poorly preserved, so the fact that there were found
no recognizable fragments of barbed harpoons, such as those which
have been recovered from Lowasera and related sites around Lake
Rudolf, does not necessarily mean that such artefacts were not
employed there. However, the bones which were preserved include

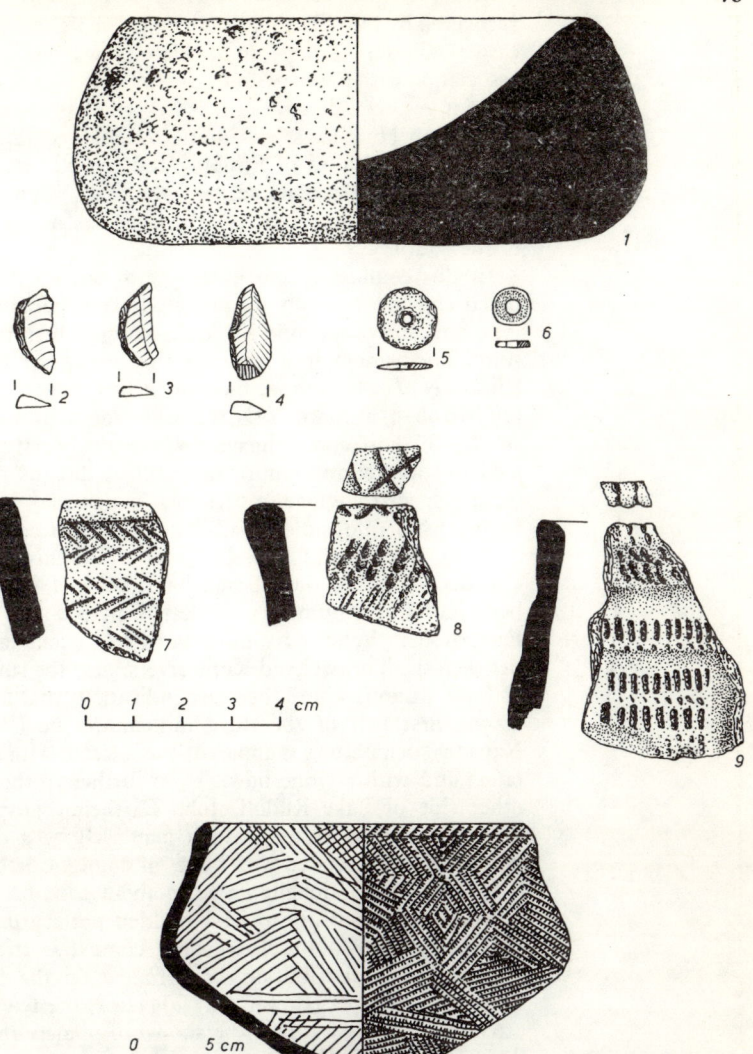

Fig. 23 1–9, artefacts from the third-to-second-millennium-bc site at North Horr; 10, reconstructed Nderit pottery vessel from Stable's Drift (after Sutton, 1973a)

none that are demonstrably of fish; and it seems likely that the already drying Chalbi Lake had by this time become too saline, as Lake Nakuru is today, to support a significant fish population. The earlier North Horr site had an area of some 25,000 square metres, and was thus over thirty times as big as the broadly contemporary fishing settlement at Lowasera. Evidently some concentrated food-resource was available to support a substantial population (cf. J. D. Clark, 1972). It is possible tentatively to suggest – although concrete archaeological evidence for this is so far lacking – that pastoralism (and, perhaps, some form of agriculture) may have been practised by the site's inhabitants.

Further confirmatory evidence for this hypothesis has recently been recovered by John Barthelme (1977) in the Ileret region near the north-eastern shore of Lake Rudolf. Here, stone bowls occur in apparent association with bones of domestic cattle and small stock. This material has not yet been dated, but it is nevertheless apparent that the Ileret and North Horr sites provide not only a geographical link between the stone bowl sites of Ethiopia and those of southern Kenya, but also a chronological one between the early fishing settlements of the Lake Rudolf basin and those of the stone-tool-using pastoralists further to the south.

In this connexion it is necessary to discuss the scattered, poorly dated and inadequately documented occurrences of an idiosyncratic type of pottery known in the archaeological literature as 'Gumban A' ware. The name Nderit ware has now been proposed for this material (Bower et al., 1977). Specimens were first recovered by Louis Leakey (1931: 198–9) at Stable's Drift on the Nderit river some 40 kilometres south of Nakuru and at the nearby 'Makalia burial site'. It is character-ized by decoration comprising hatched designs of parallel rows of closely spaced angular impressions which may have been executed by means of an obsidian spall. The designs often give the impression of being imitative of basketry (Fig. 23). Many of these vessels are also deeply scored on the interior surface. This Nderit pottery has been found on a number of widely dispersed sites in and around the Eastern Rift Valley. Its most northerly occurrence is in the area between the Turkwel and Kerio rivers, near the south-western shores of Lake Rudolf, where there are indications that it may date as early as the first half of the third millennium bc (Robbins, 1972). At Napadet such pottery is apparently associated with an exclusively wild fauna and with a stone bowl. Even further to the north and on the other side of Lake Rudolf, John Barthelme (1977) has discovered internally scored pottery which may well be a developed form of Nderit ware, associated with bones of domestic cattle and small stock, in a context provisionally dated to about 2000 bc.

The only other site to have yielded pottery described as Nderit in a comprehensible archaeological context is at the southern limit of this ware's distribution, at Seronera on the Serengeti Plain of northern Tanzania (Bower, 1973a). Here, the few sherds tentatively attributed to this ware can be shown to predate the first century bc. They occurred in the lowest levels of a small rockshelter which also contained a sparse microlithic industry and bones of an exclusively wild fauna, including a few of fish.

In the otherwise complete absence of clearly associated archae-ological assemblages, negative indications are obviously of little value; but it may be significant that Nderit pottery has not, except in the far north, been found associated with bones of domestic animals or with stone bowls (J. Brown, 1966; Cohen, 1970). These observations, if confirmed by future research, will be sufficient to set Nderit pottery apart from most of the other pre-Iron Age wares of highland Kenya. John Sutton (1974) has suggested that it may prove to be significantly earlier than the other wares, perhaps as old as the third millennium bc date indicated in the Turkwel–Kerio area. He would link it with a fishing people who exploited the waters of the Rift Valley rivers and lakes which were at that time receding from their earlier maximum heights and extents. This hypothesis seems to fit the few established facts which are available, but cannot be proved or disproved until further fieldwork has been conducted.

Nderit pottery has frequently been classed together with that of the undated settlement site at Hyrax Hill, situated on the outskirts of Nakuru town overlying a beach level some 100 metres above the present level of Lake Nakuru (e.g. Sutton, 1966). The Hyrax Hill pottery, unlike the few reconstructible Nderit vessels, is almost invariably open mouthed, and tall round-based beakers are typical. Both stamped and incised decoration occurs and shows considerable variety. Not a single characteristic Nderit sherd has ever been found at Hyrax Hill, and the present writer is not convinced that the close connexion postulated between the two wares has any validity.

The Hyrax Hill site was excavated by Mary Leakey in 1937–8 and, at the time of writing, is being re-investigated by John Onyango-Abuje. The earlier levels yielded chipped stone artefacts, mainly crescents but with a sizeable minority of scrapers, almost exclusively of obsidian. The closest affinities of this industry were said to be with the final stage of the 'Upper Kenya Capsian' from Gamble's Cave (see chapter II, above). The pottery has already been noted: examples are illustrated in Fig. 24. A settlement site with a minimum extent of 500 square metres was associated with a cemetery containing nineteen burials, each interred in a contracted position with the knees up to the chin. The nine female skeletons were each buried with stone platters or shallow bowls, and occasionally with a stone pestle also.

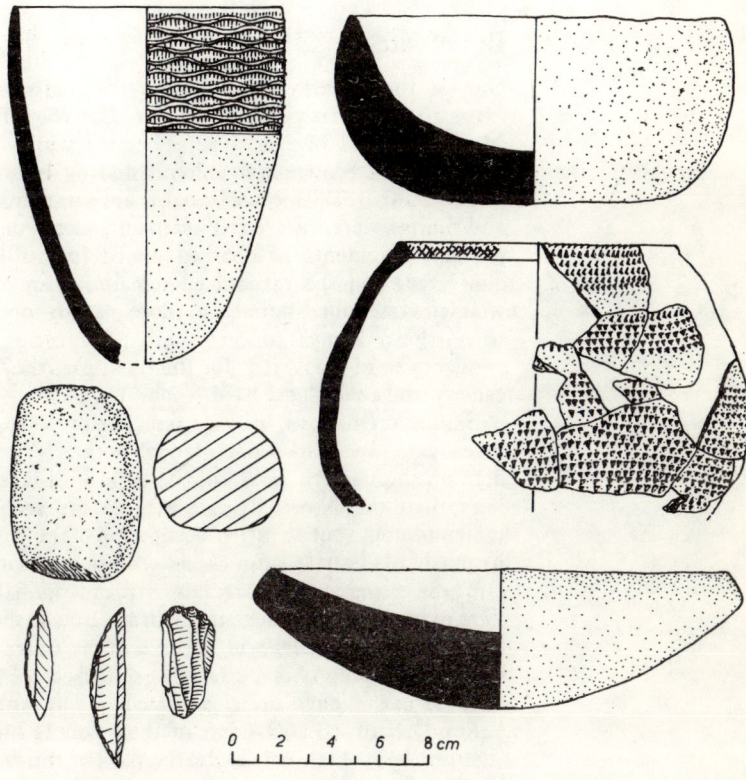

0   2   4   6   8 cm

Fig. 24 Artefacts from the early pastoral site at Hyrax Hill (after M. D. Leakey, 1945)

Each grave was delineated by large stones and roofed with a substantial cap-stone. The burials were covered by a series of adjacent low mounds of stones, forming an almost continuous stony layer over the entire burial area. The overburden of hillwash which covered the burial structure contained occasional fragments of deep stone bowls of a type not associated with the main occupation, where the bowls were exclusively of the shallow platter type (M. D. Leakey, 1945).

Abundant animal bones were recovered from the pre-Iron Age levels at Hyrax Hill, but they were all destroyed during the Second World War before detailed identifications had been made. Similarly, no radiocarbon dates have been processed. The position of the site on a 100-metre beach of Lake Nakuru merely indicates that it must date from after the water's retreat from that level: it need not have been a lake-shore fishing settlement as Sutton (1974: 541) has argued.

ARCHAEOLOGICAL EVIDENCE FROM THE RIFT VALLEY

There are several sites in southern Kenya and northern Tanzania which have yielded evidence for the practice of pastoralism by stone-tool-using peoples from around 1000 bc onwards. Sites attributed to these pre-Iron Age pastoralists include open-air villages, occupied rock-shelters and burial sites.

Burial sites

One of the earliest dated sites is that of Njoro River Cave near Nakuru, which has yielded a single radiocarbon date of about 1000 bc. Many cremated burials were associated with an obsidian industry, described as 'Elmenteitan', dominated by long blades (Leakey and Leakey, 1950). With each burial it appears that a stone bowl, pestle and mortar were interred. There were sherds of mostly undecorated pottery, fragments of charred gourd (probably wild rather than cultivated) and the carbonized remains of an elaborately decorated wooden vessel not dissimilar to those used by modern pastoral peoples in northern Kenya to carry milk. Large numbers of beads and pendants were recovered: for the most part they were made of chalcedony and other local hard stones.

Similar cremations, likewise associated with stone bowls, have been investigated by Mark Cohen (1970) at the Keringet Cave near Molo, high on the western slopes of the Rift. This level is dated somewhat later than the Njoro River Cave, to the second half of the last millennium bc; but an earlier occupation of the same site, characterized by potsherds bearing impressed decoration, is dated to about 1000 bc.

These cremation sites are, however, exceptional; and the more usual form of burial found associated with artefacts of the East African stone-tool-using pastoralists was under a stone cairn – a burial tradition which was evidently related to that practised at Hyrax Hill. Examples of these cairns have been excavated in the central part of the Rift Valley (J. Brown, 1966) and in the adjacent highlands to the west (Sutton, 1973a), as well as further to the south in the Kenyan Rift (Posnansky, 1968b). However, the most intensive research has been conducted on the cairns in the Ngorongoro Crater of northern Tanzania (Reck, 1926; M. D. Leakey, 1966; Sassoon, 1968). These are large, up to 10 metres in diameter, and often cover multiple burials. A variety of ornaments accompanied the dead, including chalcedony beads comparable with those from the Njoro River Cave, shell disc beads, quartz and ivory lip-plugs, with pierced cowries and other marine shells. The latter objects indicate some form of trade contact, however intermittent and indirect, with the Indian Ocean coast some 500 kilometres distant. Stone bowls and pestle-rubbers (sometimes paired) were recovered from most of the Ngorongoro cairns; and the pottery, where diagnostic, is comparable with that which has been recovered from other stone bowl sites. A tantalizing discovery reported by Hans Reck is of a pot filled with carbonized seeds which, unfortunately, were never conclusively identified (although Reck considered them to belong to a local wild species) and are now lost. Metal tools are conspicuously absent from all the cairns so far investigated, but flaked obsidian artefacts were recovered in most cases. The cairn excavated by Hamo Sassoon at Ngorongoro is dated by a single radiocarbon analysis to the second half of the last millennium bc.

Only rarely have animal bones been recovered from these burial cairns, but a few Kenyan sites have yielded remains of domestic cattle. Such cairns, notably that on MacDonald's farm, Nakuru and several examples excavated by John Sutton (1973a: 107–16) in the Western Highlands, are clearly the work of pastoral people; and the cattle bones have been interpreted as representing the remains of funeral feasts. The distribution of these sites is continuous with the areas in northern Kenya and Somalia where the Cushitic-speaking pastoralists still bury their dead under similar stone cairns.

Elsewhere, contemporary and comparable interments have been found in rockshelters. Examples have been described from the Njoro River (Faugust and Sutton, 1966) and from Lukenya Hill near Nairobi (Gramly, 1975a).

Settlement sites

For several decades the stone-tool-using pastoralists of East Africa were known only from their burial sites. Within recent years, however, a number of settlement sites have been investigated and have proved to be more informative concerning the details of the food-producing economy of their inhabitants. A site which may represent a very early stage in the adoption of pastoralism in east Africa is that at Long's Drift near Elmenteita, south-east of Lake Nakuru. It may be the same locality as was investigated by Louis Leakey (1931: 176–7) and regarded as the 'type site' of the 'Kenya Wilton' industry. Re-excavation by Glynn Isaac and his colleagues (Isaac, Merrick and Nelson, 1972) has demonstrated the presence of an extensive midden covering an area of between 400 and 450 square metres. A date of about 1000 bc is postulated, but the evidence is inconclusive and the true age could be considerably more recent: all that appears certain is that the midden overlies alluvial deposits which date from the middle of the second millennium bc. The rich stone industry is dominated by a large series of crescentic microliths and by short endscrapers of distinctive type. Sherds of pottery and a stone bowl were recovered, together with a ground stone axe and a perforated obsidian bead. Bones of wild animals dominate the faunal remains, although domestic cattle are represented in small numbers. The excavators consider that the site was a settlement of a sedentary population which was beginning to practise pastoralism. A similar economic basis is postulated for a site on the nearby Prospect Farm, Elmenteita, where stone bowls and bones of domestic cattle are likewise attested in a context dated to between the eleventh and the seventh centuries bc (Anthony, 1967; Cohen, 1970).

The most informative of these settlement sites is that excavated by Knut Odner at Narosura in the western escarpment of the Rift Valley south of Narok in southern Kenya (Odner, 1972; Gramly, 1974). The area of the settlement is estimated as having been at least 8000 square metres; and the presence of post-holes indicates that semi-permanent structures were erected. The plan of a subrectangular house with round corners and a possible internal partition was tentatively reconstructed. Radiocarbon dates place the occupation of the site between the ninth and the fifth centuries bc. The chipped obsidian industry was of uniform type throughout this period and was dominated by geometric backed microliths and by burins (Fig. 25). Ground stone axes and stone bowls were found, together with abundant pottery, much of which was burnished, with incised and comb-stamped decoration of distinctive type which has since been recognized from several other sites.

Narosura provides the most detailed picture yet available of the economic basis of a pre-Iron Age pastoral settlement in East Africa. Less than 5 per cent of the animal bones recovered represented wild species, and the remainder were of domestic cattle (39 per cent) and sheep/goats (57 per cent). The site is thus unique among those so far investigated because of its inhabitants' emphasis on the herding of small stock. Analysis of tooth wear showed that cattle were

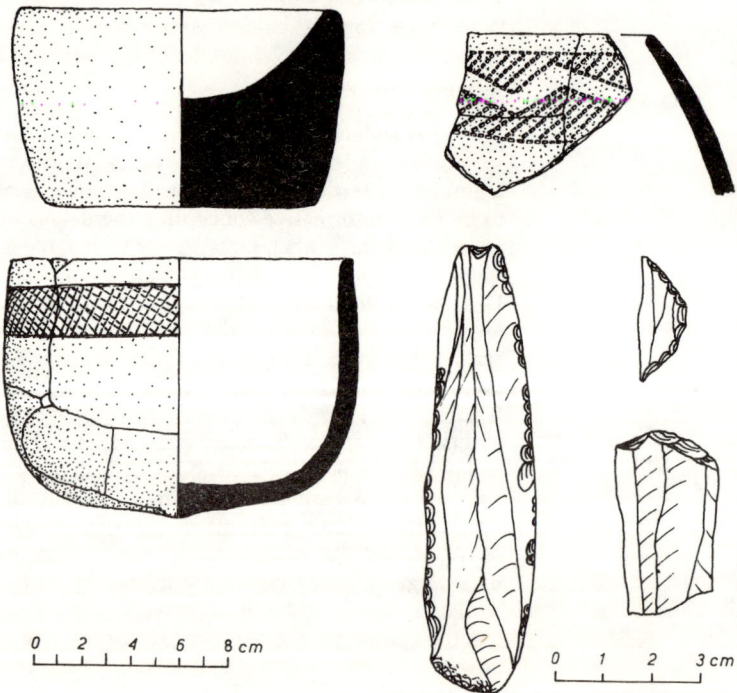

0   2   4   6   8 cm

0   1   2   3 cm

Fig. 25   Artefacts from Narosura (after Odner, 1972)

regularly allowed to attain old age, but that the small stock was frequently slaughtered while still relatively young. This is interpreted as showing that cattle were kept primarily for milk – and possibly for blood (as is the practice of the recent Maasai) – but that sheep and goats were more regularly killed for meat. These conclusions are supported by historical linguistic evidence (Ehret, 1967) which will be discussed in greater detail below. Alternatively or additionally, cattle could have been kept primarily as a source of wealth or as status possessions, as they are in many recent pastoralist societies.

Odner has suggested that the Narosura settlement was larger than could have been supported by pastoralism alone, with the clearly minimal hunting which is indicated by the faunal remains, and that irrigation agriculture may have been practised. It must be emphasized that, while there is nothing inherently improbable in this hypothesis (irrigation was practised in later prehistoric times in many parts of the Rift Valley, as will be shown in chapter IX), there is as yet no convincing archaeological evidence to support it. Grindstones were indeed recovered, but these are not in themselves indicative of agriculture, and the same is true of some obsidian blades which showed wear of a type which can be paralleled through use to cut grasses: a few carbonized seeds recovered during the excavation are exclusively of wild species. I shall return in a later section of this chapter to an evaluation of the possibility that some form of agriculture may have been practised by some of the pre-Iron Age inhabitants of East Africa.

On Crescent Island in Lake Naivasha an extensive (over 15,000 square metres) open-air settlement has been located (Onyango-Abuje, 1977). The occupation is dated to between the ninth and the fifth century bc. Finds include stone bowls, chipped – mostly microlithic – obsidian artefacts, pottery which includes many sherds reminiscent of those from Narosura, and a bossed ground stone axe. The associated animal bones are mainly of domestic species, with cattle predominating.

Further settlement sites in the Rift Valley, somewhat later in date than those described above, have been recorded at Seronera on the Serengeti Plain (Bower, 1973a) and at Deloraine Farm near Rongai (Cohen, 1972). The earliest occupation at Seronera, which yielded pottery possibly akin to Nderit ware, has already been discussed. It was succeeded, at a date subsequent to the first century bc, by an occupation by the makers of a distinctive type of pottery known as Akira ware. This remarkably delicate pottery, often burnished, is characteristically decorated with incised parallel lines forming panelled hatched designs. Comparable sherds come from widely scattered sites, including rock-shelters at Lukenya Hill, south-east of Nairobi (Gramly, 1975a). Their most northerly occurrence is reported by Robert Soper and Ari Siiriäinen (unpublished) at Kisima Farm near Rumuruti, south-east of Lake Baringo, in an area known to have been reached by trade in obsidian from more southerly parts of the Rift Valley (Walsh and Powys, 1970). At all these sites, Akira pottery is apparently associated with stone bowls, mode 5 stone industries and evidence for the herding of domestic cattle. They are also relatively late in date, being attributed to the first millennium ad. Delorain Farm is an extensive open-air site which has only been test excavated on a very limited scale. The pottery, which bears impressed decoration, is of an otherwise unknown type and is associated with a sparse obsidian industry and with faunal remains which are largely of domestic cattle, plus some small stock. The site has been dated to late in the first millennium ad.

No trace of metal was found, but the scarcity of stone artefacts suggests that this may nevertheless be an Iron Age site.

ARCHAEOLOGICAL EVIDENCE FROM THE HIGHLANDS AND THE LAKE VICTORIA BASIN

It is clear that the territory of the stone-tool-using pastoralists extended to the highlands to the east of the Rift Valley, in view of the discoveries at Lukenya Hill, noted above. Little trace of them has, however, been found at other sites in this area, and the eastern limit of their distribution has not yet been ascertained.

The Western Highlands have been somewhat better served by archaeology and both burial cairns (noted above) and rockshelter sites have been investigated by John Sutton (1973a), although open-air settlement sites are still lacking. At Tunnel rockshelter, near Fort Ternan, on the south-western slopes of the highlands, a mode 5 stone industry with undiagnostic pottery associated with bones of domestic cattle and, possibly, small stock is dated to the first millennium bc. Comparable material comes from Muringa rockshelter at Moiben further to the north, but is undated. A detailed chronological framework for the archaeology of the Western Highlands is not yet available.

Further to the west, Creighton Gabel (1969) has excavated several rockshelters on the northern shore of the Winam (Kavirondo) Gulf of north-eastern Lake Victoria, a number of which yielded evidence for occupation during the last millennium bc. Bones of domestic cattle were recovered, but there remains some doubt as to whether these were associated with a mode 5 industry or belong to a later period. Indeed, the whole question of possible pre-Iron Age food production in the Lake Victoria basin remains unanswered: some speculations will be offered below.

In much of this area the archaeological sites of the first millennium bc seem to be marked by the appearance of a distinctive type of pottery named after a site on Kansyore Island in the Kagera river (Chapman, 1967). Kansyore ware is characterized by bowls with tapered rims decorated by means of comb-stamping and zig-zag hatched incision (Fig. 26). It has been found at several sites around Lake Victoria and extending southwards as far as Iramba (Odner,

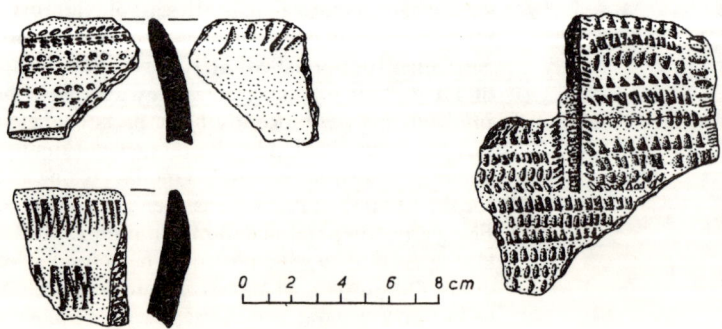

Fig. 26 Kansyore ware (after Chapman, 1967)

1971*a*) and the eastern end of Lake Eyasi (Smolla, 1956). At the 'type site' it appears to pre-date the Early Iron Age Urewe ware (see chapter VI), while Robert Soper's excavations near Mwanza on the southern shore of Lake Victoria demonstrate its association with a mode 5 stone industry, dated at Nyang'oma rockshelter to the second quarter of the last millennium bc (Soper and Golden, 1969). Generally, the distribution of Kansyore ware and that of the other pre-Iron Age pottery types described above appear to be mutually exclusive, with only a limited area of overlap in north-central Tanzania, as at Seronera and Nasera. It has generally been believed that the makers of Kansyore ware were not pastoralists but exclusively hunter/gatherers and, perhaps, fishers. John Sutton (1974) has suggested that this pottery may be a late survival, parallel with that represented further to the east by Nderit pottery, of the ceramic tradition of the earlier fishing communities of the Nile Valley and the Lake Rudolf basin. Clearly, the chronology and associations of Kansyore ware require further investigation.

Archaeological conclusions

Although the general features of the typology and chronology of the industries attributed to the stone-tool-using pastoralists of East Africa are now reasonably clear (cf. Sutton, 1973*d*), it is difficult to extract from the available data a detailed picture either of chronological development or of geographical variation. This is probably largely because research has so far been conducted piecemeal on widely scattered sites, and on a scale often too small to reveal the full picture of the individual settlement sites. On the whole, it appears that the earlier lithic industries noted in chapter II – the 'Upper Kenya Capsian', 'Elmenteitan', 'Wilton', etc. – continued with little demonstrable change through the period which saw the inception of pastoralism.

The course of study most likely to instil order into these varied pastoralist industries would probably involve thorough and detailed analysis of the associated pottery wares, as is currently being attempted by Simiyu Wandibba (Bower *et al.*, 1977). The results of such investigations as have previously been attempted along these lines have proved inconclusive (Sutton, 1964), probably because the available sherd samples are too small and have inadequate chronological control. It has not proved possible to establish any satisfactory correlation between stone industries and pottery styles using the divisions currently recognized. The picture is further confused because, despite the fact that the various wares which have hitherto been discerned are inadequately defined, archaeologists working in this field have often been willing to attribute to specific wares small collections of miniscule sherds from sites which are widely scattered through both time and space. Typological studies of other artefacts, notably the stone bowls (Merrick, 1973) and ground stone axes (M. D. Leakey, 1943; Posnansky and Sekibengo, 1959; J. Brown, 1969), although indicating once again the general range of variation, have not yielded data which could be employed in the recognition of discrete industries. There is a tendency, perhaps, for Narosura ware to be early in date and Akira ware to be later, for the larger stone bowls to occur on the more northerly sites and for the shallow bowls and platters to be early and to be concentrated along the north-eastern flank of the Rift Valley. We do not yet have a sufficient body of material from dated excavations to permit the differentiation of discrete industries among the archaeological remains of the stone-tool-using pastoralists.

The overall geographical area occupied by these people may be approximately defined. Their sites are found along the Eastern Rift Valley throughout the whole of its length in Kenya and southwards into Tanzania as far as the region of Lake Eyasi. No trace of them has been found further to the south (Sutton, 1969), although it must be admitted that the coverage of research in central and southern Tanzania has been thin. To the west their limit was the western Kenya highlands: pastoralism in pre-Iron Age times is not yet attested in the Lake Victoria basin where the archaeological associations of Kansyore ware remain imperfectly known, although stone bowls are markedly absent. In the east, no sites are recorded beyond the well-watered highlands around Nairobi and the eastern flank of Mount Kenya, where a single stone bowl has been recovered.

The evidence for economy is patchy and incomplete. The herding of domestic animals is well attested, cattle being the dominant species at all sites except Narosura. It is possible that some of the ground stone 'axes', which are not attested in East Africa on pre-pastoral sites, may have been employed to change the horn-profiles of domestic animals, as is still done with comparable artefacts in Karamoja, north-eastern Uganda (J. Wilson, 1972). The incidence of hunting varies greatly. At some places, such as Long's Drift, remains of wild animals are in the great majority: elsewhere, as at Narosura, they are very few. It is, of course, quite possible that separate groups of the same population occupied contemporary settlements at which different economic practices were emphasized: such variation may be paralleled in several modern societies in this region. Groups of hunters and groups of pastoralists might also have co-existed closely, perhaps with regular interchange of population and near identity in technology and material culture.

There is no archaeological evidence for the breed of the cattle which were herded in pre-Iron Age times in East Africa. Humped zebu are attested in the Nakuru area during the Iron Age, but Richard Wright (1961) has recorded rock paintings on Mount Elgon which depict long-horned humpless cattle akin to those shown in many of the Ethiopian paintings described in chapter III. The Elgon paintings cannot be dated, but it is tempting to suggest that they may represent the types of cattle herded by the stone-tool-using pastoralists: certainly the style of the paintings differs markedly from those which are attributed to more recent times (chapter XI, below). The evidence for milking at Narosura and Njoro River Cave has been cited above. The archaeological evidence for agriculture is scanty and inconclusive, being based on the suggested use of the stone bowls and pestles for the preparation of cereal foods, on the wear-patterns on stone tools, on settlement size and permanence, and on comparable arguments of a speculative nature.

LINGUISTIC EVIDENCE

It is appropriate now briefly to review the conclusions which have been put forward by historical linguists in order to ascertain the extent to which these may be correlated with the archaeological data. In chapter

I attention was drawn to the presence in northern Tanzania of groups of people, notably the Iraqw and Asa, who speak Cushitic languages. These people are now separated by some hundreds of kilometres from the territories of other Cushitic-speakers; and the fact that their languages belong to a distinct sub-group, named Southern Cushitic, suggests that their separation took place a long time ago. Christopher Ehret (1974a; 1968a: 161) has suggested on linguistic grounds that 'the ancestral Southern Cushitic community was formed by the assimilation of an indigenous and previously non-Cushitic-speaking population to a much smaller group of (immigrant) Cushites.... The Cushitic elements brought with them their language and the knowledge of pastoral pursuits.' Study of words of apparently Southern Cushitic origin which survive today in other languages suggests that the Southern Cushitic tongues were formerly spoken over a more extensive area including much of southern Kenya.

It is tempting to suggest that a gradual spread of Cushitic-speakers from the ancient centre of that speech in southern Ethiopia began at some time during the second millennium bc, or even a little earlier; penetrated southwards through the still relatively well-watered country on the east side of Lake Rudolf into the Kenyan Rift Valley highlands; and was responsible for the introduction to the pre-existing population of these regions of important cultural innovations, pre-eminent among which were the techniques of pastoralism. The concordance between the evidence of the Narosura faunal remains, indicating the practice of milking cattle, and Ehret's linguistic conclusions relating to this activity among the Cushitic-speakers of the Kenyan rift has already been noted. Ehret also considers (1974: 8) that the early southern Cushitic-speakers of this area may have possessed some knowledge of agriculture: this is a trait not conclusively represented in the archaeological data which are so far available, but the linguistic evidence is certainly not contradictory to that of the archaeology. John Sutton (1973a: 15) also argues that the cycling age-set system and genital mutilation practices may have been introduced to the area by these early Cushitic-speakers.

These conclusions are in full accord with the archaeological evidence which indicates that the East African stone-tool-using pastoralists followed a life-style similar in many respects to that of many modern Cushitic-speaking groups. The affinities of their pottery and stone bowls are with northern Kenya and southern Ethiopia, where burial under stone cairns is still a widespread practice among Cushitic-speaking people. The dolichocephalic physical type represented from many such burials in southern Kenya and northern Tanzania is also concordant with that of many modern Cushitic-speaking populations, although Phillip Rightmire (1975) has emphasized that these remains are probably basically Negroid rather than belonging to any essentially foreign or non-African group as has on occasion been proposed (e.g. S. Cole, 1963: 266–9; Coon, 1963, 634–6).

What, however, of the makers of Kansyore ware, found in the Lake Victoria basin further to the west? It has been suggested that these people may represent a late relict culture descended from that of the earlier fishermen of the Nile valley and the southern Sahara (Sutton, 1974). This, and the concomitant hypothesis of a possibly Sudanic speech, would certainly explain the apparent cultural dichotomy between the Lake Victoria basin and the Eastern Rift Valley during the last millennium bc. Use of an Eastern Sudanic (ancestral

Nilotic) language at this time-depth is not contradicted by such information as we have of Nilotic linguistic history (Ehret, 1971). It is also by no means impossible that some of the later pottery wares which may be detected in the Rift Valley region from the end of the last millennium bc onwards may prove to have been the work of Nilotic-speakers. The poorly understood diversity of the archaeological remains of the early pastoral communities of this time may be due, at least in part, to the interaction of Nilotic- and Cushitic-speakers. In the present state of our knowledge, however, we are here approaching the bounds of useful speculation. Guessing at the linguistic affinities of the makers of Nderit pottery would far exceed those bounds.

In conclusion, it may be stated with some confidence that a predominantly pastoral economy, perhaps accompanied by knowledge of some sort of agriculture, was introduced to the stone-tool-using peoples of highland East Africa by means of gradual and relatively small-scale movements of Cushitic-speaking people southwards from the highlands of southern Ethiopia. This process probably occupied the greater part of the second millennium bc, but may have been proceeding intermittently for many generations before the successful translation of pastoralism to the more southerly latitudes. Over much of their territory the pastoralists' initial population was probably sparse, although extensive settlement sites such as those at Narosura and Crescent Island, together with repeatedly used burial sites such as Njoro River Cave, suggest that the more favourable and better watered areas soon proved exceptions to this generalization.

We have no reason to believe that these early pastoralists derived their livelihood from their herds to anything approaching the extent which is achieved by some of the present-day pastoral peoples of East Africa. Hunting and, quite probably, some forms of agriculture were also practised to varying degrees; and several of the settlement sites of this period suggest more permanent settlement than is usual among most local pastoral peoples today. Indeed, although firm archaeological evidence for this assertion has not yet been recovered, we are probably justified in regarding the present-day life-style of East Africa's nomadic pastoralists, which is centred so largely on herds of livestock, as a relatively recent development brought about by continuing environmental deterioration (exacerbated by the activities of the pastoralists themselves) and the virtual restriction of the pastoralists to the less productive areas.

The research has not yet been undertaken that will enable us to understand the economic strategies of these prehistoric populations. We do not know to what extent the diversity in food-production practices which is attested between some sites reflects differences between distinct societies, or merely various aspects of separate settlements which belonged to an integrated socio-economic system. Far more intensive fieldwork, with more emphasis on complete coverage and site interpretation, and less concern for random sampling and the recovery of small artefact samples, will be needed before we shall even begin to understand the economic processes involved at these sites.

By the first few centuries ad, the population of the stone-tool-using pastoralists was evidently sufficiently numerous to prevent or discourage invasions of their territory by Early Iron Age Bantu-speaking folk, who were by that time establishing themselves to the west, south and east of the Rift Valley highlands, as will be discussed in chapter VI. It is significant that the stone-tool-using pastoralists do not appear to have penetrated further southwards than north-central Tanzania; beyond this area the inception of food production was intimately linked with the beginning of the Iron Age, which will be discussed at length in the following chapters.

V

꙳꙳꙳꙳꙳꙳꙳꙳꙳꙳꙳꙳꙳꙳꙳꙳꙳꙳꙳꙳꙳꙳꙳꙳꙳꙳꙳꙳꙳꙳꙳꙳꙳꙳꙳꙳

Meroe, Axum and the
advent of iron

In this chapter, attention will be given to the evidence for the advent
of iron-working technology to sub-Saharan Africa and to the early
iron-using cultures of the Sudan and Ethiopia. The respective prob-
abilities of local invention and diffusion as models to explain the
beginnings of metallurgy in this section of the continent will be
evaluated; and we shall enquire which, if any, parts of this region
may be regarded as a source from which knowledge of iron technology
could have passed to more southerly latitudes.

IRON: ORIGINS AND TECHNOLOGY

Iron is not an easy metal to work. Copper and gold both have much
lower melting temperatures and are more malleable, copper is easier
to smelt, while gold is generally found in a metallic state and thus
does not require to be smelted. On the other hand, their occurrences,
or that of their ores, are very limited compared with that of iron.
Both are soft metals better suited to the production of ornaments than
to that of tools or weapons: even bronze is not very hard. (The poems
of Homer, which were written down after the advent of iron but which
described an earlier period when weapons were made of bronze, several
times refer to the warrior's need to pause in battle in order to straighten
his bronze sword: clearly this was an inconvenience the memory of
which continued to rankle for several generations.) It is not surprising,
therefore, that in most parts of the world copper was brought into
use long before techniques of iron-working were developed, but that
iron was usually readily adopted as a replacement for many purposes
when the necessary technology became available.

In Egypt, techniques of working copper and bronze were known
from at least as early as the fourth millennium bc but, surprisingly,
iron does not appear to have been in regular use there until around
1000 BC: even then it remained remarkably infrequent for several
centuries longer (A. Lucas, 1962: 212–17, 235–43; see also Coghlan,
1956), there being no conclusive evidence that iron was actually
smelted in Egypt before the Twenty-sixth Dynasty of the seventh
century BC (Petrie, 1886: 39). Here then, as in most of Eurasia, there
was a prolonged Copper or Bronze Age preceding the Iron Age. A
comparable phenomenon may be detected in the archaeological record
of the northern Sudan and, possibly, northern Ethiopia. Further to the
south, however, Africa passed directly from the Stone Age to the Iron
Age, metallurgical techniques making their first appearance in a form
sufficiently advanced to permit the smelting and working of iron as
well as copper. This in itself provides a strong argument that metal-

lurgical technology was introduced from elsewhere at a relatively late stage in its development. Such a conclusion is supported by the chronological data, which indicate that metallurgy in sub-Saharan Africa invariably postdates its attestation throughout the Mediterranean basin.

Effective smelting of iron oxide ores by reduction requires the attainment of a temperature of at least $1100°$ C., which is more than $400°$ C. below the metal's melting point. A temperature high enough to melt iron was quite probably unattainable in the furnaces which were used in ancient times (A. Lucas, 1962: 241); but the prolonged heating of ore in contact with abundant charcoal, necessary to attain a sufficiently high temperature for reduction of the oxide ores, often enabled the iron to absorb sufficient carbon to make it technically a mild steel, which has the advantage that the repeated heating and hammering of the forging process will harden it. This is the process which was generally employed in sub-Saharan Africa during the prehistoric Iron Age.

MEROE

The most northerly region with which we are directly concerned in this book is that part of the Sudan which lies to the south of Nubia. Here, centred on the 'Island' of Meroe at the confluence of the Nile and the Atbara (Fig. 27), there was established, most probably during the sixth century BC, the Meroitic Kingdom which marks the southernmost penetration of Africa by the civilization of Ancient Egypt (Arkell, 1961; Shinnie, 1967).

From the close of the third millennium BC, the Nubian Nile valley to the north of the Fourth Cataract (at about $18°$ south) was gradually occupied by Egypt, resulting in the subjugation of the 'C group'

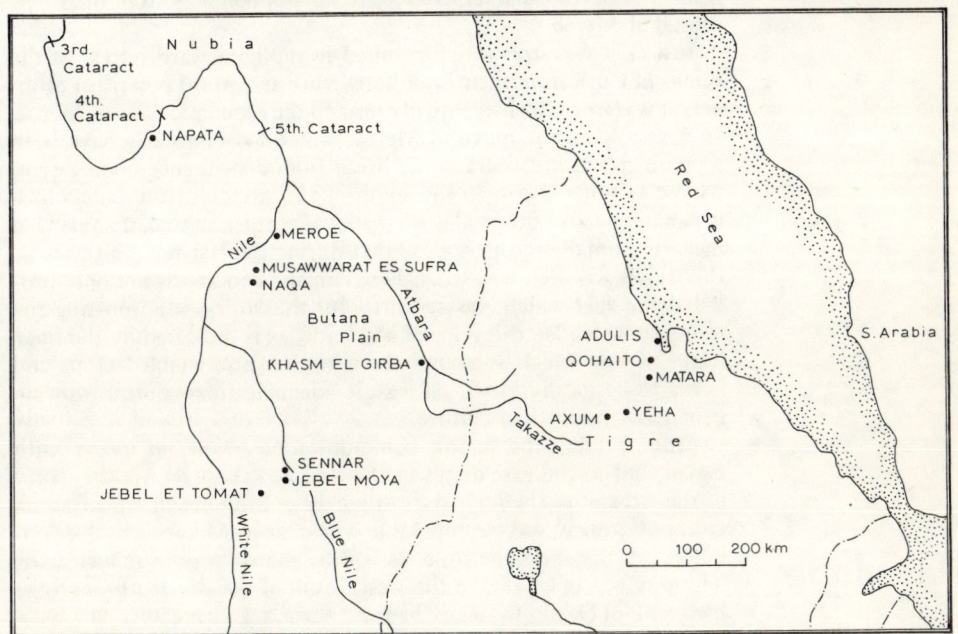

Fig. 27 Location of sites discussed in chapter V

pastoralists who have been briefly discussed above in chapter III and whose hostility to the Egyptian presence is indicated by the number and impregnability of the forts which the invaders found it necessary to erect. It is clear that the Egyptian occupation did not involve any substantial civilian presence, for the old Nubian cultures of the indigenes continued through the period with relatively little modification beyond a moderate influx of trade goods including objects of copper and, occasionally, of gold (Arkell, 1961: 77–8). Tuthmosis I, about 1580 BC, penetrated with a military expedition even further to the south – to 'valleys ... which the wearers of the double diadem (i.e. previous Pharaohs) had not seen', as his inscription at Tumbus near the Third Cataract informs us. Thereafter, the 'Egyptianization' of Nubia proceeded more rapidly and thoroughly: the region became a province of the Egyptian Empire, ruled by the 'Viceroys of Cush', and remitted regular tribute.

During the ninth century, through circumstances which remain imperfectly understood, an independent Kingdom of Cush came into existence. Its rulers were buried in the Egyptian tradition but with local modifications (Dunham, 1950). In the eighth century BC the tables were turned: the Kings of Cush conquered Egypt and established themselves as the Twenty-fifth Dynasty, Kings of Cush and Egypt. Their triumph was short-lived. In 671 BC the Assyrians invaded Egypt, rapidly gained control and placed the Twenty-sixth Dynasty in power. The relevance of this episode to the general topic of this book is that the Assyrian forces were, unlike the Egyptians and the Cushites, armed with iron weapons. Symbolically, the pyramid tomb of Taharqa, the Cushite ruler of Egypt at the time of the initial Assyrian invasion, was found to contain a single iron arrowhead wrapped in gold foil (Dunham, 1955: 12). The Kings of Cush retreated, but for another thousand years continued to rule in the Sudan, first from Napata near the Fourth Cataract, later – after about 600 BC – from their new capital at Meroe.

Just as it was iron which resulted in the homeward retreat of the Kings of Cush from their brief florescence as a world power, so probably it was iron which eventually formed the economic basis of Meroe. In a way, also, the move to Meroe, which may formerly have been a provincial centre, marked the break from dependence upon Egypt. Meroe is situated just to the south of the stretch of the Nile which is flanked by arid deserts. It is an area of regular annual, if somewhat meagre, rainfall; and it is clear that during the last few centuries BC the region was well wooded. These climatic conditions not only provided the fuel which was required for the large-scale iron-working industry which later developed at Meroe, as is indicated by the huge heaps of slag which surround the site; they also enabled crops and herds to be locally raised on a scale adequate to support a growing urban and peri-urban culture.

From Meroe, the easiest communications were no longer with Egypt, but to the east direct to the Red Sea coast or, via the valley of the Atbara, to the highlands of northern Ethiopia where an urban culture, in many ways comparable with that of Meroe, was developing at broadly the same time, as will be shown later in this chapter. The way was open also to the west, south of the desert, through the highlands of Darfur to Lake Chad and beyond. Despite its superficially Egyptian ancestry, as exemplified by the material trappings of its rulers, the Meroitic Kingdom now steadily developed and strengthened its connexions with contemporary societies south of the Sahara as well as with those of the Near East. Imports from the latter area and from the Hellenistic world including Ptolemaic Egypt were probably now brought to Meroe *via* the Red Sea coast rather than up the Nile. The territory ruled from Meroe appears to have extended southwards some 400 kilometres along the Nile at least as far as Sennar.

Meroe's increasing independence of Egypt may be seen in several fields. The Meroitic language gradually replaced Egyptian in monumental and other inscriptions. From about the second century BC, use of Egyptian hieroglyphs was abandoned: they were replaced first by a local hieroglyphic alphabet, then by a cursive script. The phonetic equivalences of many of these Meroitic symbols are now known with a reasonable degree of certainty, but the language itself still cannot be understood: even the language family to which it belongs has not been satisfactorily established although John Sharman (1974) has recently proposed some interesting correspondence with the modern Kanuri language spoken near Lake Chad. It is at about this time, too, that Egyptian imports were gradually replaced by those brought from the Near East.

Meroitic monumental architecture (Plates VIII, IX, p. 106) was much inspired by Egyptian tradition. It is best known from the 'Island' of Meroe, at the temples of such sites as Naqa and Musawwarat es Sufra (Hintze, 1962; 1968), and from the royal pyramid cemeteries at Kurru and Nuri near Napata and at Meroe itself (Dunham, 1950; 1955; 1957; 1963). The temple erected at Meroe to the Egyptian god Amun, for example, was 140 metres long (Fig. 28, p. 107), built of brick with a dressing of sandstone blocks, some of which were decorated with relief carvings in the Egyptian style (Garstang, 1912).

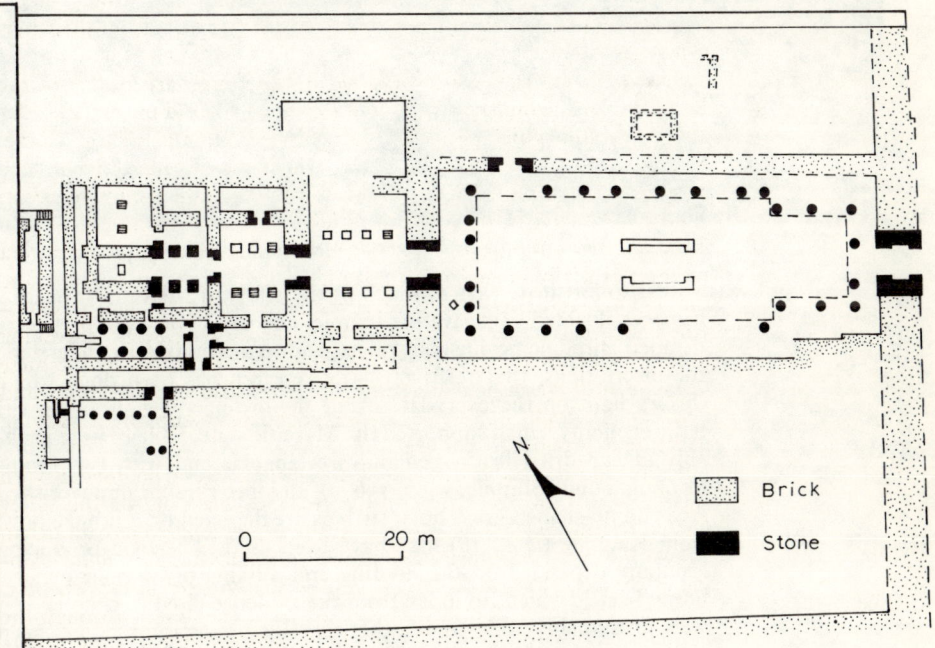

Fig. 28 Plan of the temple of Amun at Meroe (after Garstang, 1912)

Plate VIII   The 'Lion Temple' of Naqa (after Hintze and Hintze, 1966)

Plate IX   The royal pyramid-tombs at Meroe (after Shinnie, 1967)

It is unfortunate that so much of the effort of Meroitic specialists has been devoted to excavating temples and royal graves, to preparing detailed chronological lists of rulers, and to attempting to understand the inscriptions, that relatively little research has been done which throws light on the everyday life of the ordinary people or on the basic economy which supported the Meroitic state. Houses were probably of sun-dried brick, generally rectangular and with two rooms forming a unit (Shinnie, 1967: 156–7). In more rural or impoverished areas dome-shaped grass huts, such as are depicted on a bronze bowl from Karanog (*ibid.*: 18) may have been used. The food-producing economy depended on the herding and milking of humpless short-horned cattle which, to judge from the evidence cited in chapter III, were presumably of Saharan rather than Egyptian origin. Some sheep and goats were also kept. Fishing was doubtless of considerable importance. Horses were ridden and harnessed to chariots: the camel probably did not appear until late Meroitic times. Cereal cultivation emphasized millet or sorghum. Cotton was spun and woven, while fragments of cloth made of flax have also been recovered, the latter perhaps imported from Egypt. Local hand-made pottery, the style of which may be ultimately derived from 'C-group' ceramics, was in use alongside wheel-turned wares of more northerly, Egyptian or Mediterranean, type.

It is to the evidence for iron-working that most attention has been paid, but much basic research remains to be done. We still do not know just when the industry began at Meroe on a significant scale (Wainwright, 1945; Arkell, 1945; 1966; Trigger, 1969). An emerging consensus in favour of a date around the fourth century BC has been somewhat upset by the announcement of radiocarbon dates (Shinnie, 1969; 1971a: 94; in D. W. Phillipson, 1970b: 5; in Soper, 1974: 181) of which the earliest indicates an age in the sixth or fifth centuries bc – representing a true age of about 700 to 600 BC – for a sample obtained from the bottom of the largest mound, associated with fragments of iron and iron slag. It may therefore be that iron-working dates back to the time of the establishment of the royal dynasty at Meroe during the sixth century BC. Few data are available concerning the types of furnace used, but Arkell notes indications that they were tall and cylindrical, using tewels – perhaps for firing by natural draught.

Considering the scale of the iron-working, it is remarkable that so few iron tools and weapons have been found on Meroitic sites. Although part of the problem lies in the unbalanced spectrum of sites (mostly temples and royal graves) which have been excavated, it is tempting to suggest that much of the production of the Meroitic smiths was traded beyond the confines of the Kingdom. Of the finished artefacts which have been recovered, hoe, axe and adze blades, together with shears, were clearly of everyday use: weapons have been more frequently found in graves, notably arrow- and spear-heads, while swords are also depicted in the relief carvings. Almost all the iron tools are tanged rather than socketed.

From the second century AD onwards there is evidence of a rapid decline in the prosperity of Meroe. It is possible to detect two major factors which contributed to this. One, which will be described in detail below, was the rise of Axum in northern Ethiopia as a major trading centre during the second and third centuries. The second was increasing desertification in the Nile valley itself, due both to decreasing rainfall and to over-exploitation of grazing and woodland. It is generally held that the *coup de grâce* was administered by Ezana, King of Axum, in about AD 350, by which time Meroe was but a shadow of its former self. Its successors, including the so-called 'X group', will be discussed in chapter IX.

NORTHERN ETHIOPIA

It was noted in chapter I how the greater part of the population of northern Ethiopia now speaks Semitic languages, the earlier Cushitic-speakers being represented for the most part only by scattered groups of Agau. It is probable that these Semitic languages owe their presence in this region initially to the gradual infiltration of the northern highlands by agricultural people from southern Arabia, a process which seems to have occupied the greater part of the first half of the last millennium BC. As argued in chapter III, these Semitic-speakers found in northern Ethiopia a well established community which had been practising a mixed-farming economy for over a thousand years, had the use of the plough (*pace* Buxton, 1970: 36) to cultivate wheat and barley, had commenced the cultivation of local cereals, notably teff and finger millet, and herded long-horned humpless cattle which contrasted with the short-horned breeds of Arabia. It seems probable, but cannot yet be demonstrated, that use of copper had already penetrated to northern Ethiopia from the Nile valley by the time the southern Arabians arrived.

By the fifth century BC a literate urban culture had been established by these South Arabian immigrants in the fertile highlands of Tigre. The best-known site is at Yeha near Adua (Anfray, 1963*a*; Littmann, 1913, II: 78–89), where a 25-metres-long temple of this period still stands in an excellent state of preservation – a double storey building with only tiny windows, the whole being erected with large, well-dressed, stone blocks upon a stepped plinth (Plate X). Stone carvings from Yeha are in a typical South Arabian style (cf. Doe, 1971), while inscriptions employ a South Arabian Himyaritic syllabary in which the lines are read boustrophedon, i.e. alternately from left to right and *vice versa*. Of particular importance is the use of the crescent and disc, symbol of the Sabaean moon-god 'Ilumquh (Fig. 29). Associated with these objects and monuments of South Arabian origin are objects of bronze and, occasionally, iron. These include tools, weapons, and seals or cattle-brands bearing abbreviated names. Since, as noted above, there is no indubitable evidence for the use of metal in Ethiopia before the arrival of the Sabaeans, it is possible that metallurgy was another of their contributions to the culture of their adopted land. More probably however, as argued above, only iron was introduced, copper having been known previously. Iron is attested in southern Arabia from about 1000 bc (van Beek, 1969: 285, 361) and the word used for iron even in the modern Cushitic languages of Ethiopia is of Semitic origin (Leclant, 1956: 89).

Plate X   The pre-Axumite temple at Yeha (by courtesy of Neville Chittick)

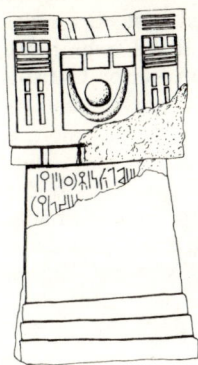

Fig. 29 Pre-Axumite sculpture (after Sergew, 1972)

Little else is known concerning this 'pre-Axumite' culture. We do not know the extent to which it impinged upon the lives of ordinary people living away from its urban and religious centres. We do not know whether Semitic speech had already replaced the Cushitic languages of the indigenes. Until archaeologists' attention is diverted to ordinary settlement sites we shall be unable to appreciate the extent of the integration achieved between the two communities, their respective contribution to its economic base and material culture, or the degree of continuity with earlier Ethiopian societies.

Around the first century AD occurred the rise to prominence of the Kingdom of Axum, its capital being some fifty kilometres to the south-west of Yeha. Although Sabaean influence was still strong at Axum, particularly in its monumental architecture, it seems likely that Axumite culture represents a fusion of southern Arabian and local Ethiopian traits to produce a more integrated whole which was able to exert influence over a far wider area than had its earlier counterpart. Other factors also contributed to the rapid rise of Axum to commercial prosperity: one of the most important was contact, through the port of Adulis on the Red Sea coast south of the present Massawa, with the Greek-dominated commercial network of the eastern Roman Empire, which was described in the first century AD in the *Periplus of the Erythraean Sea* (Schoff, 1912), and is attested archaeologically by the coins struck by the Kings of Axum from the third century AD onwards, which bear their names and titles in Greek and follow the general design, though hardly the artistic style, current in the eastern Mediterranean area at that time.

It was probably during the fourth century that the power and prosperity of Axum reached its peak. King Ezana put the finishing touches to the eclipse of Meroe, an event which is recorded in an inscription carved in Ghe'ez, a local Ethiopian language – basically Semitic, but with a strong local Cushitic element – which has remained in liturgical use to the present day. The use of this language by itself is interesting (Ezana's earlier inscriptions were in Greek, one being trilingual in Greek, Sabaean and Ghe'ez) and shows the increasing emphasis on the local element in Axumite culture, which led eventually to its almost complete isolation from the rest of the world. Before this took place, however, Ezana was converted to Christianity, which apparently became the state religion of Axum before the fall of Meroe and less than a decade after its achievement of a similar status in the Roman Empire under Constantine I (but cf. Pirenne, 1975). At Axum the change is symbolized on Ezana's coins by the replacement of the crescent and disc of 'Ilumquh by the Christian cross (Fig. 30).

Fig. 30 *Axumite coins (after Littmann, 1913): 1, pre-Christian King Aphilas, late third century* AD *(gold, Greek inscription; 2, Christian King Armah, seventh century* AD *(bronze, Ethiopic inscription)*

Most of the archaeological work which has been done at Axum has been devoted to investigation of the tombs and monumental architecture (Littmann, 1913; Chittick, 1974*b*). The grandest and most impressive of all the monuments at Axum – and, perhaps, in the whole of sub-Saharan Africa – are the monolithic stelae, over a hundred of which are situated on the edge of the present town of Axum, a town which occupies but a fraction of the area taken up by its ancient counterpart. Several of the stelae, including the largest (now fallen) which measured 33 metres in height, were carved into a stylized representation of a multi-storey building (Plate XI and Fig. 31). Base plates at the foot of some stelae appear to have been designed for the receipt of offerings. It has been generally believed that they are funerary monuments of the pre-Christian period. Neville Chittick's recent excavations have confirmed the associations of many of the stelae with tombs – some of megalithic construction – but have not yet provided conclusive dating evidence, there remaining the possibility that the monuments may be slightly more recent than was formerly believed. Metal plates set at the tops of the stelae have now disappeared, but their rivet-holes remain and much ingenuity has gone into determining (so far without conclusive success) whether the design could have been a crescent and disc or a cross (van Beek, 1967).

Early in the present century extensive remains of major buildings were excavated at Axum, but little trace of them now remains. Each

Plate XI One of the giant stelae at Axum (by courtesy of Neville Chittick)

was built on a stepped plinth comparable with that of the temple at
Yeha and which may also be paralleled at broadly contemporary sites
in southern Arabia (Doe, 1971). Both at Axum and at Matara (Littmann,
1913; Anfray, 1963b; 1965; 1967b) huge rectangular buildings with
regularly indented walls were erected to a height of several storeys,
but were perhaps not so high or so grandiose as some published reconstructions might lead one to believe. Many of them were presumably palaces or houses of the aristocracy. The walls were built
of much smaller stones than those employed in earlier times, large
blocks being reserved for the cornerstones and steps (Plate XII).
Several features of Axumite architecture have been continued in later
ecclesiastical buildings, notably the church of Debra Damo in Tigre
(Matthews and Mordini, 1959) mostly of tenth- or eleventh-century
date, which still survive and which consequently assist in the interpretation of the archaeological remains.

Other important settlements of the Axumite Empire, such as those

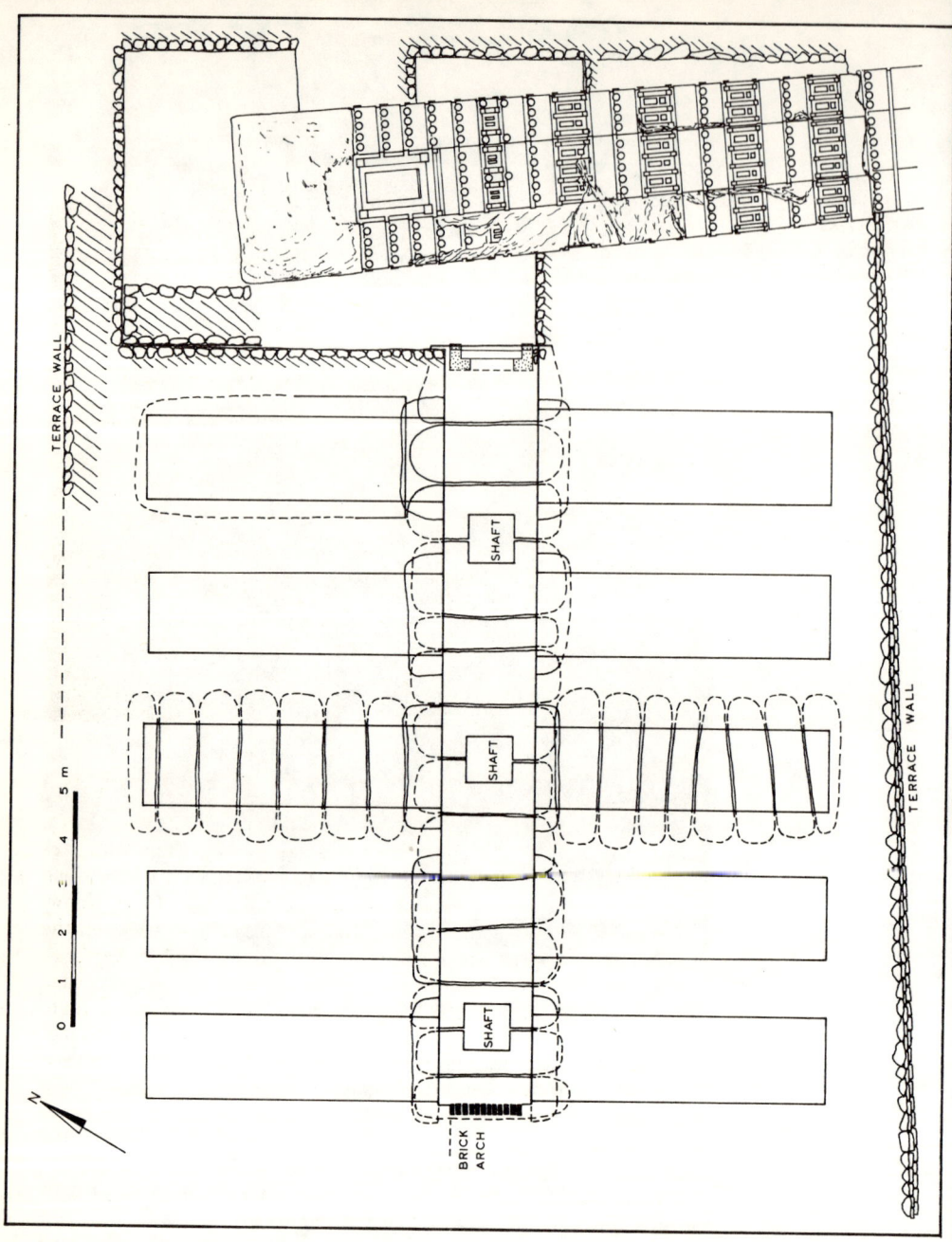

Fig. 31 Plan of subterranean mausoleum and fallen stele, Axum (after Chittick, 1974b)

Plate XII   Ruins of a late Axumite building at Dungur, Axum

at Qohaito, Matara, and, most significant of all, the port of Adulis, have received relatively little archaeological attention (Littmann, 1913; Anfray, 1967*b*; Paribeni, 1908). Significantly, most of the inland sites lie on or near the routes leading from Axum to Adulis, a route which must have carried a large volume of trade, as will be discussed below. It is interesting that Axum itself should be situated so far from the coastal outlet on which its prosperity depended. Perhaps the explanation for this is to be found in its position close to the western edge of the highlands and to the Takazze river, which provides a route to the rich lowlands of the Sudan, the Nile valley and the 'Island' of Meroe. Although there is little evidence for trade contact between Meroe and Axum, it is probable that both centres obtained ivory from the plains of Butana between the Nile and the Atbara. It may have been competition between them in this area that contributed to the final eclipse of Meroe in the fourth century AD (Kirwan, 1972*b*).

That ivory was the mainstay of Axum's external trade, along with tortoise shell and rhinoceros horn, is confirmed by several contemporary writers including the author of the *Periplus* in the first or second century (Schoff, 1912) and Cosmas Indicopleustes in the sixth (Wolska-Conus, 1968). Imports (Sergew: 1972: 73–4) included glass, metalwork and other luxury goods from the eastern Roman Empire and from further to the east: Adulis was a port of call on Roman trading voyages to India. A great trade route (Bent, 1893) ran from Adulis up the escarpment to Qohaito, on to Axum and down to the hunting grounds of the Sudan. All this territory was, by the fourth century AD, under the control of the Kings of Axum.

Once again, our knowledge of domestic economy is severely limited because of the absence of appropriate archaeological research, in the attentions of which ordinary domestic settlements have been virtually ignored. We know hardly anything, therefore, of domestic architecture or settlement patterns, and no analysis of food remains from an Axumite site has ever been undertaken. We know, however, from a literary source – Cosmas Indicopleustes – that cattle were in sufficiently good supply to be taken on trading expeditions and exchanged with the Agau for gold (Pankhurst, 1961: 40; Kirwan, 1972a). At Axum, copper, bronze, iron, silver and gold were all in use and were probably worked there. The Axumite metal-workers were particularly skilled at inlay: many of the bronze coins have parts of the design, notably the cross on the reverse, carefully picked out with gold inlay. Of ivory working we know nothing.

For several centuries Axum remained a major trading and imperial power. During two brief periods, first in the third century AD and again in the sixth, the Kings of Axum extended their rule to parts of southern Arabia. It was from Arabia, too, that Axum's power was broken as control of the Red Sea and its ports passed into first Persian and then Arab hands during the seventh century. Deprived of its outlet to its principal markets, Axum declined into obscurity. Some three centuries later, tradition relates that the capital itself was sacked by a revolt of the Agau.

THE EAST COAST

Reference has been made in the preceding section to the text known as the *Periplus of the Erythraean Sea* and to the light which it throws on international trade among the lands bordering the Indian Ocean shortly after the beginning of the Christian era. This important historical source (Schoff, 1912) was written in Greek by an anonymous resident of Alexandria. The precise date of its compilation cannot be ascertained: the closing decades of the first century AD are generally held to be probable, although some authorities have argued for a second-century attribution.

In addition to the information which he supplies concerning the external trade of Axum, the author of the *Periplus* has given us our earliest knowledge of commercial contacts with the eastern coast of Africa to the south of Cape Guardafui, which probably marked the furthest effectual penetration of the ancient or Ptolemaic Egyptians and their neighbours. It appears that traders from that part of southern Arabia now known as Yemen were, by this early date, already sailing down the East African coast as far as the modern Tanzania. The principal coastal settlement mentioned in the *Periplus*, Rhapta, is thought to have been located between the mouths of the Rufiji and Pangani rivers: that is, within the 300-kilometre stretch of coast centred on the site of Dar es Salaam (Datoo, 1970), but its remains have never been found. Sailing southwards with the north-east monsoon which blows from November to April, the Arabians brought metal and glass objects which they exchanged on the Somali coast for gums and spices and, further to the south, for ivory, rhinoceros horn and turtle shell, returning northwards before the June–October monsoon. We are told little about the inhabitants of the coast with whom this trade was conducted other than that they were tall. It may be assumed that iron, as their principal import, was not produced locally on any signi-

ficant scale, although – as will be shown in chapter VI – Early Iron
Age peoples are known to have reached the Mombasa hinterland from
the interlacustrine region by about the second century ad. The later
history of the East African coast will be discussed in chapter VII:
here, it is appropriate to return to a discussion of contemporary events
in the interior.

THE SUDANIC REGION

Concurrently with the florescence of the more developed cultures at
Axum and Meroe which in part derived from centres outside sub-
Saharan Africa, the more southerly regions of the Sudanese Nile
valley, as well as the Butana plain between the Nile and the Ethiopian
highlands, were still occupied by indigenous peoples whose material
culture continued several aspects of that of the 'Khartoum Neolithic'.
Reference has already been made in chapter III to the still unexcavated
sites at Khasm el Girba on the Atbara (J. D. Clark, 1972) which seem
to have been inhabited by a mixed-farming, stone-tool-using population whose pottery shows typological affinities to that from Esh
Shaheinab and who continued in occupation of the Butana region until
at least the end of the second millennium bc. The sites of Jebel
Moya (Addison, 1949) and Jebel et Tomat (Clark and Stemler, 1975),
between the Blue and the White Niles near Sennar, appear to represent
a survival of the same tradition until after the advent of iron.

The large-scale excavations at Jebel Moya, conducted before the
First World War, yielded enormous quantities of artefacts but little
information about their date or associations: evidence for the domestic
economy was evidently not retained. Desmond Clark's test excavations at Jebel et Tomat, some sixty kilometres to the west, place both
sites in their correct prehistorical perspective. Jebel et Tomat was
a substantial settlement site, 5 hectares in extent, which was apparently
occupied from late in the last century bc until the beginning of
the fifth century ad: it thus overlapped with, and survived, the
decline of Meroe. At both sites it is now evident that a mixed-
farming economy was practised, cattle, sheep and goats being
herded while fishing, fowling and hunting all supplemented the diet.
At Jebel et Tomat remains of sorghum were recovered: its anatomical
features show that this was fully domesticated, although it is smaller
and more primitive in appearance than that which is grown in the
Sudan today. Clark suggests that the site's inhabitants were transhu-
mant, as is the present population of the area. The pottery at both
sites retained features found in that of Esh Shaheinab, together with
some Meroitic elements: the latter are particularly strong at Jebel
Moya. Iron was present at both sites but was extremely rare. Chipped
stone artefacts of mode 5 continued in use in large numbers, apparently
throughout the occupation.

It is tempting to suggest that the inhabitants of Jebel et Tomat,
as revealed by the excavations described above, may have been representative of the peoples who inhabited much of the central and
southern Sudan during Meroitic times, and perhaps also of many of
the rural subject populations of the Empire of Meroe. In Ethiopia,
also, it is probable that many of the subjects of the Kings of Axum,
away from the urban and religious centres of the state, were peasant
farmers. In neither area, however, have the relevant sites been investigated. The absence of any archaeological data from the huge expanse

of the southern Sudan is particularly unfortunate: a tantalizing reference (Titherington, 1923) to what may eventually be found there describes large 'city mounds' in the Bahr el Ghazal Province in the far south-west of the Sudan, in what can be seen as a critical area for the elucidation of the prehistory of the earliest Iron Age in central Africa.

Possible dispersal of iron technology westwards from the Nile valley during the second half of the last millennium BC is indicated by pottery from the Ennedi region of the southern Sahara, noted by A. J. Arkell (1964) and Gérard Bailloud (1969) to bear strong resemblances to black-topped wares with thickened rims which were prevalent in the former region at that time. The pottery from this area of eastern Chad is of further interest because of its similarity to that of the Early Iron Age Industrial Complex in Bantu Africa (Inskeep, 1965; Soper, 1971a), as will be discussed below in chapter VIII. These observations make it all the more unfortunate that the archaeology of the first millennium BC in the eastern part of the sudanic belt further to the south, where communication from east to west, or *vice versa*, would at this time have been significantly easier, remains almost totally unknown.

From further to the west, outside the geographical area with which this book is concerned, comes evidence that iron was known at almost as early a date as that which is attested at Meroe. The people of the 'Nok culture' (Fagg, 1969) on the Jos Plateau of Nigeria were evidently working iron on an appreciable scale by at least the third century bc, while by some five centuries later acquaintance with metallurgy had reached southern Ghana. It has been argued that knowledge of the necessary techniques diffused southwards to West Africa from Carthaginian colonies on the Mediterranean coast quite independently of their penetration of the Sudan *via* the Nile valley (van der Merwe, 1968; Mauny, 1971). This is perfectly plausible but in the present state of our knowledge cannot be proved. Certainly, it is clear from the rock paintings that iron-using people did penetrate through the Sahara from the north and north-east (Lhote, 1953). The date at which this trans-Saharan intercourse began is difficult to establish, but it was probably somewhat earlier than the beginning of the Christian era, as postulated by Paul Huard (1966). It may be concluded that by the last few centuries BC iron technology was established through the greater part of the sudanic belt. In the more easterly regions it appears to have been derived from a Nile Valley source: whether these influences reached the regions to the west of Lake Chad before the separate advent to West Africa of metallurgical knowledge across the Sahara it is not yet possible to say.

It has frequently been postulated, notably by A. J. Arkell (e.g. 1961) that several cultural and political aspects of recent West African society are derived from Meroe (but see Shinnie, 1971b). The date in the fourth century AD which Arkell proposes for this dispersal of Meroitic traits is now seen to be far too late to be linked with the spread of iron-working technology.

In conclusion, it must be admitted that the detail so far available is not adequate to support a coherent synthesis of the inception of iron-working south of the Sahara. In general terms it appears that knowledge of metallurgy was probably widespread in the sudanic belt from the Nile Valley westwards to Nigeria by about the middle of the last millennium bc. Such evidence as we have suggests that Meroe may have played a leading part in the introduction of metallurgy to sub-Saharan latitudes. Significantly, early Meroitic iron tools are tanged, as are those in Nigeria and in Nilotic- and Bantu-speaking regions further to the south. By contrast, Axumite and other early Ethiopian tools are socketed; so it appears that the latter area did not play a major part in the transmission of metal-working techniques further to the south. Until further archaeological fieldwork has been conducted in the southern Sudan and in adjacent regions of the Central African Republic and north-eastern Zaïre, the detailed connexions between the Nile Valley metallurgists and those of more southerly latitudes will remain undemonstrated.

VI

The Early Iron Age Industrial Complex: archaeological considerations

At a level securely dated in most areas to early in the first millennium ad, there is apparent a major change in the archaeological record of the greater part of eastern and southern Africa lying between the equator and Natal. This is marked by the appearance of a characteristic pottery type which, although regional variations in style are readily apparent, is nevertheless remarkably homogeneous and throughout the whole of this vast area belongs to a single stylistic tradition. Pottery of this type is found associated with evidence for the working of metal – both iron and (in some areas) copper; and since in the whole region this is the earliest known evidence for metallurgy, the industrial complex to which these artefacts belong has been named the Early Iron Age (D. W. Phillipson, 1968a; Soper, 1971a). In most cases the Early Iron Age metallurgists appear to have been settled people practising a mixed-farming economy. In the regions of the sub-continent to the south of central Tanzania they are the first practitioners of such an economy to be recognized in the archaeological record; and it is now widely accepted that they were also responsible for the introduction of food-producing techniques into central and much of southern Africa.

THE NATURE OF THE EARLY IRON AGE COMPLEX

It will be appreciated that the contrast between the Early Iron Age Industrial Complex and its predecessors was considerably greater in the southern part of the sub-continent than it was further to the north. In the latter region settled village communities based on a pastoral economy and possibly also on the cultivation of food crops had, as shown in chapter IV, been established at least one thousand years previously. In the south, however, it appears that the Early Iron Age Industrial Complex was introduced to a region where settled existence was previously largely unknown, and where a hunting and gathering economy was practised by the entire population. Here, except in the extreme south of Africa, the Early Iron Age pottery is the earliest to occur in the archaeological record. The metallurgical practices of the Early Iron Age folk were presumably derived from a northerly origin, since in the sudanic regions – as has been shown in chapter V – knowledge of iron-working had spread during the middle centuries of the first millennium bc. The affinities of the Early Iron Age pottery tradition, although imperfectly understood, also appear to be with the sudanic regions to the north. It therefore seems reasonable to postulate a general northerly origin for the Early Iron Age Industrial Complex, although a more detailed consideration of the origins of this complex must be postponed until chapter VIII.

It has for some years been considered probable that the spread of the Early Iron Age Industrial Complex may be correlated with the dispersal of the Bantu languages. There is now reason to believe that this view, although basically correct, is an oversimplification of a process which is much more complex than was previously realized; and the whole question of linguistic and archaeological correlation in the context of the Iron Age in Bantu Africa will be discussed at length in chapter VIII. Here, we are primarily concerned with the archaeological interpretation of the Early Iron Age.

Meaningful overall synthesis of the Early Iron Age Industrial Complex is considerably hampered by the very uneven distribution of the research which has so far been conducted. Southern Kenya and Uganda are relatively well explored, although even in these areas the coverage of fieldwork has been very incomplete. There is reason to believe that the Early Iron Age Industrial Complex is not represented much to the north of this region, but the precise line of its northern frontier, particularly to the north-west, remains to be established by future research. In Tanzania work has been concentrated in the northern and especially the north-eastern parts of the country; the remaining regions, notably the south-west, are still largely unexplored. Rwanda has yielded several sites of this period, but Burundi has been little investigated. Further to the south, fieldwork in Zambia has been more intensive; the Southern Province and the areas around the main modern urban centres of Lusaka and the Copperbelt are comparatively well explored, the north and the east less so. The important region of the Luapula valley has not yet been investigated, and Iron Age research in the western part of the country is only just beginning. The Iron Age of Malawi remained virtually unknown until recent years, but extensive work in most major regions now provides a relatively clear picture of the Early Iron Age of that country. Iron Age archaeology in Mozambique is still virtually nonexistent, although it is interesting to note that one of the first occurrences of Early Iron Age pottery to be discovered in sub-Saharan Africa was found in that country by Carl Wiese in about 1907 (D. W. Phillipson, 1976a). Rhodesia, on the other hand, is probably one of the best-known African countries from the point of view of Iron Age archaeological research, although here again several important areas in the south and north-west remain largely unexplored. Iron Age investigations in South Africa are also in their infancy; but the tempo of research, especially in the Transvaal, has recently been greatly intensified. It is particularly unfortunate that the areas immediately to the west of those discussed above (the modern Botswana, Namibia, Angola and the greater part of Zaïre) remain virtually unknown to the Iron Age archaeologist, because such evidence as we have indicates that this westerly region must have played an important part in the early development of certain sectors of the Early Iron Age Industrial Complex. This is a problem to which we shall return in a later section. It will now be appropriate to present a regional survey of the archaeological evidence for the Early Iron Age Industrial Complex, before attempting a more detailed synthesis.

REGIONAL SURVEY

The following survey is arranged in terms of geographically determined groups which have been recognized primarily on the basis of typological distinctions in the associated pottery assemblages. Where the necessary data are available, I have attempted to demonstrate the nature of typological development in the pottery of individual groups and, in some cases, to subdivide the duration of the Early Iron Age into sequential local phases.

The most detailed comparison which has so far been presented of the pottery wares of the various Early Iron Age groups is that of Robert Soper (1971a). On the basis of his work, supplemented by other data which have recently become available, it is, I believe, possible to discern two distinct major divisions within the Early Iron Age of eastern and southern Africa. These divisions, for the purposes of this book, are designated the 'eastern stream' and the 'western stream' of the Early Iron Age (see map, Fig. 32). By the use of the term 'stream' I do not wish to make any implication as to the nature of the inception of Early Iron Age culture in its various regions. Although the two streams (like other Early Iron Age subdivisions) have been distinguished in the first place through studies of pottery typology, they may also be seen to be differentiated chronologically and to be marked by their differential possession of other cultural traits, as will be demonstrated in a later section of this chapter. In view of the mass of data currently available, it has been deemed advisable to present the greater part of the regional survey of the Early Iron Age archaeology in terms of the two 'streams', which involves the reader taking their existence on trust until the data have been assimilated. It is hoped that this somewhat circular approach makes up in clarity what it lacks in objectivity.

For the convenience of the reader, the hierarchy of terms used in the subdivision of the Early Iron Age should perhaps be summarized. The cultural or industrial entity is referred to in its entirety as the *Early Iron Age Industrial Complex*; it is subdivided, as noted above, into an *eastern stream* and a *western stream*. On the basis of the typology of the various pottery *wares*, several geographically restricted *groups* are recognized within each stream. Each group is named, following the accepted practice of Africanist archaeologists, after the site at which its associated pottery was first recognized and adequately described. The Early Iron Age within the territory of individual groups may, in some cases, be further subdivided, this time chronologically, by the recognition of sequential *phases*.

The Urewe group

Within East Africa, distinctive Early Iron Age material is known from three separate areas (Fig. 33). The most extensive group, known as Urewe, covers the Lake Victoria basin, extending to the south-west into Rwanda and adjacent parts of Zaïre. The characteristic Urewe ware was first recognized near the north-eastern corner of Lake Victoria, around the Winam (Kavirondo) Gulf of Kenya. It was originally known as 'dimple-based ware' after one of its most distinctive, but by no means ubiquitous, typological features (Leakey, Owen and Leakey, 1948). Urewe ware assemblages (Fig. 34, p. 123) are mainly of necked vessels and shallow bowls: the former generally have exter-

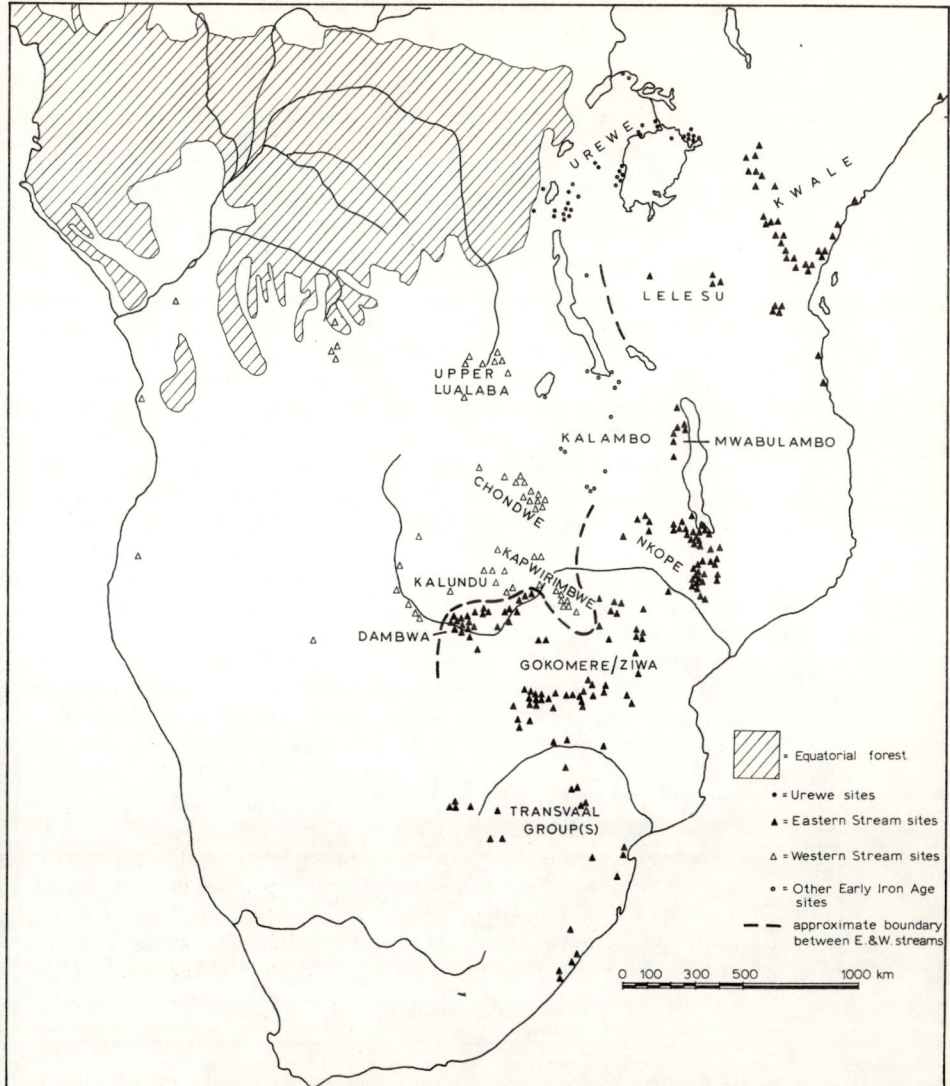

Fig. 32 Groups and streams of the Early Iron Age Industrial Complex

nally thickened rims with fluted lips, often accompanied by incised decoration on the rim-band. Grooved designs on or near the shoulder are frequently elaborate, with pendant loops, triangles, concentric circles and other motifs. The majority of the bowls bear horizontal grooving below the rim, sometimes integrated with further bands which pass under the base of the vessel to produce an overall star-like design. These vessels sometimes, but not invariably, display a small concavity or 'dimple' in the centre of the rounded base. For some time the absolute date of these Urewe settlements was inadequately known. The only radiocarbon date available (from Nsongezi rockshelter on the Kagera river in Uganda) merely indicated an age after the beginning of the present millennium (Pearce and Posnansky, 1963). It was realized that the Urewe pottery was probably considerably earlier than this, but how much earlier remained unknown until comparatively recent years.

In 1967 Robert Soper was able to reinvestigate Early Iron Age sites in the Winam Gulf area. At Urewe, radiocarbon dates were obtained which placed the habitation of the site between the mid-second and the mid-fifth centuries ad. Unfortunately, little evidence was forthcoming for the non-ceramic associations of the Urewe ware or for the nature of the site. Yala Alego, a second locality originally described by Owen, was likewise dated to somewhere between the second and the seventh centuries ad. Here, the characteristic Urewe ware was

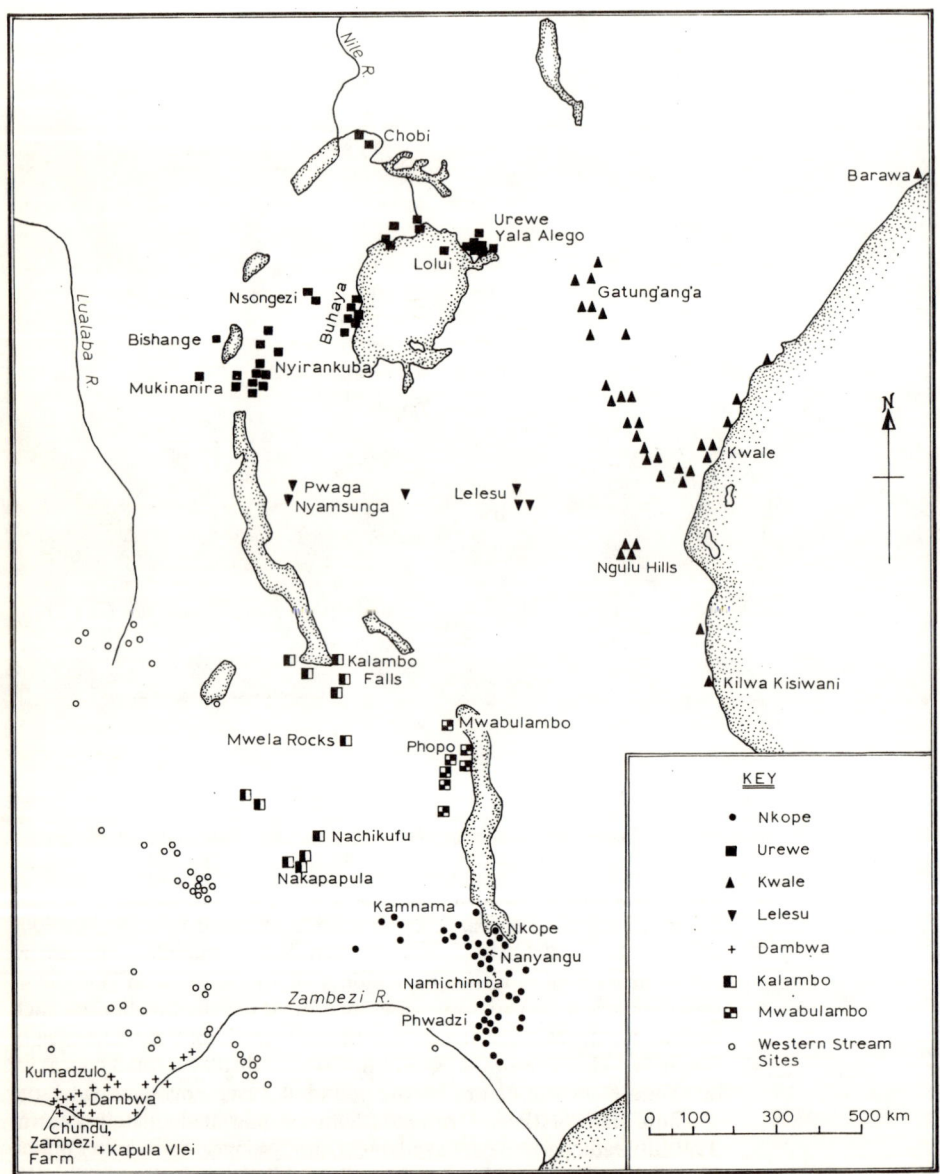

Fig. 33 Sites of the eastern stream of the Early Iron Age north of the Zambezi

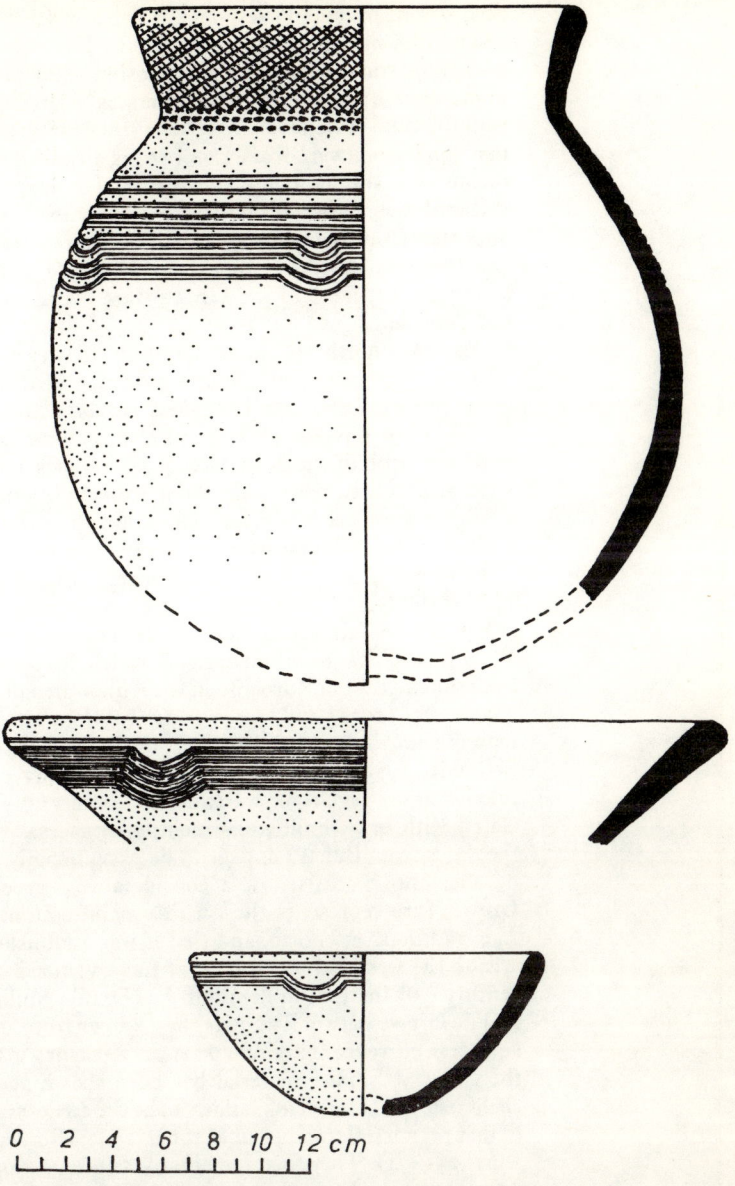

Fig. 34 Urewe ware from sites in south-western Kenya (after Leakey, Owen and Leakey, 1948)

associated with fragments of iron slag and small pieces of worked iron. Soper (1969) was thus able to demonstrate that Urewe ware was being manufactured in the area immediately north-east of Lake Victoria by the early centuries of the first millennium ad.

In Uganda, Urewe ware had been recovered from undated contexts at a number of sites in Buganda and Busoga (Posnansky, 1961). The most extensive collection, however, comes from Lolui Island in north-eastern Lake Victoria. The island was apparently not inhabited by makers of mode 5 artefacts (although there is evidence for earlier occupation, by people responsible for a mode 3 industry, at a time when Lolui was probably not an island). The Lolui Urewe ware occurs mainly in surface contexts and erosion exposures; it has also been found on the surface in rockshelters associated with schematic rock paintings and rock gongs. Merrick Posnansky (1967a; 1973) considers that the Urewe ware from Lolui spans a considerable period of time, the finer examples being the earlier. He suggests that this earlier material was either brought from the mainland or made of clay imported from the same source. The later pottery, which is cruder and less well executed, appears to be made of local clay. It is unfortunate that none of the Urewe ware occurrences on Lolui Island has been dated.

The most northerly known Urewe ware sites are located beside the Victoria Nile near the Chobi confluence downstream of Kabalega (Murchison) Falls, and have been investigated by Soper (1971b). Urewe ware was found at a number of undated localities on the northern bank of the Nile: later pottery types also occurred at these sites and consequently, although iron tools and remains of iron-smelting furnaces were located, none of these could be demonstrated with any certainty to be contemporary with the Urewe ware.

Evidence is now beginning to emerge that, in at least the western part of the Lake Victoria basin, the Urewe ware tradition was established at a significantly earlier period than it was around the Winam Gulf. Radiocarbon dates on which this statement is based have been obtained from Rurembo in the Rutare area of Rwanda by Francis van Noten (1972) and, more recently, from sites in Buhaya in the extreme north-west of Tanzania by Peter Schmidt (Sutton, 1972; Schmidt, 1975). Both these groups of sites have yielded extremely fine examples of Urewe ware; at one locality this material was associated with brick-built iron-smelting furnaces. While one or two of the dates from Buhaya appear to be exceptionally early and may well be aberrant, there is now a considerable degree of likelihood that Urewe ware represents the earliest manifestation of the Early Iron Age tradition yet known, and that it was established – at least in this area to the west and south-west of Lake Victoria – during the closing centuries of the first millennium bc (D. W. Phillipson, 1975).

The Urewe ware of Rwanda is best known from an extensive undated surface occurrence at Nyirankuba near Kinkanga in the southern part of the country. Similar material has been shown at a number of rockshelter sites, notably Mukinanira, to be the earliest pottery type to occur in that region (Hiernaux and Maquet, 1960; Hiernaux, 1962; Nenquin, 1967: 258–71). There are remarkable concentrations of iron-working debris associated with Urewe ware in Rwanda, and several sites have yielded the remains of iron-smelting furnaces. Two of these, at Ndora and Cyamakusa, are dated to between the second and the fourth century ad (Fagan, 1969a). The furnaces appear to have been tall and cylindrical, built of small wedge-shaped clay bricks which were frequently roughly decorated. The best-preserved example of such a furnace is at Bishange in eastern Kivu (Hiernaux and Maquet, 1954). It is noteworthy that, despite the frequency with which traces of iron-smelting are found associated with Urewe ware in this region, no demonstrably Early Iron Age iron tools have yet been found there. It is only in this relatively restricted part of the area of Urewe ware's distribution that these characteristic tall smelting furnaces are attested. Despite the number of sites that have been located, it appears that, in this area, the Early Iron Age settlers were not sufficiently numerous to displace the pre-existing stone-tool-using population for, at the majority of rockshelters where Urewe ware sherds have been recovered, mode 5 artefacts also occur in apparently contemporaneous association. Beyond the clear association of traces of iron-working with Urewe ware at these sites, little detailed information is yet available concerning the economy of this Early Iron Age population.

The eastern boundary of the distribution of Urewe ware appears to coincide with that of the territory occupied by the stone-tool-using pastoral folk discussed in chapter IV. It is highly probable that the latter population retained its separate identity through the greater part of the first millennium ad, with relatively little contact with their Early Iron Age contemporaries to the east and west. Only very occasional Early Iron Age sherds have been recovered from sites in the Kenya Rift Valley, and these may be attributed to spasmodic intercourse between the two populations.

The eastern stream

From this point the narrative may be conducted in terms of the two streams of the Early Iron Age to which reference has been made above. It appears that a distinct Early Iron Age variant, derived from the Urewe group, was established in north-central Tanzania to the south of the territory occupied by the stone-tool-using pastoralists. It is named after the site of Lelesu, an open site in Usandawe originally investigated by Ludwig Kohl-Larsen (1943). Lelesu ware is less well known than the other East African Early Age variants; and no absolute age determinations for it are so far available. The pottery, which comes mainly from rockshelters and surface scatters, has been described by Gunther Smolla (1956). Subsequent work at Lelesu itself by John Sutton (1968) confirms that the site is probably that of an Early Iron Age habitation. The pottery shows affinities both with Urewe ware and with the Kwale pottery discussed below: Soper (1971a) has suggested that it may be typologically intermediate between the two.

The third Early Iron Age group which has been investigated in East Africa is named after the site of Kwale, located by Robert Soper in 1966 in the Shimba Hills some 30 kilometres south-west of Mombasa. Early Iron Age pottery was recovered from a single occupation horizon which has been dated by radiocarbon to the third century ad. A tanged iron arrow-head, a fragment of slag and a piece of tewel attest the working of iron, but no further significant finds other than pottery were recovered (Soper, 1967a). Kwale ware (Fig. 35, p. 126) is characterized by very many bowls with in-turned fluted rims and flattened or slightly concave bases. Shouldered pots with incised or grooved decoration are also present. On these the rims are generally thickened and also often fluted.

Pottery closely akin if not identical to Kwale ware has been recovered from sites elsewhere in south-eastern Kenya and in the Tanga and Kilimanjaro regions of Tanzania (Soper, 1967b; Odner, 1971c). It also occurs sporadically in the eastern Kenya highlands at sites around Nairobi and in the Murang'a District, notably Gatung'ang'a (Taylor, 1966; Siiriäinen, 1971). The most southerly occurrences of this type of pottery are at four sites in the Ngulu Hills in the Morogoro District of Tanzania, recently reported by Soper (unpublished). In

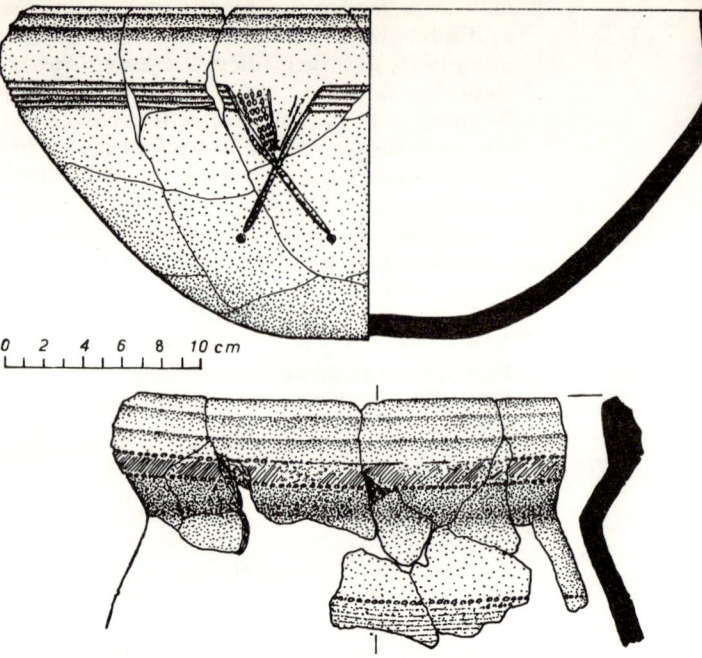

0 2 4 6 8 10 cm

Fig. 35 Kwale ware from Kwale (after Soper, 1967a)

the opposite direction, a possible extension of Kwale ware's distribution northwards along the Indian Ocean coast into what is now
southern Somalia is indicated by Neville Chittick's (1969: 122) find
of Kwale-like pottery at Barawa, over 700 kilometres from Mombasa.

It appears that, by the second century ad (D. W. Phillipson, 1975),
the makers of Kwale ware had established themselves in the hinterland of the Kenya coast, whither they presumably penetrated from
the Urewe region by means of a flanking movement around the
southern margin of the Rift Valley highlands where the stone-tool-
using pastoralists at this time held sway. Some of the inland pottery,
notably that from Gatung'ang'a, is appreciably later; and it may be
that the Early Iron Age did not reach the Eastern Highlands from
the coast until well into the second half of the first millennium ad.
Likewise, there is no indication that Early Iron Age pottery was used
on the coast itself until the closing centuries of the first millennium.

Three other sites in Tanzania have yielded Early Iron Age material.
Two of these, Pwaga and Nyamsunga, are near Uvinza to the east
of Lake Tanganyika; and the Early Iron Age occupation of this region
may be connected with the exploitation for salt of the Uvinza brine-
springs (Sutton and Roberts, 1968). The pottery, dated to around
the middle of the first millennium ad, is apparently distinct from its
two nearest neighbours, the Urewe and Lelesu wares. Its closest parallels are probably with the Kalambo ware from northern Zambia,
which will be described below. The last Tanzanian site which we must
consider as probably attributable to the Early Iron Age is Kilwa
Kisiwani, on the coast some 250 kilometres south of Dar es Salaam.
Here, Neville Chittick (1974a, II: 319–24) recognizes an 'underlying
continuity' in the styles of the locally produced pottery of his periods

Ia–II, which cover the time from the ninth century AD to the end of the thirteenth, and which apparently predate the Shirazi settlement which led to the development of the site as an important trading centre (chapter VII, below). The earliest pottery from Kilwa, that of period Ia (ninth and tenth centuries) displays many features which are characteristic of the Early Iron Age, within the acknowledged time-span of which Chittick's period Ia falls, and which do not occur in the pottery of later periods.

Studies of pottery typology enable two variants to be recognized in the Early Iron Age of Malawi. These are Mwabulambo ware in the north, named after a site on the Lufilya river and, in the south, Nkope ware which takes its name from a locality on the western shore of Lake Nyasa some forty kilometres north of Mangochi (Cole-King, 1973*a*). Although a substantial number of Early Iron Age sites is now known to be widely distributed through Malawi, the nature and location of the geographical boundary between these two pottery types is not well known. The distribution of Nkope ware extends westwards across the watershed into the greater part of south-eastern Zambia, while its spread into adjacent parts of Mozambique is attested by un-published material collected by Carl Wiese and now in the Museum für Völkerkunde, Berlin (D. W. Phillipson, 1976*a*).

Mwabulambo ware (Fig. 36) shows some strong affinities to that from Kalambo which will be described below. Undecorated vessels, particularly bowls, are comparatively frequent. Rims of all vessels are generally undifferentiated or only slightly thickened. On Nkope vessels the decoration is more elaborate and the thickening of rims is more pronounced. The resultant raised rim-band is nearly always decorated with diagonal or criss-cross comb-stamped or incised designs. On the Nkope bowls, rims are frequently pronouncedly in-turned in a way reminiscent of Kwale ware from south-eastern Kenya; on some examples these rims are fluted in the Kwale manner (Robinson, 1966*a*; 1970; 1973*a*). It is noteworthy that these Kwale-like features are more pronounced in Nkope ware than in Mwabulambo, despite the fact that the latter is geographically closer to the Kwale area. This distinction may perhaps partly be explained by the marked influence which the Kalambo ware (see p. 126, below) has clearly had upon the Mwabulambo pottery tradition. It is more probable, however, that makers of Kwale-like pottery penetrated southwards through the archaeologically unexplored country to the east of Lake Nyasa and thence inland to influence the ceramic styles at the south end of the lake. The existence of such an easterly, lowland, facies of the Early Iron Age's eastern stream is to some extent confirmed by the material, described below, recovered both from Tzaneen in the north-eastern Transvaal and from sites around Maputo in southern Mozambique, which shows a remarkable affinity to Kwale ware, stronger than that which it displays to any known pottery from the regions geographically intervening. The earliest radiocarbon dates for Malawi Early Iron Age sites are in the first half of the third century ad; and it has been shown statistically that Mwabulambo ware may have been established some-what earlier than was its southerly counterpart (D. W. Phillipson, 1975).

Only small-scale test excavations have been conducted on the majority of Early Iron Age sites so far investigated in Malawi; and correspondingly scant information is available concerning the non-ceramic artefacts (Robinson and Sandelowsky, 1968; Robinson, 1970; 1973*a*; Cole-King, 1973*b*; Kurashina, 1973). Traces of substantial structures, built of mud applied over a wooden framework (pole and *daga*), were preserved at Phopo Hill near Lake Kazuni. Iron, in the form of slag and finished artefacts, is well attested at several sites, notably at Nanyangu in the Ncheu District and at Zomba Range. Copper, on the other hand, has not been recovered. Shell beads

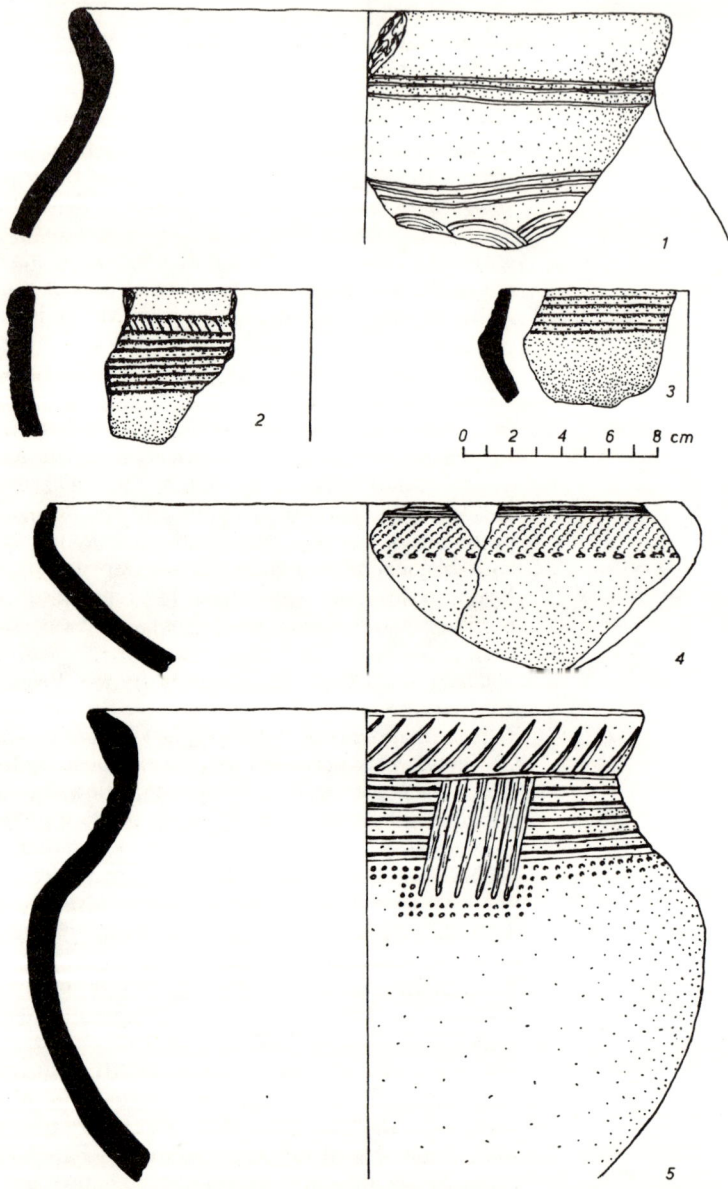

Fig. 36 Early Iron Age pottery from Malawi: 1, 2, Mwabulambo ware from Phopo Hill (after Robinson and Sandelowsky, 1968); 3–5, Nkope ware from Phwadzi (after Robinson, 1973a)

occurred in association with Nkope ware in a storage pit at Phwadze Stream in the Chikwawa District which is dated to the fifth or sixth centuries ad. The only coastal object from an Early Iron Age context in Malawi is a fragmented cowrie shell from a late Nkope site on the Namichimba Stream, Mwanya. Bones which have been identified from these sites are all of wild species.

In the Chipata District of south-western Zambia a relatively sparse Early Iron Age presence seems likewise to have been established by around the third or fourth century (D. W. Phillipson, 1976a). Here, as in northern Zambia, a population making mode 5 stone artefacts appears to have survived well into the present millennium. The only Early Iron Age village site which has so far been investigated in this area is at Kamnama near the Malawi border north of Chipata. The settlement covered an area of about 5 hectares, but its period of occupation was apparently brief. It has been dated to between the third and the fifth centuries ad. The pottery is markedly similar to Nkope ware, necked vessels being dominant, followed in frequency by bowls, about half of which have an exaggerated in-turned rim. Iron was worked at Kamnama, but no trace of copper or of trade goods was recovered.

Early Iron Age pottery akin to Nkope ware has been recorded from two sites in the Tete Province of Mozambique, but the greater part of this region is archaeologically unexplored (see, however, p. 103 above; also Newitt and Garlake, 1967). Cultural continuity across this part of the Zambezi valley at this time is, however, strongly indicated by the presence of closely related pottery in the eastern, southern and central regions of Rhodesia (Robinson, 1973b). The Early Iron Age pottery of the latter areas has been conventionally divided into two groups: 'Gokomere' and 'Ziwa'. Recent work, notably by Thomas Huffman, has shown that the distinction between these two pottery types is not well made; and they must be regarded as being at least as closely related to one another as are the Mwabulambo and Nkope wares of Malawi (Soper, 1971a; Huffman, 1971a).

The distribution of 'Ziwa' sites appears to be centred on the Eastern Highlands around Inyanga, whence it extends both westwards towards Salisbury and southwards along the Mozambique border area into the Sabi valley (Summers, 1958: 138–9; Cooke, Summers and Robinson, 1956). 'Gokomere' ware is widely distributed in the south-central area around Fort Victoria; while further to the south-west in the Bulawayo area a more distinctive Early Iron Age pottery type known as Zhizo ware (formerly 'Leopard's Kopje I') is also recognized. The often confusing changes which have taken place over the past forty years in the terminology of the Rhodesian Iron Age have been summarized and evaluated by Roger Summers (1970).

The comparatively great volume of Iron Age archaeological research which has been conducted in Rhodesia now enables us to discern a unified trend in the typological development of the Early Iron Age pottery tradition over the greater part of the country (Fig. 37). Huffman has termed the Early Iron Age ceramic tradition of the whole of Rhodesia except north-western Mashonaland (for which see p. 135, below) the 'stamped ware tradition'; but the term is open to the same objections as 'dimple-based ware' noted above (p. 104). Following more general archaeological practice, I suggest that the term 'Gokomere/ Ziwa tradition' is to be preferred. While recognizing the presence of

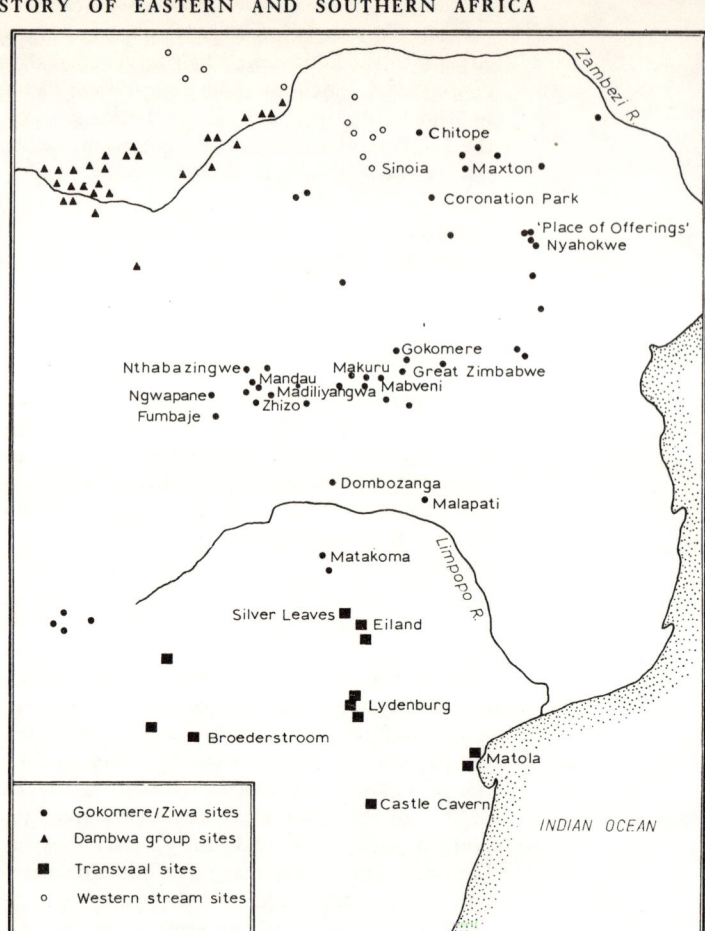

Fig. 37   Early Iron Age sites south of the Zambezi

locally recurring features of long duration, Huffman (1971*a*) proposes
a three-phase sequence of Early Iron Age development in this region.
His phase 1 is best known from such sites as Mabveni, Gokomere
and the 'Place of Offerings' which are discussed in some detail below;
Iron Age occupation of Matabeleland appears to have been sparse
at this time. Phase 2, beginning around the sixth century, shows
rather greater inter-regional diversity, being typified by the sites of
Coronation Park in the Salisbury area, Makuru in the Chibi and Fort
Victoria Districts, Zhizo in Matabeleland and Malapati in the Lowveld.
It is during this phase that Early Iron Age settlement of much of
Matabeleland first reached significant proportions, and that a north-
westerly spread of Early Iron Age culture from central Rhodesia to
the Victoria Falls region is attested. A final phase, 3, of the
Gokomere/Ziwa tradition is recognized only in the Salisbury area,
where it is named from the Maxton Farm site. The archaeological
data on which this synthesis is based may now be examined.

A particularly clear picture of a phase 1 Early Iron Age settlement in south-central Rhodesia has been provided by Keith Robinson's excavations at Mabveni in the Chibi District. Remains of three pole-and-*daga* structures were located, one of which was interpreted as a storage bin originally raised above the ground on stones (Robinson, 1961*a*). A small enclosure of dry-stone field walling and a 14-metre length of similar walling crossing a watercourse at right-angles as if to dam it could not be linked unequivocally with the Early Iron Age settlement, but are distinct architecturally from the structures of known recent date (Caton-Thompson, 1971: 23–4). A shallow midden deposit yielded pottery characterized by necked vessels with diagonal comb-stamped decoration on the thickened external rim-band, and a variety of open bowls. Clay figurines of sheep and humans were also recovered, as were beads made of iron, copper and shell. Contact with coastal trade is demonstrated by the presence of pierced marine shells and three glass beads. Sheep and (possibly) cattle (Huffman, 1975) were represented, alongside several wild species. The site is dated to some period within the first millennium ad. Artefacts from Mabveni are illustrated at Fig. 38.

Confirmatory evidence for much of the above comes from a rock-shelter at Gokomere Mission north of Fort Victoria (Gardner, Wells and Schofield, 1940; Robinson, 1963). Here, comparable pottery was associated with copper and iron fragments, imported glass beads and a complete shell of *Conus ebraeus*, an Indian Ocean species. The animal bones recovered included a horn-core of domestic goat. The Early Iron Age settlement at Gokomere is dated to between the fifth and seventh centuries ad. The earliest Iron Age occupation of Great Zimbabwe Hill (the 'Acropolis'), dated to between the third and fifth centuries for its end, is another example of a phase 1 Early Iron Age industry (Garlake, 1973*a*: 136, 153–6; Summers, Robinson and Whitty, 1961). Further occurrences of around the middle of the first millennium are reported from Cighwa Hill and Kinsale Farm (Robinson, 1967; Fagan, 1969*a*).

The phase 1 pottery in the Inyanga area shows many points in common with that described above, but is more elaborately decorated (Summers, 1958). It is characterized by pots with markedly concave necks and thickened rim-bands on which elaborate comb-stamped decoration is generally encountered, with grooving in the concavity of the neck. Comparable features are common on the bowls. Such pottery is at present best known from the 'Place of Offerings', a large undated open site on Ziwa Mountain near Inyanga, where the Early Iron Age remains were preserved mainly in shallow pits. Associated finds include iron tools, copper objects, shell beads and part of an imported cowrie shell. Millet and pumpkin seeds are apparently associated with the Early Iron Age occupation. Bones, exclusively of wild animals, were also recovered (Summers, 1958). MacIver (1906: 30–4) notes and illustrates a quantity of interesting discoveries from this site, including two ivory bracelets, but unfortunately it cannot be demonstrated whether all of these were recovered from Early Iron Age contexts.

Phase 2 developments of the Gokomere/Ziwa pottery tradition (Fig. 39) show a general modification of the more flamboyant features, while the use of haematite and graphite finishes is introduced (Summers, 1958: 134–9; 1969: 123–9). In the closing centuries of the Early Iron Age the decoration and vessel-forms become still more restrained. The process is best regarded as one of continuous change rather than

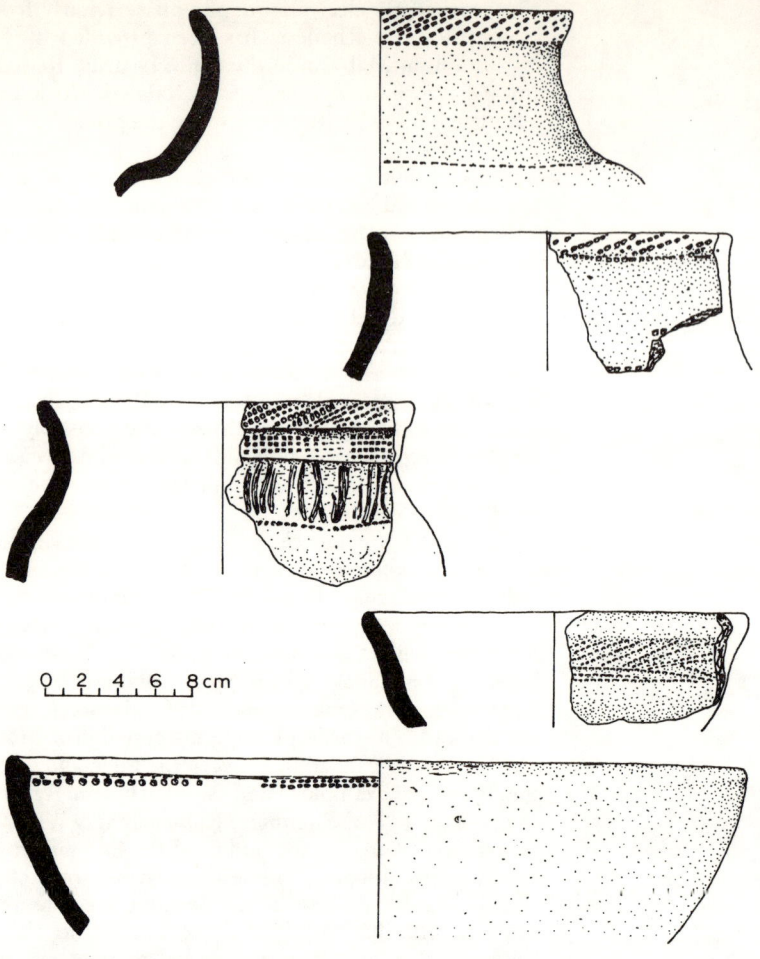

0 2 4 6 8cm

Fig. 38   Pottery from Mabveni (after Robinson, 1961a)

a sequence of easily recognizable stages. Radiocarbon dates from the
Inyanga area cover the greater part of the first millennium ad, but
they do not enable a dated sequence of the pottery typology to be
established. A date in the tenth or eleventh century for the lowest
levels of the stone-built enclosure of Nyahokwe beside Ziwa Mountain
is attributed to a final phase of the Early Iron Age in eastern
Rhodesia (Bernhard, 1961). Several human skeletons found on Early
Iron Age sites in this area are stated to show Negroid physical
characteristics (Bernhard, 1964; de Villiers, 1970).

In the Salisbury area a more detailed succession has been established, showing typological developments which clearly parallel those
described from further to the east. The site at Coronation Park, Salisbury, dated to the seventh and eighth centuries, has yielded pottery
which is attributed to phase 2 of the Gokomere/Ziwa tradition and
which is associated with remains of domestic cattle (Whitty, 1958a;
Huffman, 1973). The pottery recovered from the Golden Shower mine
at Arcturus appears to be best attributed to this phase, possibly

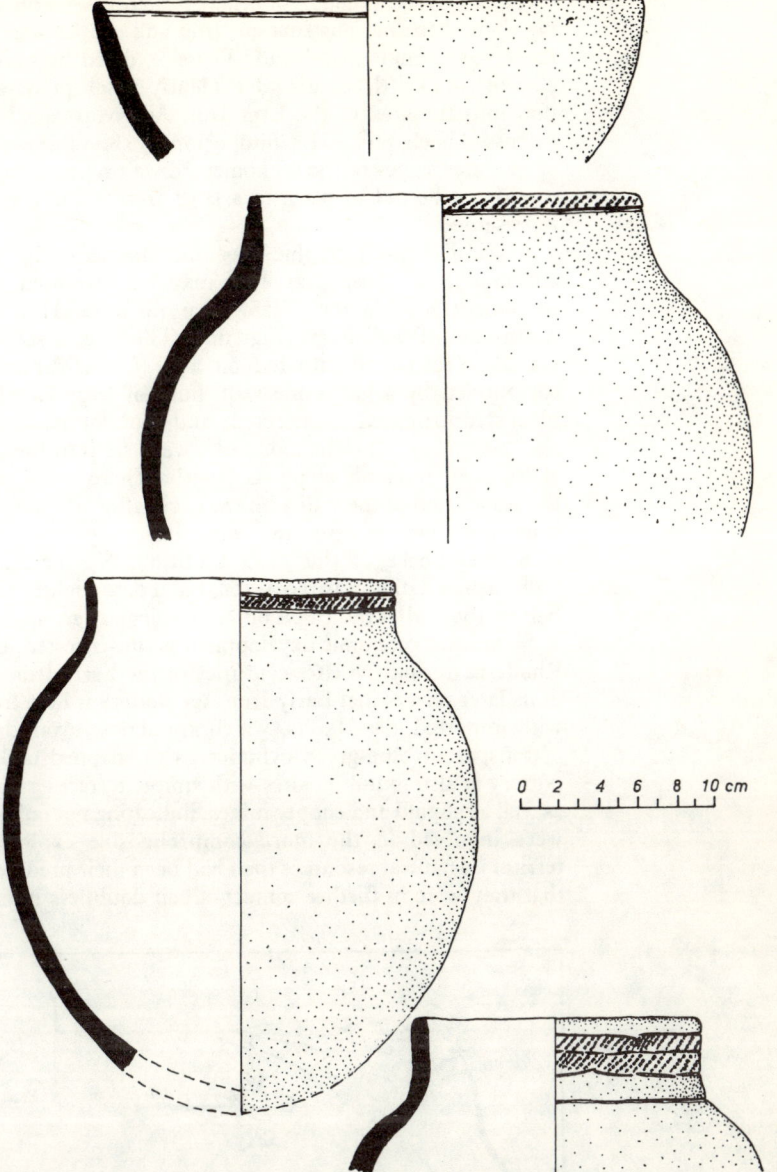

Fig. 39 Pottery from Maxton Farm (after Garlake, 1967a)

belonging to the last quarter of the first millennium ad; but this attribution and dating should be regarded as tentative pending further investigations (Summers, 1969: 43, 122; see also Huffman, 1971a). The further association of this type of pottery with prehistoric mines is discussed in greater detail below.

The site of Chitope, beside the Great Dyke about 100 kilometres north-north-west of Salisbury, represents a very extensive but briefly occupied village of the final phase (3) of the Early Iron Age in northern Mashonaland. Remains of three pole-and-*daga* houses were discovered by Peter Garlake (1969a), but there is no precise information concerning their shape or construction. Iron and copper were both rare; and there was a single glass bead. The site, dated by radiocarbon to the eleventh or twelfth century ad, evidently closely predated the introduction into the area of the later Iron Age Musengezi ware, which is discussed in chapter VII. Chitope pottery shows several characteristics of the later stages of the Gokomere/Ziwa tradition, but sherds which would not be out of place in a later Iron Age context are also well represented.

A similar stratigraphic position immediately preceding the appearance of Musengezi ware may be attributed to the phase 3 settlement at Maxton Farm near Shamva Hill, 80 kilometres north-east of Salisbury (Fig. 40). The site, also investigated by Garlake (1967a), is situated on a *kopje* the summit of which is surrounded by a low stone wall 'built of large loosely piled diorite blocks, untrimmed, unselected, and without packing or wedging' (*loc. cit.*, p. 3). Upright monoliths were set into the top of the wall at frequent intervals along its length. There is no reason to doubt the association of the wall with the occupation of the settlement which it encloses. Pottery associated with this occupation is best attributed to a final phase of the Ziwa tradition. No material suitable for radiocarbon dating was recovered, but a date slightly after rather than before 1000 ad is indicated on archaeological grounds.

Significant economic development is thus attested in north-eastern Rhodesia during the later centuries of the Early Iron Age. It is only in its later phases that Early Iron Age pottery is here found associated with imported glass beads, which are almost invariably of one type – transparent blue-green cylinders with snapped ends. Comparable pottery is also found on sites with simple terraces and stone walling, as well as at gold and copper mines, indicating not only that its makers were involved in the more comprehensive exploitation of their territory's natural resources than had been their predecessors, but also that they were in further contact, albeit doubtless indirectly, with the

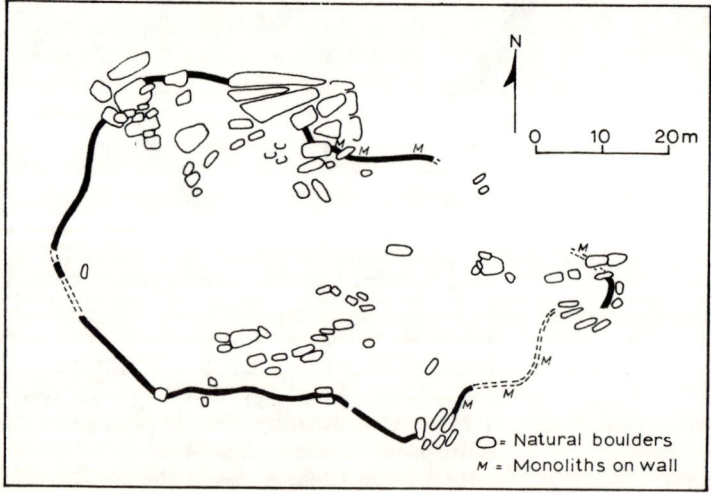

Fig. 40 Plan of the Early Iron Age stone-walled site at Maxton Farm (after Garlake, 1967a)

trade-network of the Indian Ocean. Changes in settlement patterns are also noteworthy. The sites of phases 1 and 2, like the majority of Early Iron Age sites in other areas, are almost invariably situated on fairly flat ground near water. However, of seven phase 3 sites now known in the Salisbury area, four are on hill-tops of relatively difficult access, as if defensive positions were at this time sought (Huffman, 1971*a*).

Phase 2 is poorly represented in the Chibi and Fort Victoria areas; Great Zimbabwe itself appears not to have been occupied at this time. The only site which may confidently be attributed to this phase is that at Makuru Hill near Shabani (Huffman, 1973). Its pottery shows developments from that of Mabveni which closely parallel those observed at Coronation Park. Traces of collapsed huts yielded massive *daga* fragments interpreted by Huffman as the remains of furniture comparable to that previously attested only from later Iron Age contexts. Bones of domestic cattle have been identified at Makuru.

Centred on Bulawayo, the phase 2 sites yielding Zhizo type pottery have much in common with those of the Early Iron Age industries further to the east; they are likewise probably associated with simple low stone walling (Robinson, 1966*b*). It now appears that Zhizo pottery does not represent the initial Early Iron Age occupation of the area: this is probably seen at such sites as Mandau and Madiliyangwa in the Matopo Hills where the pottery has close typological connexions both with the phase 1 wares from further to the east and with the earliest Early Iron Age material of the Victoria Falls (Robinson, 1966*c*; N. Jones, 1933). It seems likely that in much of south-western Rhodesia the Early Iron Age population remained sparse until the development of the Zhizo industry late in the first millennium. Rock art studies, summarized in chapter XI, confirm the substantial survival of stone-tool-using peoples throughout this time, especially in the Matopo Hills.

At the foot of Zhizo Hill in the Matopos a limited area of midden deposits yielded fragments of pole-and-*daga* structures and settings of stones which are interpreted as the supports for grain-storage bins (Robinson, 1966*b*: 6). The pottery is decorated primarily with comb-stamped motifs although incised designs also occur. A single radiocarbon date indicates an age between the ninth and twelfth centuries ad. At other sites which have yielded Zhizo pottery, notably Fumbaje and Ngwapane, stone terrace-walling may be contemporary, but the association is uncertain (*ibid*.: 14).

Twenty-four kilometres west of Bulawayo, a Zhizo horizon represents the earliest Iron Age occupation at the Nthabazingwe (Leopard's Kopje) site and is dated to the eighth or ninth century (Huffman, 1971*b*; 1974*a*). Associated finds include shell and glass beads, iron slag, copper bangles, teeth of sheep or goat and – less certainly associated – remains of cowpeas. Cattle bones, which were common in the overlying deposits of the later Iron Age Leopard's Kopje industry (Mambo phase), were not represented in the comparatively small faunal assemblage from the basal Zhizo horizon.

On the Nuanetsi river in the Lowveld of the extreme south-east of Rhodesia, a phase 2 Early Iron Age village site at Malapati has been dated by radiocarbon to the last quarter of the first millennium ad (Robinson, 1961*b*). Animal bones from this site have been identified as those of domestic cattle (Huffman, 1973). The pottery from this site shares affinities with contemporary wares in both Mashonaland

and Matabeleland and, through the latter, with material recovered in eastern Botswana, as at Maokagani Hill (Schofield, 1948). A few similar sherds were deposited in the Dombozanga rockshelter near Beit Bridge in the Limpopo valley around the same time (Robinson, 1964). It is thus clear that the Lowveld and Limpopo Valley, like western Rhodesia and eastern Botswana, were sparsely settled from at least phase 2 of the Early Iron Age.

The spread of the Early Iron Age Industrial Complex south of the Limpopo before the middle of the first millennium ad is now clearly indicated, but the evidence remains sparse and incompletely published, much of it only having been discovered during the last few years. (For reasons which will be given in chapter VII, I here exclude the Phalaborwa and Uitkomst finds from the Early Iron Age Industrial Complex into which they have sometimes been subsumed.)

Pottery similar to that of the Rhodesian Gokomere/Ziwa tradition has been discovered at Matakoma and Klein Afrika in the Soutpansberg of the northern Transvaal (de Vaal, 1943; Prinsloo, 1974). The latter site is dated to the fourth century ad; while the pottery from Matakoma is presumably somewhat later in view of its similarity with the dated Malapati assemblage.

Further to the south-east, at the Silver Leaves farm near Tzaneen in the north-eastern Transvaal, pits containing Early Iron Age pottery, ash-charcoal and iron slag have been discovered by Menno Klapwijk (1973, 1974). The shallow bowls with in-turned fluted rims provide a marked contrast with those from the Soutpansberg sites but show a remarkable similarity to vessels from Kwale, over 2500 kilometres to the north; and the connexion is further emphasized by several aspects of the decoration (compare Figs. 41: 1–3 and 35). Two radiocarbon dates indicate an age in the third or fourth century ad: thus the Silver Leaves site provides the earliest dated evidence for Iron Age settlement which has yet been found in South Africa. Remarkably similar pottery comes from unpublished excavations conducted by Joao Morais, Ricardo Duarte and their colleagues near Maputo in southern Mozambique.

Early Iron Age pottery apparently belonging to yet another stylistic tradition comes from Broederstroom in the Brits District west of Pretoria where investigations by Revil Mason (1973; 1974) indicate the presence of thirteen collapsed huts set in an elliptical line enclosing an area of some two hectares. Iron slag was associated with the remains of furnaces. Human skeletal remains have been described as comparable in physical type with modern South African negroids. Bones of domestic sheep, goats and cattle have been identified (Welbourne, 1973). Radiocarbon dates indicate an age in the fifth century ad. No detailed description of the pottery is yet available; but a preliminary account notes its resemblance to that from Nkope and Mwabulambo.

Further Early Iron Age sites have been located by T. M. Evers (1973; 1975) in the escarpment region of the eastern Transvaal. In the Lowveld of the Letaba District, as at Harmony, the pottery shows strong affinities to that from Silver Leaves, which lies only seventy kilometres to the north-west. Further material of this type comes from Eiland on the Groot Letaba river. Above the escarpment, however, the Early Iron Age pottery shows closer similarity to that from Broederstroom and, even more markedly, to material from the northern and coastal regions of Natal. The known sites are clustered around

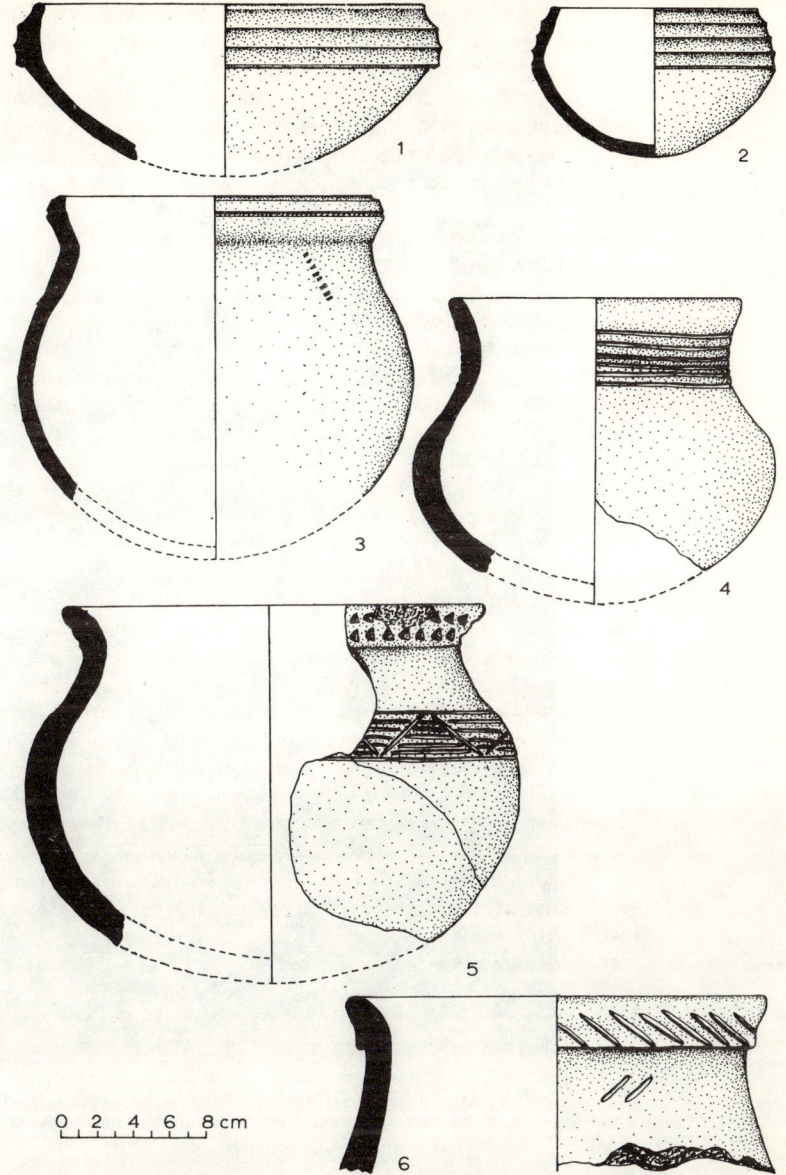

0 2 4 6 8 cm

Fig. 41 Early Iron Age pottery from South Africa: 1–3, from Silver Leaves (after Klapwijk, 1974); 4–6, from Lydenburg (after Inskeep and Maggs, 1975)

the town of Lydenburg. One of these, on the Sterkspruit, has yielded to surface collectors a rich assemblage of Early Iron Age pottery and fragments of seven elaborate terracotta heads (Inskeep and von Bezing, 1966; Inskeep, 1971; Inskeep and Maggs, 1975). The pottery assemblage consists mainly of necked vessels with banded decoration, predominantly incised, on the thickened rim bands and in the concavity of the neck. The human heads, at present unique in the archaeological and ethnographic record of the Iron Age in Bantu-speaking Africa,

Plate XIII   Life-sized terracotta head from the Early Iron Age site at Lyden-
burg, Transvaal (by courtesy of Tim Maggs and Ray Inskeep).
The scale is in centimetres

include two life-sized examples (e.g. Plate XIII) which could have been worn as masks: the others are about one third smaller and appear to have been attached to the tops of posts. There can be little doubt that they belong to the Early Iron Age; and there are good reasons for attributing them to about the fifth century ad – as indicated by the only radiocarbon date so far available from the Sterkspruit site. It is clearly a research priority that large-scale excavations be undertaken here to confirm the age of these remarkable objects and to attempt to learn something about their context and significance. Another site near Lydenburg, with pottery identical to that from Sterkspruit, has yielded bones of domestic cattle and small stock (Evers, 1975).

The Early Iron Age pottery from these Lydenburg sites is akin to that first described from occurrences on the Natal coast near Durban and designated 'NC3' by John Schofield (1935; 1936; 1948). This material is now known from more than sixty sites spread from Swaziland southwards through the Natal coastal belt as far as the Transkei. Typical assemblages come from Tongaat beach and Genozano monastery, both on the Natal coast north of Durban (Inskeep and Maggs, 1975). The only excavated and dated site is that at Ntshekane near Muden which appears from the typology of the pottery to belong to a relatively late phase of the 'NC3' tradition. The site covers an area some 300 metres in diameter and is dated to about the ninth century ad (Maggs, 1973a; Maggs and Michael, 1976). There is evidence for pole-and-*daga* houses and for a series of deep pits which contained bones of cattle, small stock and antelope, as well as large numbers of broken grindstones whose presence strongly suggests the cultivation of cereals.

The final item in this catalogue of recent discoveries in southern Africa which may provisionally be attributed to the Early Iron Age relates to discoveries at Castle Cavern near Mbabane in Swaziland. Only provisional details have so far been made available by the excavators, Peter Beaumont and Raymond Dart (in Fagan, 1967a). Sherds described as being 'typified by a carinated profile and single or multiple channelled lines lying parallel to and immediately below the rim' were found, associated with 'various types of stone mining tools, ground stone fragments, rare iron tools and "Late Stone Age" artefacts'. This material has been securely dated by radiocarbon to the fourth or fifth century ad.

This description of Early Iron Age discoveries from south of the Limpopo has, unfortunately, had to take the form of a mere catalogue of incompletely described material. Any attempt at a detailed synthesis would be premature until the archaeologists responsible for these important excavations have had time more fully to study the results of their work. For the present, it will be prudent simply to conclude that there is now a substantial body of evidence that at least two facies of the Early Iron Age Industrial Complex, both probably belonging to its eastern stream, spread into the Transvaal and some adjacent regions by the middle of the first millennium ad. One of these facies may be attributed mainly to the coastal lowlands and is represented near Maputo and at Tzaneen; another – as seen at Matakoma and Klein Afrika – was derived from the Rhodesian Plateau. The relationship of the 'NC3' sites to these others remains unclear, but some speculations will be offered in chapter VIII.

The Zambezi valley area immediately upstream of the Victoria Falls is one of the best explored regions of sub-Saharan Africa so far as Iron Age archaeology is concerned (Fig. 33). The Early Iron Age of this area has been named the Dambwa group after a site lying on the outskirts of the town of Livingstone (D. W. Phillipson, 1968a). The distribution of the Dambwa group appears to extend at least as far to the south-east as the Kapula Vlei in Wankie National Park (Robinson, 1966d), from which site remains of domestic cattle have recently been identified (Huffman, 1973). In Zambia it is largely limited to the Zambezi valley, being best known from the region between Kazungula and the Victoria Falls, although closely related pottery (unpublished, but preserved in the Livingstone Museum) comes from the regions now flooded by Lake Kariba, extending as far downstream as Chirundu.

The majority of Early Iron Age pottery collections from this region (Fig. 42) are characterized by slightly necked vessels with externally thickened rims. A band of diagonal comb-stamping or incision is the preferred decoration (Vogel, 1971*b*; 1972*a*): in many cases it is accompanied by a broad band of straight or wavy dragged lines or by designs of comb-stamping or incision in the concavity of the neck. This material shows clear affinities with contemporary phase 2 Rhodesian wares. These affinities appear to be stronger than those with the pottery of the western stream Kalundu group (see below) to the north; and it is for this reason that the Dambwa group is discussed at this position in the narrative.

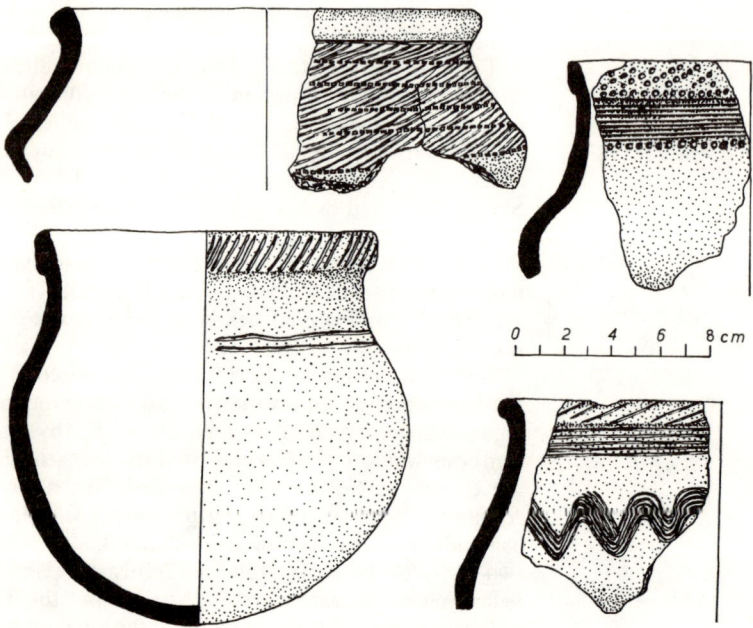

Fig. 42   Pottery from Dambwa (after Daniels and Phillipson, 1969)

The best-known sites of the Dambwa group are Kumadzulo, occupied between the fifth and seventh centuries, and the slightly later settlement of Dambwa (Vogel, 1971*c*; Daniels and Phillipson, 1969). In the Victoria Falls area Joseph Vogel has recognized four successive Early Iron Age phases on the basis of pottery typology. All these phases are attributed to a single ceramic tradition which he (1972*a*) has named the Shongwe tradition after a pre-Kololo name for the Victoria Falls. It appears that, after an initial and poorly understood phase best represented by a small collection of sherds from Situmpa Forest Station near Machili (Clark and Fagan, 1965), the main florescence of the Dambwa group probably reached the Victoria Falls region from south of the Zambezi (Vogel, 1975*a*).

The earliest Iron Age settlements in the Victoria Falls region were small and widely scattered. Their pottery was typified by necked vessels and bowls decorated with broad shallow grooving; on the former both the neck concavity and the externally thickened rim-bands are more pronounced than they are in later phases. However, by the middle of the first millennium ad much larger and more permanent villages had been established. Traces of buildings at Kumadzulo are interpreted as the remains of remarkably small rectangular pole-and-*daga* houses.

Excavations at Chundu Farm to the west of Livingstone have thrown considerable light on the local Early Iron Age burial customs (Vogel, 1972*b*; 1973*a*). The dead were buried tightly contracted in individual pit-like graves, while similar pits were dug nearby for the deposition of grave-goods. These usually comprised pairs of pottery vessels forming a covered container for a funerary cache of such objects as iron hoes, axes, iron or copper bangles, cowrie shells or shell beads. One of these caches also contained two seeds which have been tentatively identified as those of squash and a bean (Vogel, 1969). The Chundu Farm site is dated to about the eighth century ad.

Sites of the Dambwa group have yielded bones of domestic cattle and small stock, in addition to those of wild animals. Contact with the east coast trade had begun by the seventh century, as is indicated by a fragment of imported glass recovered from the ruins of one of the houses at Kumadzulo, and by the Chundu Farm cowrie shells noted above. Glass beads, however, do not occur in Early Iron Age contexts in this area. Locally made iron tools included hoes, axes, knives, bangles and spear- and arrow-points. A copper bar and bangles have also been recovered, indicating trade with copper-producing areas such as the Hook of the Kafue or the Wankie region of Rhodesia.

Our detailed knowledge of the Early Iron Age in the Victoria Falls region relates primarily to the period between the sixth and the ninth centuries ad. Indeed, the implications of recent research are that intensive Early Iron Age settlements did not begin in this area until about two centuries after its inception in neighbouring parts of central Africa. Earlier such occupants of the Victoria Falls region are attested in the archaeological record but they are poorly known and appear to have been sparse. Their historical significance is discussed on p. 137 below.

The Dambwa group inhabitants of this part of the Zambezi valley share affinities, as has been noted above, with their contemporaries and counterparts both in Rhodesia and on the Batoka Plateau of southern Zambia. The connexions with the south appear, however, to have been much the stronger; and it is on this basis that the Dambwa group is here subsumed within the eastern stream of the Early Iron Age. In the following section we shall see how the western stream Kalundu group of the Batoka Plateau was established at a date significantly anterior to the main florescence of the Dambwa group. The hinterland of the Zambezi valley in this area may thus be seen as a contact zone between the two streams. I shall return to a fuller consideration of this point in a later section of this chapter.

With the Dambwa group we may conveniently conclude our survey of the archaeological evidence for the eastern stream of the Early Iron Age. Geographically, it has been shown to extend from south-eastern Kenya, through all those parts of Tanzania where Early Iron Age settlement has so far been attested, into parts at least of northern Zambia. Further to the south it appears to have been restricted to those areas lying to the east of the Luangwa valley, that is to the modern Malawi and the Eastern Province of Zambia. Its presence to the east of Lake Nyasa has not yet been demonstrated, in the absence of any archaeological research in that region; but it must be regarded as highly probable that material similar to that from Kwale and Silver Leaves, forming a distinct coastal lowland facies of the eastern stream, will eventually be found there. All the Early Iron Age sites from south of the Zambezi (with one solitary exception, noted below, from Namibia) are attributed to the eastern stream; they are widely distributed through the greater part of the modern Rhodesia and Transvaal, as well as in adjacent parts of Botswana, Natal and Swaziland. Their southernmost limit appears to have been in the Transkei. Through the whole of this vast region, the Early Iron Age appears to have been introduced during the early centuries of the first millennium ad. Around the middle of that millennium it expanded into western Rhodesia and the Victoria Falls region, which had previously been only sparsely settled by Early Iron Age folk. Here and, probably to a lesser extent, in northern Zambia, contact was in due course established with a second stream of the Early Iron Age.

The Kalambo group

In the Northern and Luapula Provinces of Zambia only a few Early Iron Age sites have so far been discovered. These share affinities with both the eastern and western streams: it is reasonable to conclude that the area was settled from both directions. The only large village site known is at Kalambo Falls near the south-eastern corner of Lake Tanganyika (J. D. Clark, 1974). This locality has given its name to the Kalambo group to which the Early Iron Age sites of this region are attributed (D. W. Phillipson, 1968a). Characteristic artefacts are illustrated at Fig. 43. The pottery from Kalambo is abundant and distinctive. Undecorated open bowls are unusually common. Rims are undifferentiated or externally thickened; those on the necked vessels are often decorated with bands of oblique comb-stamping. Lips are frequently bevelled and may bear horizontal grooves or incised or stamped chevron lines on the bevel. Body decoration includes horizontal broad grooves which are often interrupted by pendant chevrons or loops. Comb-stamped or false-relief chevron designs are also characteristic and are often found in conjunction with other motifs. A few vessels have concave 'dimpled' bases reminiscent of those found on Urewe ware. Radiocarbon dates suggest that the Kalambo Falls site was occupied, perhaps intermittently, from as early as the fourth century ad until early in the present millennium or perhaps later; but it has not yet proved possible to demonstrate the degree of change which took place in the pottery tradition during this time. Iron-working is attested throughout the period of the site's occupation, bracelets, arrowheads and ferrules being represented (Vogel, 1971a); but there was only a single copper bangle and no other imported objects. The grindstones which were recovered are distinct from the small type found on earlier, pre-Iron Age sites, and it is thought that they were used for the grinding of grain. Several deep pits, which appear to date from the initial phases of the Iron Age occupation, are interpreted as graves, although any bones they may once have contained were not preserved. However, broadly contemporary pit-burials in southern Zambia, as at Chundu Farm (discussed above), lend some support to this interpretation.

Elsewhere in northern Zambia, Kalambo group pottery has been

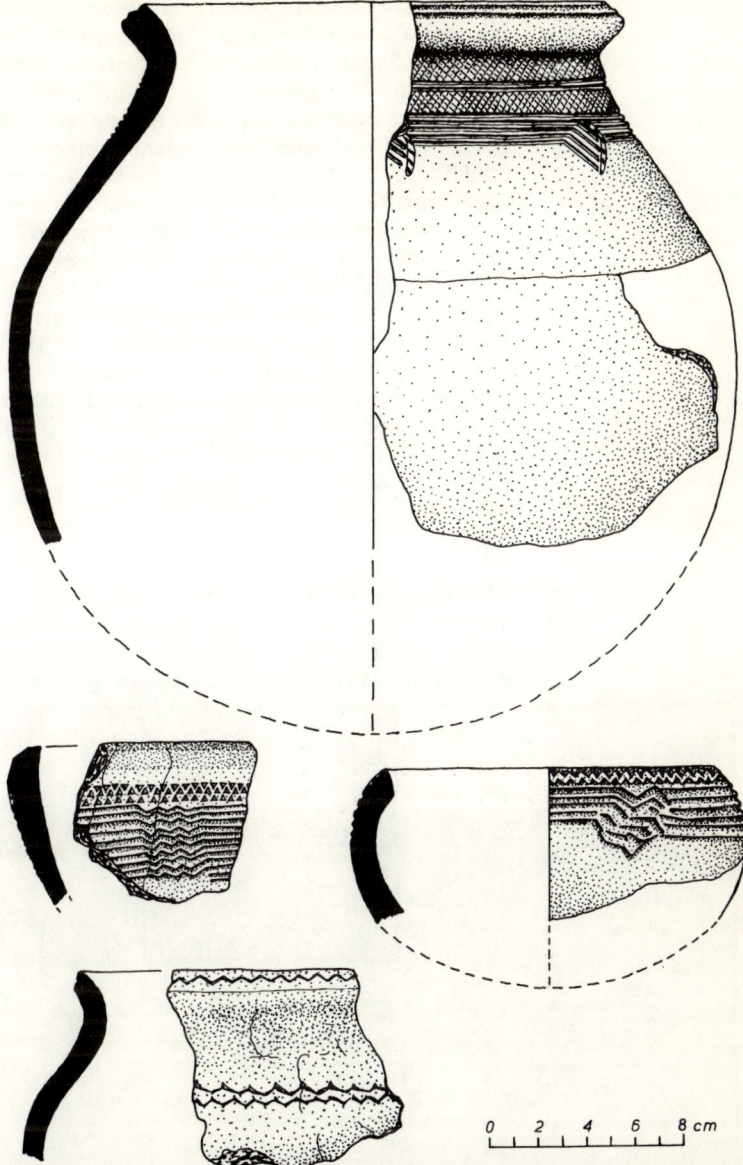

Fig. 43 Early Iron Age pottery from Kalambo Falls (after J. D. Clark, 1974)

found at open sites on the shores of Lakes Tanganyika, Mweru and Bangweulu, and also in several rockshelters scattered through the plateau country between Mbala and Serenje (e.g. Fagan and van Noten, 1964; D. W. Phillipson, 1968a; personal communication from S. Mattsson). At these rockshelter sites the characteristic Early Iron Age potsherds are found associated with mode 5 stone artefacts. It is clear that the makers of the latter continued to inhabit the area throughout the first millennium ad, and that they obtained occasional pottery vessels through contact with their Early Iron Age contemporaries. These associations are particularly clear at Nachikufu Cave near Mpika, at a rockshelter at Mwela Rocks, Kasama, and at Nakapapula near Chitambo Mission (S. F. Miller, 1969a; 1969b; D. W. Phillipson, 1969). At this last site the Early Iron Age contact is dated to the last quarter of the first millennium ad.

Northern Zambia is at present inadequately explored by archaeologists, and the account here presented may well require substantial modification in the light of future research, especially when excavations come to be conducted in the Luapula valley and in the area to the east of Kasama. The pottery collections here subsumed under the Kalambo group, although clearly closely inter-related, are more heterogeneous than those of the better-known groups from more southerly regions; and future investigations may well indicate the need for subdivision. At present, the affinities of the Kalambo group are unclear, although parallels may be drawn both with the Nkope group to the east of the Luangwa and with the Chondwe group of the Copperbelt: in this connexion it is unfortunate that the Early Iron Age of southern Tanzania and much of Shaba (formerly Katanga) remains virtually unknown.

The western stream

The territory of the Early Iron Age's western stream (Fig. 44) has been far less intensively investigated archaeologically than has that of the eastern stream. Only in central Zambia and a single small area of Shaba has any detailed field research yet been undertaken.

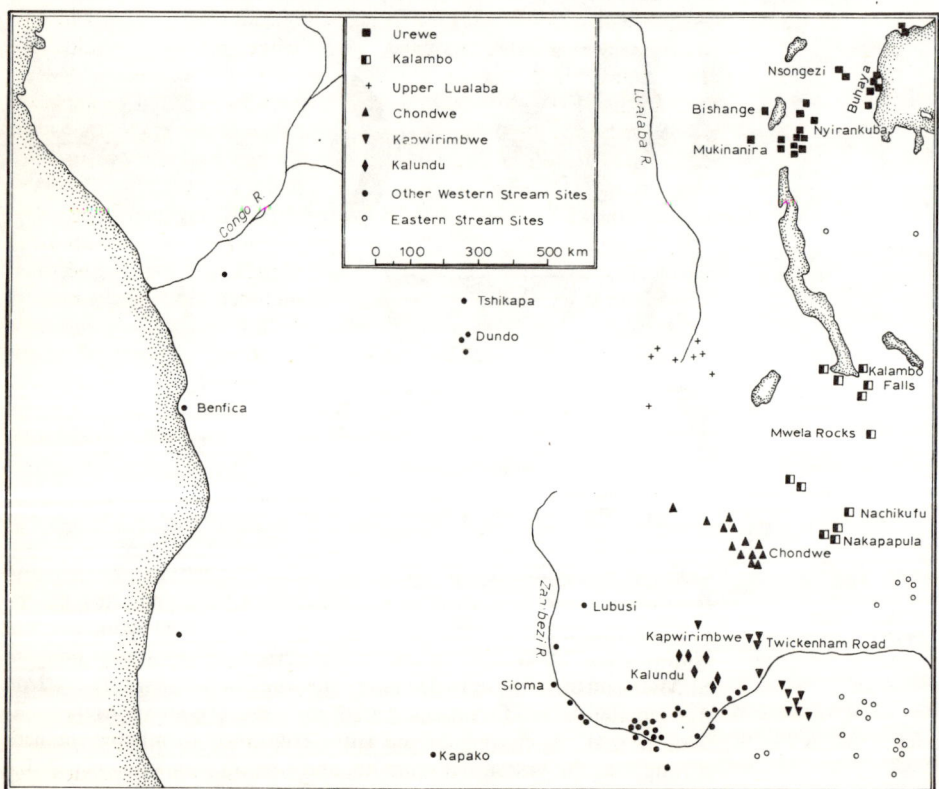

Fig. 44 Sites of the western stream of the Early Iron Age

Our knowledge of the Early Iron Age in Shaba comes almost exclusively from extensive cemeteries which have been excavated by Jean Hiernaux and Jacques Nenquin in the valley of the upper Lualaba – at Sanga on the shore of Lake Kisale and at Katoto some 140 kilometres further upstream (Nenquin, 1963; Hiernaux, de Longrée and de Buyst, 1971; Hiernaux, Maquet and de Buyst, 1973). The Sanga site is, at the time of writing, being reinvestigated by Pierre de Maret. These cemeteries appear to be of relatively late date, being placed by radiocarbon analyses somewhere between the seventh and the seventeenth centuries. However, the typology of their pottery, although distinctive, is in both cases clearly to be attributed to facies of an Early Iron Age tradition, albeit to late and highly evolved stages. Both cemeteries are extremely large – that of Sanga has been estimated to contain several thousand interments – although only 144 graves at Sanga and 47 at Katoto have been excavated.

At both sites the deceased were buried in either an extended or a lightly contracted position, on the back or side, in fairly shallow graves; those at Katoto did not exceed 2 metres in depth. All but one of the graves at Sanga were individual ones, as were the majority of those at Katoto; although at the latter site several graves contained more than one skeleton, generally in this case those of a man and a woman, sometimes accompanied by up to four children. Hiernaux has suggested that these multiple burials may indicate the sacrifice of women and children to accompany their deceased menfolk – a practice which, in one form or another, has continued in parts of the modern Zaïre and Zambia into relatively recent times, notably in connexion with the burial of chiefs (e.g. Stirke, n.d.: 69; Gouldsbury and Sheane, 1911: 185–8).

At both sites the burials were accompanied by rich and varied grave goods; at Sanga were found several pits containing grave goods but in which there was no sign of a body ever having been interred (cf. Chundu, above, p. 125). As the grave goods show significant differences between the two sites it will be convenient to discuss them separately.

At Katoto the majority of the female and child skeletons wore large quantities of twisted metal bangles and collars. Other items of personal adornment associated with the skeletons included plain ivory bracelets and pendants of copper and iron. Conus shells (*Conus prometheus*) were also found, both complete and in the form of sawn-off discs: such objects have long been, and still are, symbols of high status among many central and eastern African peoples (Harding, 1961). Cowrie shells were mostly of the Indian Ocean species, *Cypraea annulus*, with some specimens of the Atlantic *C. tenebra*. In one grave, forty-four pierced cowrie shells were found arranged in a small rectangle: presumably they were originally sewn to a piece of material which has since perished. Both cowries and conus discs were found in such a position as to suggest that they had been worn in the hair or attached to some form of head-wear. A few glass beads were also recovered.

The most abundant artefacts contained in the Katoto graves were complete pottery vessels. These were mainly straight-sided or deep, double-necked bowls, vessels with narrow, elongated vertical necks, and ring-based cups. The vessel-shapes show remarkable similarity to those of the recent Lungwebungu tradition wares of north-western Zambia, the straight-sided bowls of the two groups being particularly comparable (D. W. Phillipson, 1974; also chapter VII, below). A single bowl at Katoto had a 'dimpled' base. Almost all the pots were decorated, the most frequent motifs being interlocking loops or knots, scalloped lines of grooving, chevron lines and bands of differentially hatched triangles produced either by means of incision or comb-stamping.

There was a variety of iron tools, the majority being weapons in the form of knives, tanged spear-points, arrow-heads and battle-axes. Hoes and axes were less common and there was one single flange-welded gong – the earliest recorded archaeological occurrence of such a gong or bell of a type which has for long served as 'insignia of political leadership' (Vansina, 1969). Animal bones were included in about a quarter of the graves, generally at the side or foot of the body, but these have not yet been identified.

At Sanga, Nenquin has distinguished three successive pottery styles in the burials (Figs. 45, 46). The earliest of these is that named Kisalian. The most distinctive vessel shapes are bowls and deep, straight-sided vessels; both types frequently have an elaborately thickened, in-turned or out-turned rim which is generally decorated with pronounced horizontal grooving on the lip. Decoration elsewhere on the vessels is restrained and often restricted to a series of scalloped lines around the barely perceptible shoulder. Kisalian pottery was found in the majority of the graves at Sanga, anything from one to thirty-four vessels being interred with a single individual. It is note-worthy that these burials included several of children, and that in many cases the pottery associated with them comprised mainly small cup-like vessels of a type which differs in several significant respects from other Kisalian pottery. Since some of the non-ceramic material from these graves appears to show more affinity with that from certain later interments, it may be that these children's graves are not all contemporary with the Kisalian.

The second pottery type, which comes from six graves occurring close together in the north-western corner of the excavation area, has been named Mulongo ware. Such material has also been found at several other sites within a radius of eighty kilometres from Lake

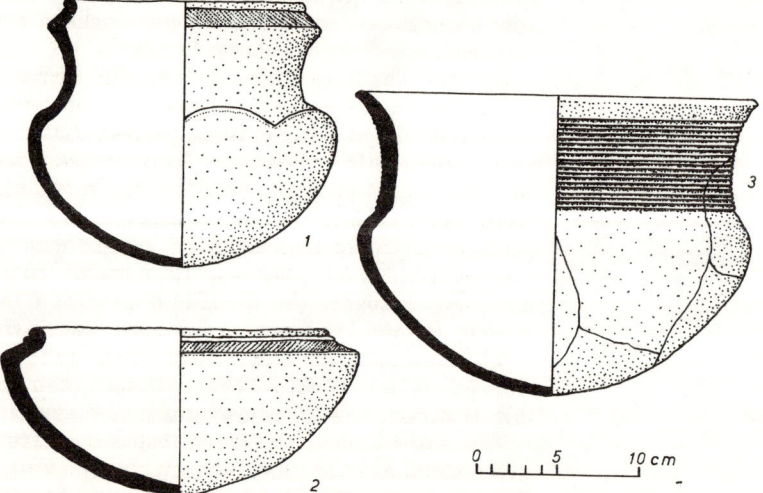

Fig. 45   Pottery from Sanga (after Nenquin, 1963): 1, 2, Kisalian; 3, Mulongo ware

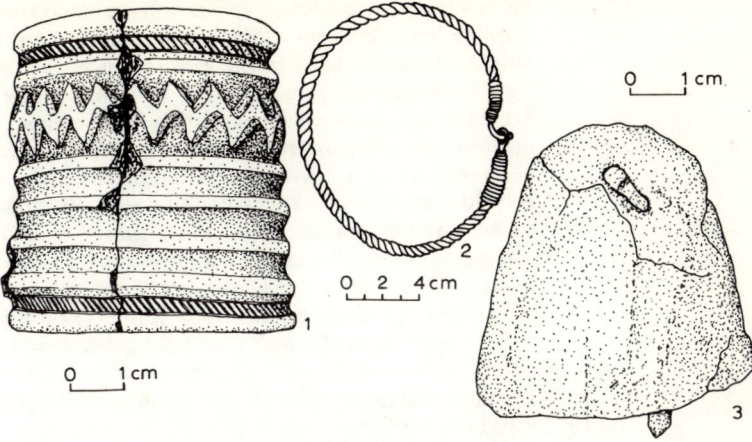

Fig. 46 Artefacts from Sanga (after Hiernaux, de Longrée and de Buyst, 1971): 1, ivory bangle; 2, copper necklet; 3, iron bell

Kisale. Nowhere, however, are the archaeological associations of Mulongo ware adequately recorded (Nenquin, 1963: 15–18). This material contains a very much higher proportion of undecorated vessels, notably bowls. The other characteristic form is a necked vessel with the concavity of the neck decorated by a broad band of horizontal parallel grooves.

The final pottery type from Sanga, 'Red Slip ware', has few typological features which would link it with the Early Iron Age Industrial Complex, but it should be noted that Hiernaux considers it to be intimately related with Mulongo ware, and it is discussed here for convenience. The vessels are primarily bowls, tall beakers and bag-shaped pots with sharply everted rims, generally undecorated but coated with a red slip and highly burnished. There are occasional beakers with grooved decoration similar to those found in Mulongo ware assemblages. The burials associated with 'Red Slip ware' are characteristically in an extended position in contrast to those of the Kisalian and Mulongo ware graves.

The non-ceramic grave goods recovered at Sanga consist mainly of metal objects, both of copper and iron. In contrast with Katoto, weapons are comparatively rare, being restricted to arrow- and spear-points; their place is taken by a greater number of agricultural implements, notably hoes and axes. Much of the metalwork from Sanga is more elaborate than any recovered at Katoto; it includes chains of copper, elaborate twisted copper belts and necklets, iron and copper bracelets, and bangles. Some of the finest copperwork was found in the graves of children, notably a loop of elaborately twisted copper from which were suspended two flange-welded iron bells. Several small bells made by this technique were recovered from other graves, apparently exclusively Kisalian, but there were no gongs such as the single example from Katoto.

The most frequently occurring copper artefacts at Sanga are small cross-shaped ingots, almost all of which came from graves containing Mulongo or 'Red Slip' ware. The crosses are characteristically rather crudely cast in an 'H'-like shape, and they vary in maximum dimension from 8 to 121 millimetres. The smallest examples (8 to 15 millimetres) occur almost exclusively in association with 'Red Slip ware', while the larger examples are predominantly found in graves with Mulongo pottery. In the majority of instances the crosses show signs of having been tied together with fibre (according to Hiernaux generally in groups of five) and they were almost always interred in or near the hand of the deceased. In only one case did copper crosses occur in a burial attributed to the Kisalian, and this was in a child's grave (no. 32 of Nenquin, 1963: 102–9), which contained atypical pottery of the type noted above; these crosses also were unusually large. The nearest known copper deposits to Sanga are around Tenke some 290 kilometres to the south. In that area there are prehistoric mines and near one of these, at Fungurume, there has been found a mould for making small crosses of the type represented at Sanga. It will be recalled that small crosses of this type were not found at Katato, despite the situation of that site in a position half way between Sanga and Tenke.

Only rare glass beads and cowrie shells were found at Sanga; these occurred exclusively with Mulongo and 'Red Slip' wares or in the children's graves of Kisalian type. Bones of animals including domestic goat were found in several Kisalian graves.

The cemeteries of the upper Lualaba have been described at length because they provide the most detailed insight we have into the non-ceramic technology and material culture of any Early Iron Age community in sub-Saharan Africa. Until a settlement site of these upper Lualaba societies has been located, however, we shall be unable to ascertain the extent to which the pottery and other artefacts from Sanga and Katoto represent an idiosyncratic funerary facies of the contemporary material culture. (Grave goods recovered by Vogel from Early Iron Age burials at Chundu in southern Zambia – see p. 125 – however, appear to differ in no significant respects from their counterparts at nearby settlement sites.) In this context it must be noted that the complete funerary vessels found in several of the Sanga graves were accompanied by broken sherds of vessels which appear to have been typologically distinct, and it is possible that this latter material will in due course be found to be representative of the domestic pottery tradition of the users of the Sanga cemetery.

At least two, and perhaps three (depending on whether one accepts Hiernaux's proposal that the Mulongo and 'Red Slip' wares represent a single category) pottery traditions are represented at Sanga, and it seems reasonably well established on stratigraphical grounds that the Kisalian is earlier than the others. Nenquin has argued an eighth-century date for the Kisalian, but in reality the radiocarbon dates cannot be held to indicate an age more narrowly defined than a seventh-to-eleventh century bracket.

Pierre de Maret has published (*J.A.H.*) a preliminary account of his re-investigation of Sanga and other nearby sites in the Upemba depression. The earliest Iron Age settlement so far discovered in this region is at Kamilamba, dated about the sixth or seventh century ad. The pottery shows strong affinities with material of the same age from western Zambia, such as Lubusi (see pp. 139, 178). The chronology of the Sanga cemetery is now much firmer than was provided by Nenquin's two radiocarbon analyses from atypical graves. The Kisalian is now shown to have begun in about the tenth century; the change to Mulongo ware (which de Maret would combine with 'Red Slip' pottery in one Kabambian tradition) was around ad 1300.

Yet another tradition is represented by the Katoto pottery which could be broadly contemporary with the Kisalian, as is suggested by the single radiocarbon date from the former site and by the presence in one of the Katoto graves of three typical Kisalian bowls. Hiernaux notes that occasional Katoto-type vessels have likewise been found at Sanga (Hiernaux, Maquet and de Buyst, 1973). These occurrences are best attributed to trade or contact between neighbouring contemporary communities whose pottery traditions, although markedly distinct, are both to be attributed to the western stream of the Early Iron Age Industrial Complex. Of the two traditions that of Katoto appears to be much more closely related to Urewe ware than does the Kisalian; and it is possible that the Katoto cemetery may eventually prove to be of significantly earlier date than that at Sanga.

In central Zambia, west of the Luangwa, two closely inter-related Early Iron Age groups are now recognized, respectively in the Copperbelt region and on the Central Province plateau around Lusaka. Both have been shown by the present writer's research to be markedly distinct from the groups described above from the north and east (D. W. Phillipson, 1976a: 209), and they appear to represent rather denser and more permanent settlement.

The Chondwe group of the Copperbelt, named from a site forty-five kilometres south of Ndola, is characterized by pottery vessels with thickened or undifferentiated rims (Mills and Filmer, 1972). Among the varied decorative motifs (Fig. 47), the most frequent and diagnostic

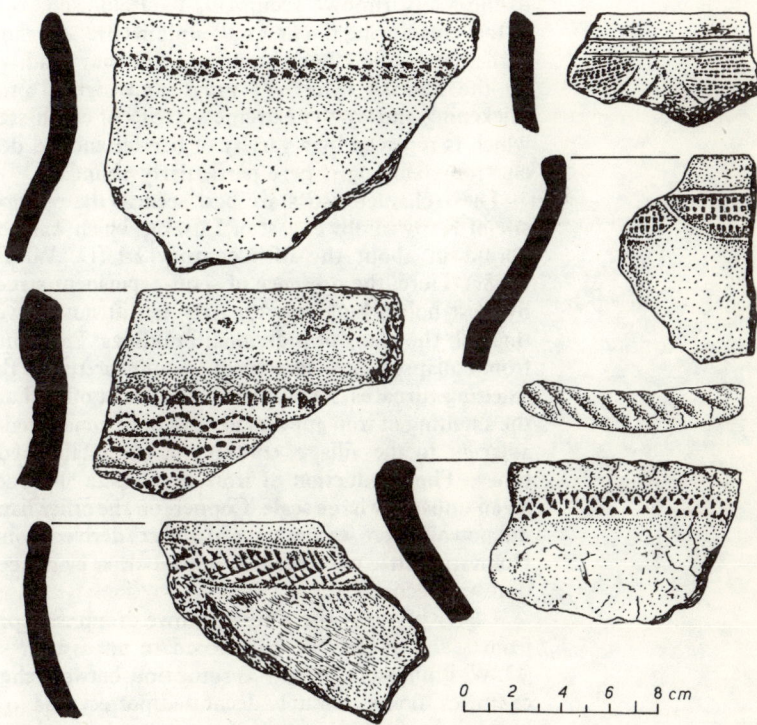

Fig. 47 Chondwe group pottery (after D. W. Phillipson, 1972a)

are lines of false-relief chevron stamping and chordate blocks of comb-stamping delineated by broad grooves. Pottery of this type has so far been recorded from several rockshelters and from over twenty open sites which are distributed alongside rivers and streams generally close to the valley edges of the upper Kafue river and its tributaries. From the modern Copperbelt the distribution of the Chondwe group spreads as far to the south as Kapiri Mposhi, but its northwards extent into Zaïre has yet to be ascertained. To the west, recent research by Michael Bisson in the Solwezi District shows that the Early Iron Age pottery of that area is distinct from that of the Chondwe group.

Only two Early Iron Age sites, Chondwe and Kangonga, have yet been excavated on the Copperbelt, and the radiocarbon dates from these range from the sixth to the eleventh century ad. Certain other sites, notably Roan Antelope near Luanshya are, however, thought – on the basis of pottery typology – to be somewhat earlier (D. W. Phillipson, 1972a). During the second half of the first millennium, the Copperbelt area appears to have been settled by a populous Early Iron Age community whose stream-side villages were generally abandoned after relatively brief occupation. Iron and copper working is indicated at many sites, but the exploitation of the area's rich copper deposits appears to have been on a small scale throughout the period of the Early Iron Age occupation. There is, however, evidence that the copper deposits attracted trading contacts from a wide area (D. W. Phillipson, 1972a).

Further to the south, on and adjacent to the Lusaka plateau, several Early Iron Age village sites have been investigated and are attributed to the Kapwirimbwe group (D. W. Phillipson, 1968a). The pottery of this area during the first millennium (Fig. 48) shows many affinities with that of the Chondwe group, but may readily be distinguished by the Lusaka material's greater incidence and degree of rim-thickening and by the extreme scarcity of comb-stamped decoration, which is replaced by a variety of banded incised designs. False-relief chevron stamping is here particularly abundant.

These characteristics are best seen in the pottery from the village site of Kapwirimbwe, east of Lusaka, which was occupied for a brief period in about the fifth century ad (D. W. Phillipson, 1968b; 1968c). Here, the presence of semi-permanent structures is indicated by post-holes, but unfortunately it did not prove possible to distinguish the plans of individual buildings. Large quantities of debris from collapsed *daga* structures are interpreted as the remains of iron smelting furnaces. At Kapwirimbwe, as at other Early Iron Age sites, the smelting of iron appears to have been conducted in or immediately adjacent to the village, contrary to the established practice of later times. The production of iron at this site also seems to have been on an unusually large scale. Copper, on the other hand, was apparently unknown. There was no trace of objects derived from the coastal trade. Domestic cattle were herded, but no other evidence for food production was recovered.

A later phase of the Kapwirimbwe group is at present best known from a site at Twickenham Road in an eastern suburb of Lusaka (D. W. Phillipson, 1970a). At some time between the ninth and twelfth centuries, fine elaborately decorated pottery was in use which clearly belongs to a development of the same tradition as was represented by the simpler, more restrained wares of Kapwirimbwe. Domestic goats were kept; and wild animals hunted. As at Kapwirimbwe, iron was

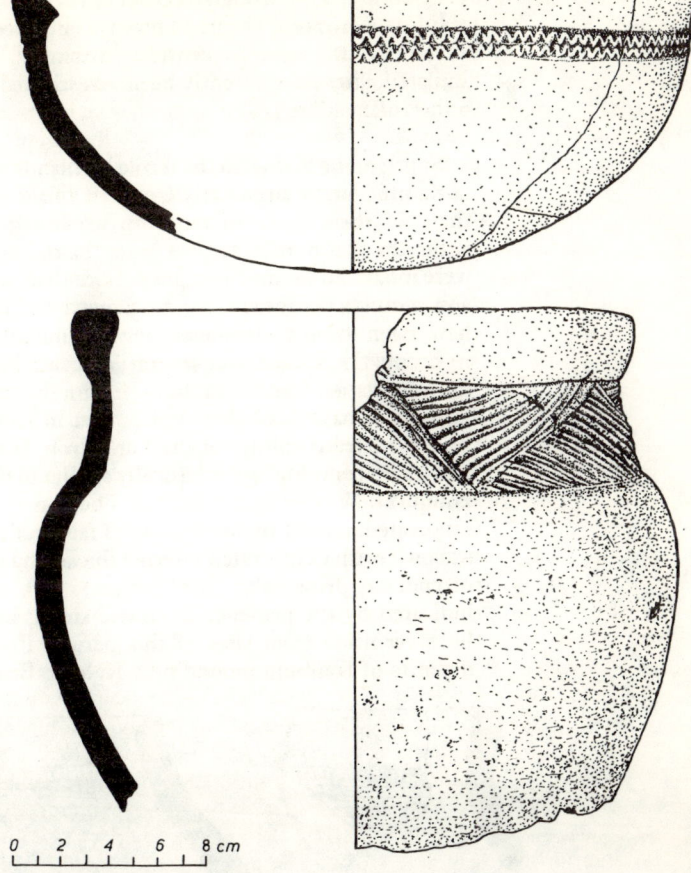

Fig. 48 Kapwirimbwe group pottery from Twickenham Road, Lusaka (after D. W. Phillipson, 1970a)

worked on a large scale; but it was only in the final phase of the Early Iron Age occupation at Twickenham Road that copper made its appearance. It is interesting to note that pottery more closely resembling that of the Chondwe group appears in the Lusaka sequence at the same time. At both Kapwirimbwe and Twickenham Road were recovered perforated pottery colanders which, it is suggested, may have been used for the preparation of salt.

The extent of the former distribution of the Kapwirimbwe group is not well known, but related pottery has been found as far to the west as Mumbwa and in the Chirundu area of the Zambezi valley. Closely related material also comes from the Mashonaland plateau in the Urungwe and Lomagundi Districts of Rhodesia, and is of interest as the only representative of the western stream of the Early Iron Age which has so far been identified from south of the Zambezi. The Early Iron Age pottery from this area of north-western Mashonaland has been attributed by Thomas Huffman to a 'Sinoia tradition', but in the present writer's view it is so similar to that from the Lusaka area that it may conveniently be subsumed within the Kapwirimbwe tradition, subject to the recognition of an element of trait-admixture through contact with the Gokomere/Ziwa group (Huffman, 1971a). The best known occurrence is at Sinoia Cave, dated to around the seventh century (Robinson, 1966e); further, as yet undated, sites have recently been investigated by both Garlake (1970) and Huffman (1971a).

South of the Kafue, in the fertile highlands of the Southern Province of Zambia, many large Early Iron Age village sites are known, but only three of these have so far been excavated. It appears that these Kalundu group villages, like some of those of the Zambezi valley, were inhabited for much longer periods than was customary elsewhere; and mounds comprising up to 3 metres of Early Iron Age deposits have been located, demonstrating continuous settlement or repeated re-occupation spread over several centuries. Early Iron Age settlement in this region seems to have begun by the early fifth century ad, and to have been denser than that in most other areas.

The material culture of the Early Iron Age Kalundu group of the Batoka Plateau (Fig. 49) is basically similar to that of the Kapwirimbwe group (D. W. Phillipson, 1968a). The pottery, however, is easily distinguished, mainly by the scarcity of false-relief chevron stamping and of bowls with exaggerated internal thickening of the rim. Some degree of contact, presumably very indirect, with the East Coast trade is indicated by the presence of cowrie shells; but glass beads have not been recorded from sites of this period. From the Early Iron Age deposits of Kalundu mound near Kalomo Brian Fagan has recovered

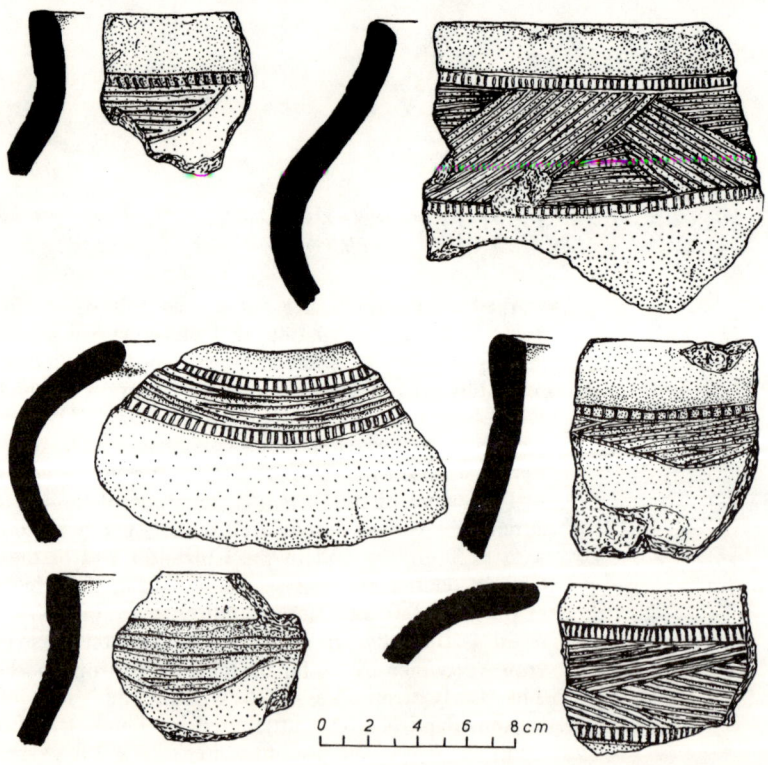

0　2　4　6　8cm

Fig. 49　Pottery of the Kalundu group (after Fagan, 1967b)

abundant animal bones, of which less than two-fifths were of domestic cattle and small stock (sheep and/or goats); hunting evidently continued to play an important part in the economy. Both iron and copper objects were recovered, but only in small quantities (Inskeep, 1962a; Fagan, 1967b).

The Kalundu group occupation of the Batoka plateau lasted until about the ninth century ad. In the Kafue valley near Namwala the Early Iron Age horizons at Basanga and Mwanamaimpa, investigated by Brian Fagan, are likewise dated to between the fifth and the ninth centuries (D. W. Phillipson, 1970b). The material from these sites has not yet been published in detail, but it appears to share affinities with both the Kapwirimbwe and Kalundu groups, the stronger connexions probably being with the former.

It now appears that there are rare occurrences of individual sherds of Early Iron Age pottery in central and southern Zambia which may predate the inception of western stream settlement. There sherds, interestingly enough, are typologically more akin to eastern stream wares than they are to their own western stream successors, to which they cannot on typological grounds be regarded as directly ancestral. They are probably closely allied to the poorly known initial (i.e. pre-Dambwa group) Early Iron Age occupation of the Victoria Falls region. These finds include those from Situmpa (Clark and Fagan, 1965), Gwisho Hotsprings (Fagan and van Noten, 1964; Fagan and Phillipson, 1965), and a single unpublished sherd from Leopard's Hill Cave near Lusaka. It will be noted that all these finds are of an isolated character and do not attest permanent settlement. It is possible that they represent an early penetration of the area by Early Iron Age folk from the east at a time, presumably during the fourth century ad, predating the establishment of permanent western stream settlement. In an earlier paper (D. W. Phillipson, 1968a) I belittled the significance of these finds: I now realize that they may be of considerable import, although in need of further study.

Our knowledge of the Early Iron Age in regions further to the west than those which have already been described is tantalizingly scanty. In Zaïre it appears that pottery closely related to Urewe ware was made at least as far west as Tshikapa in Kasai (Fig. 50). Here, four totally characteristic Urewe vessels were found during mining operations in the Lupemba Valley: their fabric indicates that they were manufactured locally, not brought into the area from elsewhere (Nenquin, 1959). Unfortunately the circumstances of this discovery are very poorly recorded, and the archaeological associations of these undated pottery vessels remain completely unknown. A short distance to the south of Tshikapa, across the Angola border, a site at Dundo Airfield has been investigated by Desmond Clark and Vicente Martins. The small collections of pottery from this and one other nearby locality are dated to the last quarter of the first millennium ad. The sherds are markedly distinct from those found at Tshikapa, but nevertheless show several Early Iron Age typological features alongside characteristics which have continued into the more recent pottery of northwestern Angola (J. D. Clark, 1968).

Further to the west, pottery of apparently Early Iron Age type comes from the cave Dimba near Mbanza Ngungu (Thysville) in lower Zaïre. This material, which shows some affinity with Urewe ware, is

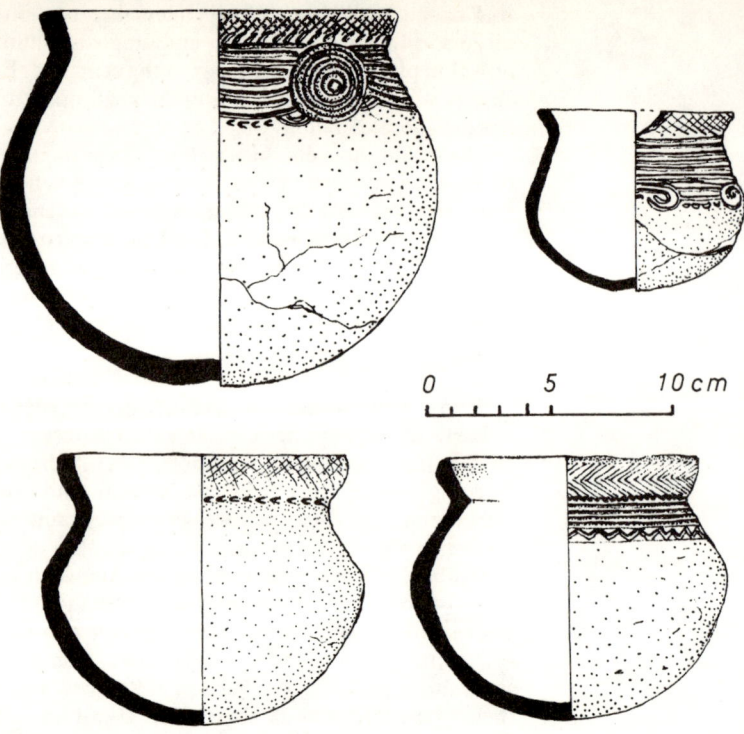

Fig. 50 Urewe ware from Tshikapa (after Nenquin, 1959)

presumably later in date than the grooved pottery (which may also show Early Iron Age connexions) found in the same area associated with the 'Leopoldian Neolithic', now dated to the last four centuries bc (de Maret, 1975; see also Fagan, 1966). It is perhaps significant, as will be shown in chapter VIII, that the distributions of this latter type of pottery and of the ground stone axes with which it is associated, do not extend southwards into Angola (J. D. Clark, 1966). Pottery of Early Iron Age affinities does, however, occur associated with chipped stone artefacts at Benfica, on the Atlantic coast near Luanda, where it is dated to around the second century ad (dos Santos and Everdosa, 1970).

In the more southerly regions of Angola and western Zambia only a scatter of isolated Early Iron Age sites is so far known. Meagre surface occurrences of undated pottery tentatively attributed to the Early Iron Age Industrial Complex have been known for some years from the upper Zambezi valley between Sesheke and Mongu (D. W. Phillipson, 1968a; Clark and Fagan, 1965). Recently, a more extensive site in this stretch of the valley, at Sioma Mission, has been investigated by Joseph Vogel (1973b), and radiocarbon dates have been obtained ranging from the fifth to the eighth centuries ad. The pottery has much in common with that of the Kalundu and Kapwirimbwe groups, particularly the former, but lacks the pronouncedly thickened rims of the more easterly material. Iron-smelting was evidently carried out at the site or in its immediate vicinity.

The only other dated Early Iron Age site from this western area of Zambia is that discovered by the present writer at Lubusi, west of Kaoma in the Kalahari Sand country lying to the east of the upper Zambezi Valley. Here, as at Sioma, the pottery vessels have rims which are undifferentiated or only slightly thickened. They are unusual for the variety of their decoration, which generally shows the combination of more than one technique on a single vessel: bands of incision, comb-stamping, impressions of metal bangles, grooves, false-relief chevron stamping, and impressions of a large triangular stamp. Lubusi is dated to the last quarter of the first millennium ad (D. W. Phillipson, 1971). Its affinities are difficult to assess, but the pottery appears to have more in common with that of the Chondwe group than with that of any other Early Iron Age groups currently recognized. It also displays a strong affinity with the modern Lungwebungu tradition pottery which is made in parts of the upper Zambezi region today (D. W. Phillipson, 1974). Recent survey work in the upper Zambezi Valley by Joseph Vogel and N. Katanekwa (1976) has shown that in this area the boundary between the eastern and western streams of the Early Iron Age was located a short distance to the south of Sioma.

In the far south-west, in southern Angola and Namibia, the available data are even more scanty. By the seventh or eighth century ad a substantial Iron Age settlement had been established at Feti la Choya, only 300 kilometres north of the Kunene (Fagan, 1965a). Iron was apparently present, but details neither of the site, discovered by Gladwyn Childs, nor of the associated pottery have been published. It is therefore not possible to tell whether this site belongs to the Early Iron Age Industrial Complex. Slightly more information is available concerning a site investigated by Beatrice Sandelowsky (1973) at Kapako in the extreme north of Namibia, close to the western end of the Caprivi Strip. Traces of iron-working, together with pottery provisionally described as resembling that from Kapwirimbwe, are dated to the ninth century ad (Sutton, 1972: 7, 14). This would appear to indicate the presence in that region of the western stream of the Early Iron Age, at least during the closing centuries of the first millennium.

It may thus be seen that our knowledge of the western stream of the Early Iron Age is much less complete, both in geographical coverage and in archaeological detail, than that of the eastern stream. The only exception to this is in the relatively restricted area occupied by the Chondwe, Kapwirimbwe and Kalundu groups in central and southern Zambia. The cemeteries of the upper Lualaba have yielded a wealth of technological data, but otherwise they illustrate only one specialized aspect of Early Iron Age culture – the burial customs. Elsewhere, but few sites are known which may be attributed to the Early Iron Age, and they have been imperfectly or incompletely investigated. They are, however, sufficient to attest the wide extent of Early Iron Age settlement in these western regions. In some places there are tantalizing indications of continuity between some western stream Early Iron Age wares and modern pottery traditions; but nowhere is the archaeological sequence sufficiently well known to illustrate this point with any certainty. In central and southern Zambia it appears that the Early Iron Age was introduced around the fifth century ad – that is, somewhat later than the date of the inception of eastern stream settlement in many areas. Elsewhere in the western zone the Early Iron Age may be dated in general terms to the first millennium ad, but no more detailed picture has yet emerged from the purely archaeological investigations with which this chapter is concerned.

CHRONOLOGY

It will be seen from the foregoing survey that the Early Iron Age pottery industries of eastern and southern Africa may be subdivided and grouped together at various levels. The above account has been presented in terms of regional groups, within several of which sequential phases may be discerned. On a broader front, it is also clear that two main streams in the spread of the Early Iron Age may be recognized on the basis of pottery typology, and also, it now appears, on that of the differential possession of domestic cattle (see below, pp. oo–oo). The eastern stream consists of the Kwale, Lelesu, Mwabulambo, Nkope, Gokomere/Ziwa and Dambwa groups as well, apparently, as all the Early Iron Age sites currently recognized south of the Limpopo. The western stream is at present best known from the sites of the Chondwe, Kapwirimbwe and Kalundu groups, as well as from those which have recently been investigated in the upper Zambezi region and from the cemeteries of the upper Lualaba. The position of the heterogeneous Kalambo group is not yet clear. Currently attributed to this group are pottery assemblages which seem variously to show features of both the eastern and western streams; and it may well be that future research will indicate that this region of northern Zambia was penetrated by Early Iron Age settlers from two distinct directions. Urewe ware can be seen as being closely related to a hypothetical direct or indirect ancestor of both streams since its typology shares affinities with both and since (as will be shown below) the available radiocarbon dates indicate that it was established at an earlier date than any of the other groups.

The relative dating of the Early Iron Age in its various regions is clearly relevant to a consideration of the separate identity of these two streams and to the direction of their spread. Since over one hundred and fifty radiocarbon dates from Early Iron Age sites are now available, a more detailed inquiry may be made than was possible only a few years ago. In a recent article (D. W. Phillipson, 1975) I have applied to Iron Age radiocarbon dates from eastern and southern Africa a modified form of a technique of presentation originally proposed by Barbara Ottaway (1973a; 1973b). This method uses the intersextile ranges of the radiocarbon dates available for any particular industry as an indication of the *floruit* of that industry. It can be shown from the data presented in Fig. 51 that the Early Iron Age *floruit* began in East Africa significantly earlier than elsewhere. Further south, throughout the territory of the proposed eastern stream, the available dates indicate that the inception of the Early Iron Age took place around the fourth century. This event appears to have taken place marginally – perhaps insignificantly – later in Rhodesia and South Africa than it did in Malawi, thus offering some confirmation to the hypothesis of a rapid north-to-south spread through this eastern region. In the Victoria Falls area, whither, as we have seen, the main Early Iron Age industry appears to have been introduced from Rhodesia, its *floruit* did not commence until the middle of the sixth

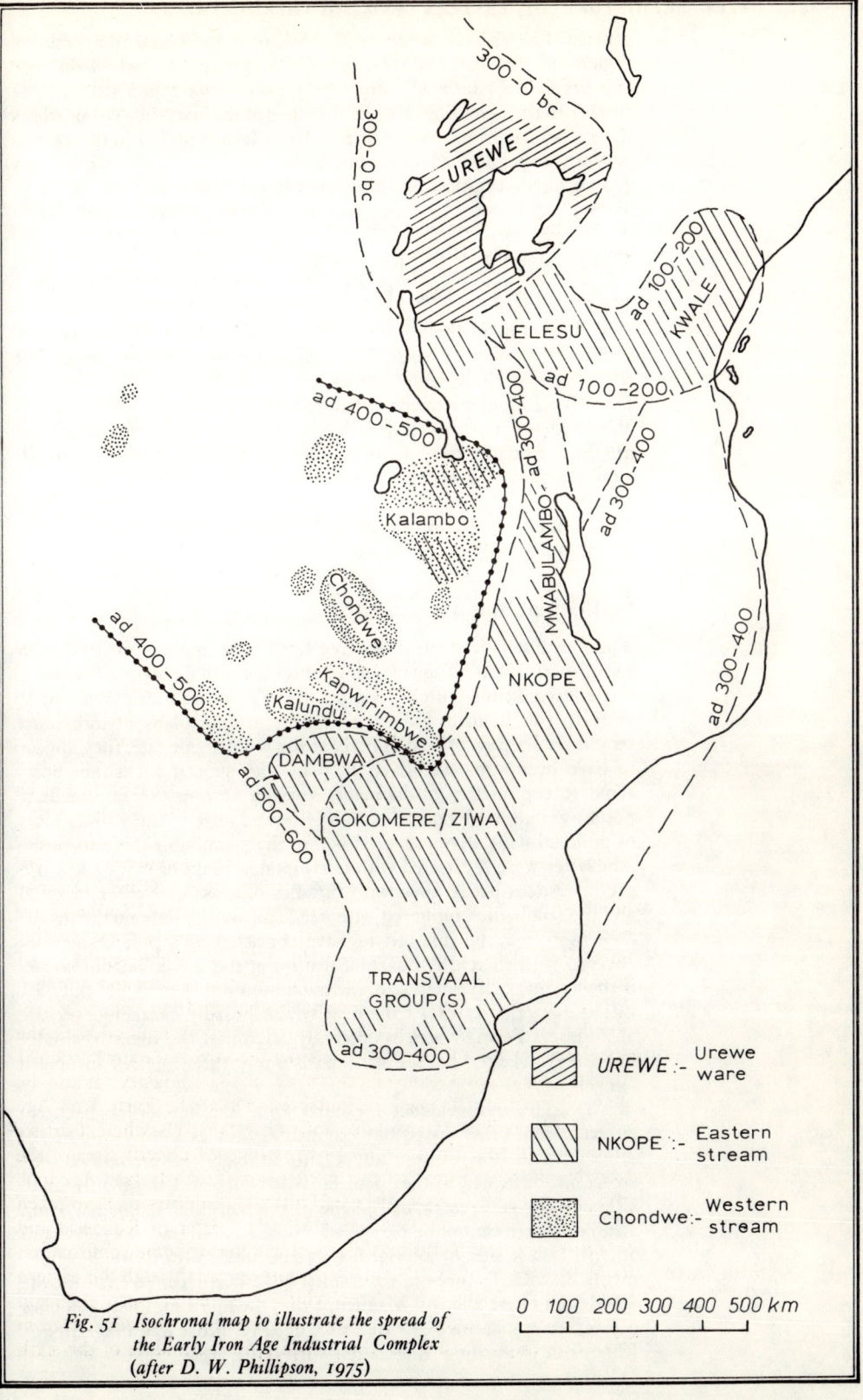

300-0 bc

300-0 bc

300-0 bc

UREWE

ad 100-200 KWALE

LELESU

ad 100-200

ad 400-500

Kalambo

MWABULAMBO ad 300-400

ad 300-400

ad 300-400

Chondwe

NKOPE

ad 400-500

Kapwirimbwe

Kalundu

DAMBWA

GOKOMERE / ZIWA

ad 500-600

TRANSVAAL
GROUP(S)

ad 300-400

UREWE :- Urewe
          ware

NKOPE :- Eastern
         stream

Chondwe :- Western
           stream

0 100 200 300 400 500 km

*Fig. 51 Isochronal map to illustrate the spread of
the Early Iron Age Industrial Complex
(after D. W. Phillipson, 1975)*

century. Elsewhere in southern Zambia, as in the central and northern regions of that country west of the Luangwa, the Early Iron Age appears to have been of significantly later introduction than it was further to the east. The intersextile range of the sixty-five radiocarbon dates available from western stream Early Iron Age sites in this region is from ad 475 to ad 966. The *floruit* of none of the Early Iron Age groups recognized in this region began before the fifth century. We shall again consider the implications of these dates in chapter VIII.

THE NATURE OF EARLY IRON AGE SOCIETY

The mass of data which has been presented in the foregoing sections enables a number of useful generalizations to be made concerning the nature of Early Iron Age society, its economy and technology. However, it must be realized that, although the quantity of the available evidence is considerable, it is derived from a very large geographical area and from sites of which the occupation is spread through almost a thousand years. Generalizations must therefore be treated with reserve, since many relevant cultural traits are now seen to have distributions which are significantly restricted either geographically or chronologically – or in both dimensions.

Settlement and architecture

The characteristic Early Iron Age settlement appears to have been a semi-permanent village of small houses made of *daga* (puddled mud, often derived from anthills) applied over a pole and wattle framework. Only in the Victoria Falls region have ground-plans of individual structures been recovered. There, at the Kumadzulo site, they appear to have been sub-rectangular in plan with substantial corner posts some 10 centimetres in diameter. Varying numbers of intermediate posts were inserted along the slightly bowed lines of the walls. Floors of puddled *daga* were prepared before the erection of the wall-posts. The latter were connected with horizontal lashings of twigs and bark, the interstices being filled with bundles of grass and other material and the whole then plastered with *daga*, apparently only on the inside. The roofs may be inferred to have consisted of a pole framework covered with thatch. A puzzling feature of these Kumadzulo houses is their remarkably small size: the maximum wall-length was only 2.3 metres (Vogel, 1971*c*). At the nearby and broadly contemporary site of Zambezi Farm, Vogel has recently recovered the plans of similar but slightly larger houses with walls some three metres in length (Vogel, 1973*a*).

No comparable evidence for Early Iron Age houses has been recovered from other areas, but fragmentary traces from a number of other sites such as Chitope suggest that the general method of construction illustrated in the Victoria Falls region was frequently used; although the sub-rectangular shape of the houses at Kumadzulo and Zambezi Farm cannot be paralleled elsewhere. No trace was observed at any of these sites of interior features or built-in furniture, but fragments of such features in solid *daga* have been recovered from the Rhodesian phase 2 site of Makuru. From the more complete evidence of later times it seems likely that such *daga* furniture was an essentially Rhodesian innovation, not shared with other areas.

The only other pole-and-*daga* structures known to have occurred in Early Iron Age villages are storage bins raised above the ground on stones or poles. Storage pits, usually bell-shaped, are also attested from several sites, such as Twickenham Road and Zambezi Farm.

At least in Zambia and further to the south, these villages occupied substantial areas and were presumably correspondingly populous: equivalent data for East Africa are not currently available. In the siting of Early Iron Age villages a marked preference (which has continued into recent times in many areas) was shown for locations close to watercourses, those near the tree-lines on valley-slopes being particularly favoured. Duration of occupation is hard to estimate on archaeological grounds, but the relative shallowness of deposits present on most Early Iron Age village sites suggests that the majority were not inhabited for more than one or two generations. This is in keeping with the supposition that agriculture played a not insignificant part in the Early Iron Age economy, for in many areas of eastern and southern Africa soil cultivated by traditional methods soon becomes exhausted, necessitating the removal of fields (and, generally, settlements) after a decade or so. This is a practice which continues in many areas to this day, being only slowly modified through the pressure of increasing population and the use of fertilizers. It is significant that regions where the Early Iron Age sites show signs of more prolonged occupation are generally those of relatively high fertility, areas such as central and southern Zambia having apparently proved as desirable to the Early Iron Age settlers as they did to their European successors some 1500 years later. It seems probable, though, that the occupation of such sites was intermittent rather than truly continuous.

Any estimate of Early Iron Age population densities would be premature. It may, however, be noted that where areas, such as the Victoria Falls region, have been intensively prospected, a substantial number of Early Iron Age village sites has generally been located. Such could, of course, be attributed to a relatively small community changing its places of residence at frequent intervals. The upper Lualaba cemeteries, however, must have served a large population. In some other areas, on the other hand, it is clear that quite contrary conditions prevailed, and Early Iron Age artefacts come primarily from rockshelter sites where they are frequently found in association with mode 5 stone industries.

We shall return in chapter X to a consideration of the nature of the interaction which took place between the Early Iron Age folk and their stone-tool-using contemporaries; here it will suffice to note that, as suggested above, there appear to have been substantial areas where the Early Iron Age population was insufficiently numerous to displace its predecessors. In these regions, such as eastern Zambia, the Limpopo valley and many parts of Tanzania, only occasional Early Iron Age villages are located; and it is suggested that the rockshelter occurrences of Early Iron Age pottery (pottery which is in all respects identical to that found in the villages) were derived either by trade or from occasional use of such sites by Early Iron Age folk for shelter or for religious purposes. Such Early Iron Age use of rockshelters is attested by the evidence of rock paintings, as will be argued in chapter XI.

In only one region of eastern and southern Africa is there any indication of the development of techniques of stone building by the Early Iron Age population; this is in the central part of Rhodesia with a possible extension to the northern Transvaal. Early Iron Age stone building was, however, invariably on a much smaller and less elaborate scale than that attained in later times. As we have shown above, it may be associated with the makers of the Gokomere/Ziwa wares as well, perhaps, as with the inhabitants of Matakoma in the Soutpansberg. Undressed stone was mainly employed for the construction of terrace- and field-walls and simple enclosures. The most elaborate form attained by Early Iron Age builders was probably of the type described above (p. 118) from Maxton Farm. The later Iron Age, as will be shown in chapter VII, brought greater elaboration and expansion to a stone-building tradition which was, however, firmly established before the close of the first millennium.

Rhodesia is far removed from the other major areas of Iron Age stone building in sub-equatorial Africa – central Angola and south-western Kenya/north-central Tanzania (de Almeida and Fraca, 1960; Lofgren, 1967; Sassoon, 1967a). Since the only architectural similarities between the stone structures in these areas and those of Rhodesia are very general and unspecialized, no connexions with these areas can be demonstrated. The absence of such stone building in regions to the north of Rhodesia, whence the Early Iron Age population must be supposed in the main to have come, suggests that its development between the Zambezi and the Limpopo should be regarded as a basically autochthonous process. Several writers (e.g. Whitty, 1957) have indicated how such a development could have occurred, perhaps in the vicinity of Great Zimbabwe. Although later stone buildings in Rhodesia were intimately connected with centres of religious and political authority, there are no indications that the few enclosures tentatively attributed to the Early Iron Age served other than purely domestic functions.

Social and political structure

The assertion is sometimes made that Early Iron Age societies lacked centralized socio/political authorities. Such statements are generally based firstly, on the alleged absence on Early Iron Age sites of objects such as iron bells and conus discs which were symbols of such authority in later Iron Age times; secondly, on the evidence of oral tradition which in many areas accounts for the imposition of chieftainship over societies which are said previously to have lacked such an institution. Both these lines of argument are open to objection – the first on the grounds that both iron bells and conus discs are preserved in Early Iron Age contexts in the upper Lualaba cemeteries, and through the theoretical difficulties of correlating the institution itself with the ritual trappings with which it later became associated. The objection to the second argument is that the traditions almost invariably relate to events which fall exclusively within the context of the later Iron Age; they are thus of little if any relevance to the Early Iron Age

The truth of the matter is that the available archaeological data are insufficient to enable useful statements to be made on the subject of Early Iron Age social and political systems. Techniques of analysis of archaeological materials have recently been developed, principally in the New World, which it is alleged can throw light on such matters; but these methods have not yet been applied in eastern or southern Africa. It has been suggested that the richness of the grave-goods recovered from the upper Lualaba cemeteries indicates the presence of chieftainship; but the size of the cemeteries and the numbers of the rich graves, even allowing for a prolonged period of use, militate against such a conclusion. The most that can be said is that these cemeteries attest the existence of considerable wealth, which was unequally distributed through the society. More light may be thrown on such non-material aspects of Early Iron Age life by other lines of inquiry, notably through the study of historical linguistics, as will be shown in a later chapter.

One aspect of religious/social custom which is well illustrated by the available archaeological data is burial. The Chundu Farm graves from the Victoria Falls region and the cemeteries of Sanga and Katoto in Shaba amply demonstrate the practice of accompanying the deceased with requirements for some form of future existence, or for the satisfaction of the spirit. Hiernaux has even interpreted the multiple interments of Katoto as indicating the despatch of women and children to accompany their departed menfolk, a custom which is attested from central Africa in more recent times. Some of the richest Sanga graves (e.g. grave 34 of Nenquin, 1963: 119–21) are those of children, perhaps indicating the important position occupied by, or attached to, the young in the community.

Food-producing economy

The economic basis for Early Iron Age society clearly lay in the production of food. Such is indicated not only by the settlement pattern of large villages concentrated in fertile areas which we have described above, but also by the remains of domestic animals and cultivated crops which have been recovered from Early Iron Age sites. So far all the sites of this period which have yielded physical remains of domesticated foods are in central and southern Africa. The data are sufficient to give a broad idea of the crops and domestic aminals exploited by the Early Iron Age farmers. It must not, however, be assumed that all the species represented were of general or widespread occurrence. In only one case, that of domestic cattle, can we adequately illustrate the limits of Early Iron Age distribution; but it may be expected that comparably restricted spreads of other domesticated food-sources may in due course be demonstrated. Few specific conclusions can be drawn concerning the crops and domestic animals which were utilized by the Early Iron Age inhabitants of East Africa.

As on archaeological sites of most periods, physical identifiable remains of cultivated food-plants are more rarely recovered from Early Iron Age associations than are the bones of domestic animals. (It is unfortunate that techniques of flotation for the recovery of seeds from archaeological deposits have but rarely been employed on Iron Age sites in sub-Saharan Africa.) The only such discoveries known are from Zambia and Rhodesia where squash or pumpkin are reported from Chundu and the 'Place of Offerings', a bean from Chundu and – probably – cowpeas from Nthabazingwe. It will be noted that these finds do not include any cereals, although sorghum is attested in southern Zambia at first millennium ad sites which are not attributed to the Early Iron Age as at Kalundu, Isamu Pati and Ingombe Ilede (Fagan, 1967*b*; 1969*b*). At several other sites occasional iron hoes and large numbers of grindstones are suggestive of the practice of agriculture. (Grindstones may, of course, be used for grinding wild seeds.) This scanty evidence merely indicates some of the crops which were tended by the Early Iron Age farmers, and there is no reason to believe that the list is at all comprehensive.

When we turn to consider the osteological remains of domestic animals, the evidence is seen to be somewhat more substantial. Bones identified as of domestic sheep and/or goats have been reported from eleven sites between Shaba and Natal (Sanga, Twickenham Road, Kalundu, Kumadzulo, Mabveni, Gokomere, Makuru, Nthabazingwe, Lydenburg, Ntshekane and Broederstroom). These sites belong to seven distinct groups including representatives of both the eastern and western streams, and chronologically they cover the whole time-span of the Early Iron Age in their respective regions. The occurrence of cattle bones, however, is more restricted. In the territory of the western stream they are recorded at Kapwirimbwe and Kalundu – sites the occupation of which goes back to the early decades of western stream settlement in central and southern Zambia. In Rhodesia and the Victoria Falls region cattle are attested at Kumadzulo, Kapula Vlei, Coronation Park, Malapati and Makuru. These are all comparatively late in date, belonging to Huffman's (1971*a*) phase 2 of the Early Iron Age: Kumadzulo is attributed to the sixth century, whilst all the others belong to the eighth century or later.

The point which should be emphasized here is that none of these eastern stream cattle occurrences predate contact with the western stream. The earliest eastern stream locality where cattle are firmly attested is the Dambwa group site of Kumadzulo, and I have argued above that the Victoria Falls region represents a contact zone between the two streams of the Early Iron Age. Kapula Vlei has likewise been attributed to the Dambwa group. Since all the other Rhodesian Early Iron Age sites where cattle bones have been recovered can be shown to post-date the beginning of the eighth century ad, in other words to be at least one hundred years subsequent to the occupation of Kumadzulo, there is no reason to attribute their cattle to other than a western stream source. Further contact between the two streams can be shown to have taken place in the northern parts of Rhodesia from at least the seventh century, for the Early Iron Age pottery of the extreme north-west of Mashonaland – as exemplified at Muyove in the Urungwe District and at Sinoia Cave in Lomagundi – shows far stronger affinities with that of the western stream Kapwirimbwe group than with any of the eastern stream material recorded from further to the south. The sample of Early Iron Age sites which have yielded cattle bones is clearly too small for any definite conclusions to be drawn concerning their distribution in either time or space. The evidence at present available does, however, appear strongly to indicate that cattle were unknown, or at least extremely rare (cf. Huffman, 1975), in early settlements of the eastern stream and that they only became common in eastern stream areas after contact had been established with the later western stream. Domestic cattle were probably herded by the western stream Early Iron Age folk from the time of their first appearance in central Africa. The archaeological indications that sheep were herded in Rhodesia before the introduction of cattle is in keeping with the evidence of the rock paintings of that country, where sheep are frequently depicted, but cattle never (C. K. Cooke, 1965; 1971*a*; Willcox, 1971*a*)

Cattle have, however, been reported from a fifth century ad context at Broederstroom in the Transvaal (see p. 120 above), as well as from the related sites at Lydenburg and Ntshekane. As will be discussed in chapter VIII, there is evidence – primarily linguistic – that domestic cattle were introduced into South Africa from a western source only indirectly derived from the Early Iron Age Industrial Complex.

Throughout the duration of the Early Iron Age the hunting of wild animals appears to have retained considerable importance as a dietary resource. This is suggested by the numbers of iron arrow-heads and spear-points which have been recovered in many areas; these easily outnumber the hoes but need not, of course, have been used exclusively for hunting. Early Iron Age sites where bones of wild animals have been recovered are much more numerous than those which have yielded remains of domestic stock; and at Kalundu Brian Fagan (1967*b*: 218) was able to demonstrate the gradual replacement of wild by domestic animal bones in the faunal assemblages from successive levels of the Early Iron Age deposits. The wild species represented on Early Iron Age sites include wildebeest and buffalo as well as many of the smaller antelopes. Fish bones have only rarely been preserved, but are recorded from Early Iron Age contexts in Malawi, as at Nkope (Robinson, 1970).

Technology

Early Iron Age technology has already been discussed at some length, and little recapitulation is necessary here. Pottery is the artefact most frequently encountered in the archaeological record and it has been described and illustrated in some detail in the earlier sections of this chapter. Here, it may merely be noted that, in several areas of eastern and central Africa where the modern pottery traditions show evidence for continuity with those of the Early Iron Age, potting is today – in contrast to the general practice among Bantu-speaking peoples – the work of men rather than women. For this reason, and through other arguments derived from a consideration of the nature of and reasons for changes in pottery traditions, I have tentatively suggested elsewhere that men may also have been the potters in many if not all of the Early Iron Age groups here recognized (D. W. Phillipson, 1974).

More detailed consideration is necessary of the evidence for Early Iron Age metallurgy. Only three metals were worked on any substantial scale; these, in decreasing order of importance, were iron, copper and gold.

Iron ore in one form or another is widespread through most regions of eastern and southern Africa; where richer ores were not available, ferricretes or limonites (bog iron) seem to have been smelted despite their low yield. There are no indications that iron ore was generally mined other than by the excavation of shallow pits; and probably the ore was often simply collected from surface exposures. The only demonstrably Early Iron Age iron-smelting furnaces are the tall, cylindrical brick-built examples from Rwanda and adjacent parts of Kivu which we have noted above. On the basis of comparison with later furnaces of similar type we may suppose that these were fired by natural draught, without the assistance of bellows. It is clear, both from oral tradition relating to later Iron Age furnaces which have been archaeologically examined and from recent experiments, that tall natural draught furnaces of this type can attain and even exceed, without the use of bellows, the temperatures of about 1100° C. required to smelt iron (e.g. Chaplin, 1961). Evidence has been cited (D. W. Phillipson, 1968d) for the attainment of temperatures in excess of 1200° C. in a furnace which was almost certainly of natural draught type.

In several regions it appears that smelting frequently took place within the confines of a village. It would thus appear that the taboos, which in later periods have ensured that this operation took place away from all contact with women, did not at that time apply.

Copper deposits have a far more restricted distribution than do those of iron; the occurrences in East Africa are exiguous and do not appear to have been exploited in early times. Further to the south the main deposits are on the Shaba–Zambia Copperbelt, in the Hook of the Kafue, in the Wankie and Lomagundi Districts of Rhodesia, in the Limpopo valley around Messina, and in the Phalaborwa area of the eastern Transvaal. In all these regions it seems probable that the copper deposits were worked during prehistoric times, but it is extremely difficult to differentiate Early Iron Age from later Iron Age activity. The problem is exacerbated by the fact that the great majority of prehistoric mines have been destroyed or severely damaged by modern large-scale exploitation; and remarkably few artefacts recovered from prehistoric workings have been preserved. No well-preserved copper-smelting furnaces of the Early Iron Age have been investigated. However, copper objects are widely distributed on Early Iron Age sites from Shaba southwards, although they are far less common than they are in the context of later periods.

Knowledge of iron-working seems to have been introduced to eastern and southern Africa contemporaneously with the arrival of the other diagnostic traits which constitute Early Iron Age culture. It cannot yet be demonstrated that copper-working technology goes back to quite such an early date, although the indications are that this was so, at least in some areas. The earliest Chondwe group sites appear to be intimately connected with copper ore deposits, although copper artefacts are not represented in the Kapwirimbwe group assemblages of the Lusaka region until the final phase of the local Early Iron Age, which is provisionally attributed to the tenth century. The presence of copper objects at Mabveni, the 'Place of Offerings' and other Rhodesian phase 1 sites indicates that copper working was practised by the eastern stream before contacts with the western stream had been established.

During the Early Iron Age copper was evidently a scarce material, only regarded as suitable for the manufacture of small items of personal adornment such as beads and bangles of thin twisted strip (Vogel, 1971a). The material was traded in the form of bars and cross-shaped ingots; of these the best examples from Early Iron Age contexts are those from Kumadzulo and from Sanga respectively. Both types of ingots are substantially smaller than their counterparts in later Iron Age times. It may be concluded that in much of central and southern Africa copper was worked on a small scale by the Early Iron Age inhabitants, but that the large-scale exploitation of this metal was a phenomenon of the later Iron Age (Bisson, 1975).

Iron Age gold mining appears to have been restricted to Rhodesia and closely neighbouring areas. Of over a thousand prehistoric gold mines which have been recorded in Rhodesia (Summers, 1969), only four have yielded any evidence for first millennium exploitation in the form of Early Iron Age pottery from within or immediately adjacent to the mines. These sites are the Golden Shower mine near Arcturus in the Mazoe valley, the nearby Three Skids Claim, the Hot Springs Claim near Umkondo in the Sabi valley and, lastly, an ore-processing site with dolly holes and crushing depressions at Three Mile Water near Que Que. In all cases the pottery is best attributed to a late phase 2 manifestation of the Gokomere/Ziwa tradition; that from the Hot Springs Claim also shares affinities with the finds from Malapati (*ibid.*: 121–41).

In the absence of radiocarbon dates from the gold mining sites, dating may only be attempted through comparison with sites of known age which have yielded similar pottery; on this basis a date for these mines between the ninth and eleventh centuries is indicated. Both the Golden Shower ancient mine and that on the Hot Springs Claim were small, consisting each of a single open stope. No finds of gold artefacts have come from stratified Early Iron Age contexts; and it is clear that gold mining was restricted to the closing phases of the Early Iron Age and that it was on a very small scale in comparison to that which was attained in later times. This conclusion is in keeping with the evidence of Arabic written records in which the first mention of gold from this region being bought on the East African coast occurs in a tenth-century context (Freeman-Grenville, 1962: 15).

The gold-mining sites from which Early Iron Age pottery has been recovered are in the eastern part of Rhodesia, in the valleys of the Mazoe and the Sabi; both these rivers provide relatively easy communications between the interior and the coast. The writings of Arab geographers leave no doubt that, from this initial period of gold mining, the metal was exported. Whether it was also used locally at this period is not yet clear. In this context it is significant that the commencement of gold mining and the introduction of imported glass beads into eastern Rhodesia (see p. 118, above) appear to have been broadly synchronous. If the two events are indeed connected, the stimulus for the development of gold mining may well have been primarily external. Roger Summers' contention (1969: 215–20) that it was specifically from India that the techniques and, by implication, some of the miners were derived is, however, unconvincing in the present state of our knowledge.

Inter-regional contacts and trade

The incomplete coverage of research has resulted in distribution maps of Early Iron Age sites which impart an exaggerated semblance of isolation to the various groups (e.g. Fig. 32 on p. 105). It is hoped, however, that the archaeological summaries presented above will have emphasized the substantial degree of contact which may be demonstrated between adjacent areas of Early Iron Age settlement and even, on occasion, over greater distances. As in more recent African societies, much of this interaction between groups probably took the form of personal contact and trade.

Joseph Vogel has drawn attention to the occurrence, in stratified

Early Iron Age Dambwa group assemblages from the Victoria Falls region, of occasional pottery vessels which cannot be duplicated at other Dambwa group sites but which would not be at all out of place in collections from other areas. Such extraneous vessels found in the Victoria Falls region may be attributed to sources both in the Lusaka area and in eastern Rhodesia (Vogel, 1971b; 1973a). It would seem unlikely that pottery was itself regularly transported over such large distances; a more probable explanation is that they are the work of potters who travelled from afar to settle, if only temporarily, in the Dambwa group villages.

Comparable occurrences of 'foreign' sherds have also been noted by the present writer in Chondwe group assemblages from the Zambian Copperbelt. The largest number of such sherds comes from the Roan Antelope site which is adjacent to a prehistoric copper working; specimens akin to material of the Nkope (eastern stream), Kapwirimbwe and Kalundu (western stream) groups were recovered. At another Copperbelt site, Luano, sherds of Kalambo and Dambwa type have been recorded (D. W. Phillipson, 1972a). It is tempting to attribute these occurrences to men coming from far afield to the mining area in order to obtain copper – a practice which is known to have continued into later Iron Age times. In view of the suggestion that Early Iron Age potting was the work of men, it is necessary to postulate neither the migration of whole households to the mining districts, nor the long-distance transport of the pots themselves. Similar inter-group contact is attested between Sanga and Katoto. This extensive trade in copper is further indicated by finds of ingots in areas far removed from the sources of the metal itself.

It may reasonably be supposed that comparable trade was established in salt at an early date, but evidence for this is hard to distinguish in the archaeological record. So far, Kapwirimbwe and Twickenham Road are the only Early Iron Age sites to have yielded remains of salt-making apparatus, although the Early Iron Age occupations of Pwaga and Nyamsunga were also probably connected with exploitation of the Uvinza brine-springs.

Contact with the coastal trade may be seen as having been slow and tentative through the greater part of the Early Iron Age, reaching significant proportions only in eastern Rhodesia at the close of the first millennium ad, when it seems to be connected in some way with the inception of gold mining. Significantly, these developments appear to have taken place at an earlier date in the south than they did in East Africa. It was probably not until the thirteenth century that Kilwa rose to be an important trading centre: before this it seems that the major entrepot on the east coast was at Sofala.

With the possible exception, to which we have already alluded, of the early Rhodesian gold trade, the dispersal of imported trade-goods (mainly glass beads) and other objects of coastal origin such as cowrie and conus shells should not be seen as implying a distinct trading system independent of the inter-group contacts of the Early Iron Age societies which have been discussed in the preceding paragraphs. In contrast to the situation which prevailed in later periods of the Iron Age, such coastal items were of rare occurrence in the interior throughout the first millennium; and they were doubtless distributed through the medium of the trading network which had been built up primarily for the distribution of local raw materials and commodities such as metals and salt.

Except on the coast itself, where very rare glass beads and some imported ceramics are found in levels of period I and II at Kilwa associated with local pottery which I would attribute to an Early Iron Age tradition, coastal materials have not yet been reported from Early Iron Age sites in East Africa. They are markedly absent even from the sites investigated by Robert Soper around Kwale, which are less than 30 kilometres from the sea. Further to the south, such items are likewise lacking from sites of the Kalambo, Chondwe and Kapwirimbwe groups and from the Early Iron Age occurrences of Malawi. In the upper Lualaba cemeteries, glass beads and cowrie shells are attested at both Katoto and Sanga, but at the latter site they apparently only occurred in the more recent graves. At Katoto both the Atlantic and Indian Ocean species of cowrie were represented, as were conus shells. At sites lying to the south of the Zambezi–Kafue line the evidence is somewhat more comprehensive. Cowrie shells are attested from early stages of the Early Iron Age settlement of the region, as at Kalundu, Chundu and the 'Place of Offerings'. The earliest occurrences of glass beads are at Mabveni and Gokomere, while a glass fragment was also recovered from Kumadzulo. Beads become more frequent in the context of phase 2 of the Rhodesian Early Iron Age both in the eastern regions and in Matabeleland. I have above tentatively linked this development with the inception of gold mining. No coastal items have yet been recorded from Early Iron Age contexts located south of the Limpopo.

It may be concluded that trading contact between the interior of eastern and southern Africa with the coastal regions and thus with the outside world remained on a very small and indirect scale through the Early Iron Age. The extant written records of the Indian Ocean trade at this time mention the export of rhinoceros horn, ivory and turtle shells. All these items could have been obtained in the coastal region and its immediate hinterland without necessitating supply-networks stretching into the interior. Neither gold nor copper, which were obtainable only further inland, are mentioned as exports until the tenth and fifteenth centuries respectively (Sutton, 1973*b*; Freeman-Grenville, 1962). These trading activities reached a far greater scale during the later Iron Age, as is described in the following chapter.

In this long chapter have been presented summaries of the archaeological evidence for the appearance in most regions of eastern and southern Africa from the equator to Natal of iron-working people who, on the basis of the close similarities of their pottery styles, are regarded as representatives of a single industrial complex. It is argued that the Early Iron Age Industrial Complex was of northerly origin and that its arrival south of the equator presents a major contrast with the earlier stone-tool-using societies. To the south of the modern Tanzania, the Early Iron Age folk were responsible for the introduction of food production, pottery manufacture and the construction of pole-and-*daga* houses.

The earliest Early Iron Age settlements appear to be those of the interlacustrine region of East Africa, associated with Urewe ware, the makers of which are shown to have been established in the country adjacent to the south-western shore of Lake Victoria by at least 300 bc. Further to the south, study of artefact typology enables two distinct streams of the Early Iron Age to be recognized. The eastern stream, which is the better known, is clearly derived from the Urewe settlements. It penetrated as far as the Kenya coast by the second century ad and southwards to the Transvaal by the fourth century. The western stream also shows Urewe affinities, although these are in most cases less marked. Sites of the western stream are dated in central Zambia from about the fifth century onwards, but may have been significantly earlier in regions further to the west. Both streams practised herding and agriculture, but it appears that, at least in more southerly areas, domestic cattle were rare or absent in the territory of the eastern stream until they were introduced through contact with the western stream. Each stream may be divided into several distinct regional groups, and study of these has revealed the local Early Iron Age antecedents of several cultural traits characteristic of the later Iron Age communities which form the subject of the following chapter.

VII

The later Iron Age in
Bantu-speaking Africa:
archaeological considerations

In many parts of Bantu-speaking Africa, the later Iron Age societies have been less intensively studied by archaeological means than have their Early Iron Age predecessors. Consequently, at least for the period before that at which oral tradition becomes a significant historical source, the centuries after about ad 1000 represent a virtual lacuna in our knowledge of later African prehistory. It is thus all the more difficult to link into a single coherent account the evidence provided by archaeology and that derived from the study of the historical traditions of extant societies. Exceptions to this generalization occur mainly where substantial sites or spectacular monuments, such as Great Zimbabwe and comparable ruins in Rhodesia, or the city-sites of the East African coast, have directed archaeologists' attentions to problems of the later Iron Age.

A significant proportion of Bantu-speaking later Iron Age societies retain oral traditions which purportedly relate to their own origins. Early historical interpretations of these traditions tended to accept many of them at more-or-less face value; and consequently it came to be believed that the history of these societies fell almost entirely within the time-depth of the extant traditions. More recent studies both by historians (e.g. Schoffeleers, 1973) and by archaeologists (e.g. D. W. Phillipson, 1974) have demonstrated not only how misleading such interpretations can be but also how archaeology, as a historical discipline in its own right, can amplify and – in some respects – confirm the testimony of oral tradition even for relatively recent periods. In many parts of the sub-continent archaeological research is currently under way which, as will be shown in later sections of this chapter, is rapidly correcting the imbalance of previous endeavours.

In this chapter, I have attempted to present an account of historical developments up to the time when written records or oral traditions take over as the principal sources upon which the historian can rely. This has resulted in somewhat uneven chronological coverage: for the coastal regions I have brought the story up to the arrival of the Portuguese at the end of the fifteenth century, but for most of the interior the techniques of the prehistorian can provide valuable information into more recent periods, as I have attempted to show. The account which follows is arranged on a regional basis, starting – both because of its relative isolation from the rest of the continent and because of its value as a point of chronological reference – with the East Coast.

THE EAST COAST

When, during the closing years of the fifteenth century, Portuguese mariners rounded the Cape of Good Hope and penetrated northwards along the eastern coast of Africa en route to India, they encountered an urban maritime civilization of the existence of which Europeans had previously remained in almost total ignorance. Spread out along the coast from the Somali coast in the north to Sofala in the south (Fig. 52) were numerous stone-built towns in which a Bantu-speaking population of mixed African and Arabian descent practised a developed Islamic culture. The economy of these ports was based upon the collection of the products of the interior regions – notably gold, ivory and skins – and their exportation into the trading network of the Indian Ocean. The chief men of these towns were, indeed, the

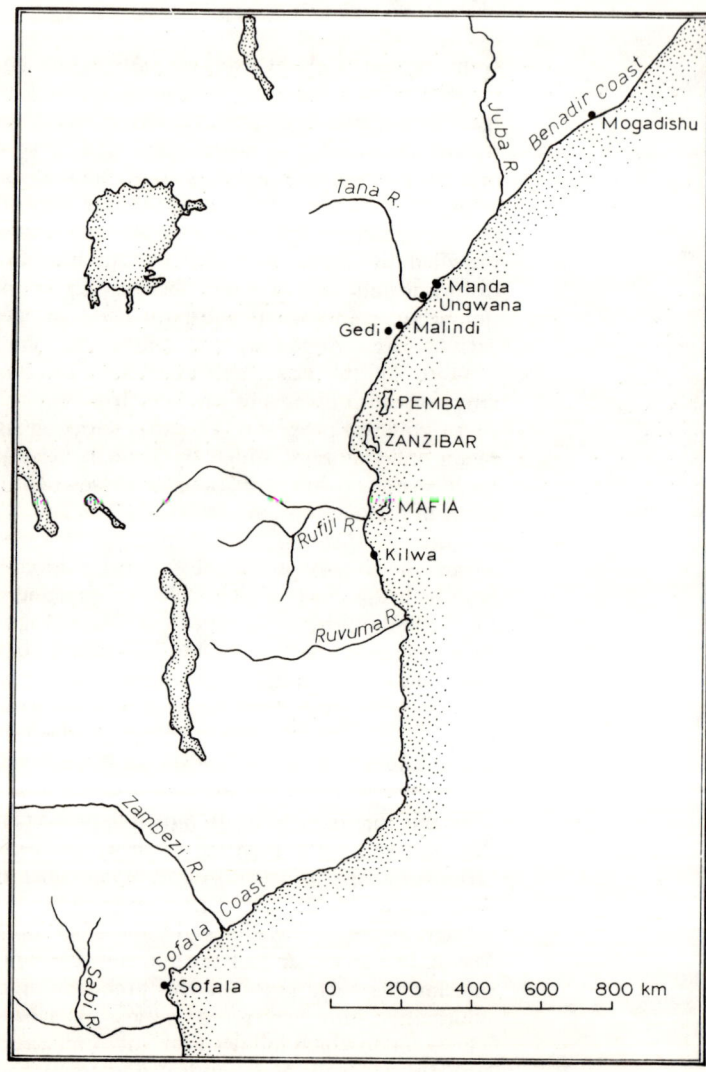

Fig. 52 Principal sites on the East African coast, 800–1500 AD

mercantile successors of the traders described some one and a half millennia earlier in the *Periplus of the Erythraean Sea*.

Despite intensive search for earlier sites, it has not yet proved possible to trace back the archaeological record of these East Coast trading societies beyond the ninth century AD. This date broadly coincides with the resumption of written references to the area after several centuries of silence following the *Periplus*. The two principal sites of this period which have been investigated – Kilwa on an offshore island some 350 kilometres to the south of Zanzibar, and Manda in the Lamu archipelago of the northern Kenya coast – provide an interesting comparison. At Kilwa, the earliest settlement revealed by Neville Chittick's (1966; 1974*a*) excavations was one of smallish rectangular dwellings with walls of mud applied over a wooden framework: there were evidently also some constructions of squared coral blocks set in mud mortar. The manufacture of shell beads appears to have been a major industry of the site's inhabitants at this time. Imported glass beads were rare. Cowrie shells were collected and may have been used as a medium of exchange. The domestic pottery, as has been noted above in chapter VI, appears to belong, or to be related, to that of the Early Iron Age Industrial Complex (Fig. 53). There are very limited quantities of imported vessels, notably those of glass and a blue-glazed ware named 'Sassanian-Islamic', which is probably of Iraqi origin. Later, probably from about AD 1000 until at least the twelfth century, a distinctive '*sgraffiato*' ware was imported: this is distinguished by decoration scratched through a pale slip to reveal the red fabric beneath, the whole then being covered with a yellowish glaze.

A marked contrast is provided by Chittick's (1967) excavations in the remains of a contemporary settlement at Manda. Comparable ceramics were recovered, but the imported wares, including glass, were very many times more frequent than they were at Kilwa. The strongest connexions of this material appear to be with the eastern shore of the Persian Gulf, where the great port of Siraf flourished at this time (Whitehouse, 1970). It is probable that at Manda stone-built houses were more numerous than they were in the contemporary occupation at Kilwa; and some of the walls investigated retained a covering of lime plaster. Around the tenth century a massive sea-wall was built along the ocean frontage of the settlement, utilizing huge coral blocks up to one cubic metre in volume. Iron-working is attested at the site; and it is possible tentatively to link this fact with a previously unexplained reference to iron mines at a place called Mulanda which is contained in the mid-twelfth-century writings of the Arabic geographer al-Idrisi (Freeman-Grenville, 1962: 20, who substitutes Malindi for Mulanda). By this time the East African coast, which had imported iron from overseas at the time of the *Periplus*, had developed its own iron industry on, according to al-Idrisi, a significant scale.

The picture which emerges from the archaeological research which has so far been undertaken is one of a chain of coastal trading settlements (including one, so far unexcavated, on the island of Pemba), established during the closing centuries of the first millennium AD, in which the bulk of the population was apparently of indigenous Iron Age stock. Trading voyages along the Indian Ocean shores, which continue to the present day exploiting the monsoon winds as they must have done since the days of the *Periplus* and before, were probably

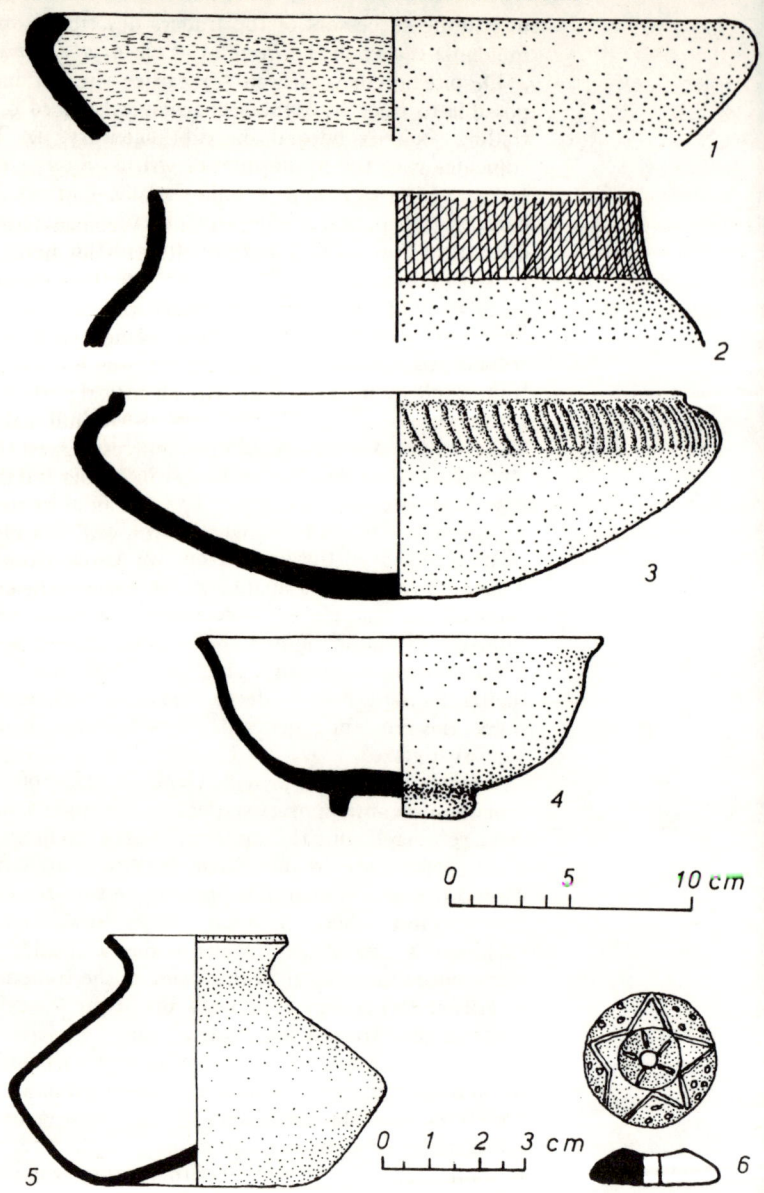

Fig. 53 *Artefacts from Kilwa (after Chittick, 1974a): 1–3, local pottery (1, 2, ninth to twelfth century; 3, fifteenth century); 4, imported celadon bowl from south China; 5, glass vessel; 6, spindle whorl*

intensified at this time and brought foreign settlers, ultimately from Arabia and the Persian Gulf region, such as may have been established at an earlier date on the Benadir coast of what is now Somalia. In the more southerly latitudes, with which we are here concerned, foreign influence appears to have been significantly stronger at Manda than at Kilwa, over 900 kilometres further to the south. It is noteworthy that the date of these coastal settlements coincides with that at which imported beads, as noted in chapter VI, are first regularly encountered in the Rhodesian interior, and it seems clear that the Sofala coast had by this time been brought within the orbit of the Indian Ocean trade network.

Fortunately, Arabic written sources, notably the work of al-Mas'udi early in the tenth century, are available to supplement the still sparse testimony of archaeology. This author refers to the indigenous people of the coast as Zenj and implies that few of them, even in the towns, had yet adopted the Moslem faith (Freeman-Grenville, 1962: 14–17). They were ruled by kings or sultans. They herded cattle, which were used as beasts of burden. Millet was their staple food, but bananas (an introduction from Indonesia) were already established, as were coconut palms on the offshore islands such as Qanbalu (Pemba). Ivory, clearly the principal export, was hunted and collected by the Zenj and shipped from the African coastal ports to Oman and onwards to India and China. Significantly, al-Mas'udi makes no mention of the export of slaves, although other sources suggest that Africans were by this date being exported to slavery in Arabia and the Persian Gulf area. It is at this period that we find the first written reference to gold 'in the land of Sofala and the Waqwaq' – a clear reference to the Rhodesian deposits which, as we know from the archaeological evidence cited above in chapter VI, began to be exploited at this time.

During the eleventh and twelfth centuries the prosperity of the coastal settlements increased, with the emphasis on the towns of the Benadir coast, especially Mogadishu. This place probably marked the approximate northern limit of settlement of Bantu-speaking peoples at this time (Cerulli, 1934; *pace* Turton, 1975): oral tradition, ethnography, archaeology and the study of place-names combine to indicate the former presence of such folk in the coastal regions far to the north of their present distribution. Through the whole coastal strip to the south of Mogadishu, the characteristic society and culture of the Swahili was doubtless already emerging. On the Benadir coast power became concentrated in the hands of people who claimed an origin on the eastern side of the Persian Gulf and who are generally known as Shirazi. It was probably during the second half of the twelfth century that these Shirazi expanded their authority southwards, settling at such places as Manda, on the islands of Pemba and Mafia, and at Kilwa, where they established a new dynasty of sultans (Chittick, 1965). It is at this time that begins the narrative contained in the so-called Kilwa Chronicle, a compendium of historical traditions probably first written down early in the sixteenth century (Freeman-Grenville, 1962: 34–49).

During the century that the Shirazi dynasty ruled Kilwa the place increased rapidly in prosperity and importance. Coins were struck by the sultans, the earliest being tiny silver pieces, weighing less than one tenth of a gram, bearing the name of al-Hasan. His successor, 'Ali ibn al-Hasan, struck first minute bronze coins, then those of the size (about 1.2 grams) more usually associated with the money of the East Coast settlements (Chittick, 1966; Walker and Freeman-Grenville, 1956; Freeman-Grenville, 1957). Stone buildings were more refined, with lime mortar taking the place of mud. Imported ceramics, including examples from China, became more frequent, as did glass beads. Spindle whorls first became commonplace, suggesting the local production of (presumably cotton) cloth. The local pottery shows much continuity with that of the previous period, with the addition of a few new types, notably carinated bowls and vessels adorned

Plate XIV   Ruins of the Swahili city of Gedi, Kenya

with bands of festooned decoration akin to that found on several later Iron Age wares in the interior.

Around the end of the thirteenth century, Kilwa came under the control of the Ahdali dynasty of sultans, probably of southern Arabian origin. There occurred at broadly the same time pronounced changes in the architecture and in the style of the local pottery. This was the great period of the coast's prosperity; and many of the smaller towns such as Gedi, Malindi and Ungwana, whose ruins (Plates XIV, XV) are scattered along the coasts of Tanzania and Kenya, were founded and flourished at this time (Kirkman, 1954; 1964; 1966). The great Moslem traveller ibn Battuta visited the coast in 1331 and has passed on to us a unique eye-witness account of its principal settlements (Gibb, 1961). At Kilwa, there was erected the great palace and emporium known as Husuni Kubwa (Fig. 54), consisting of elaborate living quarters set around a courtyard: part of the building was roofed with domes and barrel-vaults (Garlake, 1966a). The sculptured stonework displays a new refinement of decoration which may be attributed to strengthened contacts with centres of more developed Islamic civilization far to the north. The mosque was rebuilt and enlarged; and from this time onwards most of the buildings in the city were of stone. This period also saw the final disappearance of the local Early Iron Age pottery types which had survived for some three centuries longer than they did in more inland regions. They were replaced by more varieties of festoon-decorated later Iron Age wares, as well as by locally produced vessels, some of them wheel-turned, which are idiosyncratic to the coast and often imitate features of the imported wares. Imports of Chinese origin, particularly blue-green celadon porcelain, were now used in quantity. Blue-and-white porcelain became more frequent in the fifteenth century, when Arabian

Plate XV Mihrab of the Great Mosque at Gedi, probably sixteenth century

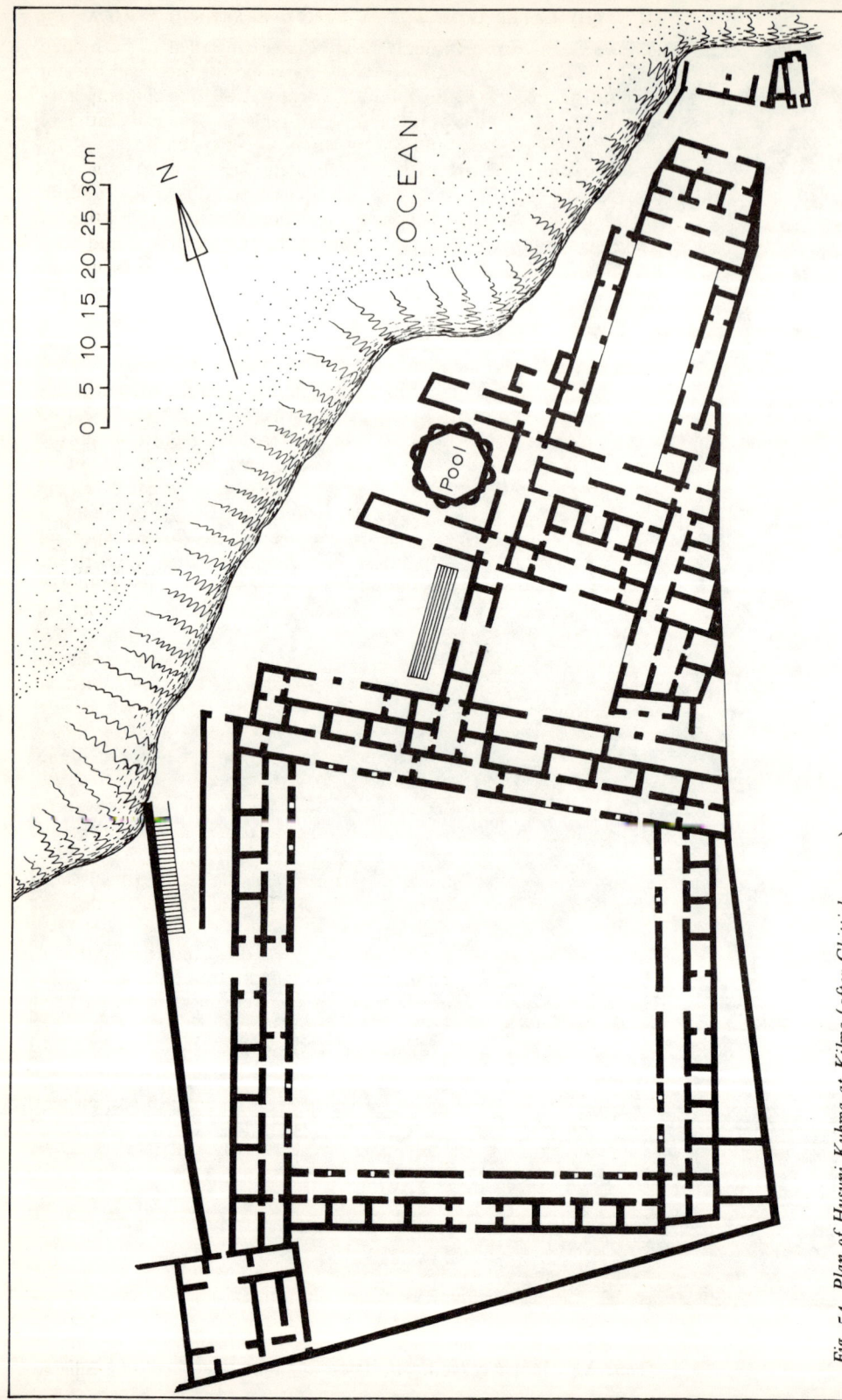

OCEAN

Pool

0 5 10 15 20 25 30 m

N

Fig. 54 Plan of Husuni Kubwa at Kilwa (after Chittick, 1974a)

imports were correspondingly rarer. Coins continued to be minted until late in the fourteenth century: the reason for their end has not been satisfactorily explained, but the event was broadly contemporary with the strengthening of local architectural styles, the elaboration of the local pottery wares and the cessation of iron-smelting.

By this time, the rule of Kilwa extended over the coast of what is now Mozambique as far as the Sofala coast near the modern Beira. Sofala appears to have been the main port for the exportation of Rhodesian gold which reached a peak in the late fourteenth and early fifteenth centuries, when the luxury imported goods represented at Great Zimbabwe (see p. 191 below) were comparable in many ways with those which were in use at Kilwa. It is tempting to suggest, but cannot yet be proven, that the trade with the interior passed the great eastern escarpment by means of the valley of the Sabi. Later, following the abandonment of Great Zimbabwe in the fifteenth century, the centre of political authority in what is now Rhodesia shifted northwards, as will be described in greater detail below, as did the main area of trade, which appears now to have followed a Zambezi valley route to the interior. The site of Ingombe Ilede near the Kafue/Zambezi confluence is best interpreted as having been inhabited by traders with Swahili (Kotakota) connexions, engaged in exporting the gold of the Mwene Mutapa by a Zambezi valley route to the east coast, Swahili penetration of the lower Zambezi being indicated from the fourteenth century onwards (Axelson, 1940: 8–10; Lancaster and Pohorilenko, 1976).

To the north of the Zambezi, penetration of the interior appears to have been on an altogether different scale: specific trade-routes cannot be identified and imported objects, even glass beads, are virtually unknown on Iron Age sites in the interior until very much later times. Here, the chief products of the interior which were of interest to the coastal traders were ivory, tortoise-shell, rhinoceros horn and game-skins: most probably these were largely obtained in the immediate hinterland of the coast, or brought thither by the interior people themselves.

Such was the civilization of the towns of the East African coast when Vasco da Gama arrived off Sofala in 1497. Within a decade, the Portuguese had established forts at Sofala and at Kilwa. At first, it was not the coast itself which interested them, nor its control of the rich trade with the interior: it was its strategic position on the sea-route to India. Gold did not for long remain a secondary consideration, however; and the Zambezi valley road to the mines was rapidly explored, with Portuguese settlements being established at Sena in 1531 and at Tete a few years later. Thus began a Portuguese presence on the east coast which was to last for more than four and a half centuries.

THE INTERIOR OF EAST AFRICA

The later Iron Age populations of the East African interior are derived from diverse origins and belong to four principal linguistic groups: Sudanic, Nilotic, Cushitic and Bantu. It is only with the last-named group that this chapter is concerned. In an area where complex processes of social and cultural interaction between Bantu-speakers and members of other linguistic groups have been under way for at least two millennia, and where we often have little if any reliable evidence for the language spoken by a given archaeological population, the selection of material for inclusion in this section has not been easy. The attempt has, however, been made in order to facilitate comparison between the prehistory of the East African Bantu-speakers and that of their counterparts further to the south. Today, the northern limit of Bantu speech follows an approximately west–east line across Uganda close to the latitude of the northern end of Lake Albert, then takes a great sweep to the south, passing close to the eastern shore of Lake Victoria, into central Tanzania. Returning northwards past Kiliman-jaro, the line encloses in the Bantu-speaking area the highlands to the east of the Kenyan Rift Valley as far as the north-eastern slopes of Mount Kenya (Fig. 55). Further areas of Kenya so included are along the coast and the valley of the Tana river.

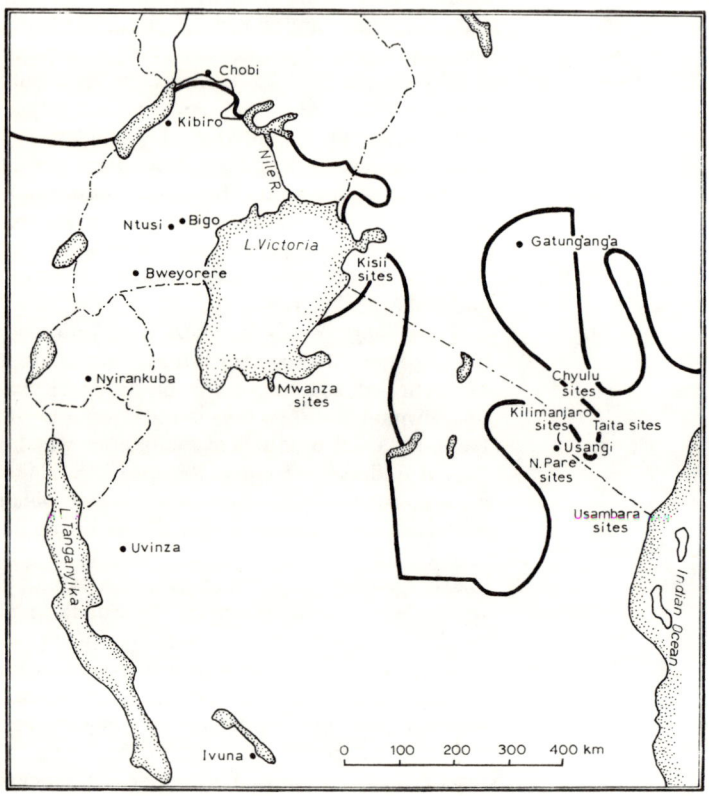

Fig. 55 East African later Iron Age sites attributed to Bantu-speakers (the bold line marks the present northern limit of Bantu speech)

In virtually no region of the East African interior has a com-prehensive archaeological succession for the later Iron Age yet been unearthed: although several scholars, notably Robert Soper, Merrick Posnansky and John Sutton, have made impressive beginnings in this study, it is not yet possible to propose a coherent synthesis comparable with those presented later in this chapter for more southerly regions. It is clear that, as elsewhere, the Early Iron Age Industrial Complex was here replaced round about the beginning of the present millennium by more heterogeneous industries represented mainly by pottery styles

which are easily distinguished from those of the Early Iron Age
(Sutton, 1972: 10; D. W. Phillipson, 1975).

Uganda and western Tanzania

In those parts of Uganda with which this chapter is concerned, the
later Iron Age pottery is characterized above all by the use of cord-
rouletted decoration (Fig. 56) such as was completely absent from the
Early Iron Age Urewe ware. The earliest dated context for this
Ugandan rouletted pottery is at Bigo in the rolling plains of western
Uganda, where it may be attributed to the period between the
thirteenth and fifteenth centuries ad (Posnansky, 1969). Comparable
pottery is made today in several of the Bantu-speaking kingdoms of
the interlacustrine region. It is interesting to note that in several of
these societies, such as those of the Ganda and Nyoro, potting is
– contrary to the general practice among Bantu-speaking peoples in
eastern Africa – the work of men rather than of women (Trowell
and Wachsmann, 1953). It seems, however, that no very clear distinction between the wares of these societies can be made on the basis
of the sex of their makers.

The oral traditions of these interlacustrine kingdoms trace their
origins to a brief period, some six centuries ago or thereabouts,
when political authority was wielded by a possibly alien group known
as the Bachwezi (Posnansky, 1966). There has been much discussion
regarding the identity of the Bachwezi and the nature of their contribution to the early history of the Bantu-speaking kingdoms of
Buganda, Bunyoro and Ankole (e.g. Wrigley, 1958; Oliver, 1963), the
details of which need not concern us here. There is, however, broad
agreement that these people were herders of long-horned cattle of the
type still associated with the Ankole, and that they were originally
speakers of a non-Bantu, probably Nilotic, language. This last point is
of importance since elsewhere in East Africa, notably in the Western
Highlands of Kenya and around the north-eastern shores of Lake
Victoria, roulette-decorated pottery is demonstrably the work of
Nilotic-speakers, as will be shown in chapter IX; and, indeed, its
manufacture is widespread at the present time in the southern and
central Sudan, where its development may be traced back to Meroitic
times (Drost, 1967: 199–200). It is most unfortunate that nowhere in
Uganda can the date of its local inception or introduction be pinpointed
with any accuracy in the archaeological record.

In one area of Uganda there is evidence for the practice of a distinct
pottery tradition of which the florescence may have partly overlapped
with the closing phases of the Early Iron Age and which apparently
preceded the first appearance of the rouletted wares. This is in the
very northernmost part of the Bantu-speaking area, on the Victoria
Nile near its confluence with the Chobi river. Here, Robert Soper
(1971b) has recovered sherds of bowls and wide-mouthed pots,
generally with thickened rims, to which he has given the name Chobi
ware (Fig. 56). The upper parts of the vessel walls are textured rather
than decorated, the finger marks of the potter and the ridges between
the individual coils with which the vessel was built up being left
unsmoothed. Finger-nail impressions and pinched-up ridges were also
employed. The stratigraphic position of this material seems reasonably
clear, but no radiocarbon dates for it are available, nor are there any
associated finds or indications of the economy of its makers.

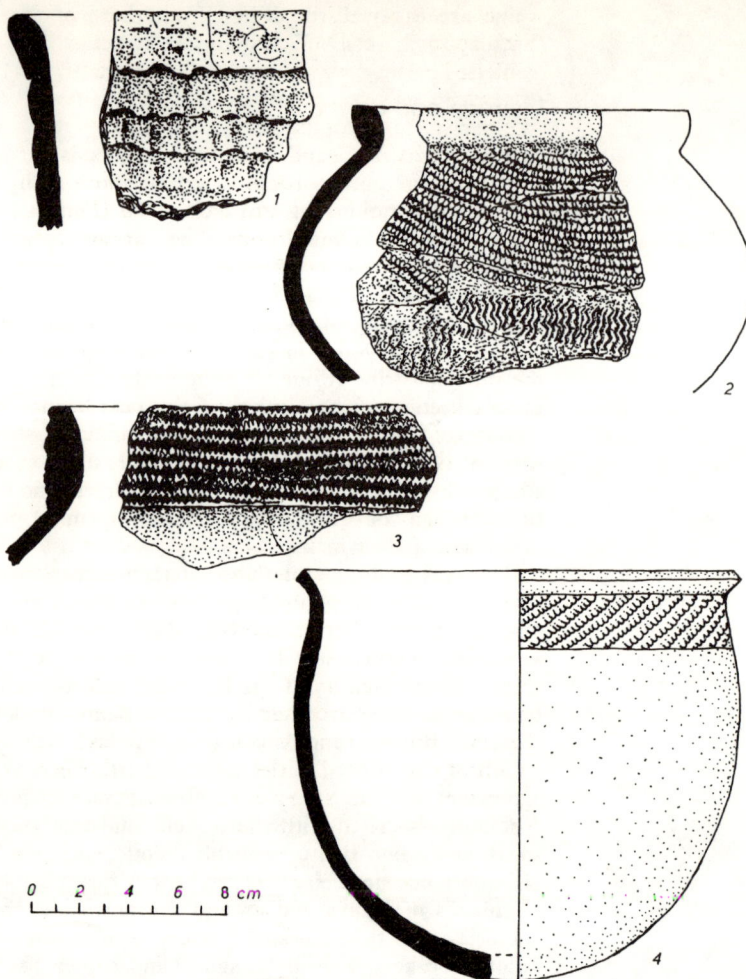

Fig. 56 Later Iron Age pottery from the East African interior: 1–3, from Chobi (after Soper, 1971b); 4, from Uvinza (after Sutton and Roberts, 1968)

It is instructive to compare Soper's Chobi ware with two other pottery occurrences in East Africa which appear to occupy a comparable place in the overall archaeological sequence. In Rwanda, 'boudiné' pottery resembling that from Chobi comes from Nyirankuba in apparent association with Urewe ware (Hiernaux and Maquet, 1960). Several sites from the Kisii District of south-western Kenya, for which a date in the first millennium ad is provisionally indicated, have yielded pottery comparable but not identical to that from Chobi (Bower, 1973b). This 'Kisii soft ware' was apparently the work of people who led a settled life and who may have been workers of iron. Although all three areas – Chobi, southern Rwanda and Kisii – are now occupied by Bantu-speakers, there are no compelling reasons for attributing these prehistoric pottery industries to speakers of such languages.

In all three areas (and, indeed through almost all the Lake Victoria basin and southwards through Rwanda and Burundi), the more recent vessels are rouletted, but in Kisii another distinctive ware decorated with applied bosses of clay intervenes before the appearance of the rouletted pottery, which may there be a relatively recent introduction. Elsewhere, as already noted, it is traceable back into the first half of the present millennium. Its association with the early developmental stages of at least some of the interlacustrine kingdoms is attested at the extensive earthwork sites of Bigo (Shinnie, 1960; Posnansky, 1969), Ntusi (Lanning, 1970) and Bweyorere (Posnansky, 1968a). These sites, recalled in oral traditions as ancient capitals, attest to the plentiful labour which their builders were able to organize. Not only do the Bigo earthworks extend for more than 10 kilometres in overall length, the supporting works such as the water-storage dams at Ntusi are equally impressive (Fig. 57). Excavations of the remains of large circular houses with elaborately constructed hearths, comparable with the chiefs' dwellings of more recent times, have been taken as confirmation that these sites served as centres for political authority in the early days of the kingdoms. The longest single developmental sequence of the rouletted pottery is at the salt-working site of Kibiro on Lake Albert (Hiernaux and Maquet, 1968): Soper and Golden (1969) have suggested that there may be a tendency for use of roulettes made of twisted cord to be earlier than those which were plaited. The distribution of rouletted pottery extends southwards to the Mwanza region on the southern shore of Lake Victoria (Soper and Golden, *op. cit.*) and further, to Uvinza on Lake Tanganyika.

At Uvinza are brine springs, the exploitation of which for salt during the Early Iron Age has already been discussed in chapter VI. Use of these springs has continued through the later Iron Age into recent times; and by the twelfth or thirteenth century ad their operators were using pottery, quite distinct from that of their predecessors, some of which bears incised decoration while the rest is

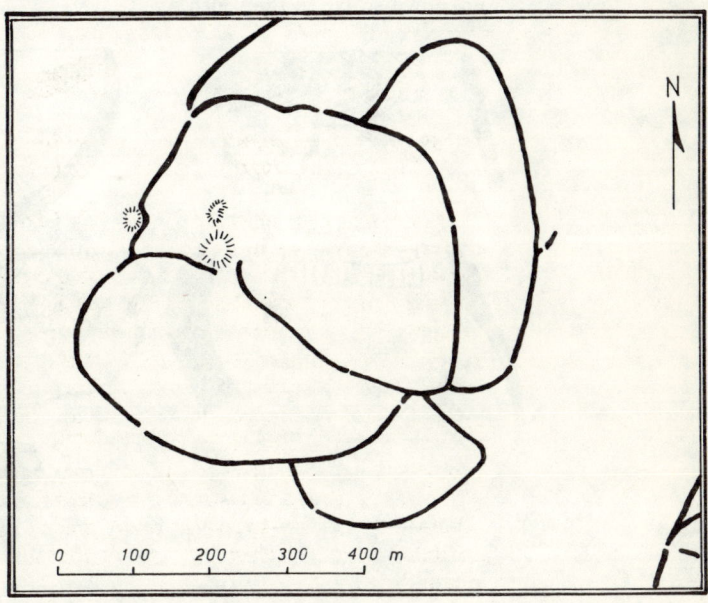

Fig. 57 Plan of the Bigo earthworks (after Posnansky, 1969)

rouletted (Sutton and Roberts, 1968). A final phase dates to the nineteenth century, when the Vinza are known to have worked the springs on a large scale. The pottery of this time is almost exclusively rouletted, the decoration being more close-set and less distinct than it was on the earlier vessels.

Southern and central Tanzania

Some 400 kilometres to the south of Uvinza, at Ivuna on Lake Rukwa, are further salt pans which have likewise been exploited for many centuries (Fagan and Yellen, 1968). Dumps dating from the eleventh or twelfth to the fourteenth or fifteenth centuries have been excavated. Here, none of the pottery is rouletted: instead there is a wide variety of decorative techniques including incision, grooving, comb-stamping and use of applied bosses or ribs (Fig. 58). Some of the vessels would not be out of place in assemblages of the later Iron Age Luangwa tradition in Zambia further to the south, while the pottery from the more recent levels is comparable with that still made in the area today by the Nyamwanga people. Domestic cattle and goats were herded by the Ivuna people, who also cultivated sorghum. Imported glass beads, generally rare on all Iron Age sites in the East African interior except the most recent, were surprisingly plentiful.

Elsewhere in southern Tanzania, the later Iron Age remains virtually unknown. John Sutton (1973c) has investigated a number of sites in the Southern Highlands where there are traces of rectangular mud-built houses associated with sparse scatters of pottery: this material is too fragmentary to permit detailed description, but it is noteworthy that rouletted sherds are completely absent. Indeed, it appears that rouletting has been adopted as a decorative technique by Hehe potters during the past century, but that it was previously unknown so far to the south.

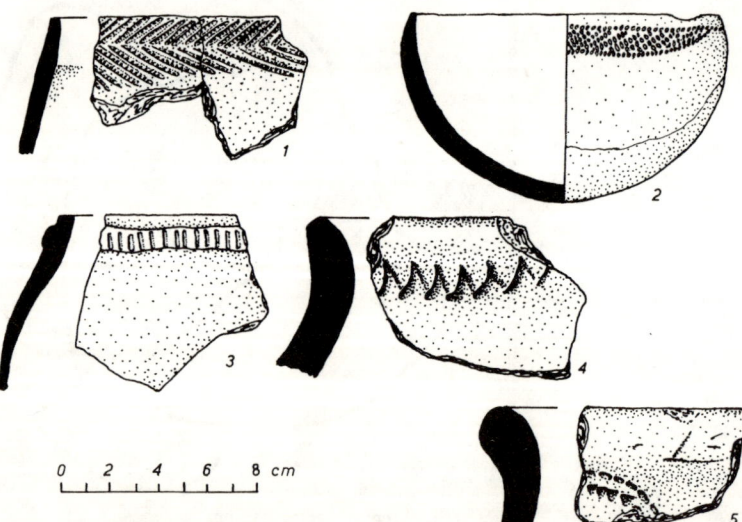

Fig. 58 Later Iron Age pottery: 1–3, from Ivuna (after Fagan and Yellen, 1968); 4, 5, Maore ware from the slopes of Kilimanjaro (after Odner, 1971c)

North-eastern Tanzania and south-eastern Kenya

It is now necessary to review the very incomplete state of our knowledge of the later Iron Age Bantu-speakers in more easterly regions of the East African interior. The greater part of central and eastern Tanzania remains unexplored by archaeologists, although in parts of Iramba and Irangi in the Central Highlands, there is evidence – as yet undated and unattributed to any specific population group – for the manufacture of cord-impressed and comb-stamped pottery before the adoption of rouletting in relatively recent times (Odner, 1971a; Liesegang, 1975). The only remaining part of Tanzania for which we have useful data is the north-east, where preliminary survey work has been undertaken on the slopes of Kilimanjaro and in the Pare and Usambara Mountains (Soper, 1967b; Odner, 1971b; 1971c). All of this area appears to have been occupied by the Early Iron Age makers of Kwale ware until at least the ninth or tenth century ad. Towards the close of the first millennium appears a distinct pottery type, known as Maore ware, which may at some sites such as Usangi Hospital in North Pare overlap with the final stages of the Early Iron Age. There is, however, no indication of assimilation between the two traditions. The Maore ware makers obtained meat from hunting and from the herding of cattle and small stock: it is probable that they were also cereal agriculturalists. They obtained beads and other shell ornaments from the coast. Pottery comparable with Maore ware comes from the Taita Hills in south-eastern Kenya. Throughout the area the archaeology of the present millennium remains obscure. There is evidence for the use of several later Iron Age pottery types with punctate, comb-stamped and wavy-line decoration, but no detailed sequences, fully analysed assemblages or well-dated sites are yet available, nor can this pottery be linked with that of any of the present peoples who inhabit the area.

The later Iron Age of the eastern Kenya highlands has only recently begun to receive archaeological attention. The greater part of the area shows evidence for a scattered occupation by makers of Early Iron Age pottery akin to, or derived from, Kwale ware. At Gatung'ang'a near Nyeri, Ari Siiriäinen (1971) has investigated a settlement dated to between the eleventh and the fourteenth century, where the pottery appears to be a late derivative of the Kwale tradition and shares several typological features with Maore ware from further to the south. Although the few chronological data which are currently available are not wholly consistent with the hypothesis, it is nevertheless tempting to suggest that Maore ware may represent a development from the Early Iron Age of the eastern Kenya highlands which spread southwards from there into what is now north-eastern Tanzania. When this pottery tradition was replaced by that of the modern Gikuyu, Kamba and Embu people, all of whom today make almost exclusively undecorated vessels often with everted squared rims, is not known; but there is no convincing evidence for any intervening tradition. Unpublished work by Robert Soper in the Taita and Chyulu areas of south-western Kenya has revealed the presence there of similar undecorated pottery, which is also of frequent occurrence throughout Ukambani. This observation lends support to those traditions which claim an origin in just this area for the Kamba and perhaps others of the Bantu-speaking people of the Kenya Eastern Highlands, there being no archaeological or linguistic evidence (except possibly in the case of the Meru, north-east of Mount Kenya) to confirm the alternative tradition which derives them from a northerly area of the coast – Shungwaya (Forbes-Munro, 1967).

In conclusion, it must be admitted that our present knowledge of the later Iron Age in the East African interior provides, at least as far as the Bantu-speaking areas are concerned, a very inadequate basis for synthesis. It is clear that there was a break from the Early Iron Age Industrial Complex which probably took place in most areas around the beginning of the present millennium, but perhaps later in the Eastern Highlands of Kenya. Throughout the later Iron Age, the Bantu-speakers of the greater part of East Africa must have been in contact with members of other language groups whose remains generally cannot be readily differentiated in the archaeological record. It has been argued that in the more westerly areas such contact with Nilotic-speakers may be indicated by the adoption of rouletting as a technique of pottery decoration. Subsequently, this practice spread much further to the south through an exclusively Bantu-speaking population, a process which is still continuing.

It is noteworthy that the most centralized and bureaucratic of the state systems developed by East African Bantu-speakers arose in the interlacustrine region where Nilotic influence was probably most pronounced, but the extent of inter-group contact involved in these political developments cannot be ascertained. In the north-east, the present social systems and economic practices of the Bantu-speakers, as outlined in chapter I, attest prolonged contact with peoples akin to those who now speak Cushitic languages, but these populations cannot yet be recognized in the archaeological record. However, linguistic studies confirm the extent of interaction which has gone on between the later Iron Age Bantu-speakers and Nilotic and Cushitic groups in these two principal regions.

Little information is likewise available on which could be based a reconstruction of the economy of the East African later Iron Age, most of the archaeological work which has so far been undertaken having been designed to obtain samples of pottery and material for dating. There is, however, sufficient scattered evidence to support a view of settlement in semi-permanent villages or scattered homesteads, a generally mixed-farming economy, and only small-scale working of metals. Long-distance trade may be inferred only in the case of salt: until very recent times there appears to have been remarkably little trade-contact with the coast. Although unattested archaeologically, an exception to this generalization must have occurred in the case of bananas, a crop of south-east Asian origin which traditionally formed – as it still does – the staple food of Buganda and some neighbouring areas. Bananas must have been established in the Lake Victoria area at an early stage of the later Iron Age if not before, in order to allow for the proliferation of local varieties which now exist there. We shall return to an evaluation of the East African data after an account has been presented of the comparable material from more southerly regions.

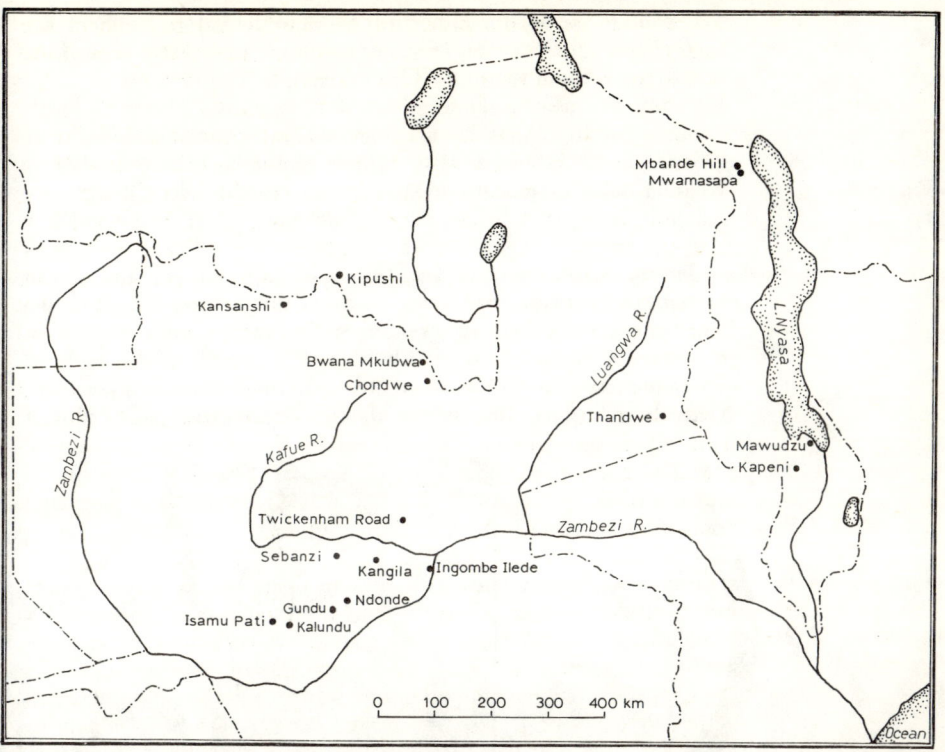

Fig. 59 Later Iron Age sites in Zambia and Malawi

ZAMBIA AND MALAWI

In contrast with that of the Early Iron Age, the archaeology of the later Iron Age of Zambia and Malawi is known only from relatively few, widely scattered parts of the region (Fig. 59). It can be shown that in several areas the various later Iron Age pottery traditions were established by early in the present millennium, and that in most cases they have been continued largely uninterrupted into recent times by the rapidly decreasing number of traditional potters.

Southern Zambia

The Iron Age sequence in southern Zambia is better known than that in any other part of the region, and this is doubtless reflected in the apparent complexity of the industrial succession. It is also here that the development of a later Iron Age pottery tradition from an Early Iron Age ancestor may best be discerned in the archaeological record. The case in point is that of the Kalomo pottery tradition; indeed, it is uncertain whether this tradition should be regarded as the earliest local manifestation of the later Iron Age or the final local representative of the Early Iron Age.

Joseph Vogel (1970; 1971*b*) has published convincing evidence for the development of the Kalomo tradition from a late phase of the Dambwa group sequence of the Victoria Falls region. Thence, around the end of the ninth century ad, its practitioners appear to have begun

to expand to the north and north-west on to the Batoka plateau where
their characteristic pottery (Fig. 60) rapidly displaced that of the Early
Iron Age Kalundu group. This transition was first noted at the
Kalundu site near Kalomo where it is, however, obscured by the
disturbed stratigraphy; it is also exposed further north at Gundu and
Ndonde in the Choma District. However, the best illustration of the
Kalomo industry as a whole is at Isamu Pati, 16 kilometres west of
Kalomo, a site which had no previous Early Iron Age occupation
(Fagan, 1967b).

Throughout the area of distribution of the Kalomo industry iron-
working appears to have been practised on a smaller scale than it
had been previously – arrow- and spear-heads, chisels, knives and
razors being the most frequently encountered tools of this material.
Hoes and axes, while present, are extremely rare. Copper, used
virtually exclusively for the manufacture of bangles, continued to be

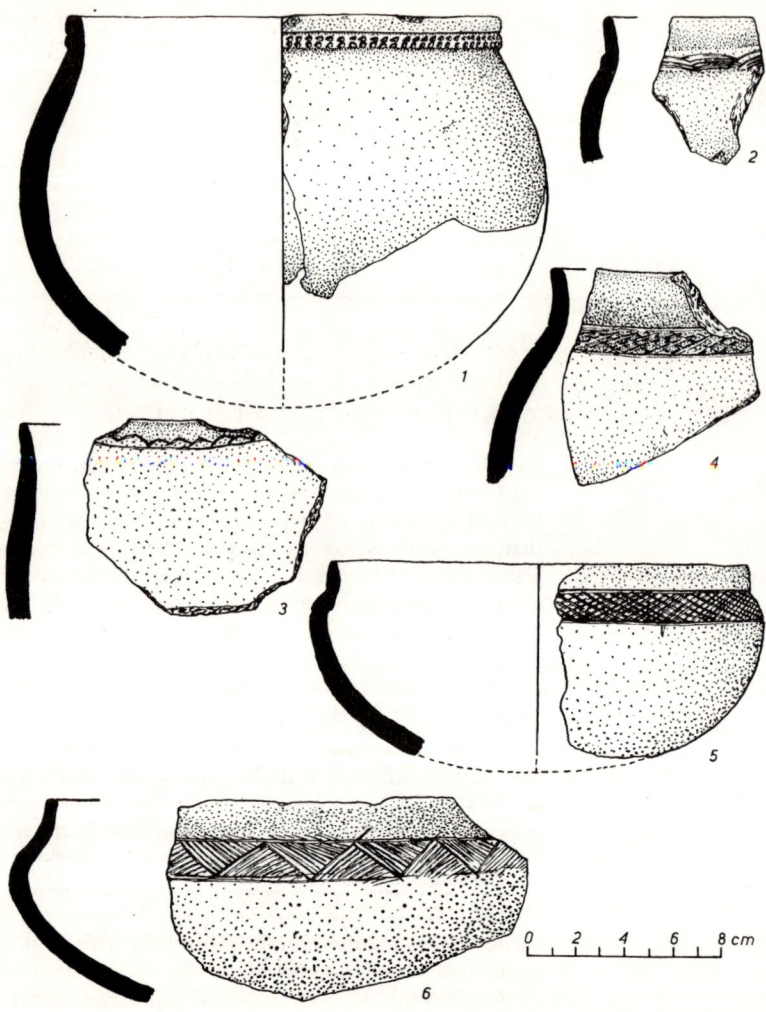

Fig. 60   *Pottery from southern Zambia (after Fagan, 1967b): 1–3, Kalomo ware;
4–6, Kangila ware*

obtained by trade, as in earlier times. Cattle and small stock form a higher proportion of the faunal material than they did in the Early Iron Age levels; domestic species now significantly outnumber wild ones, indicating a steady decrease in the importance of hunting as a source of protein. There is evidence for the cultivation of sorghum. Contact with the East Coast trade was more extensive than it had been during the Early Iron Age occupation, as is indicated by the presence of glass beads as well as conus and cowrie shells.

Many Kalomo industry villages were repeatedly re-occupied over several centuries, and this resulted in the accumulation of archaeological deposits up to 3 metres in depth. It is possible that the natural build-up of deposits was accentuated by artificial mound-building, but this is now considered unlikely. There are indications that the usual lay-out of these villages may have comprised a series of groups of circular, lightly constructed houses averaging some three metres in diameter. It has been suggested that these houses may have been arranged around open areas which could have been used as cattle kraals – a settlement pattern which has survived in southern Zambia into recent times. During the latest, post-Kalomo occupation of Isamu Pati this open area was also used for the interment of human burials. Corpses were generally buried in a contracted, occasionally seated, position. They were sometimes accompanied by one or two pots and generally wore a few iron bangles on their legs. One woman's skeleton at Isamu Pati was adorned with conus shells, glass beads and several thousands of shell disc beads in the neck and pelvic regions (Fagan, 1967*b*; Vogel, 1975*b*).

Around the second half of the eleventh century ad the Kalomo industry occupation of the Batoka Plateau appears to have come to an end. It was replaced, apparently fairly abruptly, by a southward spread of the Kangila industry from the northern areas of the Southern Province plateau. In the Kalomo area, this industry is best known from the upper levels of Isamu Pati. It spread also to the Victoria Falls region where its interface with the Kalomo industry, as at the Sinde site, is dated to around the late twelfth century ad (Vogel, 1970). This apparent time-lag of about a century between the appearance of the Kangila industry in the Kalomo and in the Victoria Falls regions is presumably a function of its southward spread. Before we proceed to discuss the nature of the Kangila industry in these southerly regions it will be well to turn to a consideration of its earlier development in the northern part of the Southern Province plateau.

The archaeological evidence for the early development of the Kangila industry is difficult to interpret. It is based largely on two sites: Sebanzi Hill north-west of Monze, and Ingombe Ilede near the Lusitu/Zambezi confluence 50 kilometres downstream of the Kariba Dam (Fagan and Phillipson, 1965; Fagan, 1969*b*). The initial occupation of Ingombe Ilede probably dates to the seventh or eighth century ad; that at Sebanzi to the same time or somewhat later. At both sites long successions of occupation took place, but the stratigraphy and chronology are somewhat unclear. The Sebanzi occupation apparently lasted into relatively recent times, perhaps until about the eighteenth century, while that at Ingombe Ilede probably ended around the beginning of the present millennium (with a subsequent re-occupation in the fourteenth or fifteenth centuries ad, to which we shall return below). The pottery at both sites is in clear contrast with that of the Early Iron Age Industrial Complex, and may be seen as ancestral to that excavated at Kangila on the plateau not far from Mazabuka.

Kangila itself was probably a single-occupation site, a village inhabited for a few decades sometime during the fifteenth century ad (Fagan, 1967*b*). It thus represents a relatively late phase of the industry to which it has given its name. The rare iron tools are basically similar to those of the Kalomo industry, and the indications are that the economies of the two groups were also directly comparable. Imported objects were not found at Kangila, but glass beads were recovered from the broadly contemporary levels of Sebanzi; and – as we shall see in a later section of this chapter – the second occupation of Ingombe Ilede shows that trade contacts between the East Coast and the Zambian interior had reached major proportions by this time.

The Luangwa tradition

The most widespread of the Zambian later Iron Age pottery traditions has been named the Luangwa tradition (D. W. Phillipson, 1974). It first appears in the archaeological record in approximately the eleventh century ad, widespread over the greater part of northern and eastern Zambia. At this time the pottery of the Luangwa tradition appears rapidly to have displaced, in their respective areas, that of the Kalambo, Chondwe, Kapwirimbwe and Nkope groups of the Early Iron Age. The nature and date of this interface is best seen at Chondwe and Twickenham Road, while confirmatory evidence has been recorded from rockshelter excavations at Nakapapula in Serenje District, and at several Eastern Province sites, most notably at Thandwe in Katete District (D. W. Phillipson, 1969; 1976*a*).

At both Chondwe and Twickenham Road, Luangwa tradition pottery (Fig. 61) makes a sudden appearance and is in marked contrast with that of the preceding Early Iron Age (Mills and Filmer, 1972; D. W. Phillipson, 1970*a*). It is at the latter site that the nature of the

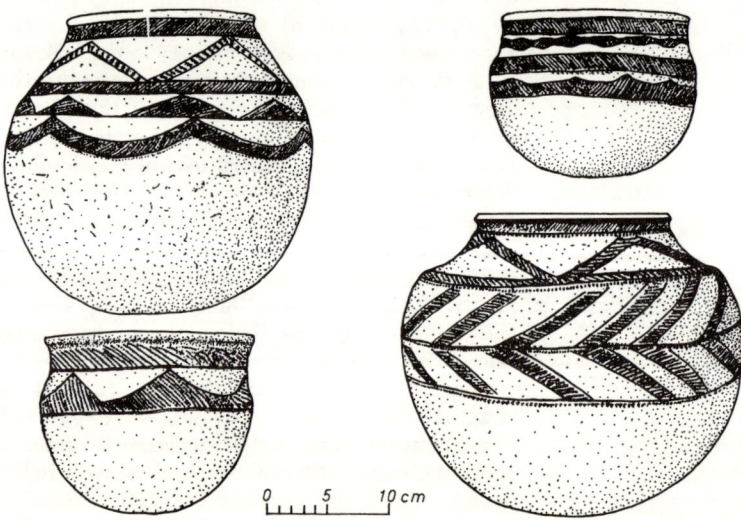

Fig. 61   Recent pottery of the Luangwa tradition (after D. W. Phillipson, 1974)

initial later Iron Age occupation is best illustrated. Deep cylindrical pits had been dug through the earlier deposits and contained abundant pottery as well as fragments of substantial pole-and-*daga* buildings. Iron slag was present, and finished tools included a razor, a bracelet and a needle. In addition to the iron bracelet, items of personal adornment comprised ivory bracelets, cowrie shells pierced for suspension or for sewing to clothing, an imported glass bead and many shell disc beads. Deeply concave grindstones were probably used for the grinding of grain. Bones of wild animals were preserved, together with those of domestic cattle and dog. Further excavations on early Luangwa tradition sites in other parts of Zambia are urgently needed to amplify these data.

Almost certainly it was the people responsible for the Luangwa pottery tradition who undertook the first large-scale exploitation of Zambian copper. We have seen how the mining and working of this metal remained at a low level during the Early Iron Age. By around the fourteenth or fifteenth centuries ad, however, there is evidence that extensive mining was being undertaken; and through these and the succeeding centuries were gradually dug the enormous mines at Kansanshi, Kipushi and Bwana Mkubwa which aroused the amazement of the early European prospectors, as well as hundreds of smaller workings mainly on the Copperbelt and around Mumbwa (Plate XVI, p. 190). Evidence was cited in chapter VI for cross-shaped copper ingots at Sanga showing a strong degree of standardization in weight, and their use as currency was tentatively suggested. In the later Iron Age, such use becomes much more strongly attested, as Michael Bisson (1975) has shown. Several types of ingot are represented (Fig. 62, p. 191) and one – a large flanged cross – is of great interest in view of its wide distribution through trade. Flanged copper crosses of this type were apparently manufactured near Kipushi on the Zambezi/Congo watershed from the fourteenth century ad onwards. It is to these later Iron Age times also that may be attributed the tall iron-smelting furnaces which still stand in many parts of northern and eastern Zambia: a typical example is shown in Plate XVII (p. 192).

As noted above, the first appearance of the Luangwa tradition over a wide area is dated to around the eleventh century ad. It survives today as the major modern pottery tradition over almost the whole of Zambia lying north and east of a line reaching from Lubumbashi to the lower Kafue. Its distribution also extends into neighbouring regions of Rhodesia, Zaïre, Malawi and Mozambique. Peoples who today make pottery of the Luangwa tradition include the Chewa, Nsenga, Ngoni, Tumbuka, Soli, Lala, Lamba, Bisa, Bemba, Mambwe and northern (Kazembe's) Lunda. Among all these people, domestic pottery of the Luangwa tradition is exclusively the work of women, although other artefacts of fired clay, such as tewels, smoking pipes and weights for fishing nets, are frequently made by men. It has been suggested that potting in Early Iron Age times was done by men; the fact that the opposite sex was responsible for pottery manufacture among the later Iron Age immigrant culture would explain the remarkable clarity of the break between the two traditions and the almost complete lack of continuity of characteristic Early Iron Age ceramic traits into the Luangwa tradition (D. W. Phillipson, 1974).

In all areas the contrast between the Luangwa tradition pottery and that of the preceding Early Iron Age is pronounced; and there is no

Plate XVI The prehistoric copper mine at Bwana Mkubwa, Zambia, as it was seen by the first European prospectors

clear evidence for a transition or integration from one to the other. It has, however, been noted that the Early Iron Age pottery which shows greatest affinity to that of the Luangwa tradition is that of the Chondwe group; and it would appear that the presently unknown ancestor of the former ware may prove to be more closely related to the Chondwe group pottery than to that of any other Early Iron Age group currently recognized.

Subsequent internal development within the Luangwa tradition is not well known. It is clear that typological change has been on a relatively small scale during the eight or nine centuries which have

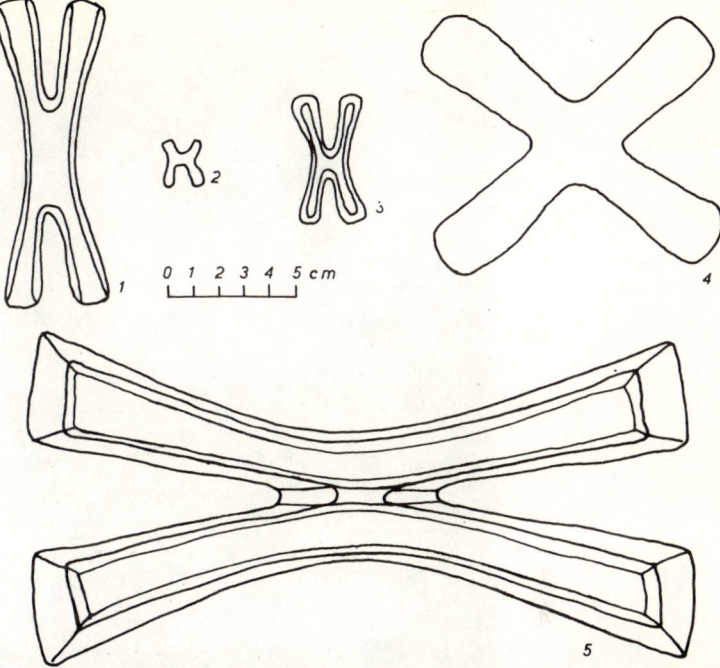

Fig. 62 *Types of copper cross-ingot from Iron Age sites in Zambia and Shaba (after Bisson, 1975): 1–3, from Sanga, Early Iron Age; 4, from the Shaba Copperbelt, nineteenth century; 5, from Ingombe Ilede, c. fifteenth century*

elapsed since the tradition's first appearance in the Zambian archaeological record. Within the last century it may be noted that there has been greater variability between pottery made by members of the various societies noted above than there has been within any individual society. The significance of this observation is discussed below.

A comparable picture is now available for the greater part of Malawi, thanks largely to research recently undertaken by Keith Robinson (1966a; 1970; 1973a; 1975). In the central area, the Early Iron Age Nkope ware appears to have been replaced, around ad 1000, by a distinctive pottery style named after Kapeni Hill in the Ncheu District. Kapeni ware has a restricted distribution and radiocarbon dates indicate an age somewhere between the early tenth and the mid-fifteenth centuries (Cole-King, 1973a). It lacks the characteristic rim thickening of Nkope pottery, and is generally decorated with grooving or incision. The later pottery of the area is known as Mawudzu ware, for which radiocarbon dates cover the period from the mid-fourteenth to the mid-seventeenth centuries. It has been tentatively attributed both by Robinson (1970: 120) and by Cole-King (1973a: 12) to the Maravi. Both Kapeni and Mawudzu pottery are clearly related to that of the Luangwa tradition, but it would be premature to subsume them within that tradition until more data are available.

In the north of Malawi, Mwabulambo ware appears to have been replaced by, or to have evolved into, that known from the site of Mwamasapa on the Rukuru river near Karonga, dated between the early eleventh and the early sixteenth centuries. It seems to be the

Plate XVII Iron-smelting furnace near Kabwe, Zambia (photograph by the late J. H. Chaplin). The scale is in inches

northern counterpart of Kapeni pottery. Here, the time-span of the more southerly Mawudzu ware is taken by a type of pottery named after Mbande Hill, Karonga, the installation place of the chiefs of the Ngonde, with which people the pottery may confidently be associated. Here again, affinities with the Luangwa tradition are marked. Throughout the Malawi later Iron Age little detailed economic evidence is available, but there have been occasional finds of teeth of domesticated cattle associated with Mawudzu ware, and seeds of sorghum with Mwamasapa pottery. Pole-and-*daga* houses are indicated at some sites, as also are less permanent beehive-shaped structures. Iron and occasional copper objects are attested throughout, and there are rare imported glass beads.

In the area of the Luangwa tradition it is possible to make useful comparisons between the testimony of oral tradition and that of archaeology. It has been noted above that there is evidence for a striking continuity of pottery tradition over most if not all of the Luangwa tradition's distribution from the time of its inception around the eleventh century up to the present day. It is reasonable to suggest that this observation is indicative of a basic continuity of population through this time.

Oral tradition testifies to the occurrence around the middle of this period – in about the fourteenth to seventeenth centuries – of large-scale migrations which resulted in the establishment of the various states and kingdoms of Lunda/Luba origin which have survived into recent times (but see J. C. Miller, 1972). However, it now appears that the migrations recalled in the oral traditions of many societies in this area were in fact relatively small affairs, and that they relate to the origin not of the whole people but of the ruling group or clan (Langworthy, 1972). There has thus been in northern and eastern Zambia (and probably also in much of Malawi) a much greater continuity of population during the past eight or nine centuries than a literal interpretation of the oral traditions would indicate. The migrations referred to in the traditional histories should be regarded as relating to the arrival of comparatively small groups of people who succeeded in setting themselves up in political authority over a part of the previously relatively undifferentiated population. This in turn led to the breaking up of this population between the various states whose origins, subsequent development and interactions are the major topics of many traditional histories.

In Malawi and eastern Zambia it is possible, as Matthew Schofeleers (1973) has suggested, to recognize the ruling Phiri clan of the Chewa as derived from an influx of people who arrived in about the fourteenth century, other clans – such as the Banda and Mbewe – having been established in the area some hundreds of years previously. This view is in accord with the archaeological evidence from eastern Zambia (D. W. Phillipson, 1976a), while in Malawi Robinson has proposed that Kapeni ware may be attributed to a pre-Phiri Chewa population.

The reflection of these state-formation processes is the tendency for Luangwa tradition pottery to show minor variation between individual societies, although the tradition itself is common to many societies which traditionally claim widely disparate origins. Even the large-scale and relatively well-documented incursions of the Ngoni into eastern and northern Zambia during the nineteenth century (Omer-Cooper, 1966) has left little mark on the archaeological record, apart from the numerous almost inaccessible sites where the indigenous population sought refuge from the Ngoni raiders. There is at this time no trace of an immigrant pottery tradition and, today, Ngoni people in eastern Zambia make Luangwa tradition pottery which is virtually indistinguishable from that of their Chewa neighbours; likewise, the Ngoni language has been almost entirely superseded by those of the Nsenga and Chewa (D. W. Phillipson, 1974).

Western Zambia and adjacent regions

To the west of the area of the Luangwa tradition, the later Iron Age archaeology presents a markedly contrasting picture. As noted in chapter VI, the Early Iron Age in this region is not well known, but the Lubusi site in Kaoma District has provided the first useful and dated collection of undoubted Early Iron Age pottery: it has been described above. There is a remarkable similarity between the Lubusi pottery and that still made in the area today. Indeed, the modern pottery tradition of north-western Zambia, which has been named the Lungwebungu tradition (D. W. Phillipson, 1974), may be regarded as displaying a marked degree of continuity with that of the local Early Iron Age as exemplified at Lubusi. The modern distribution of the Lungwebungu tradition is restricted to the Mwinilunga, Kabompo, Kaoma, Zambezi and Mongu–Lealui Districts, together with other areas of western Zambia at least as far south as Senanga and the Matabele Plain. This pottery (Fig. 63) is made by the western Lunda, Ndembu, Lovale and Old Mbunda, by the more recently established 'Wiko' peoples, and also by related peoples over a wide area of Angola. In these societies pottery manufacture is done by men just as, it has been surmised above, was the case in Early Iron Age times.

The hypothesis that the modern Lungwebungu pottery tradition is directly descended from that of the local Early Iron Age rests almost entirely on typological comparisons of collections widely separated chronologically. Recent investigations by Robin Derricourt in the upper Zambezi valley suggest that there may have been local interruption of this continuity by a distinctive pottery tradition attributed to a pre-Lovale people remembered as Mbwela (Derricourt and Papstein, 1976). The location and investigation of further sites attributed to the intervening centuries in north-western Zambia and, more especially, in neighbouring parts of Angola will be needed to test these theories before they may be regarded as proven. The westernmost site of this critical period yet known in Zambia, that from Kamusongolwa Hill near Kasempa, has yielded completely distinct pottery in an eleventh- to thirteenth-century context (Daniels, 1967). Recent research by Michael Bisson (1975) suggests that the affinities of this assemblage are with regions to the north rather than with those to the west.

The inter-relationship between the traditional history of western Zambia and the imperfectly known archaeology of that region remains far from clear. It should be noted that in this area several peoples, such as the western Lunda, claim an origin closely related to that of the more easterly societies discussed above; yet the Lungwebungu pottery tradition which the former people practise is markedly distinct from the Luangwa tradition of the latter. Here also, therefore, the establishment of states of Lunda/Luba origin clearly involved no significant disruption of the pre-existing pottery tradition; and any migration which may have been connected with the state-formation process must have been on a relatively small scale. In contrast to this, when the Kololo established their suzerainty over the Barotse Plain and downstream reaches of the upper Zambezi valley during the nineteenth century (Mainga, 1973), this was accompanied by the establishment of a new pottery tradition (Fig. 63) which has been named the Linyanti tradition (D. W. Phillipson, 1974). Wares of this type, which

are today made exclusively by women, are closely related to some
modern Tswana and Sotho types; and there can be little doubt that
they were introduced into what is now Zambia by the Kololo during
the second quarter of the nineteenth century. The Kololo were also
responsible for the introduction of the modern Lozi language which
has rapidly almost entirely replaced the earlier Luyana.

The later Iron Age in western Zambia belongs to a culture area
which extends far to the west into Angola and, probably, parts of
southern Zaïre also. Here, there is no trace of the pronounced break
in pottery traditions which is such a marked feature of the Iron Age
sequence further to the east. The significance of this observation
will be considered in detail both in a later section of this chapter and
in chapter VIII.

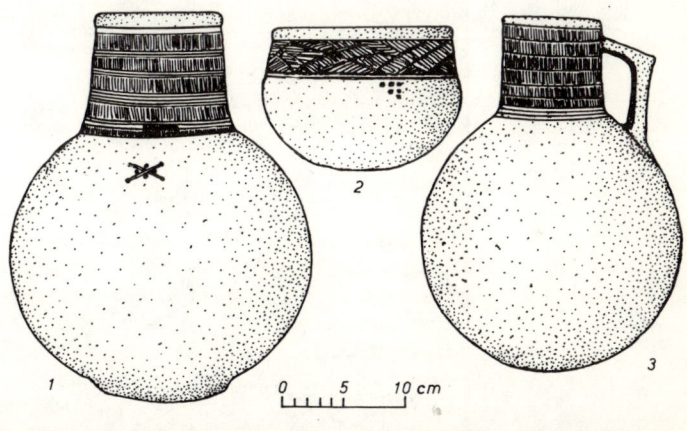

Fig. 63 Recent pottery from western Zambia (after D. W. Phillipson, 1974):
1–3, Lungwebungu tradition; 4, 5, Linyanti tradition

FROM THE ZAMBEZI TO THE LIMPOPO

The archaeological sequence of the Rhodesian later Iron Age follows a fairly uniform pattern over the greater part of the region, although the inter-relationships of the several local successions which have been investigated are not always clear. The relatively well-known material from the Bulawayo region (Fig. 64) forms a convenient start and reference point for the account which follows.

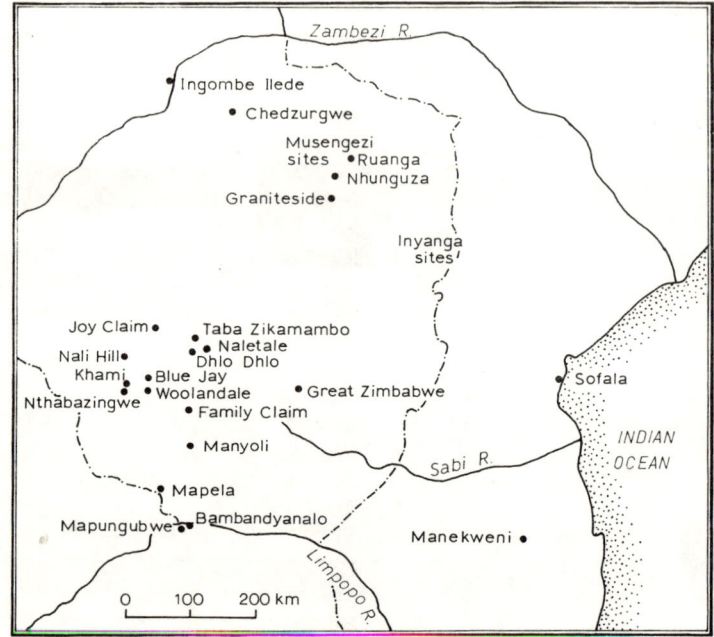

Fig. 64 Later Iron Age sites in Rhodesia and adjacent areas

Matabeleland and the Limpopo valley

It was shown in the previous chapter how an initial Gokomere–like Early Iron Age occupation of Matabeleland was replaced, probably around the seventh century ad, by a distinct but related eastern stream manifestation known as Zhizo. Zhizo was formerly regarded (e.g. by Robinson, 1966*b*) as the earliest phase of a tripartite local industrial succession known as the Leopard's Kopje industry – the latter name being a translation of Nthabazingwe, a rocky outcrop near Khami, 20 kilometres west of Bulawayo. Subsequent research by Thomas Huffman (1971*b*; 1974*a*) has demonstrated conclusively that Zhizo does not belong to the same industrial tradition as do the two following phases: he proposes – and the same scheme will be adopted here – that the Leopard's Kopje tradition is exclusively of the later Iron Age, and that it began with the Mambo phase (formerly known as Leopard's Kopje II) in the eleventh century ad.

The Mambo phase is best represented by Huffman's (1974*a*) excavations at Nthabazingwe, where it overlay a Zhizo horizon. Detailed plans of circular houses were recovered: these appear generally to have been some 3 metres in diameter. Their walls were formed of vertical poles 8 to 12 centimetres thick, heavily plastered with puddled clay (*daga*). A similar material, finely finished, was used for the floors which, in some cases, incorporated features such as a circular fireplace surrounded by a *daga* kerb, a low bench and a shallow socket which may have been used as a pot-stand. Almost certainly these houses had conical thatched roofs which extended beyond the main wall to form a narrow verandah supported by an outer ring of posts. Comparable structures are still made in parts of Rhodesia today. Settings of stones noted in the Mambo horizons at Nthabazingwe are tentatively interpreted as the supports for grain-bins. There are no Mambo sites with which traces of stone walling are indubitably associated.

Mambo pottery (Fig. 65) presents a sharp contrast with the preceding Early Iron Age Zhizo material. Characteristic vessels are necked, with tapered rims: decoration is more frequently incised than comb-stamped and involves bands of looped or triangular motifs, often accompanied by a high burnish. Iron was worked at or near Nthaba-zingwe, but finished tools were few, including a hoe and an arrow-head. Occasional copper bangle fragments were also recovered. Contact with the coastal trade is indicated by occasional glass beads.

The mixed-farming economy of the Mambo folk is clearly illustrated in the archaeological record. Remains of sorghum, finger millet, ground beans and cowpeas were recovered. Animal bones were predominantly of domestic species with (in contrast to the situation in earlier times) those of cattle greatly outnumbering those of sheep and goats. The importance of cattle is further attested by the presence of numerous clay figurines, comparable with those from the contemporary or slightly later levels at Great Zimbabwe, on which humps and long horns are clearly apparent. A second class of figurines represent women with pronounced buttocks and spread legs: breasts and navel are sometimes cursorily represented, but the head and arms are completely ignored. Scarification of the torso is often indicated.

The second phase of the later Iron Age Leopard's Kopje industry, as re-defined by Huffman (1974a), is known as Woolandale after a farm of that name near Bulawayo, but the best illustration of its archaeology is that obtained by Huffman (*ibid.*) at Blue Jay/Bunting Close in suburban Bulawayo. It is differentiated from the Mambo phase primarily by the typology of its pottery, which shows an increased frequency of incised decoration at the expense of comb-stamping, while looped curvilinear designs become significantly more frequent. Spindle whorls, presumably indicating the manufacture of cotton cloth, make their first appearance in the Rhodesian archaeological record at this time (Huffman, 1971c). Several Woolandale sites near Bulawayo, notably Mambo Umboza and Nali Hill (Robinson, 1966b) are associated with stone walling. The Woolandale people were evidently involved in gold mining, since sherds of their pottery have been recovered from several ancient workings, notably those at the Joy Claim near Lonely, and the Family Claim at Filabusi (Summers, 1969), while Keith Robinson (1966b) has reported the discovery of a crucible containing traces of gold in Woolandale levels at Taba Zikamambo. Imported glass beads are more common than they were on earlier sites. Unfortunately, only one radiocarbon date for the Woolandale phase is yet available: it indicates an age in the thirteenth and fourteenth centuries and comes from the type-site near Bulawayo.

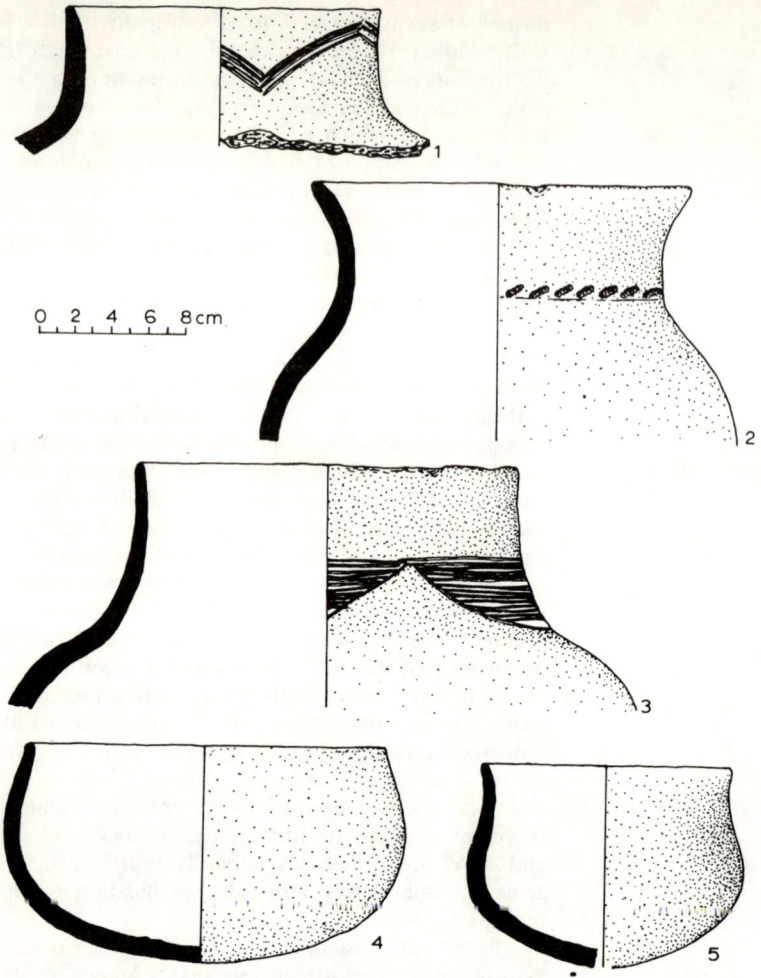

0 2 4 6 8cm

Fig. 65 Pottery of the Leopard's Kopje industry (after Robinson, 1966b): 1, 2, Mambo phase; 3–5, Woolandale phase

The distributions of both Mambo and Woolandale sites are centred on Bulawayo and extend westwards to beyond the Botswana border and southwards to the vicinity of Gwanda. Further to the south, as far as the Limpopo valley, are found sites which show a comparable process of development and which are now regarded as representing a southern facies of the Leopard's Kopje industry, divided into two phases – Bambandyanalo and Mapungubwe – which parallel the Mambo–Woolandale succession of the Bulawayo area (Huffman, 1974a).

The Bambandyanalo phase is best represented at the type-site (also known as K2) on the Transvaal side of the Limpopo valley near the Shashi confluence west of Messina (Gardner, 1963), where the occupation is now very securely dated to the eleventh and twelfth centuries ad. The large (200 metres across) mound of settlement debris is interpreted as representing successive occupations of circular huts built around a central kraal area. The associated pottery tends to be finer than its Mambo counterparts from the Bulawayo region, and shows an emphasis on bowl and beaker forms (Fig. 66). Its predominantly incised decoration presents elaborations of motifs described above from Nthabazingwe. Iron objects were extremely rare. Over seventy human skeletons were recovered, mostly from flexed burials associated with pottery vessels. Alexander Galloway (1959) has stated that these remains display 'not a single specifically Negro feature' but, more recently, Philip Rightmire (1970) has shown by multivariate analysis that a sample of seven of these individuals all fall within the range of metrical variation shown by modern South African Negroes – as, indeed, do all the skeletons which have been recovered from Leopard's Kopje contexts. This is in keeping with the completely Iron Age culture which is indicated for the inhabitants of Bambandyanalo, as Brian Fagan (1964) has emphasized. Extension of Bambandyanalo-type settlement north of the Limpopo valley is shown by finds described by Peter Garlake (1966) from Venzo Kopje near the Shashi/Shashani confluence.

At the nearby hill-top site of Mapungubwe (Fouché, 1937; see also Fagan, 1964), the initial occupation was virtually identical to that at Bambandyanalo. In the later levels, dated to the fourteenth or fifteenth centuries ad, the pottery is further elaborated and includes a number of remarkably shallow, finely burnished bowls. Iron, including hoes, arrow- and spear-heads, is more frequent, and spindle whorls – as on the contemporary Woolandale sites of the Bulawayo region – make

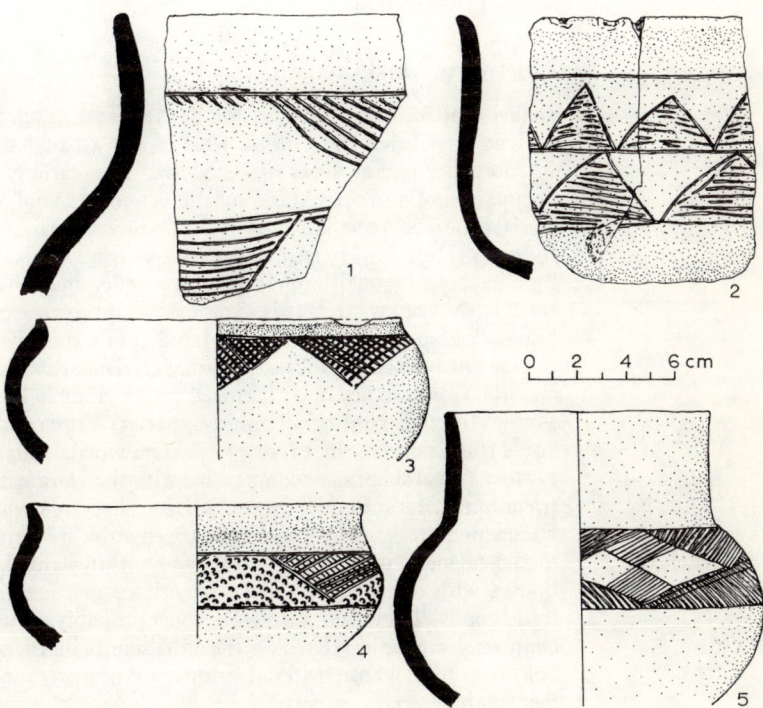

Fig. 66 Pottery from the northern Transvaal (after Fouché, 1937): 1, from Bambandyanalo; 2–5, from Mapungubwe

their appearance. *Daga* houses were more substantial and elaborate than they had been in earlier times (Gardner, 1963: 20): some had verandahs and walled courtyards. Human burials contained abundant glass beads as well as ornaments of copper and gold. Gold foil was affixed with tiny tacks to wooden objects including animal figures, bowls and staffs or clubs. There is also evidence for the working of ivory. Cultivation of sorghum and cowpeas is attested while, as at Bambandyanalo, both cattle and small stock were herded.

One hundred kilometres up the Shashi river lies the site of Mapela, contemporary and closely comparable with Mapungubwe. It is situated atop a 100-metre-high hill which was elaborately terraced to provide defences and level sites for building substantial *daga* houses. At this Mapungubwe phase settlement, Peter Garlake (1968*b*) sees evidence not only for the use of organized labour on a significant scale, but also for social stratification, indicated by the contrast between the central solidly constructed houses and the more flimsy ones on the periphery of the site. Here, in the context of the Leopard's Kopje industry of south-western Rhodesia, there are attested socio-political developments which parallel those of the broadly contemporary phase of the Great Zimbabwe industry further to the north-east. Events subsequent to the fifteenth century in this southern Leopard's Kopje area are not well known. An unexcavated site at Manyoli near West Nicholson, south of Gwanda, may represent a third phase of the Leopard's Kopje industry in this region, contemporary with the westward penetration of the Great Zimbabwe tradition which introduced the Khami phase to the Bulawayo area, as will be described later in this section.

Northern Mashonaland

Before embarking on a discussion of the Great Zimbabwe industry, it will be well briefly to outline what is known of its contemporaries in more peripheral areas of Rhodesia. The earliest later Iron Age occupation of northern Mashonaland is known mainly from a series of burial grounds in the Salisbury area. These are attributed to the Harare industry (Huffman, 1971*a*). The most extensive site is that investigated by Elizabeth Goodall (1962) at Graniteside, and dated to about the thirteenth century ad. Bowls and necked vessels recovered from these graves are sparsely if at all decorated, but extensive use was made of graphite burnishing (Whitty, 1958*b*; Garlake, 1967*b*). Contemporary material from further north, centred on the Sipolilo District, is known as the Musengezi industry (Robinson, 1965). Both open sites (Garlake, 1973*b*) and burials in caves (J. R. Crawford, 1967) are recorded. Pottery vessel shapes are comparable with the Harare material, but the predominantly stamped decoration is more frequent and graphite burnishing less so. The makers of Musengezi ware were cattle-herding mixed-farmers who lived in relatively insubstantial pole-and-*daga* houses with earth floors and apparently owned few metal objects or trade goods. They were displaced, most probably around the fifteenth century, by people related to the inhabitants of Ingombe Ilede (see below, p. 193), whose material culture was in many ways distinct from that of their predecessors.

Inyanga

In the far east of Rhodesia, the Inyanga highlands to the north of
Umtali were the scene of an extensive occupation by irrigation-based
terrace agriculturalists (Summers, 1958). Some of their remains appear
to date from the sixteenth to the eighteenth centuries, but the age of
their inception has not yet been demonstrated. In addition to terraces,
trackways, irrigation channels and associated works which cover a
total area of several hundreds of square kilometres, there are various
other stone-built structures. Most frequent, especially on high ground,
are subterranean stone-lined pits some six metres in diameter and three
metres deep, each reached by a sloping passage, which are interpreted
as stock-pens. Elsewhere are several types of enclosures of free-
standing walls, some evidently designed for domestic use, others
clearly defensive 'forts' with square loop-hole apertures in the solidly
constructed walls (Plate XVIII). The material culture associated with
these later Iron Age Inyanga sites indicates a substantial community
of mixed-farming peasants living in virtual isolation from their contemporaries in other regions. Their crudely made, incision-decorated
pottery represents a complete stylistic break from the Early Iron Age
Ziwa ware which was made in the region during the first millennium
ad. Iron was used for the manufacture of hoes, spear- and arrow-
heads, razors and thumb-piano keys: copper and imported beads were
both rare. The cultivated crops included bulrush millet, finger millet,
sorghum, ground beans, cowpeas and cucurbits: cattle and small stock
were herded.

Plate XVIII Stone-built 'fort' at Inyanga

The Great Zimbabwe tradition

It is against the background of these basically peasant communities of the later Iron Age in western, northern and eastern Rhodesia that we should view the rise and development of the Great Zimbabwe tradition in the central plateau regions. The ruins of impressive stone buildings at Great Zimbabwe itself, 28 kilometres south-east of Fort Victoria, have been the cause of much speculation and inquiry on the part of outsiders and European settlers for over a hundred years. Several accounts (e.g. Summers, 1963; Garlake, 1973*a*) are available for those interested in the history of research, fantasy, and prejudice which has been inspired by the Great Zimbabwe ruins: here, I shall attempt to summarize the latest findings and conclusions and to set them in the context of the general later Iron Age archaeology of southern Africa.

The buildings of Great Zimbabwe – the word *Zimbabwe*, derived from the Shona, means either 'stone houses' or 'venerated houses' – were erected on a steep-sided rocky hill and an adjacent valley floor in a well-watered fertile area near the south-eastern scarp of the Rhodesian plateau. The whole ruin field covers almost half a square kilometre. On the hill (known for many years as the Acropolis), the huge natural boulders have been linked by short sections of dry-stone wall built of neatly coursed, dressed blocks to form a series of inter-connected enclosures (Plates XIX, XX). In the valley is a series of larger, free-standing walled enclosures which in several cases surrounded a complex of circular *daga* houses linked to each other by short sections of stone wall (Fig. 67). One such enclosure, the so-called 'Temple' or 'Elliptical Building' (Plate XXI), stands out from

Plate XIX The western enclosure of the Hill Ruin at Great Zimbabwe

the others through its size and regularity of design: its complex also includes a solid conical tower ten metres high and nearly six metres in diameter at the base (Garlake, 1973a: 15–50).

The stone walling at Great Zimbabwe and related sites incorporates three styles of masonry, distinguished by the quality of the coursing and dressing of the constituent blocks. Study of the structural inter-relationship of walls of different styles enabled Anthony Whitty (1957) to establish that the poorly coursed walls were the earliest, followed by finely coursed ones of carefully dressed blocks. These were some-times elaborated by means of chevron or other designs of different sized blocks let into the walls. The uncoursed masonry was the most recent. The finest walling in the great enclosure reaches a height of some 10 metres and is up to 5 metres thick at the base. Such walls were pierced by narrow doorways roofed with stone or wooden lintels over which the upper courses of the wall continued without a break. The internal structures were often finely built of solid *daga* without an internal pole framework: the outer walls reached a height of over a metre, and the conical roof was supported on poles outside the line of the walls. Internal features and furnishings, also of *daga*, were much elaborated and reached a peak of craftsmanship rarely seen with this material in other parts of sub-Saharan Africa.

It is important not to over-estimate the complexity of the Great Zimbabwe stone architecture. Peter Garlake (1973a: 15-50) has pro-vided a clear and concise summary, with excellent illustrations, and emphasized that 'the methods of construction and bonding were extremely rudimentary ... lines, levels and plumb-bobs would have been unnecessary and even impractical over walls that curved continu-ously and whose faces often sloped backwards' (*loc. cit.*: 16–17). The

Plate XX Detail of the doorway shown in Plate XIX

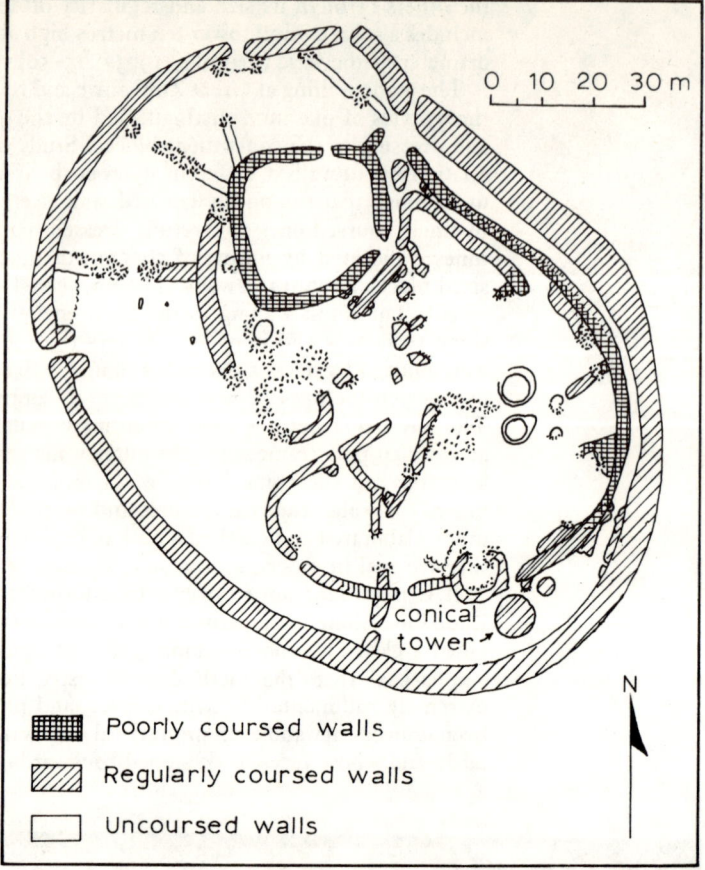

O 10 20 30 m

conical
tower

N

▓ Poorly coursed walls

▨ Regularly coursed walls

☐ Uncoursed walls

Fig. 67   Plan of the Great Enclosure at Great Zimbabwe (after Garlake, 1974)

doorways, stairs and platforms are all of forms which may readily
be traced back to those of simpler structures whose purely African
origin has not seriously been doubted, and ultimately to structures
in materials other than stone. The stone structures were not roofed.
Even the conical tower and the decorated walls, although showing
considerable refinement of execution, are basically simple in con-
ception and technology. Detailed study shows that the architecture
of Great Zimbabwe is a logical and refined development of a demonstrably African technology, in which no foreign influences may readily
be discerned.

The chronology of Great Zimbabwe itself still rests upon an inadequate foundation, particularly for the earlier periods. Only four
radiocarbon samples have been dated from securely stratified contexts;
and in each case the standard deviation of the result spans three
centuries. For a more accurate chronology, we must still resort to
correlations with more numerous and precise radiocarbon determinations which have been obtained from other sites, or to the evidence
provided by datable imported objects.

Excavations on the hill at Great Zimbabwe by Keith Robinson in
1958 revealed a succession of pottery styles which were used as the

Plate XXI The interior of the Great Enclosure, showing the conical tower, Great Zimbabwe

basis on which five phases of occupation were distinguished (Summers, Robinson and Whitty, 1961). The earliest of these belongs to the Early Iron Age, as has been noted above (p. 115), and is not associ-ated with any form of building in stone. Phases II to IV are now considered to represent developments of a single later Iron Age tradi-tion which began at Great Zimbabwe around 'the tenth and eleventh centuries, perhaps late in this period' (Garlake, 1973a: 182). The associated pottery (Fig. 68) is generally attributed to the Great Zimbabwe tradition (Garlake, *op. cit.*) or, less happily, to the 'Ruins tradition' (Huffman, 1971a). Phase II pottery, now sometimes referred to as Gumanye ware, is not well known, but the characteristic vessels are necked, generally undecorated, and have tapered rims which con-trast with the almost invariably thickened ones of Gokomere/Ziwa and other Early Iron Age wares. It is clearly intimately related to the broadly contemporary Mambo ware which marks the first mani-festation of the later Iron Age in Matabeleland: there are also strong similarities with the earlier occurrences of the Luangwa tradition in Zambia (p. 172, above), in which undecorated vessels are likewise predominant (Mills and Filmer, 1972). The earliest, poorly coursed, stone walling at Great Zimbabwe appears to be associated with the somewhat later but clearly derivative phase III. There is general agreement that the earliest occurrence of this phase dates to about ad 1300. The pottery displays a finer finish, the vessels characteristic-ally have more pronounced shoulders and vertical necks: decoration remains uncommon but includes bands of interlocking incised tri-angles. The buildings of this time were relatively simple walled en-closures and platforms which supported pole-and-*daga* structures much more substantial than those of earlier periods.

All the more elaborate structures, including the finest coursed stone architecture and the solid *daga* buildings, are attributed to the fourth phase. Formerly thought to be relatively recent, this has now been shown by Peter Garlake (1968*a*) to belong to the fourteenth and fifteenth centuries. All the substantial stone buildings at Great Zimbabwe were thus erected within a period of little more than two

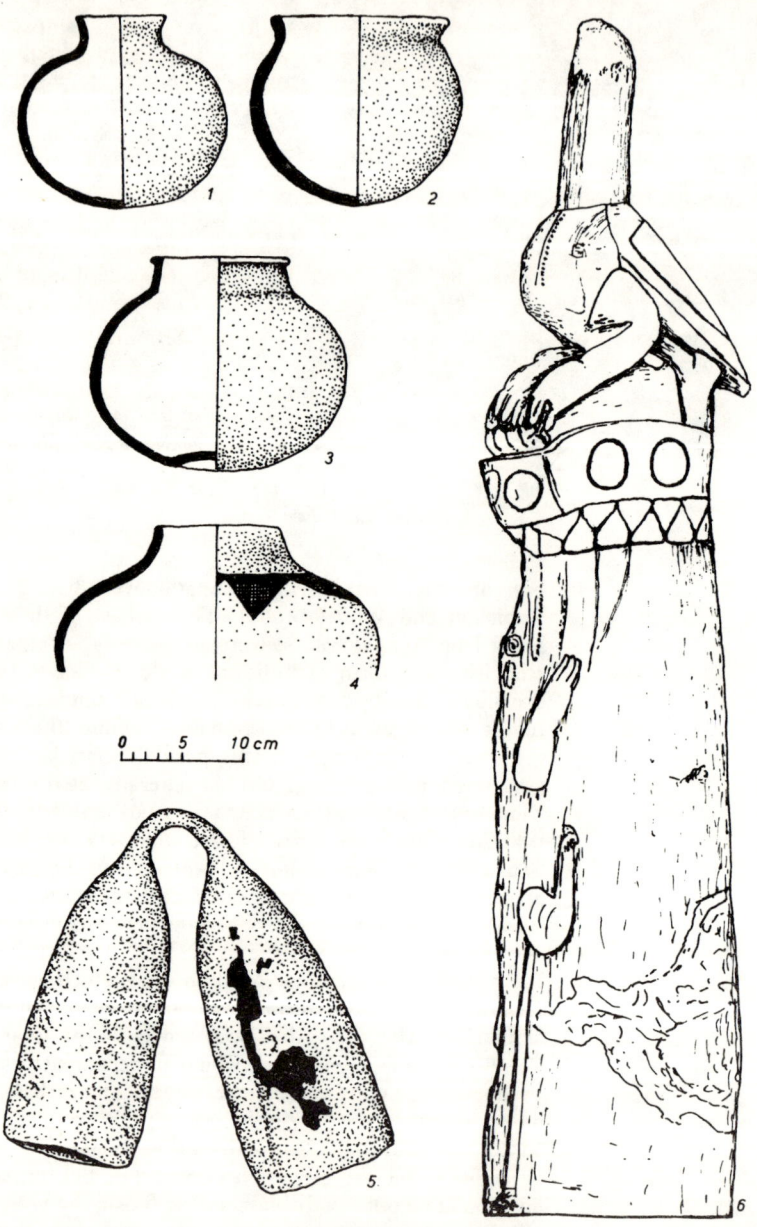

Fig. 68 *Artefacts from Great Zimbabwe (after Garlake, 1973a; 1974): 1, 2, pottery, 'period II'; 3, 4, pottery, 'period III'; 5, iron gong; 6 (not to scale), soapstone monolith*

hundred years, and the site had already declined in importance by the time the Portuguese penetrated the interior of Mashonaland in the first half of the sixteenth century. Indeed, Joao de Barros, writing in 1552 but quoting slightly earlier sources, describes a structure which can only be the great enclosure at Great Zimbabwe as being already ancient (Abraham, 1966; Garlake, 1973a: 51-3).

Economically, as well as technologically, the inhabitants of Great Zimbabwe appear to have followed development processes remarkably parallel to those of the Mambo and Woolandale folk in the area further to the west (Jaffey, 1966; Robinson, 1966f; Garlake, 1973a: 157). The distinctiveness of the later phase at Great Zimbabwe is due largely to the great florescence of the architecture which, as will be shown below, may be linked to the development of a powerful and strongly centralized political authority, and to a much greater degree of contact with the Indian Ocean trading network. Presumably these latter developments were interconnected to some degree, although it is not easy to separate cause from effect (*pace* Huffman, 1972). The trade objects recovered at Great Zimbabwe came originally from a variety of sources: Persian and Chinese glazed pottery, Near Eastern glass, tens of thousands of glass beads, cowrie shells from the East African coast and many other items attest the far-reaching contacts of the site's inhabitants during the fourteenth and early fifteenth centuries (Garlake, 1973a: 131–5). Imported objects are far more frequent here than at other contemporary and related sites in Rhodesia, so it is reasonable to conclude that Great Zimbabwe served as a centre for the trade in the products of the interior for those available from the coast. This hypothesis is strengthened by the presence at the site of gold objects, iron gongs and copper ingots, all of which are more typical of other regions.

So far in this narrative, the Great Zimbabwe site has been considered in virtual isolation. It is in fact one – by far the largest and most elaborate – of over one hundred and fifty comparable stone structures which are widespread through the granite regions of the Rhodesian plateau. Many of these ruins are small and, like Great Zimbabwe, they were clearly not sited in specifically easily defensible positions (e.g. Caton-Thompson, 1931: 121–62; Wieschoff, 1941; Robins and Whitty, 1966; Rudd, 1969; Garlake 1973b). A closely related, unusually large site has recently been investigated by Peter Garlake (1976) at Manekweni on the coastal plain of southern Mozambique. While the occupation of some of these sites may have begun as early as the beginning of the twelfth century ad, their florescence clearly took place during the fourteenth and fifteenth centuries. All have yielded pottery similar to that from contemporary deposits at Great Zimbabwe, indicating a close relationship between their inhabitants and the people of the latter site. In this context it is highly significant that, at Ruanga Ruin in northern Mashonaland, Garlake (1973b) observed that the stone building was erected directly over a peasant settlement of the Musengezi tradition (see p. 184, above). He considers it probable that the Musengezi people continued to live there and to practise their traditional technology even after the establishment of the alien Great Zimbabwe presence. Here, clearly, is archaeological evidence for the imposition – apparently peaceful – of centralized authority over a widespread and diverse peasant population – an authority which kept to itself control of the profitable coastal trade on which the prosperity of its capital at Great Zimbabwe was so largely based.

At Nhunguza Ruin, also in northern Mashonaland, Garlake (1973b) excavated the remains of a large circular *daga* house divided into three areas or rooms: respectively a large open area, a room containing a single *daga* seat, and a third secluded room with a stone platform fitted with sockets (Fig. 69). 'This hut seems to have been one in which a single authority backed, literally as well as symbolically, by ritual or religious emblems, held court. Such authority could well have been the basis on which the enclosures were established and maintained' (Garlake, 1973a: 164).

As in many Bantu-speaking states, political and religious authority appears here to have been intimately connected. Oral tradition is consistent in linking Great Zimbabwe with the worship of Mwari, the supreme god of the Shona-speaking peoples. Garlake (1973a) argues convincingly that the conventional fourteenth-century dating of the Mbire, the first Shona immigrants, based as it is on genealogical evidence, is several centuries too late and that the Mbire advent more probably occurred within the ninth- to thirteenth-century bracket proposed by Donald Abraham (1962). A link between the Mbire and the first stone buildings of Great Zimbabwe is therefore an acceptable hypothesis, although concrete supportive evidence is so far lacking. It is thus now possible to dispose of a persistent popular misapprehension about Great Zimbabwe – the site's supposed position as the capital of the Empire of Mwene Mutapa (Monomotapa). The title of Mwene Mutapa was assumed by an Mbire ruler of the early fifteenth century, Nyatsimba Mutopa, who was responsible for transferring the seat of his authority northwards to the middle Zambezi valley while retaining control of the southern provinces, Guruhuswa

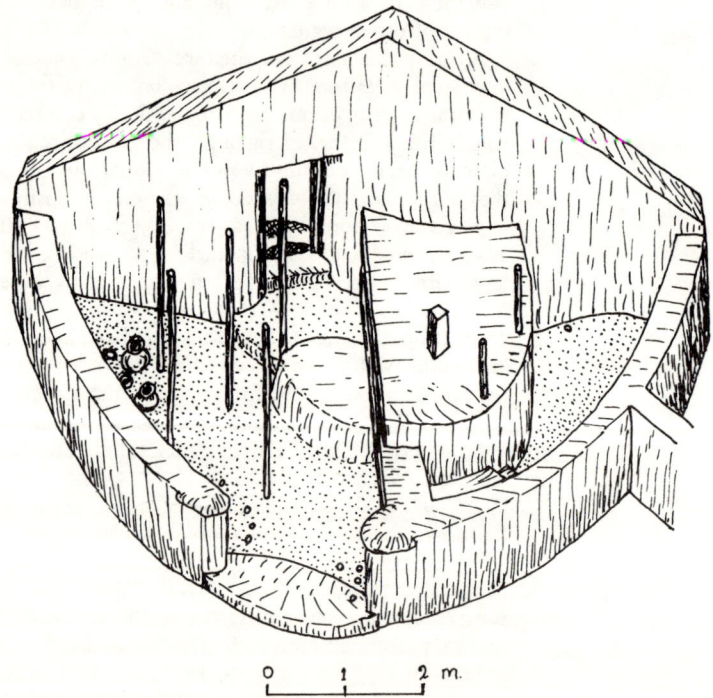

0   1   2 m.

Fig. 69   *Reconstruction of the main building at Nhunguza, northern Mashonaland (after Garlake, 1973b)*

in the area of the modern Matabeleland, and Mbire in southern Mashonaland, ruled respectively by the dynasties of Changamire and Torwa. The two latter areas, however, broke away from the Mwene Mutapa during the reign of Mukombero Nyahuma, son of Nyatsimba Mutota's son Matope. It is obvious that this process must be linked to the fifteenth-century decline of Great Zimbabwe which is so clearly indicated in the archaeological record. The Monomotapa described and visited by the Portuguese during the sixteenth and seventeenth centuries was a comparatively small state centred on northern Mashonaland.

Ingombe Ilede

It is against the background of this northwards shift in the distribution of power and wealth on the Rhodesian plateau that we can best interpret a cluster of sites in northern Mashonaland and at Ingombe Ilede in the adjacent stretch of the Zambezi valley just upstream of the Kafue confluence. The first occupation of Ingombe Ilede has been discussed on p. 171 above: it was re-occupied for a fairly brief period most probably in the late fourteenth or early fifteenth centuries. The re-occupation is marked by the presence of many finely made thin-walled bowls (Fig. 70), but most of our information is derived from a series of elaborate graves dug down into the earlier deposits (Fagan, 1969b; Phillipson and Fagan, 1969). The corpses, interred in an extended position, wore large numbers of bangles, mainly of copper, occasionally of iron and in one case of gold. Corrosion of the copper bangles had, in several places, ensured the preservation of cloth. Bark cloth and woven cotton have been identified, both probably of local manufacture, although a sample of unusually fine cotton cloth has tentatively been identified as being of Indian origin. Further decorations worn by the Ingombe Ilede corpses included conus shells from the East Coast, one of which had a backing of hammered sheet gold, gold beads and tens of thousands of imported glass beads. The other grave goods were predominantly of African origin, although they indicate far-ranging trade contacts over a substantial area of what is now Zambia and Rhodesia. These items included bundles of thick copper wire, lengths of copper bar, large, flanged, cross-shaped copper ingots weighing between 2.3 and 4.5 kilograms, and iron hammers, tongs, and drawing plates used for the production of copper wire (Plate XXII, p. 211). Also there were thin elongated iron hoes buried at the heads of the corpses, and single iron gongs formed by welding together two beaten sheets of metal (Fagan, 1969b). These discoveries amply demonstrate the metal-working ability of the inhabitants of Ingombe Ilede at this time, or that of neighbouring peoples with whom they came into contact.

The characteristic pottery of the later settlement of Ingombe Ilede has not been reported from any other major site in Zambia, although its decoration shows some degree of affinity with that of the Luangwa tradition, discussed above. To the south of the Zambezi, however, this pottery has been recovered from several sites in the Urungwe District on the northern plateau of Mashonaland. These sites are dated to a slightly later period than Ingombe Ilede, and have also yielded large numbers of copper crosses identical to those from the latter site. It may be concluded that Ingombe Ilede and the related Rhodesian sites were connected with a well-organized trade system, for which there is also evidence in early Portuguese records, involving the metal-producing areas both of Mashonaland (Garlake, 1970) and of the Zambia/Shaba Copperbelt where production of copper crosses identical to those from the Ingombe Ilede sites is attested from the fourteenth century ad (Bisson, 1975). This ties in with the evidence noted on p. 161 above for penetration of the Zambezi valley by coastal traders prior to the advent of the Portuguese, and is in accord with the view that this route to the coast gradually replaced that of the Sabi further south, on which Great Zimbabwe's prosperity had largely depended.

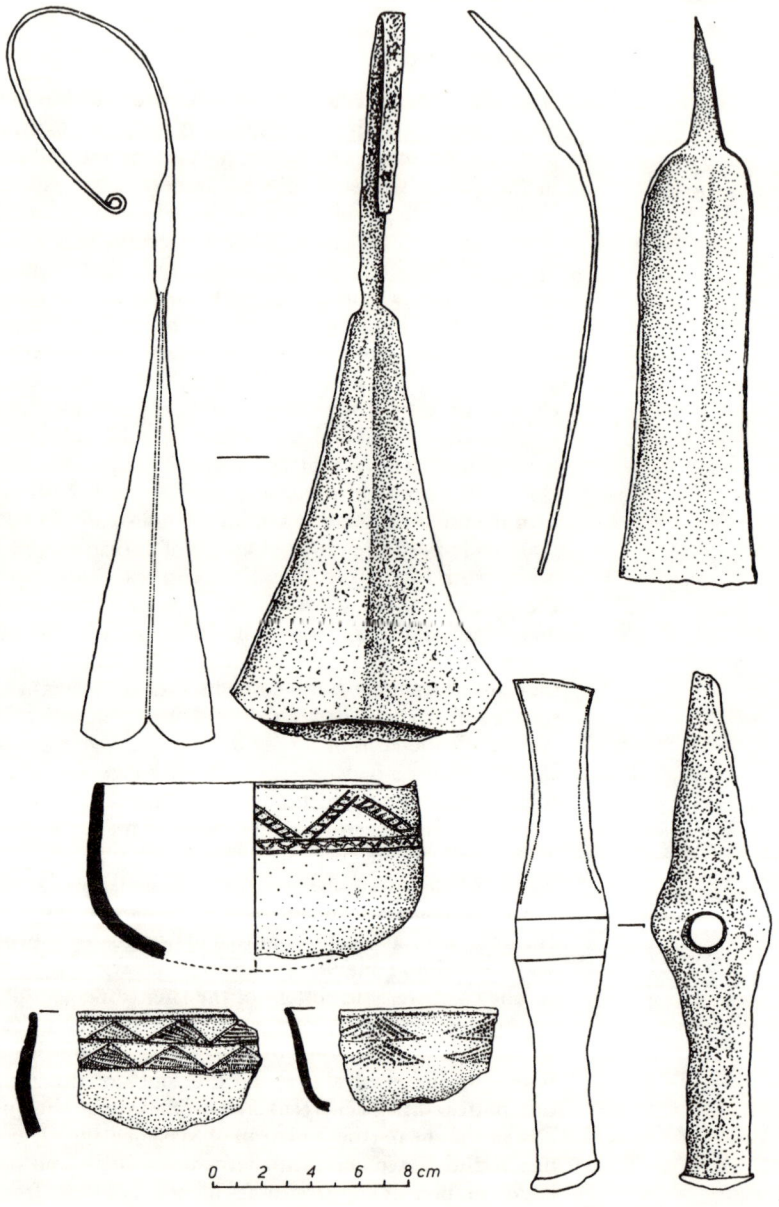

Fig. 70   Artefacts from Ingombe Ilede (after Fagan, 1969b)

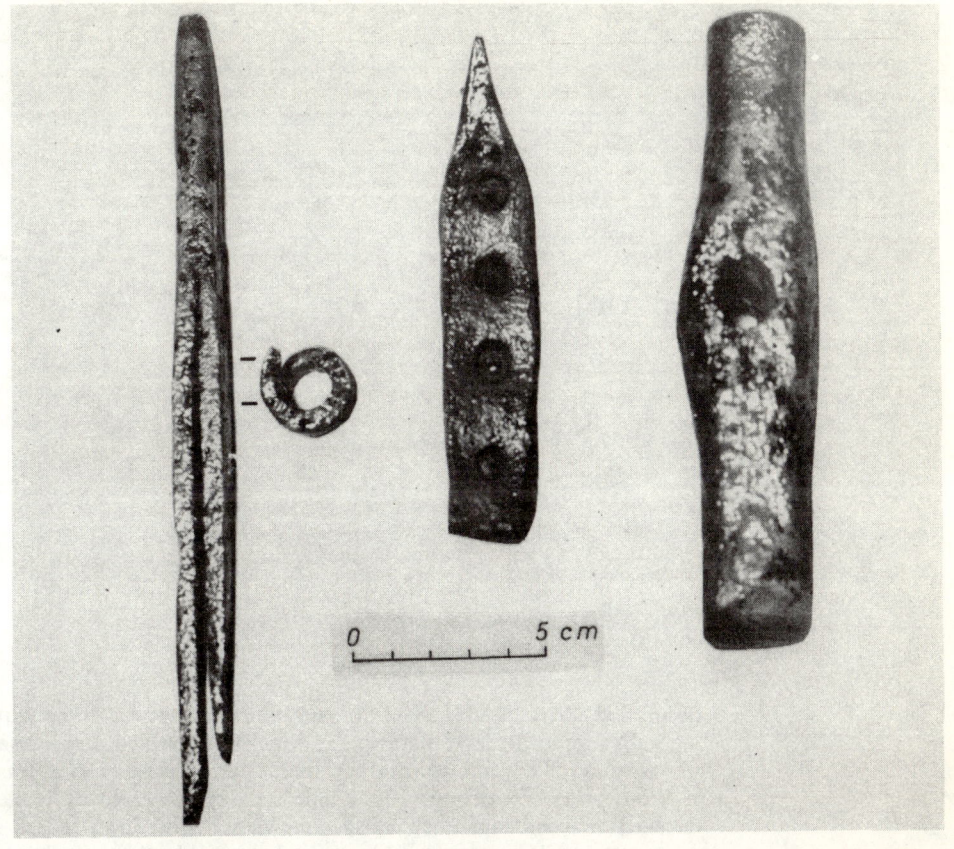

Plate XXII   Metal-working tools from burials at Ingombe Ilede. From left to right: tongs, wire-drawing plate and hammer (by courtesy of M. S. Bisson)

Khami and the Rozwi

Further to the west, in Matabeleland, the area formerly occupied by the Leopard's Kopje folk witnessed significant developments during the late fifteenth and sixteenth centuries which may be interpreted as due to the penetration of the region by people related to the final inhabitants of Great Zimbabwe. Possible precursors of this penetration are suggested by still unexcavated ruins such as Chumnungwa and Umtwarte (Garlake, 1973*a*: 166). The main phase of substantial stone building in this area saw the erection of some sixty-five complexes within a clearly circumscribed area centred on the Matopo Hills: the best-known examples are those at Dhlo Dhlo, Naletale and Khami. They are distinguished from earlier sites such as Great Zimbabwe by the virtual absence of free-standing walls. Instead, well-dressed blocks were set in neat courses, often incorporating elaborate bands of

Plate XXIII Decorated stone wall at Naletale

decoration (Plates XXIII, XXIV) to form massive terraces and retaining walls supporting level platforms on which thick-walled *daga* houses were erected. This architectural tradition clearly has its roots at least as firmly in the local Leopard's Kopje area, as witnessed by earlier terraced constructions such as that at Mapela Hill (p. 184), as it does in the building styles of Great Zimbabwe. The pottery of these sites, best known from Keith Robinson's (1959) long campaign of excavations at Khami, marks a significant break with the preceding Woolandale material: vessels with tall pronounced necks are characteristic, especially those decorated with elaborate polychrome designs produced by the use of graphite and haematite (Fig. 71). Only very occasional sherds of this latter type have ever been found at Great Zimbabwe (Caton-Thompson, 1931: 48–9).

The prosperity of these Matabeleland sites probably reached a peak during the seventeenth and eighteenth centuries, when oriental and European imports were received in quantity, some of it indicating frequent intercourse with the Portuguese who are known from their own written records to have established trading posts or 'fairs' on the northern Mashonaland plateau during the sixteenth and seventeenth centuries (Garlake, 1969b). In view of the dating of these Khami-related sites and their clear connexion with Great Zimbabwe, there can be little doubt that they are the archaeological manifestation of the Rozwi Kingdom of Guruhuswa ruled by the Changamire dynasty, the historical significance of which has been discussed above (p. 193). During the seventeenth century, the Rozwi power increased. The Portuguese were expelled from Mashonaland and both Sena and Sofala were attacked; but by the early 1800's decline had set in and the Rozwi state was overrun by the Matabele.

Plate XXIV Khami ruins

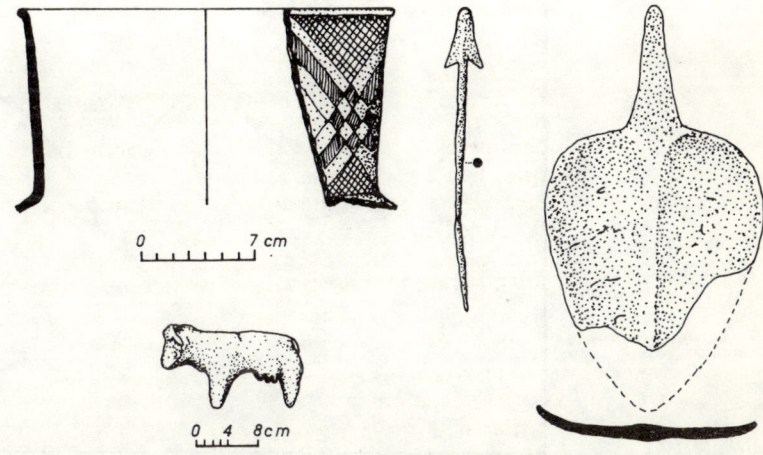

0 _____ 7 cm

0 4 8cm

Fig. 71 Artefacts from Khami ruins (after Robinson, 1959)

SOUTH OF THE LIMPOPO

Systematic study of the archaeology of the South African later Iron Age is, to all intents and purposes, a phenomenon of the last decade, and its pace is steadily accelerating. Very few definitive reports have yet been made available on the work which has so far been undertaken; and the synthesis here presented must therefore be regarded as extremely tentative and provisional.

In this part of the continent, we are once again on the frontier of the territory occupied by Bantu-speaking people: they are known from historical sources to have penetrated by the seventeenth century at least as far to the south as the general line connecting Windhoek in Namibia with Port Alfred on the south-east coast of the Cape Province (Inskeep, 1969). Beyond lived varied Khoisan-speaking groups, some of whom were hunters, others pastoralists: they and their interactions with the Bantu-speakers will be discussed below in chapter X. It will be convenient in this section to divide the territory of the later Iron Age Bantu-speakers into two zones: the highlands of the interior and the coastal lowlands to the east of the Great Escarpment and the Drakensberg (Fig. 72).

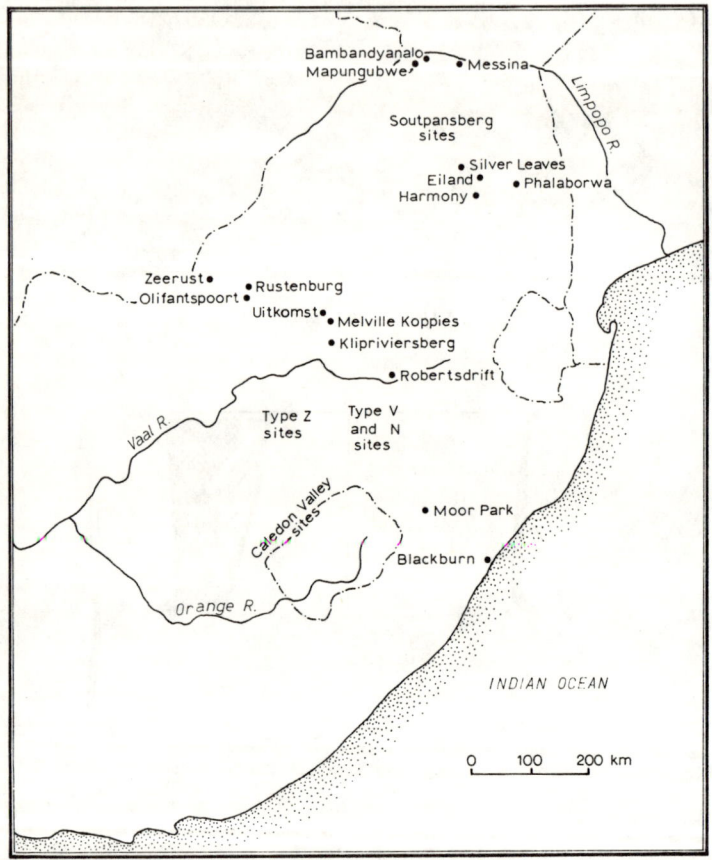

Fig. 72 Later Iron Age sites in South Africa

The Transvaal and Orange Free State highlands

The great density of Iron Age archaeological sites in the Highveld, especially that of the characteristic stone-walled enclosures, has been vividly demonstrated by aerial survey (Mason, 1968a). Over huge areas of now largely treeless grassland are scattered roughly circular walls of varying sizes – some of them evidently huts, others stock pens or kraals, others again compound walls enclosing a number of smaller structures. Stone was almost invariably obtained in the immediate vicinity of the sites and was generally used undressed. In the Transvaal Highveld such settlements are particularly numerous, especially in the south where Revil Mason has investigated later Iron Age sites in the Magaliesberg valley and on the Witwatersrand.

Recent work has provided indications that techniques of stone building may not have been practised in the earliest phase of the Transvaal later Iron Age, but that there are strong links in pottery styles, settlement types and economy between the two phases. The later Iron Age evidently began at broadly the same time as it did in regions further to the north, if credence can be placed on a single radiocarbon date in the eleventh century ad for a small iron furnace at Melville Koppies, Johannesburg (see also D. W. Phillipson, 1975). Associated with this furnace were a few potsherds bearing bands of oblique comb-stamped decoration (Mason, 1971). Comparable pottery comes from several village sites in the Olifantspoort area further to the west (Mason, 1974), where up to twenty circular houses were set around an open area which evidently served as a kraal for cattle. Each house contained a raised bench or platform adjacent to the fireplace, and most had several shallow depressions in the floor which presumably (as at Nthabazingwe) served as pot-stands. A particularly interesting feature which has not been observed on later Iron Age sites in other areas is a deep cylindrical hollow in several house floors: there was evidence that this had formerly held a small wooden mortar, presumably used for the preparation of foods such as millet, seeds of which were recovered in a number of localities. No radiocarbon dates for these Olifantspoort sites are yet available, but Mason considers that they were occupied during the first half of the present millennium.

The later sites known from this region are mainly stone-walled enclosures of which literally thousands may be traced on aerial photographs. Individual structures range from simple hut-circles to complex settlements incorporating huts, stock pens and linking or encircling walls. These structures have not yet been investigated in sufficient detail on the ground for us to be able to distinguish any temporal trends in their architectural development. Radiocarbon dates for them range from the seventeenth to the nineteenth century; and there is abundant evidence in the writings of early European travellers (e.g. Campbell, 1822; Moffat, 1842) that stone-walled sites were still inhabited both in the southern Transvaal and in eastern Botswana during the first decades of the nineteenth century. Their abandonment in many areas probably dates from the Difaqane – the northwards diaspora of Nguni-speaking people under Msilikazi in the 1830's. Mason (1962; 1965; 1967; 1968a; 1971; 1974) has published numerous plans and general accounts of the southern Transvaal sites, but the only relatively full excavation report is that by Robin Derricourt and Michael Evers (1973) of a settlement at Robertsdrift near the confluence of the Vaal and Klip rivers south-east of Johannesburg. The walls there have well-built outer and inner faces retaining a rubble core: a site plan is shown in Fig. 73. At Robertsdrift, as at comparable sites investigated by Mason at Klipriviersberg and Olifantspoort, it appears that most of the smaller stone-walled enclosures served as stock pens, houses being of *daga* construction with conical thatched roofs. Cattle, sheep and goats were herded, while the cultivated crops included sorghum. Iron and copper artefacts of local manufacture occur, along with glass beads and, on the most recent sites, other imported objects mainly of European origin.

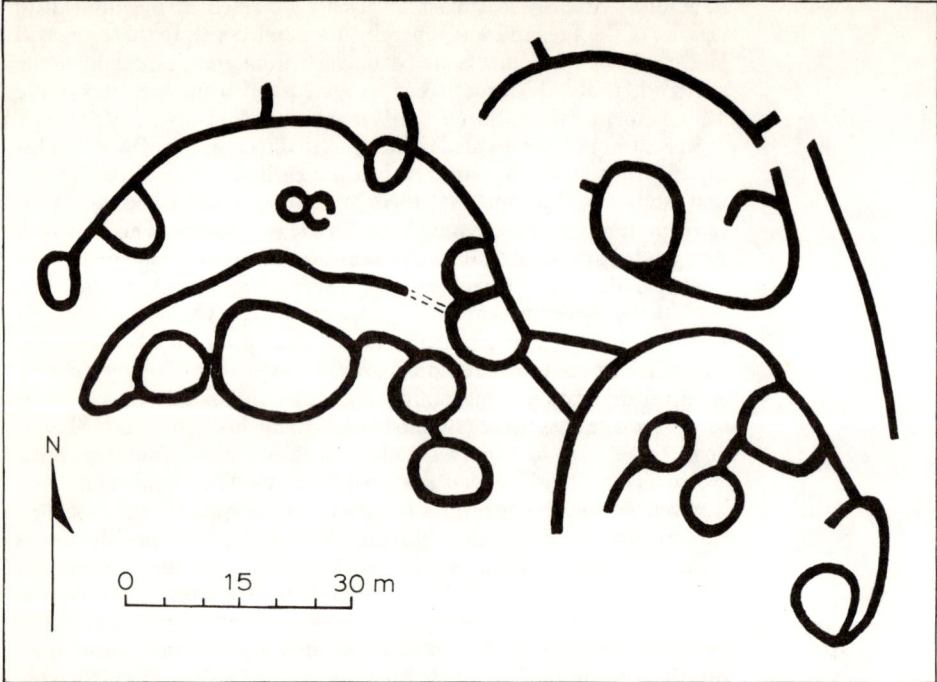

N

0   15   30 m

Fig. 73 *Plan of stone-walled settlement site at Robertsdrift (after Derricourt and
Evers, 1973)*

Pottery found on these southern Transvaal sites is of a type which
has been known for many years and is named after the Uitkomst cave
(Mason, 1962) some thirty kilometres north-west of Johannesburg,
but of which no detailed analysis has ever been undertaken. Decoration
is banded and generally comb-stamped, while rims are usually tapered
and may be slightly everted (Fig. 74). It has frequently been stated,
or tacitly assumed, that Uitkomst pottery is one of the most southerly
known representatives of the Early Iron Age Industrial Complex (e.g.
Soper, 1971a). However, it now seems almost certain that the affinities
of the Uitkomst material are to be found within the later Iron Age
rather than in the Early Iron Age Industrial Complex as it is at present
defined. The original and highly tentative Early Iron Age attribution
(Mason, 1962: 430) was made at a time when the Iron Age successions
of the areas to the north were still poorly known. The later Iron Age
typological affinities of the Uitkomst pottery are in keeping with the
available chronometric data which indicate an age exclusively within
the present millennium. The same is true of a less well known but
clearly related ware found on comparable sites further to the north-
west, principally around Rustenburg and Zeerust. It is known as Buispoort ware and is characterized by the use of punctate decoration
immediately below the rim. No very clear description of Buispoort
pottery has, however, ever appeared; and it is possible that the distinction between it and Uitkomst ware is more apparent than real
(Inskeep, 1969).
    We know much less about the later Iron Age archaeology of the
more northerly regions of the Transvaal lying between the area des-

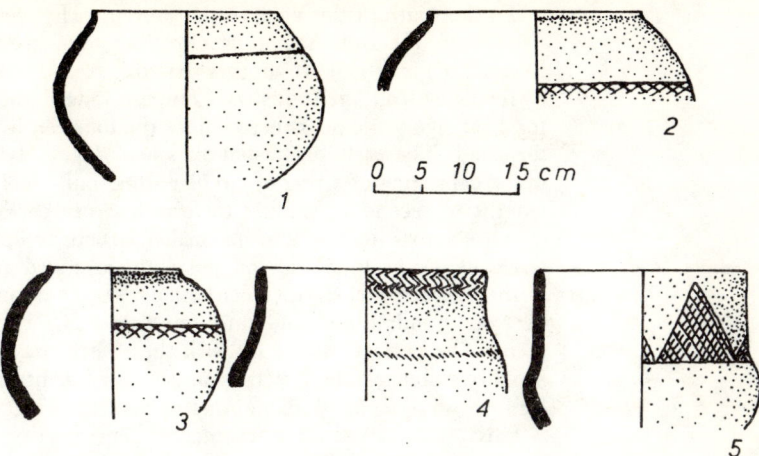

Fig. 74 Later Iron Age pottery from Eiland (after Evers, 1975): 1–3, Phala-borwa type; 4, 5, earlier type

cribed above and the Limpopo valley sites of Bambandyanalo and Mapungubwe. Much of this territory was traditionally occupied by Venda peoples; and it is here that the techniques of building stone-walled enclosures have been preserved and practised up to the present century (Kirby, 1956; Mason, 1968*b*). Concerning the date at which these techniques were first adopted we remain ignorant, but it is noteworthy that the buildings of this area, as preserved most frequently in the Soutpansberg, are not primarily the spacious farmsteads seen in the south, but are more compact, often surrounding only a single dwelling, after the pattern of the Rhodesian sites (de Vaal, 1943; Mason, 1962). It is tempting to suggest, but it cannot yet be demonstrated conclusively, that some at least of these buildings date back to the time of the Mapungubwe settlement. The later Iron Age pottery found associated with these Soutpansberg sites shows vessel forms comparable with those of Uitkomst and Buispoort wares, but its decoration is distinctive, comprising mainly bands of incised hatched designs. This same ceramic tradition is continued today by both Venda and northern Sotho groups (Mason, 1968*b*; van der Merwe and Scully, 1971).

A final aspect of the Transvaal later Iron Age of which mention must be made is the mining of iron, gold, tin and copper. There is evidence that all four metals were worked on a substantial scale, and traces of prehistoric mines are widespread (Trevor, 1912; Baumann, 1919). Unfortunately, most of these ancient workings were destroyed through modern mining or prospecting operations before archaeological investigations could take place, although the work of van Warmelo (1940) in the Messina area provided some information about prehistoric copper-working techniques. Recent research in the eastern Transvaal lowlands, to be discussed below, provides indications of the range of evidence which has been lost on the Highveld. The point to be emphasized is that over the great part of the Transvaal a relatively dense population of mixed-farmers exploited the area's mineral resources for many centuries prior to the Difaqane, long predating the advent of the Voortrekkers.

To the south of the Vaal, in the southern Highveld of the Orange Free State, the Iron Age archaeology has been investigated by Tim Maggs (1973b; 1976). It appears that this region was not penetrated by the Early Iron Age Industrial Complex: indeed, there is no evidence for Iron Age settlement there before the fourteenth or fifteenth centuries ad. The earliest attested sites are Maggs' 'type N settlement units' consisting of a ring of circular stone-built enclosures linked by lengths of secondary walling to form a larger enclosure, 60 metres or more across, into which the smaller structures opened. There are traces of insubstantial clay or grass huts arranged around the edges of these larger enclosures. Such units generally occur in groups; and over one hundred are sometimes found in a single continuous settlement. The pottery associated with these sites consists of bowls and roughly globular pots, generally undecorated or bearing crude comb-stamped designs in bands or rows of pendant triangles.

Later, in the sixteenth or seventeenth centuries, 'type N' settlements were replaced by, or converted into, those of the much more numerous 'type V', distributed over a more extensive area including most of the best and most adequately watered arable and grazing land around the upper reaches of the Vaal. 'Type V' settlements are clearly derived from those of 'type N', but are on a more open plan, lacking the outer surrounding wall. Some of the huts were now built of stone and had corbelled roofs constructed of undressed stone blocks (see Walton, 1951; 1965). Maggs (1976: 323) notes that settlements were 'often spaced out along a ridge . . . there is no specialization or ranking among the units, although sometimes a particularly large one with small ones around it suggests the home of a headman or chief'. The pottery from 'type V' sites shows greater variety than did that of the earlier period: comb-stamped decoration is finer but less commonly employed, generally in conjunction with a red ochre burnish. The cruder vessels were now decorated by a variety of impressions below the rim. Related remains, less well known, occur in the Caledon valley on the border with Lesotho.

Further to the west and at a slightly lower altitude are found stone-built settlements of an essentially different form, 'type Z', dated from the sixteenth or seventeenth century onwards. The circular huts had a mud wall covered with a conical thatched roof supported on poles. The huts, which were arranged around a group of large primary enclosures presumably serving as stock pens, each had a semicircular walled courtyard at front and rear (Maggs, 1972). It seems that the front courtyard was used as a food preparation area, while that at the rear held grain storage bins and served as a general work and storage place. The inhabitants of this relatively dry region apparently depended more on stock raising and less on agriculture than did the residents of the 'type N' and 'type V' settlements described above. The associated pottery, although utilizing comparable forms, bears distinctive banded decoration in chevrons, pendant loops or triangles, executed either by grooving or by application of ochre. There are excellent grounds for linking these 'type Z' sites with the ancestors of the modern southernmost Tswana, while those of types 'N' and 'V' further to the north-east can be shown to have been inhabited by people from whom certain Sotho groups, such as the Fokeng and the Taung, claim to be descended.

The Transvaal Lowveld and Natal

To the east of the Great Escarpment, the lowland areas of the Transvaal bordering on southern Mozambique contain later Iron Age sites which have been known for several decades (e.g. van Hoepen, 1939), but it is only recently that detailed research has begun to produce a coherent picture. It is in this region that the Early Iron Age remains, as discussed in chapter VI, indicate a culture-zone distinct from that of the Highveld. The dichotomy in the later Iron Age is much less pronounced: comparable stone structures are found in both regions, although in the escarpment and, to a lesser extent, in the Lowveld, stone-built terraces are a frequent feature.

Of particular interest as providing a chronological framework for the Lowveld is the research at Phalaborwa directed by Nikolaas van der Merwe. Here, iron and copper were mined from late in the first millennium ad. Unfortunately, no diagnostic artefacts appear to have been associated with the earliest mine-shafts; and it is not until the eleventh-century occupation of the site known as Kgopolwe 3 that the dated pottery sequence begins. Throughout, this represents a single later Iron Age tradition which has continued with, according to the excavators, remarkably little modification until the present (van der Merwe and Scully, 1971). The assemblages are described as comprising open bowls and globular pots decorated with incised bands of hatched triangles: such vessels are still made by several groups of the north-eastern Sotho.

Throughout the later Iron Age occupation of the Phalaborwa region, settlement appears to have been concentrated on the rocky hills which are here scattered across the veld. Many of the slopes were terraced with stone-built retaining walls and most of the terraces supported one or (rarely) more circular houses, two to three metres in diameter. The walls were of pole-and-*daga* construction; the *daga* floors generally had a central hearth depression. Domestic cattle dominate the faunal remains, with goats, chickens and a variety of wild species. The presence of grindstones and iron hoes, as well as the terraced hill-sides, make it likely that agriculture was practised although wild marula nuts, as today, evidently provided a significant part of the vegetable diet.

Mining for copper was conducted on a substantial scale and evidently provided the focus for Iron Age settlement of the Phalaborwa area. The technique employed included the sinking of shafts, the driving of horizontal passages, and open trenching. Iron gads and stone hammers were the tools most generally employed. In view of the scale of the mining, it is remarkable that only a few finished copper objects, mostly ornaments, have been found at Phalaborwa. Iron was also worked in the area, the ore being collected from the surface rather than mined.

That the Phalaborwa mines were not isolated phenomena in the Transvaal Lowveld has been demonstrated by Evers and van den Berg (1974) at Harmony, near the foot of the escarpment some 80 kilometres to the west. Here, open trenches followed the outcrop of the copper ore, shafts and stopes then being excavated to follow the strike. A radiocarbon date suggests that the mine was probably in operation by about the thirteenth century ad. Industrial activity during the later Iron Age also included the manufacture of soapstone bowls which were used locally for the evaporation of brine: a nearby village site yielded pottery akin to that from Phalaborwa (Evers, 1975). Comparable salt-extraction and settlement sites are recorded at Eiland, further to the north on the Groot Letaba river. Here and at the nearby site of Silver Leaves, Tzaneen, the Early Iron Age levels noted in chapter VI were overlain first by an occupation containing pottery comparable with that of Mapungubwe and dated to the eleventh or twelfth century ad (Klapwijk, 1973), and then by a deposit of Phalaborwa pottery.

Detailed investigations into the later Iron Age archaeology of Natal are only just beginning. The pioneer pottery classification of John Schofield (1948), which has for long formed a useful frame of reference, is now seen to need drastic revision. At Blackburn, Oliver Davies (1971) has investigated a site on coastal dunes overlooking Umhlanga Lagoon some 15 kilometres north of Durban, which has yielded evidence for a somewhat unusual later Iron Age settlement dated to about the eleventh century ad. This was evidently a village of large, insubstantial dome-shaped houses some 5 metres in diameter, perhaps comparable with the 'beehive' huts of the recent Nguni which are made of osier hoops covered with grass or matting. Iron was worked, and the pottery – mainly jars and bowls with tapered or slightly everted rims, rarely decorated except for occasional banded comb-stamping or rim-nicking – is clearly of later Iron Age type. The only food refuse that was recovered consisted of sea shells and occasional fish bones.

Inland, near Estcourt, Davies' (1974) excavations at Moor Park have revealed a more typical later Iron Age settlement, dated to about the thirteenth or fourteenth century ad. The site lies atop a prominent rocky ridge which had been surrounded by a roughly built wall of boulders. Within the wall, several clearings and terraces had been made on the stony hillside, and here were recovered poorly preserved remains of houses which may have been roughly rectangular rather than circular: if this was so, they are unique in the later Iron Age as currently known from regions to the south of Tanzania. One piece of *daga* floor retained impressions of a woven grass mat. The site's inhabitants herded cattle, hunted game and cultivated sorghum. Iron tools were used, but there is no evidence that metal was worked within the settlement. The pottery, including bowls, jars and globular necked pots, has characteristically tapered rims. Many vessels are undecorated, others bear banded stylus impressions on the wall or on top of the rim (Fig. 75).

In the more southerly regions of Natal, as in the Transkei, little adequately documented archaeological information is yet available concerning the later Iron Age. It is nevertheless abundantly clear from the study of Xhosa traditions that settlement of the area by Bantu-speakers has an antiquity well in excess of four centuries (M. Wilson, 1969b). Robin Derricourt (1972) has recorded evidence for domestic cattle at Middledrift in the Ciskei as early as the eleventh century ad, but it appears that the associated artefacts were not of Iron Age type. Until such time as further research is undertaken, all that may usefully be said is that, during the period between the eleventh and the sixteenth centuries, later Iron Age peoples spread southwards through Natal as far as the Kei river, and that it may have been they who were responsible for passing domestic animals to the stone-tool-using folk further to the south-west. The question of contact between

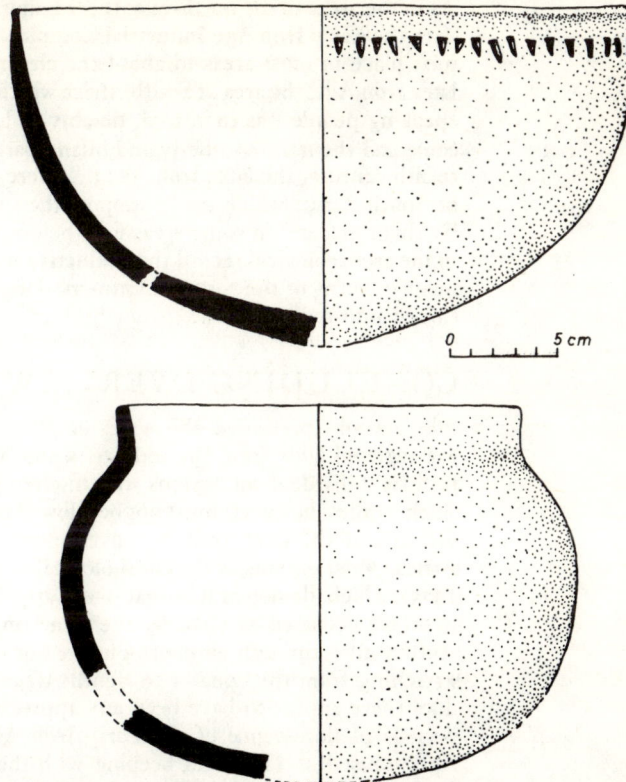

0   5 cm

Fig. 75 Pottery from Moor Park (after Davies, 1974)

Iron Age people and the stone-tool-users will be discussed in greater detail in chapter X.

Far to the west, in southern Angola and northern Namibia, settlement by Bantu-speaking peoples must also have taken place. Reference was made above (p. 139) to the substantial Iron Age site at Feti la Choya, only 300 kilometres north of the Kunene, where the prolonged occupation evidently began as early as the seventh or eighth century ad. In Okavango, northern Namibia, the only later Iron Age site which has yet been investigated is at Vungu Vungu, where pottery belonging to the same tradition as that of the area's modern Bantu-speakers is dated to the seventeenth century (Sutton, 1972). Further to the south, the stone-tool-using inhabitants of the Brandberg were evidently in contact, by early in the present millennium, with people who knew how to work copper (MacCalman, 1965). Clearly, as a basis for synthesis, these data are woefully inadequate. The prehistory of the Bantu-speakers in the regions now occupied by such peoples as the Ovambo and the Herero is a subject for future research. All that can be said at present is that, linguistically, the affinities of these people are with the areas to the north, in highland Angola, where settlement by Bantu-speaking folk is demonstrably of long standing.

Despite the inadequate coverage of research, a comprehensible picture of the South African later Iron Age is now beginning to emerge.

As in the areas to the north-east, there is apparent a pronounced break with the Early Iron Age Industrial Complex – a break which evidently took place in most areas in about the eleventh century ad. With the later Iron Age, the area of South Africa which was inhabited by Bantu-speaking people was increased, notably in Lesotho, the Orange Free State and the more southerly and inland parts of Natal. By the seventeenth century, the later Iron Age folk were settled in almost all parts of South Africa which could support their mixed-farming economy. By this time, and in some areas long before, there may be recognized in the archaeological record the distinctive material culture and settlement patterns of the several Bantu-speaking groups which have continued into recent times.

CONCLUDING OVERVIEW

The account presented above has emphasized the idiosyncracies of the regional later Iron Age industries and has in some cases pointed to their individual connexions with modern Bantu-speaking societies. Such studies, however, must not be allowed to mask the many unifying features of the later Iron Age over much of eastern and southern Africa. Most striking is the chronological evidence (D. W. Phillipson, 1975) which demonstrates that the Early Iron Age/later Iron Age interface occurred at virtually the same time – during the eleventh century ad – through an enormous area of the eastern half of Africa stretching from the equator to South Africa. In no part of this area does there appear to have been any appreciable overlap between the periods of florescence of the Early Iron Age and of the later Iron Age industries. This is in keeping with the archaeological evidence for the sharp break and lack of continuity between the respective pottery traditions.

Through the greater part of this eastern zone there may be detected a certain element of typological homogeneity in the later Iron Age pottery. The characteristic thickened or in-turned rims of the Early Iron Age wares became extremely rare; and the majority of later Iron Age pottery vessels had undifferentiated or tapered rims. Undecorated vessels, particularly at the beginning of the later Iron Age, were more frequent than they had been in earlier times. Decoration tended to be more areal, rather than banded, and was concentrated on the body of the vessel instead of on the rim. Comb-stamping was the characteristic decorative technique from southern Tanzania southwards. To the north, the rouletted decoration which was now dominant in many areas was, it has been argued above, derived from a northerly source among the Nilotic-speaking peoples, and spread steadily southwards during the past five or six centuries. Before that time it appears that the later Iron Age pottery in the Bantu-speaking parts of East Africa, although distinct and more varied, was more closely similar to its counterparts further to the south. In the whole of this region, the only Early Iron Age pottery tradition which bears any appreciable typological resemblance to this later Iron Age material is that of the Chondwe group. In this connexion it may be significant that in the general area of Zambia west of the Luangwa the inception of the later Iron Age appears to have been slightly earlier – by a matter of a few decades – than it was elsewhere. These observations lead to the hypothesis that, if the basic homogeneity of the later Iron Age is accepted, it may have been derived from an Early Iron Age ancestor of the western stream more closely related to the Chondwe group than to any other Early Iron Age group which is currently recognized. In many areas of southern Africa it is clear that the economy of the later Iron Age rested much more heavily on the herding of domestic cattle than did that of earlier times; and it will be recalled that cattle were, in the Early Iron Age, initially restricted to the territory of the western stream.

It must not be imagined that the suggestion here put forward is for a sudden and total eclipse of the Early Iron Age in the eastern half of sub-equatorial Africa by a largely alien later Iron Age successor. Clearly, there are instances of local successions which gave rise to indigenous later Iron Age industries rooted in the Early Iron Age tradition of their particular area. The most obvious examples, which have been noted above, are the Maore and allied wares of the Eastern Highlands of Kenya, the Mwamasapa ware of northern Malawi and – possibly – the Kangila pottery of southern Zambia. These are, however, isolated cases. Likewise, there is clear evidence that local technological specialisms were in some areas passed on from the Early Iron Age folk to their later Iron Age followers, as was most notably the case with the stone architecture of Rhodesia. Nevertheless, the cultural and chronological integrity of the later Iron Age in this eastern African later Iron Age must not be underestimated.

In view of the sharpness of the break with the Early Iron Age, and the rapidity with which it took place over a huge area, it is hard to avoid the conclusion that the inception of the later Iron Age was due to the arrival of a new population element. It is unnecessary to postulate that population movement took place on such a scale as completely to replace the existing communities, for recent instances have been recorded where a relatively small-scale migration has resulted in a sudden and complete change in the pottery tradition analogous to that attested at the Early Iron Age/later Iron Age interface. The Kololo incursion into the upper Zambezi valley of western Zambia during the nineteenth century, for example, involved whole families to a total of not more than thirty thousand souls (E. W. Smith, 1956), yet resulted in the rapid installation of the Linyanti pottery tradition in place of the earlier Lungwebungu tradition (D. W. Phillipson, 1974). Even more significant in the long term was the adoption by the indigenous majority of the language of the invading minority. In this case, it is doubtless relevant that, whereas Lungwebungu pottery was made by men, that of the Linyanti tradition was the work of women. It is noteworthy that later Iron Age pottery today is, in almost all areas, manufactured by women. It was suggested above (p. 147) that potting during the Early Iron Age was probably a male task. This contrast could explain the remarkable clarity of the break in pottery styles which is evident in almost all areas during the eleventh century.

Although archaeological evidence from more westerly areas is very incomplete, it does suggest a situation markedly different from that described above for the eastern half of the sub-continent. Here, there is no sign of a break between the Early Iron Age pottery tradition and those of more recent times: indeed, in some areas – such as parts of north-western Zambia – it seems that direct continuity may be demonstrated. Over how great an area this generalization holds good it is not yet possible to say.

Several lines of archaeological argument thus point to the conclusion that the later Iron Age industries of the eastern half of equatorial Africa to a large extent owe their origin to a movement of population from an area in or near what is now the Shaba Province of Zaïre. Significantly, on the Zambian Copperbelt which is the archaeologically well-explored area nearest to Shaba, the known distribution of Chondwe group sites suggests that a significantly greater density of Early Iron Age population built up in this part of the western stream's territory than was the case elsewhere. This (as will be shown below in chapter X) resulted in the more rapid disappearance as a distinct entity of the earlier stone-tool-using population. Possible contributory factors to this population expansion were the greater inherent fertility of the region, the greater variety of food resources which the western stream folk had at their disposal (including cattle and, probably, a variety of West African food crops), a possibly sparser indigenous population, and the rich copper deposits which attracted wide-ranging trade-contracts during Early Iron Age times, including some from the territory of the eastern stream.

Plate XXV   A clapperless iron gong, north-western Zambia

Such an origin in what is now the Shaba Province of Zaïre is in keeping with the evidence of several more specialized cultural traits which, at least in south-eastern Africa, are associated with the later Iron Age. For example, flange-welded iron gongs (Plate XXV) have for many centuries been employed as 'insignia of political leadership' (Vansina, 1969) in later Iron Age societies in this region, as at Great Zimbabwe (Garlake, 1973*a*: 133–4) and at Ingombe Ilede (Fagan, 1969*b*). The earliest archaeological occurrence of such objects, and the only one which appears to belong to the Early Iron Age, is at the upper Lualaba cemeteries of Sanga and Katoto in Shaba. In so far as oral traditions relating to the early movements of later Iron Age peoples can be distinguished from those of their more recently established rulers, an origin in this region is compatible both with the clan histories themselves and with the relative ease with which later migrants from the same general region appear to have succeeded in establishing themselves in political authority over the earlier arrivals.

Such a reconstruction of the processes which gave rise to the later Iron Age societies receives, as will be shown in the following chapter, a substantial degree of confirmation from linguistic studies. It also explains how several widely scattered areas proved receptive to the establishment of remarkably similar systems of centralized political authority during more recent centuries, as is recorded in the oral traditions. The formation of these states, and other less centralized polities, was intimately linked with the emergence of distinct 'tribal' groupings within a later Iron Age population which had previously been relatively homogeneous. Since a prime function of many oral traditions, as noted above in chapter I, is to uphold political authority, it is hardly surprising that they frequently reflect the origins of the political systems, rather than that of the population as a whole. They undoubtedly have the effect of exaggerating the unity of many societies. If these factors are borne in mind, it will be seen that the archaeological conclusions presented above are in no way contradictory to a careful interpretation of many traditions of 'tribal' origin which have been recorded within the last few decades. It will also be seen that it is in most cases meaningless, if not positively misleading, to attempt to trace back into prehistoric times the identity of individual societies or 'tribes'.

VIII

❧❧

The Iron Age of the Bantu-speaking peoples: archaeological and linguistic considerations

It has been noted in chapters VI and VII that the study of historical linguistics is capable of yielding data bearing upon many of the same problems as were illustrated by the archaeological observations relating to the Early and later Iron Ages in eastern and southern Africa. The correlation has frequently been made and, on occasion, somewhat acritically accepted, between the spread of Iron Age culture into sub-equatorial Africa and the dispersal of people speaking Bantu languages (e.g. Oliver, 1966; Huffman, 1970: in the latter work the additional assumption is made that it is specifically with the spread of the 'Eastern Bantu' languages that the inception of the Early Iron Age is to be linked). The correlation is largely based on circumstantial evidence, the main arguments being, firstly, that in this part of Africa, both today and in the recent past, the distributions of Iron Age culture and of the Bantu languages have been broadly conterminous, there being strong indications that indigenous non-Bantu speakers did not – on the whole – practise full Iron Age culture. Secondly, the close degree of linguistic similarity which may be demonstrated between Bantu languages spread thoughout the sub-continent indicates that they are probably derived from a common ancestor within the comparatively recent past, a similarly brief antiquity and common ancestry being attributed to the Iron Age industries on the basis of archaeological evidence. Such a broad and generalized correlation is, however, of little value if we are to attempt to make maximum use of linguistic data to amplify the archaeological evidence for the eastern and southern African Iron Age.

Linguistic evidence, properly interpreted, may not only be expected to amplify the available archaeological data, but it should also be able to throw light on aspects of the prehistoric past not normally illustrated by archaeology. Tracing the ancestral forms and processes of spread of the Bantu languages may be expected to indicate basic features of the nature of whatever societies spoke these ancestral dialects, as well as the possible locations of their early developmental stages.

The evidence of historical linguistics in most of sub-Saharan Africa is, however, of an order significantly different from that provided by archaeology. The artefacts and their associations which comprise the raw data of archaeological research were made by the actual prehistoric populations whose history we are attempting to unravel. They are frequently recovered from primary contexts, from the sites where they were deposited by their makers. Usually, they can also – within relatively narrow limits – be dated in terms of an absolute chronology. When we turn to linguistics, however, we find that in eastern and southern Africa a markedly contrasting situation prevails. Until very recent centuries the African languages of this region were unwritten; and, apart from infrequent instances where early European or Arabian travellers recorded local items of vocabulary, we have no primary contemporary sources for the linguistic forms which were in use before the advent of writing. In eastern or southern Africa, the earliest Bantu language to be written appears to be Swahili, originally recorded in Arabic script: the oldest undoubted evidence for written Swahili dates to the second decade of the eighteenth century, although certain documents which survive only in nineteenth-century texts were probably originally composed as much as three hundred years before. Arabic sources extending back to the tenth century – and European ones to the seventeenth – record words which could have belonged to Swahili or to some other Bantu language (Whiteley, 1969: 28–141).

It is, of course, possible to attempt the reconstruction of earlier linguistic forms from those which have been recorded in recent times; and one can, less confidently, argue from the present distribution of modern forms for the approximate areas where the ancestral dialects were spoken. These are, however, secondary data since we have no significant linguistic records for the greater part of this area before the eighteenth century, and precious little before the closing decades of the nineteenth. This does not in itself invalidate the hypotheses which may be reached: it merely emphasizes that they should be treated with the reserve due to all secondary data. This point will be emphasized when we come, in a later section, to discuss some of the widely different conclusions which professional linguists have drawn from these data..

One of the more severe limitations of linguistics as a source of historical information in the context of eastern and southern subequatorial Africa is the absence of an accurate absolute chronology. Ancestral forms may be reconstructed, but there is at present no firm foundation for ascertaining the period of time during which they were spoken. The linguistic data may sometimes be made to supply a relative chronology showing the postulated sequential stages of development of linguistic forms and – less certainly – their progressive areas of distribution; but the linguistic evidence for the absolute time-scale against which these developments took place is generally exceedingly slender. Our views on the speed of long-term linguistic development are, of necessity, based on languages which have a long written history; and there are good reasons to believe that writing may, in many cases, have a retardative effect on the rate of linguistic change. It is thus possible that some conventional views of the lengths of time necessary for the evolution of recent African languages from their reconstructed ancestral forms may prove to be substantial overestimates. In the final resort, the best approximation to an absolute chronology for the development of an unwritten language must come from correlation between its linguistically determined stages and a dated archaeological succession.

The line of argument followed in this chapter will therefore be firstly to survey the purely linguistic evidence for the development and spread of the Bantu languages and the various historical implications which have hitherto been drawn from this. Next, an attempt will be made to correlate these linguistic patterns with the archaeological data which have been presented in chapters VI and VII. A general overview of the Iron Age history of eastern and southern Bantu-speaking Africa will lastly be presented, drawn from both linguistic and archaeological sources.

BANTU LANGUAGE DEVELOPMENT

The general pattern of language-distribution in sub-Saharan Africa has been outlined in chapter I. It is with the Bantu languages that we are here primarily concerned; the area in which they are spoken today is shown on the map at Fig. 4, p. 7. The most comprehensive and widely accepted classification of African languages, that of Joseph Greenberg (1963a), sees Bantu as a part of a larger Niger–Congo language family. This family includes also the majority of the languages spoken today in West Africa south of the sudanic belt; but the Bantu section is by far the most widespread and internally homogeneous. It may therefore reasonably be assumed that the dispersal of the Bantu languages has been a comparatively recent phenomenon in terms of the development of the Niger–Congo family as a whole.

Concerning the area where the earliest reconstructible form of the Bantu languages was spoken, most researchers would now subscribe, at least in basic outline, to the views of Greenberg (1963a; 1972), who places their homeland close to the north-western limit of their present distribution. Not only is this the area where there is found the greatest diversity among the modern Bantu languages, there is also a marked degree of similarity – both in vocabulary and in grammatical form – between the Bantu languages and other (non-Bantu) tongues spoken in this particular area. Indeed, there is some disagreement among linguists as to whether certain languages spoken in this region, such as Tiv, should be included in Bantu or not (Greenberg, 1974).

It may be noted in passing that the significantly different reconstruction of the origin and early development of the Bantu languages originally proposed by Malcolm Guthrie is now seen to require major revision (Greenberg, 1972; Ehret, 1972). Guthrie (1967–71; 1962) postulated a 'proto-Bantu nucleus', from which he believed all the modern Bantu languages to be derived, located near the centre of the savannah belt lying to the south of the equatorial forest. There is now a substantial consensus of agreement that any centre of dispersal in this region must have belonged to a relatively late stage of Bantu language development, and have been responsible for the diaspora of only a restricted number of these languages, notably those spoken today over the eastern half of the Bantu area (Heine, 1973; Henrici, 1973; Dalby, 1975). In view of this re-evaluation of Guthrie's work it is now necessary to reconsider those constructs of Bantu prehistory (e.g. Oliver, 1966; Huffman, 1970; Oliver and Fagan, 1975) which have relied heavily upon Guthrie's original hypothesis.

Recently, Bernd Heine (1973) has attempted a classification of the Bantu languages completely independent of that by Guthrie. David Dalby (1975) has also presented a detailed review and evaluation of Guthrie's work, in the light of the varied criticism to which it has

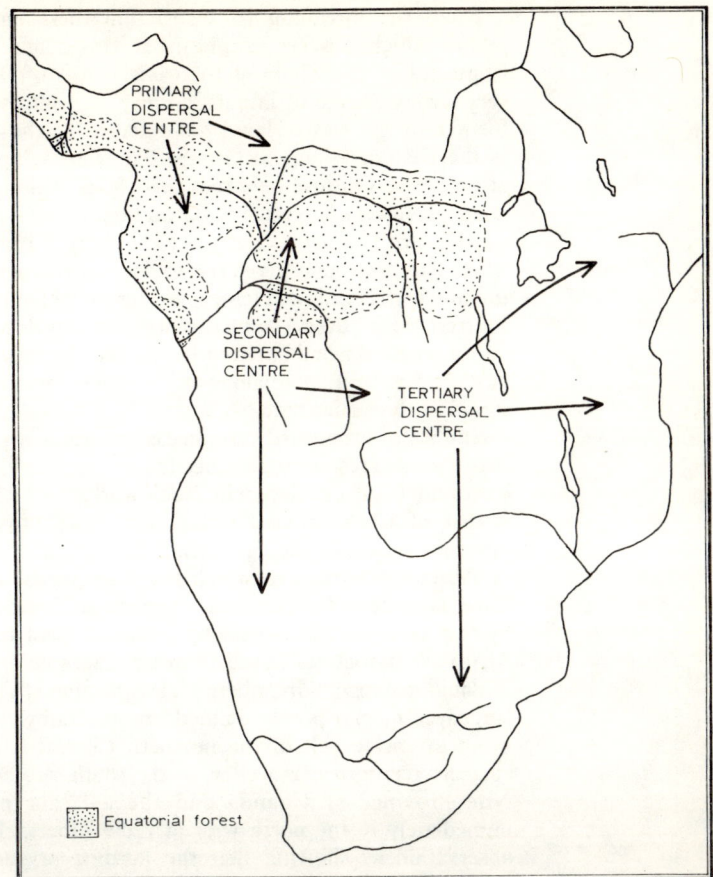

Fig. 76 Schematic representation of Bantu language dispersal (based on Dalby, 1975)

been subjected by others. There has emerged a broad consensus of opinion in favour of a linguistic developmental sequence along the general lines indicated in Fig. 76.

An initial centre of proto-Bantu speech was located in the far north-west of the present Bantu area, most probably in what is now central Cameroon. Languages ancestral to those surviving today in the Aruwimi–Ituri areas then dispersed eastwards from this centre along the northern margin of the equatorial forest. Perhaps at broadly the same time a southward expansion brought Bantu speech to the island of Macias Nguema Biyogo (Fernando Po) and, eventually, via a river and/or coastal route, to the south-western margin of the forest. From here, both Dalby and Heine agree that Bantu languages were first introduced southwards into Angola and Namibia, giving rise to modern languages such as Herero and Umbundu. Following Heine (1973), these latter languages may be referred to as the Western Highland Group. Subsequent developments gave rise to a further centre of such speech in the Luba-Upper Kasai area (broadly coinciding with that of Guthrie's 'nucleus'). It is from this last centre that the modern Bantu languages of the eastern half of the sub-continent are, almost without exception, derived.

From the foregoing reconstruction there emerge the following points which deserve emphasis at this stage. Firstly, the Bantu languages of the whole of the eastern half of Bantu Africa show a very strong degree of linguistic unity, in contrast with those spoken further to the west. Heine has referred to these eastern languages as the Eastern Highland Group. Far from being a primary division of Bantu, as Guthrie believed, this clearly belongs to what must be, relatively, a very late stage of Bantu linguistic development. Secondly, this Eastern Highland Group is to be derived from a westerly source, which had previously given rise to Bantu settlement in western Angola and northern Namibia (Heine's Western Highland Group). Thirdly, in contrast with these essentially western developments, a spread of Bantu languages had apparently reached the interlacustrine region of East Africa, by a route along the northern margin of the forest, at a significantly earlier date.

Studies of loan-words of non-Bantu origin which are preserved in Bantu languages have also been used to illustrate the sequence of Bantu linguistic development. Such work, of which the most intensive is that of Christopher Ehret (1967; 1968b; 1973) is of additional interest because of the light which it may throw on the transmission of the cultural traits to which the loan-words relate. For example, Ehret considers that the names applied to domestic cattle and sheep by the modern Bantu-speaking populations of much of this part of Africa are probably derived from languages belonging to the Central Sudanic group of Greenberg's classification. (The Central Sudanic languages form a poorly defined group (Dalby, 1976), today spoken in an extensive belt of the northern Central African Republic and adjacent territories, as well as in the south-western Sudan, the West Nile Province of Uganda and the adjacent part of Zaïre lying immediately to the north-west of Lake Albert.) Ehret interprets his observation as showing that the herding of sheep and cattle was introduced into southern and eastern Africa by Central Sudanic-speaking people, at a time previous to the main expansion of the Bantu-speakers.

Now, if we accept the commonly held correlation between the dispersal of the Early Iron Age and that of the Bantu languages, then the view that both cattle and sheep were brought to south-central Africa before the Bantu languages had spread to that region is at variance with the archaeological evidence which, as we have seen, shows that cattle, goats and sheep were apparently introduced throughout the region during the Early Iron Age, although cattle were – at least in south-central Africa – originally restricted to the territory of the western stream. It may here be reiterated that, throughout the area of the Early Iron Age Industrial Complex, there is no archaeological evidence for the prior practice of food-production techniques by any of the stone-tool-using populations. I shall return later in this chapter to a discussion of Early Iron Age origins as revealed by archaeology, and to an inquiry as to how these may be correlated with the linguistic evidence.

Returning to a consideration of the Eastern Highland Bantu languages, the approximate present distribution of which is shown in Fig. 77, we find that, although their essential unity and homogeneity *vis-à-vis* other Bantu languages are widely accepted, few linguists have undertaken detailed work on the nature of their clustering and inter-relationship. The most recent attempt, that of Ehret (1973), is based

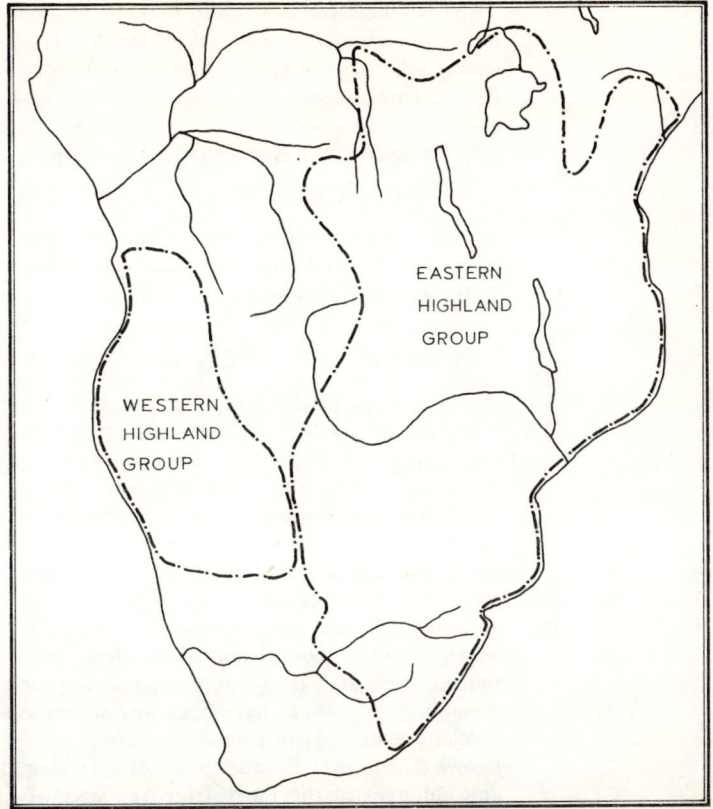

EASTERN
HIGHLAND
GROUP

WESTERN
HIGHLAND
GROUP

Fig. 77   Present distributions of the Western Highland and Eastern Highland groups of the Bantu languages (based on Heine, 1973)

almost exclusively on loan-word studies: its results should be regarded as tentative pending further research by other scholars using different methodologies. While agreeing with Heine (1973) and Dalby (1975) that the Eastern Highland languages are derived from a common ancestor which was spoken somewhere in the broad region of what is now south-eastern Zaïre, Ehret distinguishes two major subdivisions – which we may term northern and southern – the geographical division between which roughly follows the line from the southern end of Lake Tanganyika to the northern extremity of Lake Nyasa. The northern branch seems to have given rise to the modern Bantu languages of Kenya and most of those of Tanzania as far to the south as the areas now occupied by the Yao and the Makonde. The southern branch is seen as ancestral to the languages of northern and eastern Zambia, Malawi, Rhodesia, and much of Mozambique, as well as to the South-East Bantu languages spoken to the south of the Limpopo.

The South-East Bantu languages have been subjected to more intensive study: they are seen to form a single interlocking dialect network which is believed to have developed within the area of its present distribution (Ehret *et al.*, 1972). The implication of these studies is that the South-East Bantu languages separated from the rest of the southern branch of the Eastern Highland Group at a relatively early date, and that since that time they have developed in close contact with each other but isolated from the related languages spoken further to the north. The main exception to this generalization is that strong affinities are apparent between Venda, which is a member of the South-East Bantu cluster, and Shona, which is not.

INTERPRETATIONS AND CORRELATIONS

It is now appropriate to inquire how the linguistic data summarized above may be correlated with the archaeological reconstructions which were presented in chapter VI and VIII.

The origins of the Early Iron Age Complex

We have seen in the foregoing chapters that many of the cultural traits of the Early Iron Age Industrial Complex represent major innovations within most of the area of its distribution. In virtually every region where the necessary research has been undertaken, the Early Iron Age (whether of the eastern or the western stream) may be shown to have been introduced in a fully fledged form, both in its various components and as a viable cultural entity. In no part of the Early Iron Age area has any pottery been found which may be regarded as in any way typologically ancestral to the Early Iron Age wares; through most if not all of Africa south of central Tanzania, indeed, the Early Iron Age pottery is the earliest known. Likewise, metallurgy appears to have been introduced as a fully developed and efficient technology into an area where previously even a rudimentary knowledge of its techniques was totally lacking. The domestic animals and cultigens of the Early Iron Age were of species not previously known in the southern regions of the sub-continent; however, during the first millennium bc – as has been shown in chapter IV – domestic cattle and small stock were herded by the stone-tool-using folk of the Rift Valley and adjacent regions of Kenya and northern Tanzania. (It is not yet known whether these pre-Iron Age pastoralists also cultivated food crops.) The conclusion thus seems inescapable that the Early Iron Age Industrial Complex was introduced into most if not all of its area of distribution by means of a rapid and coherent movement of population which brought with it a fully fledged but largely alien culture, the formative processes of which had taken place elsewhere.

The origins of the Early Iron Age Industrial Complex must be sought in an area where its various component traits are represented in the archaeological record at an appropriate time-depth – that is, during or before the middle centuries of the first millennium bc. It will be pertinent also to inquire whether separate developments may be discerned in such an area, which could have given rise to the two streams of the Early Iron Age which we have noted above. It is to be anticipated that the source area may prove to be geographically closer to the region of Urewe ware (centred near Lake Victoria) than to that of any other of the Early Iron Age variants which are currently recognized. This is because, as has been shown, the Urewe ware tradition was established at an earlier date than the other groups, and because it may also be seen as fairly closely related typologically to the common ancestor of the two streams of the Early Iron Age which spread into more southerly latitudes.

It is clear that the origins or ancestors of the Early Iron Age

Industrial Complex are not to be sought in any part of Africa to the south of central Tanzania or, indeed, anywhere within the known distribution of that complex itself. It is not practicable to envisage the East African stone-tool-using pastoralists, discussed in chapter IV, as being directly ancestral to the Early Iron Age mixed-farmers. Not only did the former group lack all knowledge of metallurgy, but their pottery seems to belong to traditions quite distinct from that of the Early Iron Age. Indeed, linguistic evidence suggests that their most significant contribution to the Early Iron Age economy may have been the practice of milking cows (Ehret, 1967).

It follows from the above, as a logical conclusion, that the origins of the Early Iron Age may be expected to have been located either to the north or west of the interlacustrine region, or outside Africa, to which continent some aspects of Iron Age culture may, it has sometimes been tentatively suggested (e.g. Oliver, 1966; Posnansky, 1968c), have been introduced via the Indian Ocean coast. It will be convenient to discuss the latter suggestion first. Of possible extra-African sources, Indonesia has been the candidate most frequently and plausibly put forward; but the suggestion may be discounted for a number of reasons. Firstly, no convincing typological parallels may be drawn between Early Iron Age pottery and any known ware from Indonesia or other region bordering the Indian Ocean. Secondly, there is no evidence, archaeological – in the form of pottery or other excavated artefacts – or linguistic, for the former presence of Indonesian settlers in eastern or southern Africa. This is in contrast to the position in Madagascar where such influences are well documented, but only from the second half of the first millennium ad (Vérin, 1966). It is at this time that iron makes its first appearance in the Malagasy archaeological record; it is associated with pottery which appears to bear no resemblance to that of the mainland Early Iron Age. Such mainland cultural traits as xylophones and certain types of boat have, however, been claimed to be of Indonesian origin or inspiration (A. M. Jones, 1964; 1969). The introduction of these limited technological influences to the African mainland cannot be dated, but is very unlikely to have preceded the inception of Indonesian contacts with Madagascar. Likewise, several food plants now growing in sub-Saharan Africa are believed to be of Asiatic or Indonesian origin; they are now held either to be of very general and ancient distribution or, in other cases, to have been introduced into eastern Africa from the coast in comparatively recent times. These considerations, and the clear seniority of the mainland material, effectively disprove an extra-African or Malagasy origin for the Early Iron Age Industrial Complex, or for African metallurgical techniques.

A probable partial exception to the above conclusion is demonstrated by consideration of banana cultivation in the interlacustrine region. Here, a substantial number of local varieties have developed, indicating a considerable antiquity for the crop. Since bananas, which are of south-east Asian origin, are known to have been grown on the East African coast by early in the tenth century AD, as has been shown in chapter VII, it must be regarded as probable that they were introduced to the interior regions before the end of the Early Iron Age.

To the north and north-west of the interlacustrine region, however, a markedly different situation prevails. The prehistory of these areas during the last few millennia bc has been discussed in chapters III and

V. It has been shown how, by at least the second millennium bc, a mixed-farming economy had been established in most of the broad Sudanic belt which stretches across Africa between the southern fringes of the Sahara and the northern limits of the equatorial forests. The food-crops cultivated by the Early Iron Age farmers further to the south were, probably without exception, of species originally domesticated in the Sudanic region. Domestic goats, sheep and cattle are also all attested here during the last two millennia bc. The two early centres of iron working in sub-Saharan Africa, Nok in Nigeria and Meroe on the Nile, are situated adjacent to the Sudanic belt through which knowledge of metallurgical technology doubtless diffused rapidly, though in which direction has not yet been ascertained.

Throughout this area the pottery of this time, although at present very inadequately investigated, also reflects a common industrial tradition. The broad generic similarity between southern African Early Iron Age pottery and certain West African wares was originally pointed out by Gertrude Caton-Thompson (1931) and has recently been reaffirmed by Merrick Posnansky (1968c). More specifically, Ray Inskeep (1965) has drawn attention to the Early Iron Age affinities of some of the pottery from Wanyanga Kebir in northern Chad illustrated by A. J. Arkell (1964). Closer parallels for the Early Iron Age pottery, with which we are here primarily concerned, are provided by material recovered from the Ennedi in Chad and attributed to the time – presumably around the middle of the first millennium bc, as was argued in chapter V – when iron working techniques were spreading among the local stone-tool-using farming communities (Soper, 1971a; see also Bailloud, 1969). This and other, quite closely related, material from Batalimo in the Central African Republic and from Chad (de Bayle des Hermens, 1975; Coppens, 1969; Courtain, 1969) represents a ceramic tradition which could have been ancestral to that of the Early Iron Age Complex. Despite our as yet scanty knowledge of the archaeology of the central part of the Sudanic belt, the accumulated evidence is now very strong that it was somewhere within this general region that was located the population which ultimately gave rise to the Early Iron Age Industrial Complex.

Now, the greatest archaeologically attested extent of the Early Iron Age Industrial Complex is to the south of the equatorial forest – on the opposite side from that on which it is argued that the complex's formative processes took place. How did it arrive at the southern savannah? The forest itself is not well suited to the practice of a mixed-farming economy such as that of the Early Iron Age. Indeed, the inherent improbability of even a rapid traverse by a farming people through several hundreds of kilometres of low-lying forest separating two regions of high, open grassland makes it unlikely that the Early Iron Age Complex, as such, reached the southern savannah through the equatorial forest.

The alternative route, of course (as pointed out by Thurstan Shaw in 1969), circumvents the forest in a direction first easterly, then turning to the south. In the initial section of this proposed route we find, east of Lake Chad, an area where the pottery of the first millennium bc is strongly suggestive of that of the Early Iron Age. Adjacent to this region are those where Central Sudanic languages are now spoken, and where, it may be proposed on linguistic grounds, the Early Iron Age folk could have obtained their domestic cattle and sheep. Here, also, is one of the few places where the Early

Iron Age pottery tradition has continued to the present day (Soper, 1971c). Lastly, around Lake Victoria, in the region where the south-ward turn must have occurred, we find the sites of Urewe ware.

The Urewe sites of the interlacustrine region belong to the Early Iron Age variant which is geographically closest to the proposed source area. Urewe is shown by the available radiocarbon dates to be the earliest of the known Early Iron Age groups. Robert Soper's analysis showed that, of all the Early Iron Age wares, Urewe pottery retains the highest proportion of characteristics which one would expect to find represented in a common ancestral tradition (Soper, 1971a). Data discussed in chapter VI confirm that this holds good for both the eastern and the western streams of the Early Iron Age. Whether one or the other or both of these streams stem directly from the Urewe group, or from an as-yet-undiscovered Urewe-related industry located somewhere to the north-west of the interlacustrine region, it is not possible to say.

The identity of the Early Iron Age language(s)

Difficulties and some discrepancies are, however, encountered in reconciling these archaeological data with the conclusions relative to the economic development of eastern and southern Africa which have generally been drawn from linguistic studies. It has frequently been assumed, either tacitly or explicitly (e.g. Huffman, 1970), that it is with the dispersal of the eastern Bantu languages (i.e. those of Heine's Eastern Highland Group) that the spread of the Early Iron Age Industrial Complex is to be correlated. However, as has been shown above (p. 213), the linguistic evidence points very strongly to a westerly source, south of the equatorial forest, for these Eastern Highland languages. This is in contrast with the north-eastern origin demonstrated for the Early Iron Age by the archaeology. This super-ficially contradictory evidence derived from archaeological and lin-guistic studies may be reconciled if, contrary to the general opinion, the modern Bantu languages of the Eastern Highland Group are to be correlated with the later rather than the Early Iron Age (D. W. Phillipson, 1976b). This hypothesis will be discussed in greater detail below.

It remains to discuss the possible identity of the language or languages spoken by the practitioners of the eastern and western streams of the Early Iron Age Industrial Complex. One candidate, at least for the eastern stream, is the Central Sudanic speech claimed by Ehret (1974b) to have been that of the people who introduced food production into eastern and southern sub-equatorial Africa. This may, however, be discounted for a number of reasons. Not only is the distribution of the relevant Sudanic loan-words retained in the modern Bantu languages not conterminous with that of the Early Iron Age (or with that of its eastern stream), but this hypothesis would involve accepting the presence over an enormous area of southern and eastern Africa of a Central Sudanic-speaking population surviving until less than a millennium ago. It is highly improbable that such a population could have existed so recently and yet left so little archaeological or linguistic trace of its specifically Sudanic character.

It is far more likely that the languages of the Early Iron Age people were Bantu, and descended (at least as far as the eastern stream is concerned) from those which can be shown to have passed, at a relatively early date, along the northern margin of the forest to the Lake Albert region. These languages are represented today by the Nyali and Mbuti tongues, spoken in an area of extreme north-eastern Zaïre where an Early Iron Age pottery tradition still survives (Soper, 1971c). Adjacent people, such as the Mangbetu, speak Central Sudanic languages. It may be postulated that the Sudanic loan-words relating to domestic animals and other topics were originally dispersed through these Early Iron Age languages and passed thence into the recent Bantu languages of the Eastern Highland Group. This hypothesis obviates the need to assume the presence in sub-equatorial Africa of Sudanic-speaking people during or before the Early Iron Age.

Both archaeology and linguistics thus point to the area to the north-west of Lake Albert as that where the formative processes of the Early Iron Age Industrial Complex took place. Unfortunately, the archaeology of this region is virtually unknown. It may be supposed that it was in this general area that the early Bantu speakers obtained from their Central Sudanic-speaking neighbours the domestic cattle and sheep (and the words used to name them), which they in turn spread through eastern, central and southern Africa. Goats, being known by a name common to almost all the Bantu languages, may be regarded as having been in the possession of the Bantu-speakers for an even longer time – since the dispersal from their north-western homeland. These contact processes may have occupied many centuries, perhaps most of the first millennium BC. Cultural differentiation within the Early Iron Age, reflected both in the pottery tradition and in other cultural traits, may be attributed partly to early distinctions to the north of the equatorial forest, and partly to environmental and other factors effective in the course of their subsequent dispersal.

It remains to inquire whether this hypothetical Early Iron Age Bantu language was spoken throughout the area of distribution of the Early Iron Age Industrial Complex, or just by the members of its eastern stream. Could the western stream Early Iron Age folk have spoken a language derived from the early southward spread of Bantu speech which, as shown in Fig. 76, penetrated from Cameroon to the southern savannah through the western equatorial forest or along the Atlantic sea-board? It would appear probable that they did, at least in some areas, for – if the dating here proposed for the easterly spread of Bantu across the northern fringes of the forest is even approximately correct – the western languages must have been spoken in the south-western savannah at broadly the same time as that at which a local Early Iron Age presence is attested. On the other hand, there are also arguments in favour of a pronounced similarity with the language(s) of the eastern stream, a similarity much stronger than may be explained simply through reference to derivation from a common Cameroon homeland.

The development of the western stream

Central Sudanic loan-words, such as are argued above to be derived from the Early Iron Age languages whose speakers adopted them in the northern savannah, are detected by Ehret (1973) in the modern languages of areas where the Early Iron Age belonged to the western stream. Indeed, it will be argued below, cattle – together with the Central Sudanic loan-word used to name them – were apparently introduced into much of the Eastern Highland area from the western stream of the Early Iron Age. The pottery tradition of the western stream shows strong affinities (but not so marked as that displayed by the eastern stream pottery) to that of Urewe. It is tempting to suggest that the Tshikapa site near the border between Zaïre and Angola, noted above (p. 137), may represent an early spread of the Urewe tradition, perhaps accompanied by a full Early Iron Age mixed-farming metallurgical economy, to the territory where the western stream of the Early Iron Age subsequently arose. Here, in what is now north-western Angola, contact would have been established with the speakers of those Bantu languages which spread southwards to the southern savannah directly from their Cameroon homeland (Fig. 78).

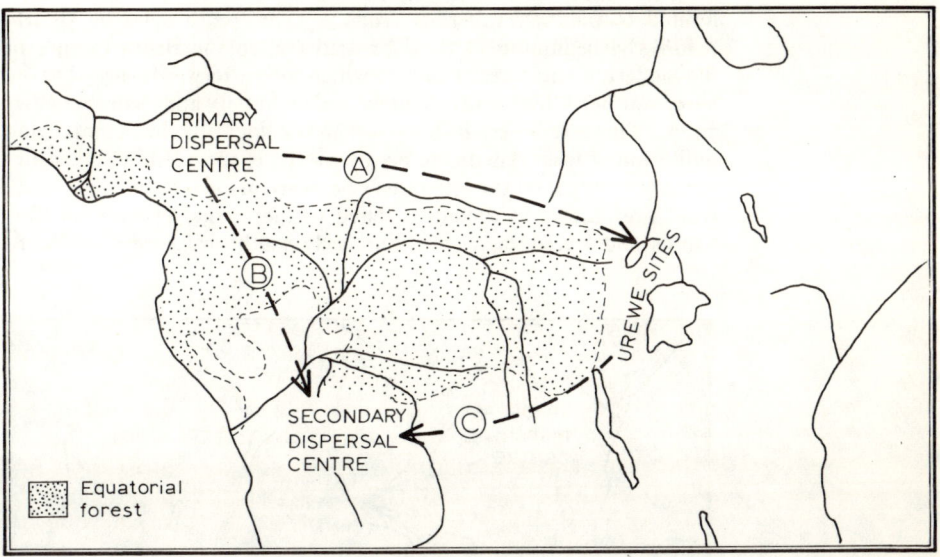

Fig. 78 Suggested routes of Bantu-speaking people to the southern savannah (for key, see text, pp. 221–2)

This latter, southward, spread may be recognized in the archaeological record in the discoveries from Fernando Po described by Martin del Molino (1965), notably in the pottery, dated to the first millennium ad, which displays a strong Early Iron Age affinity. It is associated with a developed mode 5 'Neolithic' chipped stone industry, characterized by the presence of finely ground stone celts. Comparable celts, associated with grooved pottery resembling that of the Early Iron Age appear in the so-called 'Leopoldian Neolithic' in the lower Zaïre region by about 200 bc (Mortelmans, 1962e; de Maret, 1975). It is not known whether these Fernando Po and lower Zaïre folk herded domestic animals. In view of the difficulty, noted above, involved in the passage of such creatures through the equatorial forest, it may be suggested that the balance of probability is that at least the latter group were not herdsmen – except possibly of goats, whose presence in the Cameroon Bantu homeland is attested linguistically. The ground stone celts of these people might have been used in connexion with an agricultural system based primarily on the cultivation of non-cereal crops. It is probable that this early southward spread of Bantu-speakers

(Fig. 78, B) comprised people with a pre-metallurgical 'Neolithic' technology: whether and to what extent they were food-producers remains to be ascertained.

It is noteworthy that, although this 'Neolithic' industry reached the southern fringe of the forest at the lower Zaïre and at the Stanley (Malebo) Pool, it did not penetrate the more open savannah of northern Angola (J. D. Clark, 1966). Doubtless this latter area was then already occupied by the Early Iron Age herdsmen and cereal agriculturalists who had circumvented the forest from the interlacustrine region (Fig. 78, C), bringing with them an Urewe-related pottery tradition, as is represented at Tshikapa. The fusion of these two traditions of common origin – the one metallurgical, pastoral, and practising cereal agriculture; the other non-metallurgical and with an agriculture perhaps limited to planting tuberous crops – gave rise, around or shortly before the beginning of the Christian era, to the Bantu culture of the modern Kongo area, a culture which soon afterwards spread to the more southerly highlands of present-day Angola and Namibia (Fig. 79, A). This area is very little known archaeologically, but a tantalizing indication of what remains to be discovered is provided by the occurrence at Benfica, on the Atlantic coast near Luanda, of possibly Early Iron Age pottery in a context dated to the second century ad (dos Santos and Everdosa, 1970). The early southward spread of Bantu

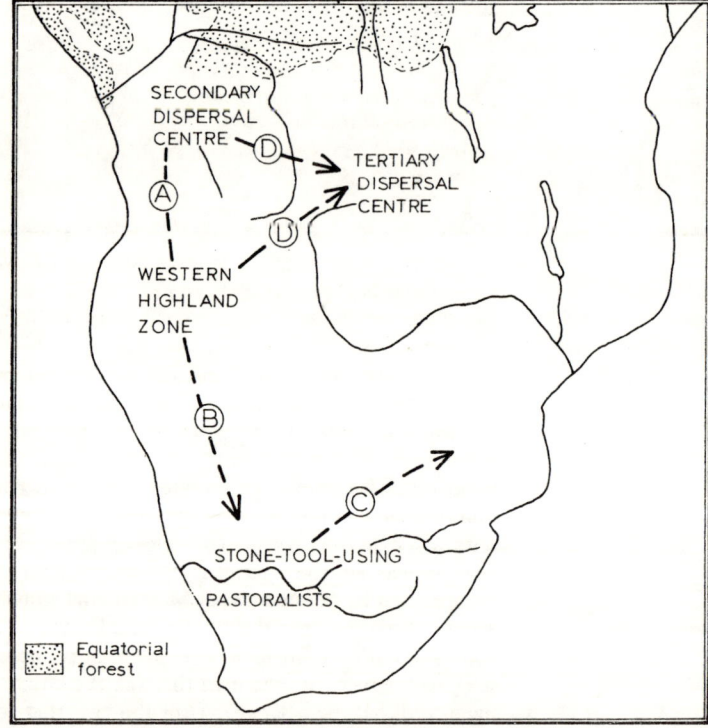

Fig. 79 *Suggested dispersal-routes of Bantu-speaking people in the southern savannah, showing also the proposed transmission of domestic cattle to stone-tool-using pastoralists of the Cape and thence to the Early Iron Age inhabitants of the Transvaal (for key, see text, pp. 222–3)*

speech through this area is, however, attested linguistically by the languages of Heine's Western Highland Group.

This Western Highland group of early Bantu-speakers, seen by both Heine and Dalby as derived ultimately from the Cameroon Bantu homeland *via* a westerly route along the Atlantic coast or through the forest, can be regarded as the most probable source of the domestic stock (sheep and, possibly later, cattle) and of the pottery technology which are now known to have been adopted by the (presumably Khoisan-speaking) inhabitants of the western and southern Cape in the early centuries of the Christian era (Fig. 79, B). The archaeological evidence on which this statement is based will be discussed below in chapter X. These Khoisan-speakers were in turn responsible for the introduction of cattle to the eastern stream Early Iron Age occupants of the Transvaal around the fifth century ad (Fig. 79, C). This hypothesis agrees with the suggestion, noted above in chapter VI, that this transfer may have been accompanied by that of the Khoisan loan-word for 'cow' (which may be of ultimate Central Sudanic origin) which is preserved in the modern languages of the South-East Bantu dialect cluster (Sotho, Venda, Xhosa, etc.) of the Eastern Highland Group.

A final expansion of the western stream of the Early Iron Age (Fig. 79, D) took place from the western highlands in an easterly direction, bringing Iron Age culture to the area of western and central Zambia, with adjacent parts of southern Zaïre, where its presence is attested in the archaeological record from about ad 500. It is here that the archaeology of the western stream has been most intensively investigated (see above, pp. 133–6); and it is here that its practitioners came into contact with the eastern stream people along their common boundary in central Zambia and northern Rhodesia, as indicated in Fig. 32 (p. 105).

The spread of the eastern stream

In the foregoing survey of the western stream we have passed beyond the time when the eastern stream of the Early Iron Age expanded rapidly southwards from its homeland in southern Kenya and northern Tanzania. It is necessary, therefore, for us to retrace our steps chronologically and to consider the routes by which the eastern stream was dispersed in sub-equatorial Africa. Here, the archaeological evidence is more comprehensive; and the isochronal map (Fig. 51) presented and discussed in chapter VI (p. 141) shows the general trends quite clearly, notably the rapid southward expansion through Malawi and eastern Zambia to Rhodesia and the Transvaal during the fourth century, followed some two hundred years later by a further spread into south-western Zambia. In certain areas it is now possible to suggest some refinements to the somewhat general picture provided by the isochronal map. Within the eastern stream there is a particularly strong affinity between the Kwale ware of coastal south-east Kenya and north-east Tanzania and the Nkope pottery found in the southern regions of Malawi. Although the contemporary eastern stream pottery of northern Malawi (Mwabulambo ware) is geographically closer to Kwale, it is typologically more distant.

One is tempted to postulate that the region to the east of Lake Nyasa also played an important part in the transmission of Early Iron Age culture into southern Africa. It is perhaps possible to discern a dim reflection of this in the close linguistic affinity between Swahili, Yao and (to a lesser extent) Nyanja (Henrici, 1973); for it is note-worthy that Swahili has much more in common with these southerly languages than it does with its Bantu neighbours within East Africa, such as Gikuyu and Kamba. While the eastern stream Early Iron Age of Rhodesia is clearly derived from the area to the west of Lake Nyasa, that of the north-eastern Transvaal (Klapwijk, 1974) is almost certainly best attributed to the Kwale-Nkope continuum. A late phase of this is probably represented by the pottery from the earliest Iron Age occupation of Kilwa (Chittick, 1974a). Only intensive archaeological research in Mozambique will clarify these important questions.

A broadly parallel southward dispersal of Early Iron Age culture to the west of Lake Nyasa and east of the Luangwa river is indicated archaeologically. This would have been the route by which the eastern stream of the Early Iron Age reached what is now Rhodesia. It is also discernible to the linguists in the distribution of a particular form of the word for 'sheep'. Ehret notes how forms of this word (*-bil-) are found distributed today 'west of Lake Malawi, southwards into Rhodesia even into parts of South Africa, and west up the Zambezi' (Ehret, 1968b: 219). One notes how closely this parallels the route postulated above, on completely independent archaeological grounds, for the spread of the Early Iron Age herdsmen who introduced sheep (but, significantly, not cattle) into this part of Africa. The linguistic distribution even mirrors the later extension of the eastern stream of the Early Iron Age into the Victoria Falls region of southern Zambia.

It is clear that the eastern stream, taken as a whole, was well established throughout this area for a significant period before contact was established with groups which I attribute to the western stream. In its early stages, the eastern stream appears in many areas to have lacked certain elements of the full Early Iron Age culture, such as domestic cattle and some of the more sophisticated metal-working tech-niques, which are represented on sites of the western stream. The greater cultural wealth of the western stream may perhaps be attributed partly to developments in its homeland which took place after the inception of the southward spread of the eastern stream, and partly to innovations within the north-western Angola (Kongo) area where the fusion of two distinct population elements, in conjunction with autochthonous factors, gave rise to the western stream.

It should be noted that our information concerning the absence of domestic cattle on eastern stream sites is derived exclusively from the regions to the south of the modern Tanzania. Identifiable faunal remains have not yet been recovered from Early Iron Age sites in East Africa; and it is possible that future research will demonstrate that cattle were herded, for example, by the makers of Kwale ware. Tentatively, the absence of cattle on more southerly sites of the eastern stream may be attributed to the wide tsetse-infested belts of southern Tanzania through which the eastern stream folk must have passed in their passage southwards.

What was the language spoken by the eastern stream Early Iron Age people? It follows from the previous section (p. 220) that it was a Bantu language derived from the early eastward spread of Bantu from Cameroon to the interlacustrine region (Fig. 78, A) which became enriched *en route* by the addition of a number of Central Sudanic loan-words relating particularly to food-production and metallurgical techniques. This was the language which the eastern stream introduced to eastern and southern Africa: it has since been submerged by the more recent expansion of the languages of the Eastern Highland Group from a southern Shaba centre of dispersal (D. W. Phillipson, 1976*b*). Such a hypothesis involves acceptance of the view that there were two distinct strata of Bantu speech in much of eastern sub-equatorial Africa, with an Early Iron Age language which had its origins to the north of the forests being replaced by those of the later Iron Age Eastern Highland Group which were of essentially westerly derivation. Indeed, Wilhelm Mohlig (personal communication) has recently discovered linguistic traces of just such a superposition, while David Dalby (1976: 25) admits the possibility that there may have been 'geographically overlapping waves of Bantu expansion in the east, associated with the Early and later Iron Age respectively'.

The inception of the later Iron Age

It was shown above in chapter VII how the later Iron Age industries of the eastern half of sub-equatorial Africa from southern Kenya to the Transvaal display a strong element of typological unity, and how they first appeared in the archaeological record of almost all areas at a date which approximates to the second half of the eleventh century ad. Through the greater part of their area of distribution the later Iron Age pottery wares make a seemingly sudden appearance and present a marked typological contrast with the preceding Early Iron Age ceramics. It has been suggested that the Luangwa tradition and, by implication, the related later Iron Age industries found both to the north and to the south may have developed from a western stream Early Iron Age predecessor located in the general area which is now south-eastern Zaïre. By contrast, the second-millennium pottery traditions from more westerly regions, as exemplified by the Lung-webungu tradition, display a much greater degree of continuity with their Early Iron Age forebears. It is logical to conclude that many of the later Iron Age industries of the eastern part of the sub-continent may owe their development to a large-scale expansion of population from Shaba area around the beginning of the present millennium.

It has often been assumed, for reasons not specifically stated, that the spread of the Eastern Highland Group of Bantu languages was concomitant with the dispersal of the Early Iron Age (e.g. Huffman, 1970; 1974*b*). The place of the more westerly Bantu languages in this model does not appear to have been considered. It is, however, important to note that, while the Early Iron Age Industrial Complex was widespread in regions where both western and eastern Bantu languages are now spoken, the distinctive later Iron Age industries, in so far as they are now known, were largely restricted to the eastern part of the sub-continent. It is probable that the establishment of the closely inter-related Eastern Highland Group in its present area was associated with the inception of the later Iron Age rather than with any earlier event. This would attribute to these languages an antiquity of approximately one thousand years instead of the two millennia which have conventionally been allocated.

Some degree of support for this hypothesis is available from Ehret's (1973) view of the developmental processes of the Eastern Highland languages. The linguistic evidence for placing the original ancestral dialect (his 'proto-Eastern Bantu') in eastern and south-eastern Zaïre accords with archaeological data which, as noted above, suggest that the Luangwa tradition and related later Iron Age industries may have developed from an Early Iron Age predecessor in broadly this same general area. It is tempting to suggest that the presence of the root *-gombe (cow) in the loan-word set which serves to characterize Ehret's 'proto-Eastern Bantu' may be especially significant in view of the archaeological evidence that cattle were originally restricted to the western stream of the Early Iron Age, which was located in that same area which Ehret sees as the homeland of his 'proto-Eastern Bantu' (but cf. Dalby, 1976). The spread of 'proto-Eastern Bantu' may be provisionally correlated with the expansion which ultimately brought the western stream herdsmen into contact with the eastern stream and resulted in the transfer of cattle to the latter population. A date around the third quarter of the first millennium ad is indicated on archaeological grounds for this contact, and is – I submit – not unacceptable linguistically.

It is with the emergence of the northern and southern divisions of the Eastern Highland Group that the later Iron Age correlation becomes clearest. As noted above, the geographical division between the two linguistic groups runs roughly from the south end of Lake Tanganyika to the north end of Lake Nyasa and thence south-eastward. This is in remarkable agreement with the archaeologically known division in the distribution of the later Iron Age pottery traditions. To the south of the Tanganyika–Nyasa line, in the territory of the southern languages, is found a series of closely interrelated later Iron Age ceramic industries, notably those of the Luangwa tradition in northern, central and eastern Zambia and in neighbouring countries, together with the related wares in Rhodesia, Mozambique, Botswana and South Africa. The appearance of these industries is securely dated to around the eleventh century ad. The rapidity of this process is attested both by archaeology and by linguistic studies, one view being that the spread of the ancestral Shona and South-East Bantu-speakers south of the Zambezi and 'the development of two centres of spread of Bantu speech and ideas in the north and south respectively of that span of country must have been accomplished within a very short time, perhaps only two or three centuries' (Ehret et al., 1972: 15).

Were we to accept the conventional attribution of the Eastern Highland languages to the bearers of Early Iron Age culture, we would be forced to concede that the almost equally widespread and rapid inception of the later Iron Age industries has left no significant mark on the pattern of linguistic distribution in eastern and southern Africa. Nowhere are the complications raised by such a concession clearer than in the regions south of the Zambezi. Here, several writers have proposed correlations between the Rhodesian later Iron Age and speakers of Shona, and between the makers of the Uitkomst pottery and early Sotho-speakers (Fagan, 1965b; Ehret et al., 1972; Huffman, 1974b). The relative isolation of South-East Bantu from the time of its inception south of the Limpopo, which has been postulated on linguistic grounds, is an archaeologically acceptable hypothesis only if we concede the later Iron Age correlation: isolation from the arrival of the Early Iron Age is highly improbable in view of the broad later Iron Age continuity which has been demonstrated in chapter VII. The linguistic evidence for some degree of contact and interaction between early speakers of Shona and those of Venda is paralleled by the archaeological connexions at the appropriate time-depth between

Bambandyanalo and other northern Transvaal sites with the Rhodesian Mambo industry.

Turning now to eastern Africa north of the Tanganyika–Nyasa corridor, the picture is far more complex. Basically, there is no objection to correlating the later Iron Age wares of this region, which display a much greater heterogeneity than do those in the south, with the speakers of the northern division of Eastern Highland Bantu. The typology and chronology of the later Iron Age pottery is in this region much less clearly understood than is the case in the south, although the inception of the later Iron Age appears in both regions to be very closely contemporary. It is clear that several distinct pottery traditions are represented in the East African later Iron Age and, as noted in chapter VII, there are indications that at least one of these was derived ultimately from the north, from speakers of Nilotic languages, from which sources they were subsequently adopted by the Bantu-speaking peoples in whose dialects Nilotic (and Cushitic) loan-word sets are likewise apparent (Ehret, 1973). Linguistically, the pattern is also complicated by the apparent survival of earlier Bantu linguistic forms, both in the interlacustrine region and in some coastal languages.

There is thus abundant evidence to link the spread of the Eastern Highland Bantu languages with that of the later Iron Age. This may best be demonstrated in areas to the south of southern Tanzania but, in view of the basic homogeneity of the Eastern Highland Group and of the chronological evidence outlined in chapter VII, is most probably true of more northerly regions also.

CONCLUDING SUMMARY

It is now appropriate briefly to summarize the conclusions which have been drawn regarding the development and spread of the Bantu languages and the correlation between this process and the Iron Age archaeological succession. The reconstruction which is proposed is of sufficient complexity to merit presentation in tabular form, with reference to Figs. 80 and 81 (pp. 244, 245).

Stage 1   By 1000 bc
        Early development of Bantu speech in the Cameroon area among a stone-tool-using population which, at a relatively early date, obtained domestic goats and may have adopted some form of agriculture.

Stage 2a   c. 1000–400 bc
        Some of these Bantu-speakers dispersed eastwards along the northern fringes of the equatorial forest. In the process, they came into contact with mixed-farmers who may have been speakers of ancestral Central Sudanic languages and from them, through a relatively prolonged period of contact, adopted the herding of domestic cattle and sheep, as well as the cultivation of certain cereal crops, notably sorghum. Almost certainly it was at this stage also that knowledge of metal-working techniques was acquired by the Bantu-speaking people.

Stage 2b   c. 1000–200 bc
        A second Bantu-speaking population penetrated southwards from Cameroon to the area south of the lower Congo. These were stone-tool-using people making pottery and ground stone arte-

facts, and may have brought with them knowledge of those food-production techniques with which their ancestors had been acquainted in the Cameroon area.

Stage 3   *c.* 400–300 bc

The Bantu-speakers noted at (2a) above, who had previously spread eastwards from the Cameroon area, established an Early Iron Age culture in the interlacustrine region, where they are represented in the archaeological record by sites yielding Urewe ware.

Stage 4   *c.* 300–100 bc

Some Urewe ware-makers spread around the flank of the equatorial forests to the southern savannah and then westwards to the lower Congo area, where they were responsible for introducing many aspects of Early Iron Age culture to the other group of Bantu-speakers noted at (2b) above who had moved directly southwards from Cameroon to the lower Congo area. This co-alescence subsequently gave rise to the western stream of the Early Iron Age.

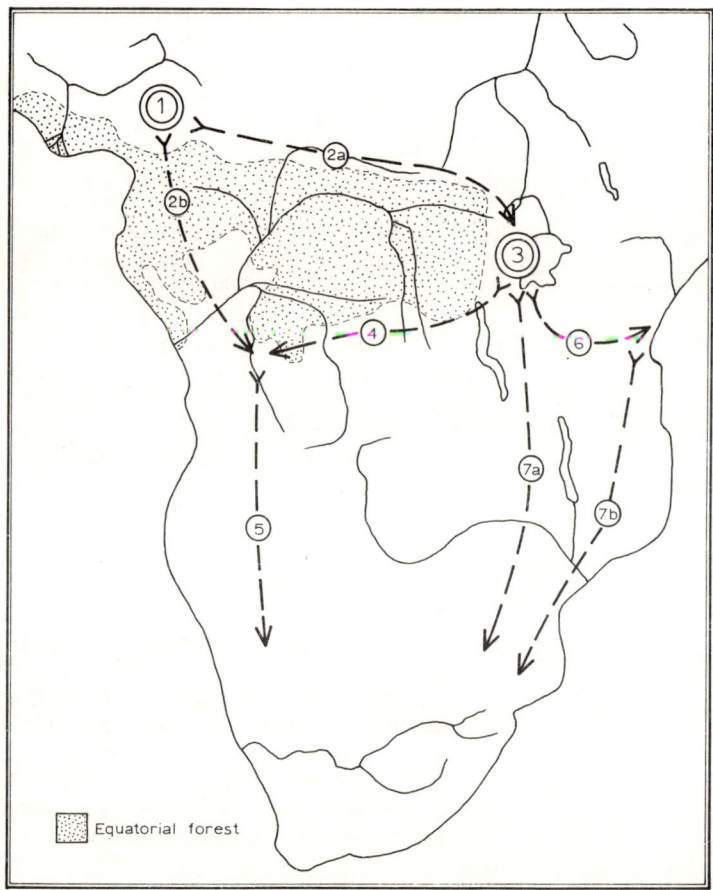

Equatorial forest

Fig. 80 Stages 1–7 in the dispersal of the Bantu-speakers (for key, see text, pp. 227–30)

Stage 5   *c.* 100 bc

A southward spread of the western stream brought the Early
Iron Age culture from the lower Congo area through Angola into
northern Namibia, accompanied by Bantu languages of the
Western Highland Group.

Stage 6   *c.* ad 100–200

The eastern stream of the Early Iron Age, descended from those
Urewe ware-makers who had not moved westwards to the lower
Congo area, penetrated southwards and eastwards from the inter-
lacustrine region to the coast of southern Kenya and northern
Tanzania, establishing settlements characterized by Kwale ware.
The speech of these and other eastern stream communities was
descended from that of the original eastward spread of Bantu-
speakers noted at (2a) above.

Stage 7a   *c.* ad 300–400

A major southward expansion of the eastern stream from the
interlacustrine region passed through the highlands west of Lake
Nyasa to the Transvaal. Passage through tsetse-infested country

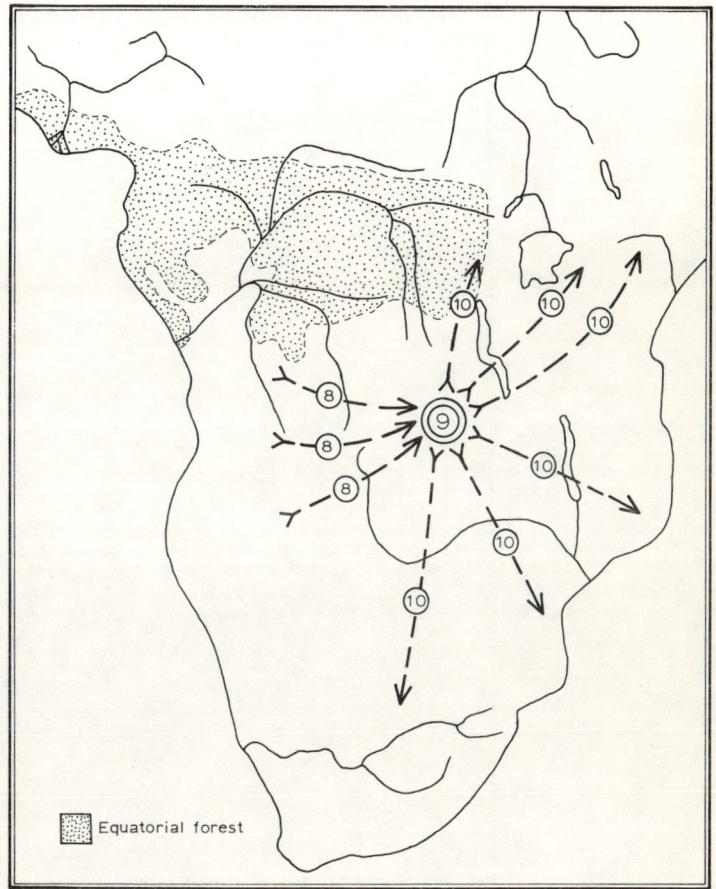

*Fig. 81   Stages 8–10 in the dispersal of the Bantu-speakers (for key, see text,
p. 230)*

in southern Tanzania probably deprived all these eastern stream colonists of their cattle.

Stage 7b   *c.* ad 300–400

A parallel southward expansion brought the eastern stream's lowland facies from the Kwale area, east of Lake Nyasa, to southern Mozambique and the eastern Transvaal.

Stage 8   *c.* ad 400–500

Peoples of the western stream expanded eastwards into Shaba and western Zambia. In the latter area, contact was established with the eastern stream folk.

Stage 9   *c.* ad 500–1000

A substantial increase in Early Iron Age population occurred in Shaba, with concomitant economic, technological and socio-political development, giving rise to the later Iron Age cultures, practised by peoples speaking Bantu languages of the Eastern Highland Group.

Stage 10   *c.* ad 1000–1100

Expansion of speakers of Eastern Highland languages from Shaba introduced later Iron Age culture to the eastern half of the subcontinent.

✣✣✣✣✣✣✣✣✣✣✣✣✣✣✣✣✣✣✣✣✣✣✣✣✣✣✣✣✣✣✣✣✣✣✣✣✣✣✣

The final prehistoric and early historic societies of north–eastern Africa

The three previous chapters have been devoted exclusively to the Iron Age of the Bantu-speaking people, and it has been shown how the substantial population movements which resulted in these people's establishment over the greater part of eastern and southern Africa lying to the south of the equator have also lent a strong element of homogeneity to the last two millennia of the region's prehistory. Further to the north, however, the events of the same period were far more complex, involving constant interaction of peoples with several diverse backgrounds and life-styles. It is to this area, stretching from the southern borders of Nubia southwards to the northern edge of the territory settled by the Bantu-speakers, and from the Nile valley and the Western Rift to the Indian Ocean, that we must now turn. Here, as already noted in chapter V, the advent of iron did not mark such a sharp break in the archaeological sequence as was the case further to the south: it is thus not appropriate to recognize a distinct Iron Age and to discuss it in isolation from the contemporary or preceding stone-tool-using societies. This chapter is therefore concerned with the prehistory of the last two thousand years, seen as a whole. It will discuss (so far as is permitted by the exceedingly scanty evidence which is yet available) the development and inter-actions of the diverse inhabitants of this region – irrespective of language; whether they were hunters, fishers, pastoralists, or mixed-farmers; stone-tool-users or workers of iron.

THE SUDAN

In the northern half of the Sudan, the period following the final collapse of the Kingdom of Meroe (see chapter V) was marked by disintegration and extensive shifts of population, as peoples from the outlying areas of the former kingdom moved into its heartland. This period, from the fourth to the sixth centuries AD, is represented in the archaeological record by sites and artefacts attributed to the 'X-group' – a population whose historical identity has never been demonstrated completely satisfactorily. It is possible that they were the people known to the Romans as Nobatae: Nubians who, perhaps in the late fourth or early fifth century (rather than earlier, as was formerly thought), were encouraged to settle in the Nile valley to act as a buffer protecting the southern frontier of the Roman Empire beyond Aswan (Kirwan, 1974). Archaeologically, the 'X-group' people are known principally from their graves. At the earlier cemeteries in the north (e.g. Emery and Kirwan, 1935), the culture which is revealed retains strong Meroitic influences.

Later, around the second half of the sixth century, the area was converted to Christianity by missionaries from Constantinople. At broadly the same time, three distinct Nubian kingdoms emerged (Fig. 82): Nobatia centred near Wadi Halfa, Makurra with its capital at Old Dongola, and Alwa in the south, ruled from Soba on the Blue Nile, some thirty kilometres upstream of the modern Khartoum (Monneret de Villard, 1938). It is only the last-named that falls within the area with which this book is primarily concerned.

Little more than half a century after the Nubians' adoption of Christianity, they were cut off from the missionaries' homeland, the Byzantine Empire, by the Arab conquest of Egypt which took place in about AD 640. From then on, for almost seven hundred years, the forces of Islam were kept at bay by a combination of military strength and the payment of tribute; and Christian Nubia developed in virtual isolation from the outside world. Archaeological studies of this period have recently made great advances through excavations conducted before the flooding of much of the Nubian Nile valley by construction of the Aswan High Dam (Shinnie and Shinnie, 1965). The most spectacular discoveries have been those of Kazimierz Michalowski (1962; 1964) at Faras near Wadi Halfa, where a cathedral has been unearthed,

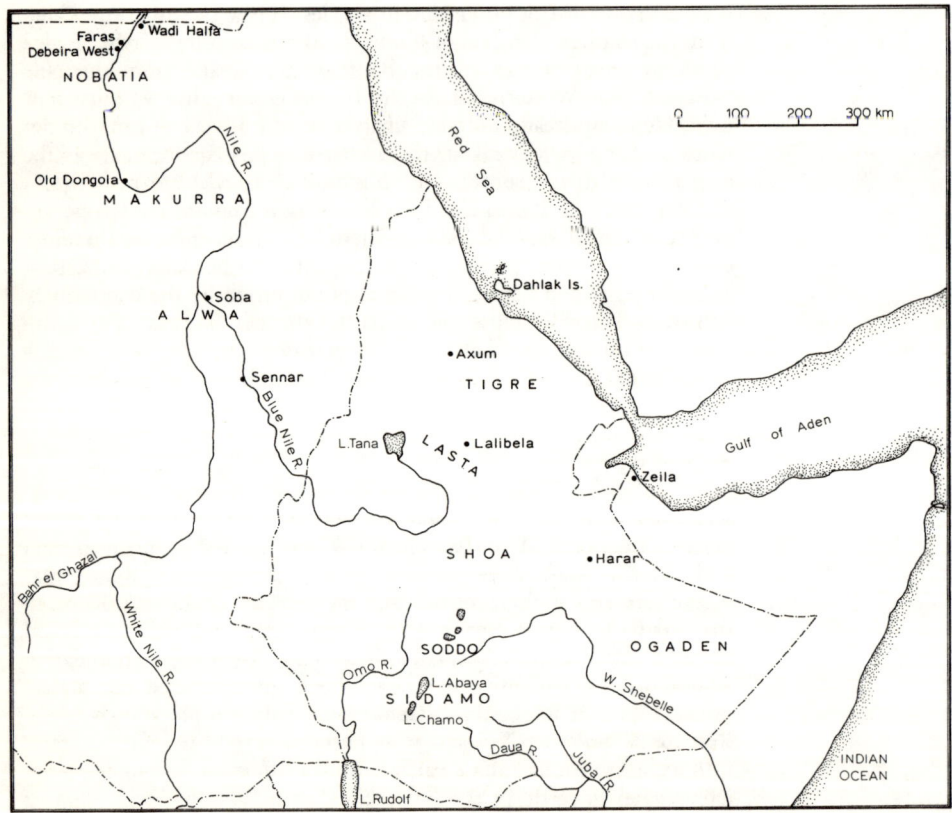

Fig. 82   Later Iron Age sites in Ethiopia and the Sudan

built of mud brick following the plan of a Byzantine basilica, and decorated on the interior walls with magnificently preserved frescoes, also in a Byzantine style. The secular side of life in Nubia at this time is best illustrated by Peter Shinnie's excavations at Debeira West not far to the south of Faras. This site was evidently a well-organized town of several hundred inhabitants occupied between the seventh and thirteenth centuries (Shinnie, 1963; 1964). The mud-brick built dwellings, often of two storeys, had vaulted roofs. The town had a centralized drainage system. The excavator has drawn attention to the similarity which life there must have had to that which has continued in the region into recent times: diet and agricultural methods (including irrigation by water wheel) show remarkably little change. The Nubian language belongs to the Eastern Sudanic branch of Greenberg's classification (Greenberg, 1963a; Trigger, 1966). Medieval Nubia was a literate society, and their own language continued to be written in Coptic Greek letters until as late as the twelfth century. (Nubian has survived into recent times only in enclaves in the Nile valley, surrounded by areas where Arabic is now spoken.)

Towards the end of the seventh century the two more northerly kingdoms of Christian Nubia, those of Nobatia and Makurra, combined to form the Kingdom of Dongola. This for several centuries appears to have surpassed its southern counterpart, Alwa, both in riches and in strength. The Dongolans on several occasions made major inroads into Egyptian territory. Finally, in about AD 1320, the Kingdom of Dongola was conquered by the Mamluk-ruled Egyptians and laid open to invasion by desert Arabs from the west. By this time, Alwa had greatly increased in prosperity. Late in the tenth century its capital, Soba, was described as having splendid churches and other buildings, surrounded by fertile fields. Cattle, horses and camels were herded. This prosperity was cut short by the rise of the Moslem Fung Empire, with its capital at Sennar on the Blue Nile upstream of Soba. The Fung finally conquered Alwa and laid waste Soba in about AD 1504. Our knowledge of the Fung, such as it is, is derived mainly from written sources (O. G. S. Crawford, 1951; Holt, 1963 and references): their expansion thus provides an appropriate point at which to close an account of the later prehistory of the Sudan.

NORTHERN ETHIOPIA

Away from the Nile valley, the other centre of Christian culture in north-eastern Africa was in the highlands of Ethiopia. The Axumite Kingdom of that region has already been described in chapter V, and it will be recalled that this predominantly Semitic-speaking kingdom was overthrown late in the tenth century AD by a revolt of the indigenous Cushitic-speaking Agau. Before this, however, during the closing centuries of the first millennium, the Agau of the mountainous area known as Lasta, east of Lake Tana, had been brought within the orbit of Christian Axumite culture; and it was here, around the beginning of the twelfth century, that a new ruling group – the Zagwe dynasty – arose and re-established centralized political authority over what was left of Christian Ethiopia (Sergew, 1972).

Our knowledge of Zagwe-ruled Ethiopia is lamentably incomplete. Such written documents as have survived from this context are almost exclusively liturgical or hagiographical. There are passing references in contemporary Arabic writings, but they are, on the whole, difficult to interpret. The monuments of the period are virtually all ecclesiastical, most notable being the subterranean rock-cut churches of the Zagwe capital, Lalibela (Bidder, 1959; Gerster, 1970). These remarkable churches (Plate XXVI) retain, transformed into a more permanent form, many Axumite architectural features; and their style clearly owes far less debt than was once thought to foreign influences or artisans. Rock-hewn churches in a similar tradition are widespread in the mountains of Tigre, further to the north and closer to the heartland of the former Kingdom of Axum (Buxton, 1971). Archaeological investigations have not been conducted on settlement sites of this period, but there are no grounds for believing that the general life-style differed significantly from that which prevails in the greater part of the region today. The period from the eleventh to the thirteenth centuries was one of almost total isolation for Christian Ethiopia, which was by this time virtually surrounded by Islamic people who, particularly in the regions to the east and south-east, were steadily increasing in power. Late in the thirteenth century, a chief of the Semitic-speaking Amhara from Shoa seized power from the Zagwe and established a new dynasty of rulers based on the fertile plains lying to the south of the bend of the Blue Nile. Despite their claims to be descendants of the old Axumite dynasty, this southward shift in the centre of power in fact represented a significant break with the old order. The subsequent history of the Ethiopian Empire, at least so far as its central regions are concerned, lies beyond the scope of this book.

Plate XXVI The rock-hewn church of Abba Libanos, Lalibela

SOUTHERN ETHIOPIA, THE HORN AND THE ADJACENT REGIONS

When we turn our attentions to the areas lying to the south and south-east of Ethiopia's Christian heartland, we are once again in territory where written records, except for passing references in external sources, are unknown until very recent periods. Lamentably, archaeological research here has hardly begun, and consequently only a very bare and tentative account can here be offered of the later prehistoric centuries in what is now southern and eastern Ethiopia and Somalia. The modern peoples in this region speak exclusively Cushitic languages, and there is virtually no surviving linguistic trace of any earlier, non-Cushitic, tongues having been used there. It may reasonably be concluded, therefore, that Cushitic-speaking groups have occupied these regions for several millennia. This is in keeping with the discussion presented in chapter III of the inception of food production there. It will be recalled that chapter V made no mention of the inception of iron-working in southern Ethiopia or in Somalia. This is because such evidence as we have suggests that iron was of relatively recent introduction to this region, as will be discussed below.

During the closing centuries of the last millennium BC and for several hundreds of years afterwards, the stone-tool-using Cushitic-speaking folk inhabiting the roughly diamond-shaped region demarcated by the Ethiopian Rift Valley, the Indian Ocean coast of Somalia and the northern Kenya plains continued to practise the technology and way of life of their forebears, virtually unaffected by the literate societies of the Nile valley and of northern Ethiopia which have been described above and in chapter V. Mode 5 stone artefacts and hand-made pottery are the principal objects surviving in the archaeological record which may reasonably be attributed to this period, although it must be stressed that dated excavated assemblages are still not available. Agriculture, supplemented in some areas by the herding of domestic animals, would have been the mainstay of the economy in the better watered highlands, notably in the Southern Highlands of Ethiopia, in much of which a fairly settled life-style would have been practicable. In the drier regions to the south and east, the economy must be supposed to have been more exclusively pastoral, supplemented by agriculture in the valleys of such rivers as the Omo, Daua, Juba and Webi Shebelle. There is evidence from northern Kenya that the areas suitable for agriculture were formerly more extensive than they are today; and the same is probably true of other areas also. In some places, too, it is reasonable to assume that pockets of hunter/gatherers survived long after the inception of food production in the region as a whole. Fish are today avoided by most Cushitic-speakers, but it appears from Desmond Clark's (1954: 282–90) investigations on the eastern coast of Somalia that groups of fishers have been settled along the shore for a long period, both before and after the coming of iron, the Rer Manyo being their modern counterparts (Grottanelli, 1975: 73).

Archaeological remains which may be attributed to the last two thousand years in southern Ethiopia and in all parts of Somalia except the coastal belt, although undoubtedly existing in large numbers, have only been investigated in a very cursory fashion – if at all. There is an almost complete absence of data with which a chronological framework could be constructed. In Sidamo, surrounding the southern

Rift Valley Lakes – Chamo and Abya, large numbers of sculpted monoliths, often phallic or crudely anthropomorphic in shape, have been recorded (Azais and Chambard, 1931; Anfray, 1975). On the basis of the weathering to which the unburied specimens have been subjected, it seems reasonable to suggest that they are, as a class, older than the flatter slab-like monoliths, often carved with abstract curvilinear designs or with unmistakable representations of metal weapons, which are frequently seen on graves a little further to the north, in Soddo (Fig. 83). Whether the phallic monoliths date to before the advent of metals is not yet known, nor, it must be emphasized, is it yet possible to propose an estimate of the date at which the inhabitants of southern Ethiopia first became acquainted with metallurgical techniques.

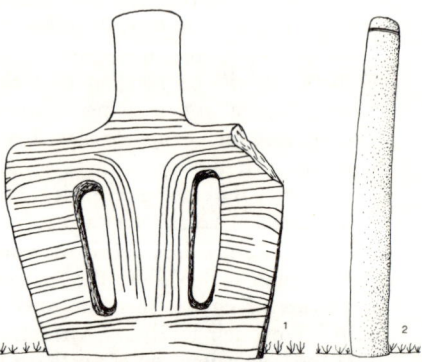

Fig. 83   Megaliths in southern Ethiopia (not to scale): 1, in Soddo (after Anfray, 1975); 2, in Sidamo (after Azais and Chambard, 1931)

To the north-west, around Harar, are found funerary monuments which evidently belong to a related tradition. Here, Azais and Chambard (1931) report graves with small burial chambers roofed with a single stone slab. Other structures in this region include large cairns, stone-lined subterranean pits, and upright monoliths. Recent investigations by Roger Joussaume (1971; 1975) have demonstrated that some at least of these monuments post-date the introduction of iron. Some similar monoliths, probably later in date and generally marking smaller, simpler graves, bear incised inscriptions in Arabic characters. The date of these latter monuments is unlikely to be earlier than the ninth century AD, in view of what we know from contemporary written sources about the spread of Arab culture inland from the Dahlak Islands and from Zeila during the closing centuries of the first millennium (Trimingham, 1952). Ruined towns with massive stone-built walls are sited in many defensive positions in the Harar area. They have as yet been investigated only cursorily, but most probably belong to this period of Islamic expansion.

In the low-lying plains of northern Kenya (Fig. 84), an archaeological succession is beginning to emerge through unpublished research conducted by the present writer. It is evident that the stone-tool-using pastoral peoples continued in occupation of the region until at least the fifth century ad, or even more recently in some places. At North Horr II, a large open settlement – occupied, perhaps intermittently, during the second half of the first millennium ad and the first half of the second – was situated on the shore of the Chalbi Lake, which was by this time shallow and greatly shrunken from its former

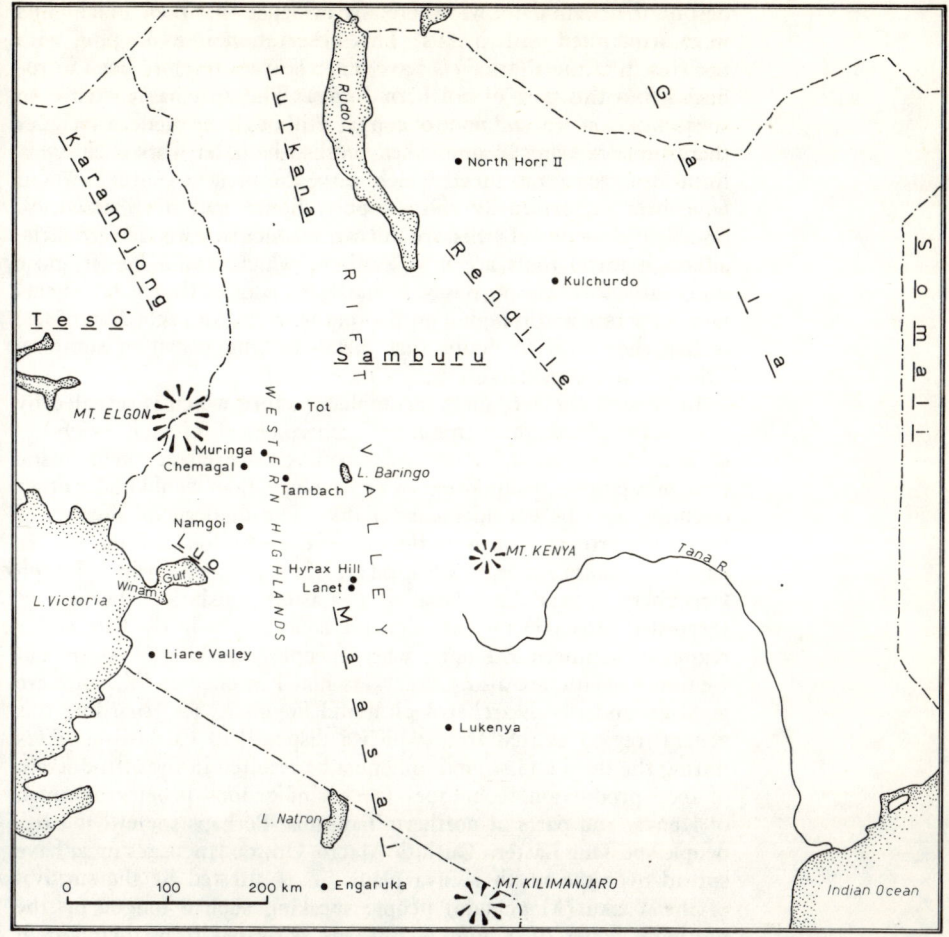

*Fig. 84 Non-Bantu sites of the last two millennia in East Africa. The present
locations of selected peoples are shown underlined*

extent. The inhabitants of this site practised a mode 5 microlithic
technology which continued many typological and stylistic features
of the much older nearby settlement which has been described above
in chapter IV (pp. 71–3). The pottery, on the other hand, showed considerable development and included fine red-burnished wares with
incised decoration executed after the clay had hardened. Some two
hundred kilometres to the south-east, on Mount Marsabit just outside the present forest edge, is Kulchurdo rockshelter, occupied during
the fifteenth century ad by people making a stone industry which differed markedly from that of North Horr II, backed microliths being
virtually absent and replaced by crude scrapers and heavily utilized
flakes: pottery was here extremely rare. It is tempting to attribute these
distinctions in material culture (to which geology and raw material
availability doubtless contributed) largely to the different life-styles
which the sites' respective environments would have supported, the
settled lake-shore existence of the North Horr folk contrasting with the
nomadic life of the inhabitants of the arid mountain slopes.

It is noteworthy that neither at North Horr II nor at Kulchurdo, despite their late date, was there any evidence that their inhabitants were acquainted with metals. This observation is in keeping with the view that metal artefacts have but relatively recently been introduced into this part of northern Kenya. The area has virtually no sources of iron ore, and none of copper. Although the modern societies there support many accomplished smiths, the latter work exclusively from imported scrap metal which, until the present century, would have been in extremely short supply. Some traditional activities, notably the digging of wells, are still carried out using wooden artefacts, although metal tools are now available which would be far more serviceable for these purposes. It may be concluded that metal objects were very rare in this region until a very few centuries ago. There is no reason, however, to doubt that metal-working began in southern Ethiopia at a considerably earlier date.

In view of the extremely incomplete picture which is revealed by the woefully inadequate amount of archaeological research which has so far been conducted, it is necessary to place more reliance on linguistic evidence, largely unsupported by archaeology, than would under other circumstances be considered advisable. The modern inhabitants of Somalia, northern Kenya (to the east of Lake Rudolf) and the greater part of southern Ethiopia are speakers of the languages which Joseph Greenberg (1963a) has classified as Eastern Cushitic. The area of greatest diversity in modern Cushitic languages is in the Rift Valley region of southern Ethiopia, where peoples speaking Western and Central Cushitic are also present. As noted in chapter IV, there are good grounds, both archaeological and linguistic, for regarding this general region as that from which a dispersal of Cushitic-speakers during the third and second millennia bc resulted in the introduction of food-production techniques to the indigenous peoples of much of Kenya, and parts of northern Tanzania. Perhaps somewhat later, people speaking Eastern Cushitic Macro–Oromo languages must have spread over the north Kenya plains, as is attested by the survival of the Yaaku (Mogogodo) people speaking such a tongue on the northern slopes of Mount Kenya, far separated from their kin in southern Ethiopia (Greenberg, 1963b).

The next stage in the linguistic development of the region was marked by the arrival of speakers of the ancestral Somali–Rendille language into an area which 'probably extended from Lake Rudolf on the west to the Benadir coast on the east, and from the Tana river on the south to probably the Ogaden, or possibly Harar, on the north. In this general lowland area, which in time came to include the easternmost Horn, the Somali internal dialect differentiation took place' (Fleming, 1964: 84). The existence on an island in Lake Abaya of a language (Baiso) more closely related to Somali and Rendille than it is to its more immediate neighbours suggests a possible general area from which this dispersal may have taken place. The date at which – or the period through which – this Somali diaspora occurred is not easy to ascertain. Clearly, it involved people who were predominantly pastoralists rather than agriculturalists (Heine, 1976). It probably took place before the introduction of the camel: an event which may, very tentatively, be placed around the middle of the first millennium AD if not before. Fleming (1964) has argued that the Somali-speakers were already present in what is now southern Somalia before the arrival there of Bantu-speaking people from the south. The latter event has been shown in chapters VI and VII to have occurred most probably within the period between ad 300 and 800. This view of the dispersal of the Somali peoples contrasts with the older view, based on a literal interpretation of Somali oral traditions and the inconclusive evidence of Arabic accounts of the coastal region, which regarded the Somali as having spread southwards from the northern areas of the Horn about a thousand years ago (e.g. I. M. Lewis, 1960).

Most recent of the major folk movements of north-eastern Kenya and Somalia has been the rapid southward expansion of peoples speaking Galla and related languages, including Gabbra and Boran. The majority of the Galla-speakers still live in the highland areas of southern Ethiopia but, within the last six or seven centuries, groups of them have expanded southwards through what is now north-eastern Kenya and Jubaland as far as the lower reaches of the Tana, thus effectively dividing the Rendille to the west from the closely related Somali to the east. Oral traditions and recent written records concerning the interactions of Galla and Somali relate mainly to fluctuations in the territory of the respective groups since the time of the main southward thrust or thrusts of the Galla (H. S. Lewis, 1966; Turton, 1975). The former contiguity of the Rendille and Somali is indicated by the presence of the Boni, speaking a language apparently closely related to Rendille–Somali, in territory which is now completely surrounded by Galla (Fleming, 1964). Despite this, Galla and Rendille–Somali are fairly closely connected branches of Eastern Cushitic, and it is reasonable to suggest that they owe their origins to the same general area.

The historical reconstruction outlined above, and in particular its chronology, must be regarded as highly tentative and provisional until such time as it can be amplified or modified by archaeological evidence. At present, the sparse archaeological data at our disposal are inadequate either to prove or to disprove the basic hypotheses suggested by linguistic studies. This is hardly surprising in view of the nature of the societies under study, with their migratory life-style, meagre and largely perishable material culture, and low population density. The traces which are left behind by recent settlements of people such as the Gabbra and Rendille comprise, for the most part, burial cairns and simple circles of stones placed so as to strengthen the base of temporary shelters (Plates XXVII, XXVIII, p. 256). Where there is no wood with which to make stock enclosures, corrals and pens are built of stone. Pottery is rarely used by these nomadic peoples, being replaced by lighter (and perishable) wooden vessels or baskets. For the centuries which have passed since the abandonment of stone-tool manufacture, therefore, the archaeological record is exceedingly scanty.

THE NORTH-WESTERN PARTS OF EAST AFRICA

The latest stages of the prehistory of the areas further to the west show significant differences from the picture outlined above. In this generally better watered region, agriculture played a much more significant part in the economy. The people with whom we are here concerned were almost exclusively speakers of Nilotic languages. The later Iron Age Nilotic-speakers in Uganda have partly been discussed in chapter VII above, in connexion with their interaction with their Bantu-speaking contemporaries.

Plate XXVII *A recently abandoned pastoral settlement in northern Kenya. The scale is in decimetres*

Plate XXVIII *An abandoned pastoral settlement in northern Kenya. Note the absence of imperishable artefacts: all that remains of the former house is a circle of stones and the fireplace. The scale is in decimetres*

Elsewhere, our most detailed archaeological data come from John Sutton's (1973a) investigations in the Western Highlands of Kenya. Much useful information on settlement patterns and economic practices has been recovered, but unfortunately we still lack a comprehensive chronological framework. As noted in chapter IV, this area was occupied by stone-tool-using, pastoral people during the last millennium bc. It is likely that, at this time, the Western Highlands formed an extension of the culture-area of the adjacent Rift Valley to the east; and it may be that, like their contemporaries in the latter region, the early pastoralists of the highlands were speakers of a Southern Cushitic language.

The date at which knowledge of iron came to the Western Highlands remains difficult to ascertain. It is not even certain whether the first Iron Age settlement there was the result of the arrival of a new population element, or whether metallurgy spread by diffusion to the earlier stone-tool-using pastoralists. Although the evidence is exclusively secondary, it seems more likely that it was the coming of the Southern Nilotic-speakers, presumably at some date during the first millennium AD, which was responsible for the introduction of iron. It is possible, if unlikely, that the Southern Nilotic-speaking Iron Age folk may have been established in the Western Highlands before the advent of the Bantu-speaking makers of Urewe ware to the Lake Victoria littoral immediately to the south. Virtually no archaeological remains have been located which may reasonably be attributed to the early phases of Southern Nilotic settlement in the Western Highlands; and such are urgently needed to support or modify the complex pattern of developments and migrations which has been proposed from linguistic sources by Christopher Ehret (1971). The area to the north-west of Lake Rudolf, whence it is suggested that the Southern Nilotic-speakers may have come, remains completely unexplored archaeologically.

Ehret's hypothesis, in general outline, is that the Southern Nilotic-speakers, who originated in an area near the modern borders of Kenya, Sudan and Ethiopia, spread southwards into the Western Highlands and there displaced an earlier Southern Cushitic-speaking population whose counterparts, however, continued to occupy the adjacent parts of the Rift Valley for some time longer. This Southern Nilotic language of the Western Highlands was ancestral to the modern Kalenjin dialects which are still spoken there today. A continuation of the spread of the Southern Nilotic-speakers into north-central Tanzania gave rise to a formerly widespread population whose language was ancestral to that of the modern Tatoga.

Although the detailed succession of events in this area during the first thousand years AD remains obscure, it is clear that by the first half of the present millennium a distinctive local culture had arisen in the Western Highlands. The settlement pattern of dispersed homesteads, characteristic of much of the area today, may already be recognized. Sites of these homesteads are marked by roughly circular depressions, usually between five and ten metres in diameter, the edges of which were in some cases lined with dry-stone walling. These structures are conventionally known by the somewhat misleading term 'Sirikwa holes', after the name given to an earlier population to which they are attributed by oral tradition. They are now known to have been defensible semi-subterranean cattle folds. Such structures are widely distributed, usually in groups of two or three, associated with the remains of circular houses built of mud applied over a framework of poles and interwoven lathes. Typical examples have been excavated by Sutton at Namgoi near Kapsabet, Muringa, Chemagel and at Tambach: at the last-named site the associated houses were built of stone.

That the later Iron Age economy of the Western Highlands was not exclusively pastoral is indicated by the presence of systems of field terracing, as at Tambach, and by several substantial irrigation works, most notable of which is that at Tot in Marakwet where carefully excavated furrows many kilometres long lead water down and across the Cherangani escarpment. The most highly developed irrigation works are found only in the more northerly parts of the highlands.

The material culture recovered from these Western Highlands sites is both sparse and simple. Pottery is characteristically roulette-decorated, but is more restrained both in vessel shape and in adornment than its counterparts further to the west. Typical vessels are tall and bag-shaped, often with handles or lugs, presumably for suspension. Iron, used mainly for arrow-heads and spear-points, is rare, as are beads, whether imported or local.

During the middle centuries of the second millennium AD, builders of 'Sirikwa holes' appear to have spread eastwards from the highlands and to have settled in much of the elevated portion of the Rift Valley, where they at least partially displaced the earlier pastoral folk who had until this time maintained their stone-tool-making technology little modified through contact with Iron Age peoples. This movement is attested archaeologically by the presence of numerous 'Sirikwa holes' in the Rift Valley. Examples have been excavated at Hyrax Hill and at Lanet, both near Nakuru (M. D. Leakey, 1945; Posnansky, 1967b). The latter site has been dated by radiocarbon to about the sixteenth or seventeenth century AD. At Hyrax Hill bones of zebu cattle were recovered, providing a rare view of the type of domestic stock which was raised in prehistoric East Africa. Roulette-decorated pottery of Western Highlands type (Fig. 85) is widespread on sites in the Rift Valley and in areas even further to the east, as at Lukenya Hill near Nairobi (Gramly, 1975a).

It is evident that this settlement of the Rift Valley was short-lived, being brought to an end by the southward expansion of the Eastern Nilotic-speaking pastoral Maasai in the late seventeenth or eighteenth century. These Maasai settled through a wide stretch of the Eastern Rift Valley as far to the south as central Tanzania, as well as on the high Laikipia plateau between Mount Kenya and the Nyandarua (Aberdare) Range. They further encroached on the territory of the Southern Nilotic-speakers by penetrating into the Western Highlands themselves and settling on the Uasin Gishu plateau near the modern Eldoret. It is not clear whether this great incursion represents the first penetration of speakers of Eastern Nilotic so far to the south, or whether the pastoral Maasai had been preceded by other, related, folk not yet differentiated in the archaeological record from the Southern Cushitic-speakers, as Alan Jacobs (1972) and others have suggested. Be that as it may, it is clear that the period about three centuries ago was one of major southward expansion by Nilotic-speaking peoples: movements broadly contemporary with that of the pastoral Maasai took place further to the north and north-west, in the areas now occupied by such peoples as the Samburu, Turkana, Teso and Karamojong. Also connected in some way, as yet imperfectly understood, was the more gradual arrival in the region around the

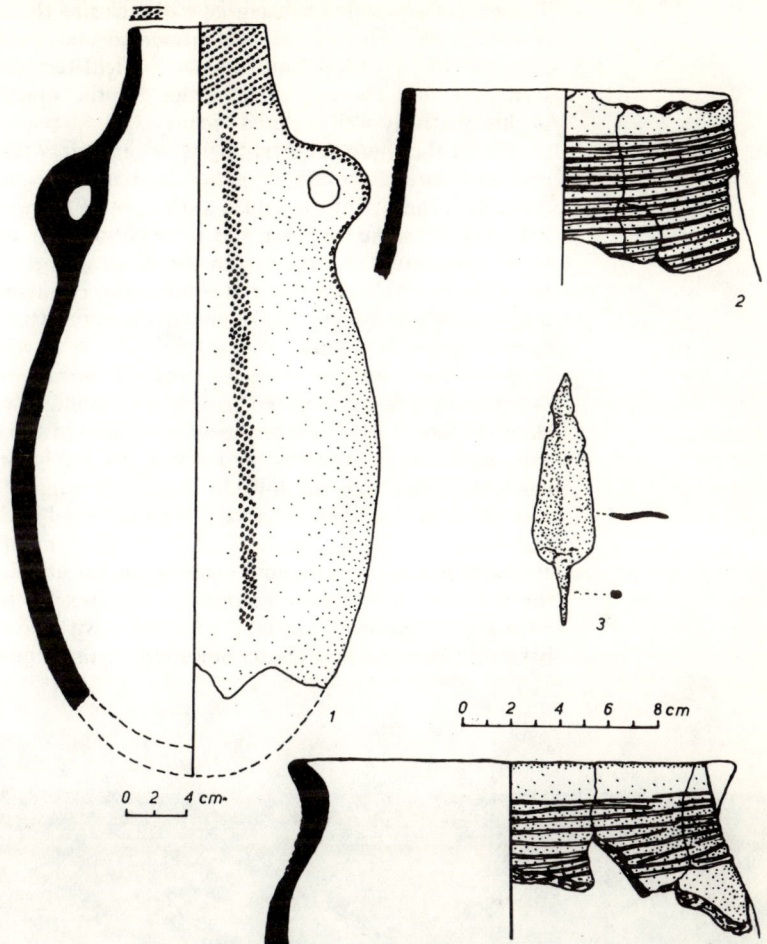

Fig. 85   Artefacts from Lanet (no. 1, after Posnansky, 1967b) and Engaruka (nos. 2–4, after Sassoon, 1966)

Winam (Kavirondo) Gulf in south-western Kenya of Western Nilotic-speaking people ancestral to the modern southern Luo. These Luo are the southernmost representatives of a very numerous linguistic group now living in much of northern Uganda and in the southern Sudan centred on the Bahr el Ghazal: an origin in the latter region is indicated by their oral tradition (Ogot, 1967), but has not yet been tested archaeologically.

In south-western Kenya, the Western Nilotic-speakers occupied territory which was previously settled by speakers of Bantu and, in part, Southern Nilotic languages; and considerable mingling of their cultural traditions has taken place. In recent times the traditional pottery of this area has been almost exclusively roulette-decorated, but with broader, more globular vessel-shapes than were the norm further to the north-east, and generally lacking the distinctive handles of the latter area. Stone-built stock enclosures are also found both north and south of the Winam Gulf (Lofgren, 1967), but are larger, free-standing structures than the 'Sirikwa holes' described above.

There was frequently a substantial wall enclosing the whole homestead (Plate XXIX). One of the best preserved and most elaborate sites is in the Liare Valley, South Nyanza. Field terrace walls are to be seen here, but there is no evidence for the practice of irrigation in this relatively well-watered vicinity.

It is in the more southerly parts of the Rift Valley that the most extensive and elaborate irrigation systems are encountered. Pre-eminent is the site of Engaruka, at the foot of the western wall of the Rift between Lake Manyara and Lake Natron in northern Tanzania. Here, the waters of streams flowing down into the dry Rift Valley from the relatively well-watered Ngorongoro Highlands were diverted into an elaborate system of stone-lined furrows and used to irrigate over twenty square kilometres of small fields, each of which was divided from its neighbours by lines of stones or terrace walls. Along the upper margin of the irrigated area, which extends for nine kilometres along the foot of the Rift escarpment, are scattered seven distinct village sites, each now represented by a series of roughly circular platforms partly cut back into the hillside and partly supported by a terrace wall. Their siting appears to have been designed both to aid defence and to leave the greatest possible area available for cultivation. Clearly, agriculture was the economic mainstay of Engaruka's economy, and the discovery of remains of sorghum indicates one of the crops that were grown (Sassoon, 1967a). It is not known whether the site's inhabitants were also herders of domestic animals, although the presence

Plate XXIX   A stone-walled homestead near Gogo Falls, South Nyanza, Kenya (by courtesy of Laurel Phillipson)

of large circular stone enclosures which may be the remains of stock pens lends some support to the view that they were. Several of these enclosures are, however, demonstrably later than the main irrigation system, and consequently may date from a period when decreasing water supply was necessitating a partial abandonment of agriculture.

There remains some uncertainty concerning the date of the Engaruka settlement and associated works. The flow of water at the present time is inadequate to irrigate the whole area that was formerly treated. Radiocarbon dates obtained by Hamo Sassoon (1971) include two in the first millennium ad, although of the remaining seven none indicates an age prior to the fourteenth century ad. Since there is no evidence for more than one period of construction (except in the case of the isolated enclosures), it appears reasonable to conclude that there was some poorly defined occupation of the area during the first millennium, but that the main irrigation-based settlement dates from a single period between six hundred and two hundred years ago.

The material culture of Engaruka's inhabitants was extremely simple. The predominant pottery type was decorated with horizontal parallel incisions below the rim, and is not at present known from other sites in this region, although comparable sherds come from further north in the Rift Valley, around Lake Baringo and in the Turkana District of north-western Kenya. Iron objects were not common, comprising mainly beads and tanged arrow-heads. Other beads were of shell, bone and occasionally copper, with the number of imported glass specimens being unusually high for a site in the East African interior. This last observation, taken with the presence of several cowrie shells, lends some support to the view that the main occupation of Engaruka was of relatively late date.

It remains to discuss the identity of Engaruka's inhabitants in the light both of the archaeological evidence described above and of our overall knowledge of the East African later Iron Age. Irrigation agriculture is today practised in the same region of northern Tanzania by the Bantu-speaking Sonjo, but their works are on a completely different scale from that of Engaruka, their pottery is quite distinct from that recovered at the latter site, and their traditions indicate connexions with the areas to the north-east, not with Engaruka. As has been shown above, some of the Nilotic-speaking Kalenjin of Kenya's Western Highlands still irrigate their fields; and in the past the practice seems to have been both more widespread and on a larger scale. The connexion with Nilotic-speakers is paralleled in the affinities of the Engaruka pottery, although it must be emphasized that this is not similar to the roulette-decorated wares of the Kalenjin themselves. An attribution to a Cushitic-speaking population must also be considered, for this region of northern Tanzania is linguistically one of the most complex in Africa, and is today inhabited by peoples speaking Bantu, Nilotic and Cushitic languages, as well as by the possibly Khoisan-related Hadza. Although it is not impossible that Engaruka will eventually prove to have been inhabited by a Cushitic-speaking people, it must be admitted that at present such an attribution appears unlikely. The question must still be left open: the present writer believes, however, that the most likely candidates are a Southern Nilotic-speaking people, perhaps related to the Tatoga. In the present state of our knowledge, the most important lesson to be learned is that, within the last thousand years, the divisions between the diverse later Iron Age inhabitants of East Africa have been breaking down.

So much cultural borrowing and assimilation has taken place that it is in many cases difficult to follow individual threads through the tangle of interaction that is evident at this period.

An attempt has been made in this chapter to summarize our very incomplete knowledge of the prehistory of eastern Africa north of the 'Bantu line' during the past two and a half millennia. For the sake of completeness, brief mention has been included of Christian Nubia and Ethiopia, although these cultures fall outside the main topic covered by this book. The main emphasis has been on the areas further to the south, where contact with these literate cultures appears to have been minimal.

In southern Ethiopia, northern Kenya and Somalia the period here discussed has been one of progressive desiccation, leading to increasing emphasis on pastoralism throughout the region. The sites that have been investigated are too few and too widely scattered to allow the reconstruction of an archaeological sequence: in northern Kenya at any rate it appears that iron was scarce until very recent times and that varied stone-tool industries continued in vogue until the middle of the present millennium. Correspondingly greater trust must therefore be placed upon linguistic evidence, and it is suggested that the Somali-speakers probably originated in the area east of Lake Rudolf and dispersed from there to the north and east. Further to the west, in the areas now occupied by Nilotic-speakers, it is only in the extreme south that any relevant archaeological research has yet been undertaken, and even here no adequate chronological framework has been erected. The Iron Age occupation of Kenya's Western Highlands may be attributed to Nilotic-speakers ancestral to the modern Kalenjin; while related people may have been responsible for the impressive irrigation works at Engaruka in northern Tanzania. The area to the north, centred on the southern Sudan, remains one of the major *lacunae* in our knowledge of later African prehistory.

X

༺ ༺

The final stone-tool-users of sub-equatorial Africa

In the preceding five chapters an account has been presented of the inception and development of the iron-using, food-producing societies whose direct descendants form the major part of the modern population of eastern and southern Africa. Two principal processes of cultural development have been recognized, and the areas where they operated have been shown to be quite well defined geographically.

In the more northerly regions, which may be regarded approximately as those lying to the north of the equator, techniques of food production were, during the last three millennia bc, gradually adopted by peoples whose technology was still at a pre-metallurgical stage. It has been argued in chapters III and IV that relatively few large-scale movements of population took place in connexion with these spreads of pastoralism and of agricultural practices. The same appears to have been the case when knowledge of metallurgy came to these stone-tool-using farmers during the last few centuries bc.

Further to the south a markedly contrasting situation prevailed. As shown in chapters VI, VII and VIII, knowledge of food-production, pottery and metal-working was introduced by means of massive and rapid population movements into regions where these traits were previously unknown. This process brought into contact with one another two essentially disparate populations: the stone-tool-using hunters and gatherers who were described in chapter II, and the incoming Iron Age folk. It is the processes of contact and interaction between these peoples which form the subject of this chapter.

EAST AND SOUTH-CENTRAL AFRICA

The very imperfect state of our knowledge of the diverse populations of East Africa during the first millennium ad has been discussed in the previous chapter. It is probably a function of the environmental diversity of the region that such varied populations were able to survive there in relative isolation from each other. Since many of the pre-Iron Age inhabitants were pastoralists and some – possibly – agriculturalists, the contrast between the early Iron Age arrivals and the stone-tool-using indigenes was somewhat less marked here than it was further to the south. Thus, for example, the early pastoral folk of the Rift Valley regions of southern Kenya and northern Tanzania continued to practise their mode 5 lithic technology in relative isolation from their Iron Age contemporaries in surrounding regions for many centuries – probably until early in the second millennium ad. Many more detailed excavations on sites of this period, to supplement the few widely scattered investigations so far undertaken, will be required before a comprehensive view may be obtained of the complex cultural interactions which must, nevertheless, have taken place between the different population groups.

It is only from regions further to the south that we are yet able to understand the processes of contact and interaction which took place between the Iron Age immigrants and the pre-existing stone-tool-using peoples, who here were exclusively hunters and gatherers. It was shown in chapter VI how the Early Iron Age Industrial Complex was introduced through most of south-central and southern Africa, from Zambia and Malawi southwards to the Transvaal, Swaziland and southern Mozambique during a remarkably brief period around the fourth century ad. In many parts of this region there is abundant evidence from both archaeology and oral tradition that the mode 5 stone-working technology of pre-Iron Age times survived for long after the inception of metallurgical practices. In some areas, occupation by users of chipped stone tools continued until very recent times indeed, although the degree of this survival varied according to the nature and intensity of the local Early Iron Age presence.

In Zambia, late survival of mode 5 stone-tool-using communities is best represented in the archaeological record by the later stages of the Makwe Industry (see p. 40, above) in the eastern part of the country, and by the contemporary industries, from further to the north and west, which are conventionally classified collectively as 'Nachikufan III' (S. F. Miller, 1969a; 1973; D. W. Phillipson, 1976a). It is important to realize that there is no evidence for the adoption of any sort of food-production economy on the part of the people responsible for these stone industries. Several detailed analyses of industrial successions in northern and eastern Zambia, such as that from Nakapapula rockshelter in the Serenje District (D. W. Phillipson, 1969), indicate that no significant typological changes took place during the period of contact with the Early Iron Age folk, such as would be expected had there been any appreciable change in the economic practices of the stone-tool-users as a result of such contact. The steady continuation of the microlithic industry, showing only gradual typological development in keeping with trends which were already apparent before contact with the newcomers was established, suggests that cultural contact was restricted. On the other hand, some form of contact between the stone-tool-using hunter/gatherers and the incoming agriculturalists is attested by the presence of occasional sherds of characteristic Early Iron Age pottery in virtually all the rockshelters and other sites which were occupied by the former peoples at this time.

Associated with these late stone-tool industries are found artefacts – notably ground-stone stools and pottery – which in some other regions, such as West Africa, have been regarded as indicative of the practice of a food-producing economy. As was noted in chapter II, ground-stone axes have a very high antiquity in Zambia, being attested at least as long as the 'Nachikufan II' industries of between the eighth and the sixth millennia bc. They are clearly an integral part of all the subsequent stone industries in the territory of the 'Nachikufan' traditions, and there is no reason to believe that they were at any time associated with food-production. The 'Nachikufan III' pottery is now seen to be typologically and stylistically indistinguishable from that of the local Iron Age industries; and it, like that recovered from Makwe Industry contexts, must be regarded as having been obtained

by the stone-tool-users through contact with their Early Iron Age
and later Iron Age contemporaries, rather than as being an integral
part of the material culture of the makers of the 'Nachikufan III'
or Makwe industries. There is clear stratigraphical evidence that microlithic industries of Makwe and 'Nachikufan III' type continued until
several hundred years after the inception of the later Iron Age
around the eleventh century ad.

Periodic use of even those rockshelters which continued to be frequented by the makers of the mode 5 stone artefacts is attested for
such Iron Age activities as metal-working. Schematic rock paintings
which – as will be shown in chapter XI – are now considered to
have been connected with Iron Age initiation and other religious
ceremonies, are further indications of the Iron Age people's physical
presence in the same sites as were still sometimes frequented by their
stone-tool-using contemporaries.

In the Zambezi valley near Livingstone, Joseph Vogel's (1975a)
investigations of the Iron Age succession have shown that the distribution of Iron Age settlement did not extend from the valley slopes
to the sandy soils of its floor until about the eighth century ad. In
view of the evidence for the late but undated survival of mode 5 stone
industries in this stretch of the valley (L. Phillipson, 1975; J. D. Clark,
1950b; Fagan, 1967b), it is tempting to suggest that, in this area,
the earlier population may have held its own for some centuries against
the advance of the Iron Age immigrants.

In those parts of central Zambia where the Early Iron Age is attributed to the western stream, a markedly contrasting situation appears
to have prevailed, for here there is hardly any evidence for the survival
of stone-tool-using communities for any significant length of time after
the arrival of the Iron Age settlers. For example, the succession of
mode 5 stone industries at Leopard's Hill Cave on the Lusaka plateau
is shown to have come to an end around the fifth or sixth century
ad, at broadly the same time as the establishment of Early Iron Age
settlement in the area (S. F. Miller, 1969b; D. W. Phillipson,
1968b). It is clear, as was noted above in chapter VI, that the population
densities of the Chondwe, Kapwirimbwe and Kalundu groups were
significantly greater than those of their eastern stream counterparts
beyond the Luangwa. Furthermore, these Iron Age folk, unlike those
of the eastern stream, were herders of cattle as well as of small stock
from the time of their arrival in what is now Zambia. Their competition
for territory with the stone-tool-using hunter/gatherers would thus
have been all the stronger; and the latter population would thus have
been more rapidly displaced or assimilated.

Further to the west, in the upper Zambezi valley of western
Zambia, Iron Age penetration seems once again to have been sparse.
Manufacture of mode 5 stone artefacts continued into at least the
fifteenth century ad, and it is possible that their makers also undertook the manufacture of pottery. The sherds in question, from Kandanda, are readily distinguished from their Iron Age counterparts by
their crumbly fabric and by the use of an organic temper (L. Phillipson, 1976).

The demography of this period in Rhodesia is less clear. Survival
of a predominantly mode 5 stone-working technology into the period
of Early Iron Age settlement is nevertheless attested at several sites,
notably Calder's Cave near Gokwe and the caves of the Matopo Hills
(C. K. Cooke, 1963a; 1966; N. Jones, 1933). As in Zambia, the archaeo-

logical evidence on which this statement is based consists primarily of sherds of Early Iron Age pottery associated with the most recent occurrences of microlithic industries. Confirmation is provided by studies of the rock paintings which, in the late phases of the stylistic sequence (as will be demonstrated in chapter XI), depict scenes in which Iron Age people engage in economic practices evidently different from the artists' own (e.g. C. K. Cooke, 1959; 1964a). At least in the greater part of the Rhodesian plateau it appears that, as in parts of central and southern Zambia, the stone-tool-using hunter/gatherers had been displaced by, or assimilated into the society of the Early Iron Age folk before the close of the first millennium ad. Elsewhere, the mode 5 industries survived the inception of the later Iron Age, as is best illustrated at the Limpopo valley sites of Dombozanga and Mpato (Robinson, 1964; Cooke and Simons, 1969).

It is now necessary to turn to a consideration of the nature of the contacts and interactions which took place between the stone-tool-using hunter/gatherers and the incoming food-producing Iron Age people. It is clear that the two populations maintained, to a large extent, their separate identities throughout the period of their co-existence. At virtually no Early Iron Age village sites except that at Kalambo Falls (J. D. Clark, 1974: 52) have chipped stone artefacts been recovered. In all the excavated rockshelters which were occupied during the appropriate centuries, on the other hand, mode 5 artefacts occur in substantial numbers associated with potsherds which are individually identical in every way to those found at the local Early Iron Age village sites. The most obvious interpretation of these facts is that the Early Iron Age immigrants were the sole makers of this pottery, but that they did not make chipped stone artefacts; while the indigenous population continued to practise their mode 5 stone-working technology, and obtained pottery from their Early Iron Age neighbours. The identity of the sherds from the rockshelters with those from the villages is such as to preclude the possibility that the indigenes ever manufactured this type of pottery themselves.

The clearest indication that techniques of pottery-manufacture may have been adopted by some of the mode 5 stone-tool-using peoples of south-central Africa comprises the small collections of sherds conventionally classed as 'Bambata ware'. The name comes from the cave in the Matopo Hills where pottery of this type was first described by John Schofield in 1940. Bambata ware is now known to occur at some ten sites widely distributed in most areas of Rhodesia except the north-west and the Zambezi valley (e.g. Bernhard, 1963; Robinson, 1966c; 1964; Schofield, 1940; C. K. Cooke, 1963a), but it has not been reported from neighbouring countries. Arguments linking it with pottery types from regions as far to the north as Kenya (Robinson, 1966a; Summers, 1967) are unconvincing. Bambata ware has been found almost exclusively in caves and rockshelters in association with mode 5 stone industries and also, on several occasions, with Early Iron Age pottery from which, however, it is typologically distinct. Radiocarbon dates for Bambata ware range from the third/fourth to the eighth/ninth centuries ad. It is thus contemporary with the local Early Iron Age pottery tradition. There is no evidence at all to suggest that Bambata ware predates the arrival of the Early Iron Age people in Rhodesia. The characteristic thinness and elaborate stamped decoration of Bambata ware (Fig. 86) indicate its separation from the Early Iron Age tradition, but occasional features of rim decoration suggest

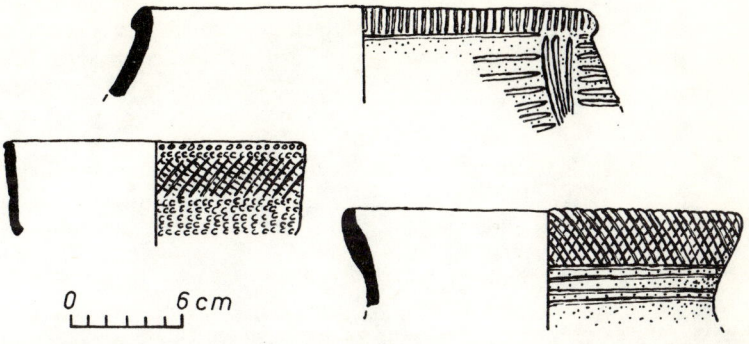

Fig. 86 Bambata ware (after Robinson, 1966c)

some degree of inspiration from the latter source. While the status and affinities of Bambata ware remain problematical, the most reasonable interpretation of these finds appears to be that first proposed by Roger Summers (personal communication): that they may represent the adoption or imitation by some of the stone-tool-using folk of Rhodesia of the pot-making technology of their Early Iron Age contemporaries.

When all these factors are taken into account, it is found that the most satisfactory interpretation of the occasional interactions which must have taken place between the stone-tool-using hunter/gatherers and the Early Iron Age food-producers is that of temporary client relationships. Such a situation may still be observed in several areas of southern Africa (e.g. Silberbauer, 1965; M. Wilson, 1969d; see also Harinck, 1969) and also in more northerly regions between various groups of Twa and their neighbours (d'Hertefelt, 1965). An area of south-western Zambia provides a vivid example. Here, on the arid plains between the Zambezi and Mashi rivers, small groups of Hukwe 'Bushmen' still continue a wandering hunting existence similar to that of their stone-tool-using ancestors. The Hukwe do not themselves make pottery or smelt iron: they obtain both these commodities from their Lozi and Subiya Bantu-speaking mixed-farming neighbours in the Zambezi valley. Meat, skins and labour are the main items which the Hukwe exchange for the products of their neighbours. For much of the year contact between the two groups is, in this sparsely populated region, rare. At certain seasons, however, groups of Hukwe emerge into the Zambezi valley and enter into a temporary client relationship with individual villages of Subiya, where they render hunting and herding services in exchange for food and other village products. Through this process, some groups of Hukwe have recently begun to grow their own crops, or even to own a few head of cattle. At Hukwe settlements away from the Zambezi valley (Plate XXX, p. 268) are seen several artefacts which were produced by Subiya craftsmen. Despite this increasing rate of acculturation, the wide cultural and social divergence between the two groups is recognized by both; and there is little integration. Such a model provides a plausible explanation of the archaeological data which have been recorded from several areas of south-central Africa.

Plate XXX   A Hukwe settlement in south-western Zambia

Evidence was cited above which indicates that the final eclipse of the stone-tool-using folk took place at markedly different times in the various regions of south-central Africa. In parts of the territory of the Early Iron Age's western stream, and in much of Rhodesia, the beginnings of Iron Age settlement seem quite rapidly to have resulted in the disappearance of the Stone Age hunter/gatherers as a distinct population entity – probably during the third quarter of the first millennium ad. Elsewhere, most notably in northern and eastern Zambia and apparently – in Malawi and in the Limpopo Valley, the two peoples appear to have continued to practise their traditional economies until long after the inception of the later Iron Age in the eleventh century ad. This interpretation of the archaeological evidence is in keeping with the oral traditions of the regions (J. D. Clark, 1950c; Rangeley, 1963) which are believed to relate to the last remnants of the stone-tool-using hunters and gatherers and which emphasize their lack of regular contact with the later Iron Age folk. It seems that their final extinction as a separate population took place, at least so far as northern and eastern Zambia is concerned, around the seventeenth century AD (S. F. Miller, 1969b; D. W. Phillipson, 1976a: 197).

The final disappearance of the hunting peoples may be attributed to the greatly increased and rapidly expanding population of the later Iron Age, with its increased economic emphasis on the herding of domestic animals, which has been discussed above in chapter VII. With the passage of time, these factors would have restricted the ability of the stone-tool-users to practise their traditional way of life; client relationships would have become more frequent and more permanent, resulting in the breakdown of the social and economic divisions between the two groups. This in turn must have led to the absorption of the last of the Stone Age hunter/gatherers into the society of the now far more numerous later Iron Age farmers.

SOUTHERN AFRICA

In parts of this region, the contact between Iron Age immigrants and their stone-tool-using contemporaries resulted in a variety of complex archaeological situations, some of which present a marked contrast with those which prevailed in more northerly regions. As has been noted in chapters VI and VII, Iron Age settlement in South Africa before the fifteenth century AD was virtually restricted to the region lying to the north and east of a line extending roughly from the vicinity of Windhoek to around Port Alfred on the south-east coast (Fig. 87, p. 270). It will be argued in this section that cultural traits of Iron Age origin spread far beyond this line and were there adopted by makers of chipped stone artefacts who did not themselves come into direct contact with Iron Age people. Here, as in East Africa and the regions further to the north, we find evidence for the practice of pastoralism and the manufacture of pottery by some of the makers of the local mode 5 stone industries, others of whom retained the hunting and gathering economies of their ancestors. Unlike the early East African pastoralists, however, these southern herders evidently obtained their knowledge of domestic animals and pottery, albeit indirectly, from an Iron Age source. Such is the diversity indicated by our very incomplete archaeological knowledge of the stone-tool-using peoples of South Africa during the past two or two and a half millennia that it will be appropriate here to present a brief regional survey before attempting an overall synthesis.

The western and southern coastal regions

These coastal regions form a convenient starting point: not only was it apparently here that Iron-Age-derived cultural traits were first adopted by the South African stone-tool-using communities, but it is also from the south Cape coast that we have our largest body of reliable excavation data. Chapter II, above, contained an account of the Wilton Complex of mode 5 industries in this region; and it was noted that through the first millennium bc the backed microlith component of these industries was gradually replaced by varied unstandardized scraper forms and by casually utilized flakes. Although there are few carefully excavated assemblages of this period which have been adequately analysed and dated, it appears highly probable that there was no single developmental process throughout the region leading to the gradual growth of the chipped stone industry and the abandonment of backed microlith manufacture (Fig. 88, p. 271). Instead, it seems likely that the inhabitants of some sites retained a true mode 5 technology until some time after the arrival of the first European colonists at the Cape of Good Hope, while elsewhere the production of backed microliths had been virtually abandoned as early as 1000 bc. It may be anticipated that some coherent pattern in this variation may emerge once the economic bases of the various settlements has been elucidated and when we know more concerning their respective environments and exploitation patterns.

It is through this varied spectrum of stone-tool-using communities that pottery makes a fairly sudden and widespread appearance at a date now shown to be very close to the beginning of the Christian era. The sherds which have been excavated from late Wilton contexts are indistinguishable from those which are found on the surface of coastal

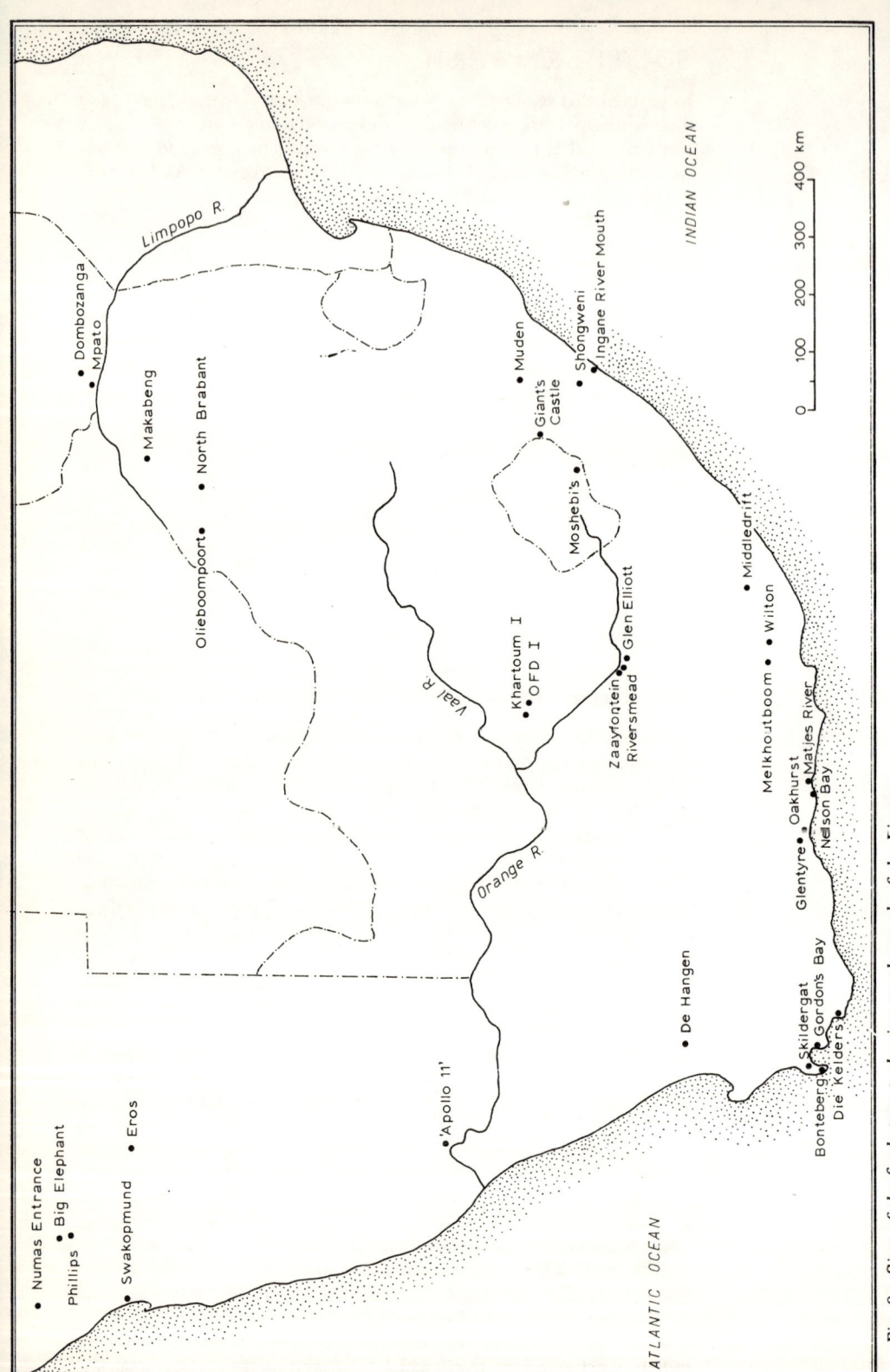

Fig. 87 Sites of the final stone-tool-using peoples south of the Limpopo

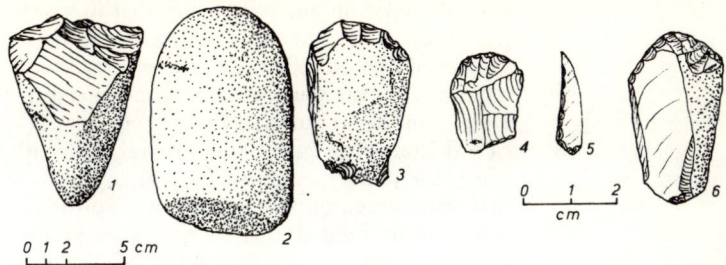

Fig. 88 *Artefacts of the final stone industries of the southern Cape: 1–3, from Gordon's Bay (after van Noten, 1974); 4–6, from Wilton (after J. Deacon, 1972)*

middens from Swakopmund in Namibia southwards to the Cape peninsula and eastwards along the south Cape coast (Rudner, 1968). Their fabric is characteristically gritty and poorly fired. Most vessels have a pointed base and are shouldered, with a relatively narrow neck (Fig. 89). Bosses or pierced lugs, presumably for suspension, are a frequent elaboration on the shoulder of these vessels. Decoration is not common but, where present, consists generally of grooved or incised parallel lines below the rim. Despite its simplicity, there can be little doubt that this pottery was developed from an established ceramic tradition. Since no traces of any earlier manifestations of such a tradition have yet been found anywhere in South Africa itself, it is reasonable to assume that its formative developmental processes must have taken place elsewhere (see below, p. 259).

It does not appear that any significant change in the typology of the Wilton stone industry was synchronous with the beginning of pottery, the crudescence to which allusion was made above having begun considerably earlier. At the Wilton rockshelter, for example, Janette Deacon (1972) has obtained a radiocarbon date in the fourth or third century bc for a developed phase of the mode 5 industry in which backed microliths are infrequent in contrast with earlier phases, being replaced by sidescrapers and utilized flakes. This phase pre-dates by a considerable margin the introduction of pottery. At the Nelson Bay Cave at Plettenberg Bay a date in the first century ad comes

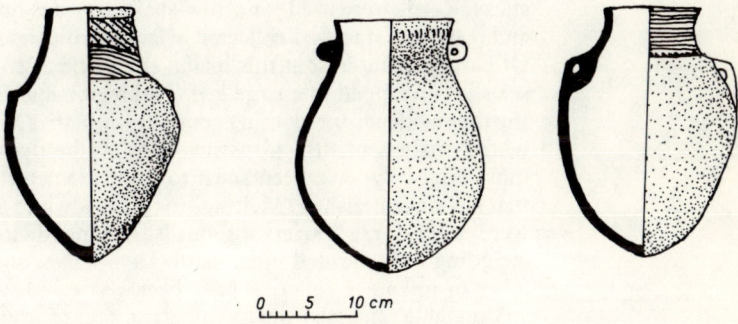

Fig. 89 *Pottery from the Cape coastal regions (after Rudner, 1968)*

from the level immediately below that in which pottery first appears (Sampson, 1974: 309). The late continuation of these pottery-associated Wilton industries is best illustrated at De Hangen in the mountains of the south-western Cape inland from Saint Helena Bay. Here, John Parkington and Cedric Poggenpoel (1971) have described a rich Wilton occurrence, dating from the fifteenth century ad onwards, where the pottery evidently belongs to the same general tradition as that represented on the earlier sites. Further excavated Wilton sites which have yielded this type of pottery are those at Oakhurst, Glentyre, and Melkhoutboom (Schofield, 1938; Fagan, 1960; H. J. Deacon, 1969). At Skildergat on the Cape peninsula a similar occurrence is associated with gunflints, imported from Europe and subsequently reworked (Jolly, 1947; 1948).

At some coastal sites, the trend towards the production of crude flakes and scrapers proceeded so far that backed microliths were totally unrepresented. These sites are found along the same extensive stretch of coast as are the late microlithic industries; and there was evidently a prolonged period of overlap, covering at least two thousand years, between the florescence of these two industrial facies. In some places, such as Bonteberg shelter on the Cape peninsula and a shell-midden at Gordon's Bay some 40 kilometres to the east, production of backed microliths had evidently ceased well before the advent of pottery (Maggs and Speed, 1967; van Noten, 1974). At the latter site, indeed, it appears that a completely non-microlithic tool kit was in use by the end of the second millennium bc. Excavations by Frank Schweitzer (1970) in a coastal rockshelter at Die Kelders about 160 kilometres south-east of Cape Town show the introduction of pottery during the first few centuries ad. The majority of sites containing this non-microlithic pottery-associated industry are coastal shell-middens, of which very few have been scientifically excavated (Rudner, 1968; Sampson, 1974). The sherds which they have yielded come from vessels apparently indistinguishable from those recovered in late Wilton contexts; and there can be no doubt but that the wares from both groups of sites belong to the same tradition.

These sites of the final stone-tool-using peoples of the southern Cape coastal regions are remarkable for the fine preservation of organic remains, resulting in an unusual insight into the technology of their perishable artefacts as well as into the vegetable diet of their inhabitants. At De Hangen, for example, were found pieces of sewn leather which may represent part of a tailored garment or a quiver for arrows. Wooden artefacts include fire-drills, pegs and digging-sticks. Reeds were used for arrow-shafts, various fibres for nets, cords and matting. Grass was collected in large quantities for use as bedding. Of particular interest at this inland site is the discovery of a parcel of sea shells wrapped in a large leaf (Parkington and Poggenpoel, 1971). Further evidence for clothing comes from Matjes River and Oakhurst, where settings of discoid ostrich-eggshell beads were noted, which must originally have been sewn to some garment, such as an apron, that has since perished (Meiring, 1953; Goodwin, 1938). Marine shells were used for a variety of beads and pendants. Bone artefacts including awls, headed pins, mattocks or adzes, and carefully carved tubes of unknown function have been recovered from several sites.

Vegetable remains from the montane sites of Melkhoutboom (H. J. Deacon, 1969) and De Hangen include much material which is best interpreted as derived from collecting wild foods. A detailed knowledge of the local vegetation is indicated by the range of species which were collected: corms, tubers, fruits, nuts and seeds were all exploited. At De Hangen the presence of domestic rye and of the castor oil plant, both non-indigenous species, demonstrates acquaintance with plants which must have been introduced by the early European settlers.

Analyses of the faunal remains show that a variety of resources was exploited by the inhabitants of these sites. At many of the coastal localities the species represented are almost exclusively fish and marine molluscs. Indeed, at several middens – such as that at Gordon's Bay as well as, apparently, at the numerous unexcavated examples spread along the Atlantic coast of Namibia and South Africa – shells are virtually the sole constituent of the faunal assemblages. In most cases the species represented are those which are still most common in the immediate vicinity of the site; and it may be concluded that the middens represent settlements temporarily, but often repeatedly, sited for the exploitation of specific shell-beds. Examination of the crayfish remains from Bonteberg (Grindley, 1967) has shown that the population was probably heavily exploited. Fishing was also widely practised; and at Oakhurst fish bones became progressively more frequent in the later stages of the Wilton occupation, being accompanied by a reduction in the numbers of backed microliths represented in the stone industry. No fish-hooks, such as would indicate the use of lines, have been reported; but it seems likely that nets were used as well as traps. It is probable that, by at least late Wilton times, tidal fish-traps, such as still continue in use on the south-western and southern Cape coasts, had been constructed in many of the shallow inlets (Goodwin, 1946; Avery, 1975). These traps consist of stone-built barriers behind which fish are stranded by the retreating tide. Similar structures were doubtless used on the lower reaches of suitable rivers, as they are in many areas of southern and south–central Africa at the present time (Plate XXXI, p. 274).

Mammalian remains are also found, especially on the inland sites such as Melkhoutboom and De Hangen. Bones of small creatures are by far the most common: at the latter site over ninety per cent of the individuals represented were hyrax or tortoise. During recent years there has been discovered incontrovertible evidence for the presence of domestic sheep at sites in the south-western Cape which date from the early centuries ad (Schweitzer and Scott, 1973). Sheep bones associated with chipped stone artefacts have now been reported from a total of seven sites in the Cape Province; and at four of these radiocarbon evidence suggests a date in the first half of the first millennium ad. Frank Schweitzer (1974) considers that the initial introduction of domestic sheep took place at about the beginning of the Christian era (see also Avery, 1974; Klein and Scott, 1974; Humphreys, 1974). All these are recent discoveries; and it is only in the case of Die Kelders, south-east of Cape Town, that fully documented details are yet available. Here, the relevant sample consists of several hundred bones, and there are indications that these are definitely of sheep and not of goat. The large numbers of young animals represented, and the high proportion of males, strongly suggest that the inhabitants of the Die Kelders site were themselves herders of sheep, not merely obtaining these animals from other herders in the vicinity by theft or raiding. The Die Kelders sheep occur at a level which is securely dated to about the fourth century

Plate XXXI Fish traps in northern Malawi

ad and which post-dates the first appearance of pottery at the site. Other bones from this deposit have been identified as those of domestic cattle, but further confirmation is required before this attribution can be regarded as certain.

The picture revealed by archaeology of the inhabitants of the western and southern coastal regions of South Africa during the past two or three thousand years is concordant with that recorded in the writings of the early European settlers at the Cape of Good Hope during the seventeenth century (Schapera, 1933; Goodwin, 1952). In 1653 Jan van Riebeeck was able to distinguish three groups among the indigenous inhabitants of the Cape Town area: 1 – strandlopers who were gatherers of shellfish and of wild vegetable foods, 2 – herders of cattle and sheep, 3 – fishermen who also owned herds of cattle (Thom, 1952). It is not apparent, however, whether these groups represented three separate populations or a single society following seasonally differentiated economic patterns.

Precisely the same problem is encountered when we attempt to interpret the available archaeological evidence; and there remains a strong element of disagreement between South African prehistorians as to the extent to which separate development is attested in the Cape coastal regions during the past three millennia. Garth Sampson (1974: 403–5), for example, would exclude those stone industries which lack backed microliths from the Wilton Complex and attribute them to a distinct 'Strandloper' population. Other researchers (e.g. Inskeep, 1967; H. J. Deacon, 1969, 1972) prefer to regard these industries and those of the later phases of the Wilton as representing different specialized – perhaps seasonally differentiated – activities of an essentially homogeneous population. More specifically, migration from winter settlements on the coast to more inland territories during the summer has been proposed; and Parkington and Poggenpoel (1971) have indeed demonstrated through study of the tooth-eruption patterns of hyraxes that the inland rockshelter of De Hangen was mainly occupied during the summer months. Furthermore, primarily winter settlement of at least some coastal sites has recently been demonstrated (Shackleton, 1973).

In the light of our present knowledge, it seems probable that both views represent an oversimplification of what may have been a complex series of interconnected processes of social differentiation and economic specialization. It would be logical to assume some basic distinction between the activities carried out at sites where backed microliths were produced and those conducted at places lacking such artefacts. Differences in the raw materials available are insufficient to explain the industrial variation now demonstrated on sites which were contemporaneously occupied. However, such economic evidence as we have shows that a comparable range of activities was practised at many sites with each type of industry, although there is a tendency for backed microliths to be very rare if not completely absent at settlements which relied mainly on shellfish for their subsistence base. There is certainly no reason why the inhabitants of such settlements should not, on occasion, have followed a hunting and gathering way of life and produced the artefact types appropriate to this, for it can be demonstrated that the people who inhabited the inland regions did maintain at least intermittent contact with the coast. A further argument for the absence of any sharp or permanent demographic divisions is the close stylistic similarity of the pottery found on the various sites in the region.

It is safest for the present to regard the final stone-tool-using population of the Cape coastal areas as representing the descendants of the Wilton people who from about 1000 bc, if not earlier, embarked on processes of economic specialization – perhaps in part as a response to population increase – which are mirrored in the differing typologies of the stone industries found on sites of this period. During the first three or four centuries ad there were adopted by these people two cultural innovations of foreign origin – the manufacture of pottery and the herding of domestic sheep and probably cattle. As has been argued in chapter VIII, it is likely that both these traits were introduced through contact in what is now southern Angola or northern Namibia with the western stream of the Early Iron Age Industrial Complex. Pottery and domestic animals did not spread concurrently through the stone-tool-using population, for at some sites the former precedes the latter, while elsewhere the reverse order is indicated. Pottery was evidently virtually ubiquitous on sites in this region by at least the end of the first millennium ad, while domestic herds are only relatively rarely represented in faunal assemblages of pre-colonial times. For the last fifteen or sixteen centuries, therefore, to the economies based on hunting, gathering, fishing and shellfish collection was added that dependent on pastoralism. We have no evidence that any of these economies was ever practised to the exclusion of all others; and each doubtless contributed in varying degrees, according to seasonal and cultural factors as well as geographical location, to the subsistence of the final Wilton populations. It is noteworthy that there is no evidence that knowledge either of metallurgy or of plant cultivation spread to these people before the advent of the European colonists. Such were the antecedents of the 'Hottentot' peoples encountered by the Portuguese and the Dutch at the Cape of Good Hope in the sixteenth and seventeenth centuries.

Namibia

In more inland areas of Namibia the archaeological sequence remains obscure, which is particularly unfortunate in view of the important role which this territory evidently played in the transmission of domestic animals and pottery-making techniques to the stone-tool-using peoples further to the south. As in the Cape, most archaeologists have divided the stone-tool industries of the last three thousand years into two distinct groups: 'Wilton', with large numbers of backed microliths, and others in which scrapers form the dominant element and from which microliths are virtually or completely absent. It appears from preliminary accounts of excavations conducted by W. E. Wendt (1972), notably in the Erongo Mountains and at the 'Apollo II Cave' near the Orange–Fish confluence, that industries of both types were partly contemporary with one another, at least during the last five or six centuries. There are as yet no clear indications as to when the scraper industries first appeared in Namibia. At the Numas Entrance Shelter in the Brandberg, Rona MacCalman (1965) has investigated a 'Wilton' occurrence, of about the eleventh century ad, which is overlain by a scraper industry akin to that for which the name 'Brandberg Industry' has been proposed by Jalmar Rudner (1957; 1973). Two sites in the Erongo Mountains – Phillips Cave and the Big Elephant Shelter – have, however, yielded radiocarbon dates in the last two millennia bc for comparable scraper industries (Martin and Mason, 1954; Clark and Walton, 1962; Fagan, 1967a). It may thus eventually be demonstrated that the two industries had in Namibia an overlap of comparable duration with that demonstrated above for their counterparts in the Cape.

In addition to the makers of these stone industries, there is now archaeological evidence – albeit only from northern Namibia – for the presence of peoples belonging to the western stream of the Early Iron Age Industrial Complex, as noted in chapter VI. The only Early Iron Age settlement so far investigated, that at Kapako near the Angola border, is dated to about the ninth century ad; but there is no reason to believe that this represents the earliest Iron Age penetration of what is now Namibia.

Undecorated, pointed-based pottery is attested at the Eros shelter near Windhoek from the second century ad (D. W. Phillipson, 1970b: citing Beatrice Sandelowsky and Rona MacCalman). There is thus evidence from the northern half of Namibia for the presence of pottery, closely resembling that found on coastal sites further to the south, at a time-depth concordant with the hypothesis that the Cape coastal pottery was derived from a north-westerly origin. The belief that domestic sheep and cattle, the appearance of which in the Cape seems to be linked closely with that of the pottery, is as yet without archaeological confirmation from Namibia, other than the undated testimony of the rock paintings which depict fat-tailed sheep but not, so far as is at present known, cattle (Inskeep, 1969: 23).

Further data are, as a high priority, needed on the introduction of domestic animals into what is now Namibia. Such research may be expected to throw light not only on the southernmost representatives

of the Early Iron Age's western stream, but also on the affinities and
early history of several of the territory's pastoral peoples, such as the
Herero, which have for long been subjects of speculation.

The interior and eastern regions of South Africa

In chapter II it was noted that scraper-based stone industries may
have continued in vogue in the Transvaal during the last few
millennia bc. There is good evidence that they survived for several
centuries the arrival of the first Iron Age settlers south of the Limpopo.
Most probably the sparseness of Early Iron Age occupation of the
Transvaal ensured that, at least in some areas, relatively little contact
took place between the indigenes and the new arrivals. This may be
illustrated by the discovery of stone scraper industries which lack
associated pottery, dated as late as the end of the first millennium ad
at Olieboompoort and Makabeng (Mason, 1962). It is not before the
second millennium ad, after the inception of the later Iron Age, that
we have archaeological evidence for the presence of stone-tool-using
societies which appear to have been in regular contact with their Iron
Age contemporaries.

It is necessary to emphasize the sparsity of published information
which is yet available concerning the archaeology of the Transvaal
during the first thousand years AD. Such work as has been undertaken has been concentrated on the Early Iron Age settlements
described and discussed in chapter VI: the contemporary sites of their
stone-tool-using neighbours have so far received very little attention.
Only in adjacent Swaziland, at Castle Cavern, have we evidence of
contact between Stone Age and Iron Age peoples as early as the
fifth century ad (Fagan, 1967a; Dart and Beaumont, 1968). It must
be admitted that the slender archaeological evidence which we have
is inadequate either to support or to refute the hypothesis propounded
in previous chapters (especially on p. 223) that it was through
contact with local Khoisan-speaking peoples, south of the Limpopo,
that the eastern stream Early Iron Age inhabitants of the Transvaal
obtained their domestic cattle, and that it was from the same source
that certain items of vocabulary relating to cattle-herding came to the
south-eastern Bantu languages. Clearly, further research is required.

For the second millennium the data are a little more plentiful. The
most informative site for our present purposes is the North Brabant
rockshelter in the Waterberg of the north-western Transvaal, investigated by Murray Schoonraad and Peter Beaumont (1968). Here, the
stone industry is of particular interest in view of the presence of some
backed microliths, such as are not yet attested in the Transvaal except
in very late contexts (Malan and van Niekerk, 1955; Mason, 1962).
Associated metal fragments and beads of glass and porcelain provide
chronological implications which are confirmed by the presence of later
Iron Age pottery akin to that from Bambandyanalo. In view of
the almost complete absence of industries containing backed microliths further south in the Transvaal (except in the Vaal valley itself,
bordering on the Orange Free State), it is tempting to suggest that
the North Brabant occurrence should be linked with those on the
Rhodesian side of the Limpopo valley. Here, as noted above, mode 5
technology continued to be practised until a few centuries ago, being
finally replaced by scraper-based industries of Transvaal affinities,
such as are represented in the extreme south of Rhodesia at Mpato

(Cooke and Simons, 1969) and in the most recent levels at Dom-bozanga (Robinson, 1964).

In Natal, although several sites have been investigated which appear to belong to the period under review, few have been adequately published or subjected to radiocarbon dating. In the coastal lowlands are found industries of scrapers and utilized flakes which show little significant difference from those of the south Cape coast. Such an industry is best represented in a midden at Ingane River Mouth, some 30 kilometres to the south of Durban (Schoute-Vanneck and Walsh, 1959). The site's inhabitants were both hunters and fishers. Only a single sherd of pottery was recovered; but nearby middens, which are probably somewhat later in date, were evidently inhabited by Iron Age peoples, as has been noted in chapter VII.

Further inland, the most recent chipped stone industries are those which have conventionally been classed as 'Smithfield N'. They are not dissimilar to those described above from the Transvaal, but contain a significantly higher proportion of concave or strangulated scrapers (Goodwin, 1930). The best published assemblages of such industries, albeit undated, come from a rockshelter and open site near Muden (Farnden, 1965). At the Giant's Castle rockshelter in the Drakensberg, Alex Willcox (1957) was able to demonstrate the presence of pre-pottery and pottery-associated phases of this industry; but about 100 kilometres to the south-west, at Moshebi's shelter in eastern Lesotho, a microlithic industry appears to have survived until after the advent of pottery late in the first millennium ad (Carter, 1969; Carter and Vogel, 1974).

To date, the chronology of the later stone-tool-using inhabitants of Natal remains very poorly understood, as does their economy and general life-style. A most tantalizing insight into both questions is provided by Oliver Davies' (1975) recent excavations at Shongweni South Cave some 40 kilometres inland of Durban. The stone industry from this site is crude and sparse, scrapers being by far the most frequent implement type. Pottery occurred down to a level which is dated to the beginning of the second millennium bc, as did remains of millet, both *Eleusine* and *Pennisetum*. The pottery is too fragmentary to permit comparison either with local Iron Age wares or with those found associated with other stone industries further to the south. The Shongweni evidence for the high antiquity of pottery in this region, and for the cultivation of cereals in pre-Iron Age times, is contrary to all other evidence at our disposal for the inception of pot-making and food-production in southern Africa. It will be prudent to suspend judgement on these discoveries until confirmatory data are available from other sites.

Little archaeological research has yet been undertaken in the Transkei and Ciskei, despite the area's clear importance as a frontier zone marking the furthest southward expansion of Bantu-speaking Iron Age people in pre-colonial times. Recent work by Robin Derri-court (1972) at an open-air occupation site at Middledrift on the Keiskamma river has demonstrated that the stone-tool-using peoples of the region had acquired both pottery and domestic cattle by the beginning of the present millennium. For a more detailed picture of social and economic interactions between the southernmost Iron Age folk and their stone-tool-using neighbours it is necessary to turn to the interior.

In the arid regions of the South African interior, in what is now

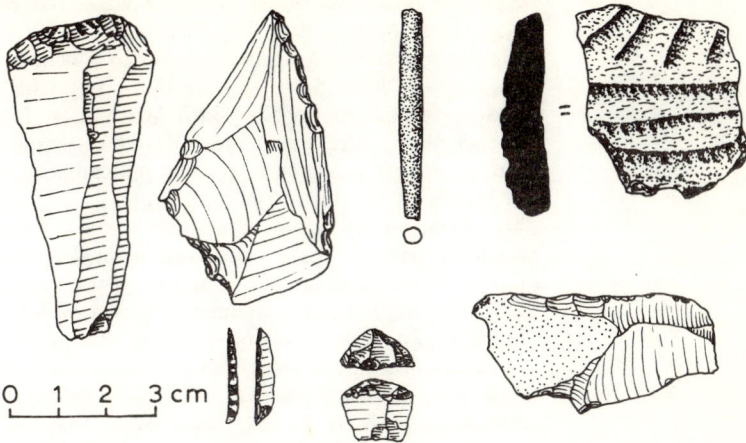

Fig. 90   Artefacts from Glen Elliott (after Sampson, 1967b)

the Orange Free State and northern Cape, microlithic industries appeared only at a relatively late date, as has been noted in chapter II (J. Deacon, 1974). Their development has been most clearly illustrated by Garth Sampson's (1967a; 1967b; Sampson and Sampson, 1967) excavations at sites in the middle Orange area (Fig. 90).

During the last two millennia bc, the stone industries of this region, as exemplified at such rockshelters as Glen Elliott, Riversmead and Zaayfontein, were dominated by large numbers of backed microliths, notably crescents, together with diminutive scrapers. The first fifteen centuries ad saw a continuation of the mode 5 character of the industries, with the crescents gradually giving way to increased numbers of backed blades and the small scrapers yielding to larger blade-end examples which, in contrast to their earlier counterparts, appear to have been used unhafted. Around a thousand years ago, the assemblages became enriched by the presence of pottery, glass beads, and occasional metal objects which presumably indicate contact, whether direct or indirect, with an incoming Iron Age population. Finally, the backed microlithic element was replaced by a proliferation of blade-end scrapers and bone points. This last industry probably appeared in about the seventeenth century AD, and survived into very recent times.

The better-watered mountain regions, such as those of Lesotho and adjacent parts of the Orange Free State and Natal, probably saw an inception of Wilton-like industries broadly contemporary with the corresponding event on the southern Cape coast. In Lesotho and neighbouring areas the levels marked by the first appearance of pottery are also distinguished by the presence of small, neatly made, tanged bifacial arrowheads (Carter, 1969; Humphreys, 1969).

The earliest pottery found on Wilton sites in the South African interior is markedly distinct from that described above from the coastal regions. Well-made, thin-walled, round-based undecorated bowls are characteristic (Sampson, 1974: 329). It is highly improbable that these vessels represent the handiwork of the Wilton people themselves, in view of the advanced techniques employed in their manufacture and the absence of any evidence for local development of the appropriate technology. For typological reasons they cannot be regarded as derived from the coastal ware. The remaining and most likely hypothesis is that they were acquired through trade or other contact with the Iron Age settlements to the north. This pottery from the Orange Free State and northern Cape bears much stronger resemblances to that of the South African later Iron Age than it does to that of the Early Iron Age Industrial Complex; and the dates of around the beginning of the present millennium for its appearance are in keeping with this attribution. Here, as was shown above also to have been the case in Zambia and Rhodesia, the advent of Iron Age artefacts seems to have been accompanied by no major change in the mode 5 technology of the makers of the associated chipped stone industry, or in their economic practices which centred upon the hunting of a wide variety of small animals.

Several centuries later, more pronounced changes took place. Following the establishment of dense Iron Age settlement in the northern Free State, as described above in chapter VII, a marked shift is attested in the artefact assemblages of the stone-tool-using folk further to the south, resulting in the almost complete disappearance of backed microlithic tools and their replacement by a proliferation of scrapers. These are the industries which earlier investigators (e.g. Goodwin and van Riet Lowe, 1929) dubbed 'Smithfield C' in the mountains of Lesotho and the eastern Free State: they have recently been reinvestigated by Sampson (1970). At several sites, notably Glen Elliott and Zaayfontein, these 'Smithfield' scraper industries overlie final manifestations of the microlithic Wilton: it appears that the interface between them dates to about the seventeenth century AD.

It is useful to speculate on the reasons for this apparently rapid change in the local chipped stone industries, since no major economic shift is attested in the archaeological record. Anthony Humphreys (1972) has pointed out that the typological shift to the 'Smithfield' was accompanied by an altered preference in raw material use which, however, followed continuing trends that had been under way for many centuries previously. If, indeed, the relatively sharp break which Sampson (1974) has proposed between the Wilton and the 'Smithfield' industries in this area is confirmed by subsequent research, it may be necessary to postulate the arrival of a new, albeit related, tradition from a neighbouring area such as the Transvaal, perhaps brought about as a reaction to population expansion among the Iron Age peoples further to the north.

At several sites in the middle Orange area, notably Glen Elliott, these 'Smithfield' industries are associated with rock paintings which appear to depict domestic cattle. No bones of such creatures have, however yet been recognized in the faunal assemblages, which represent exclusively wild species, including several types larger than those which were exploited by these people's Wilton predecessors. As Sampson (1974: 383) has pointed out, there are excellent grounds for identifying the makers of the 'Smithfield' industries with the last of the 'Bushmen' hunters who, as testified in the historical records, raided widely for cattle belonging to their European and Bantu-speaking neighbours.

To the west of the main region here discussed, in the Riet valley of the south-west Free State, as well as in adjacent areas of the Cape, it appears that a people making chipped stone artefacts of the type described above as 'Smithfield' adopted a settled pastoral life-style identical in many respects to that of their Iron Age contemporaries

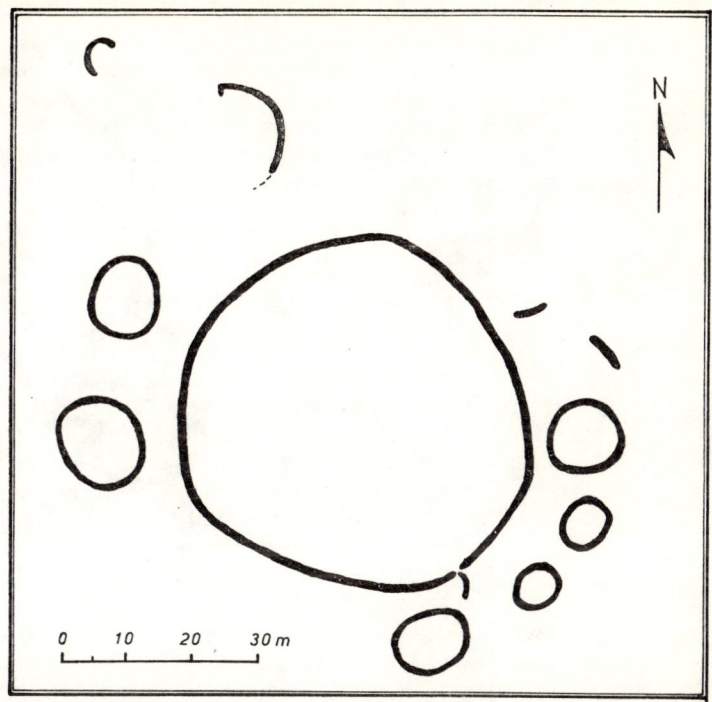

Fig. 91   Plan of the 'type R' settlement at Khartoum I (after Humphreys, 1973)

on the higher ground to the north-east. They occupied stone-walled settlements (known as 'type R'), each consisting of a large roughly circular enclosure, some 50 to 80 metres across, surrounded by several smaller ones (Fig. 91). Examples have been excavated by Tim Maggs (1971*b*) and by Anthony Humphreys (1973), respectively known as OFD 1 and Khartoum 1. They yielded almost exclusively undecorated pottery and, in the latter case, occasional iron objects of types well known from Iron Age sites in the north-eastern Orange Free State. Cattle and small stock were herded and a variety of wild species, mostly small, were hunted. Here is an interesting contrast with the Iron Age sites, where large antelope were the preferred prey of the hunters (Maggs, 1975): the stone-tool-using inhabitants of these 'type R' sites evidently retained their traditional hunting preferences after their adoption of pastoralism. At OFD 1, elaborate human burials have been described (Humphreys and Maggs, 1970). Both this site and Khartoum 1 are dated to the period between the sixteenth and the beginning of the nineteenth centuries ad.

Elsewhere in the Orange Free State and northern Cape, it appears from the archaeological record that the 'Smithfield' folk had a relationship with their Iron Age neighbours which differed markedly from that which their Wilton predecessors had enjoyed. Dense Iron Age settlement, especially in the northern Free State, was, as noted in chapter VII, now pressing southwards into the territory of which the Wilton people had formerly been the sole inhabitants. Raiding, stock theft and mutual hostility (Fig. 92) replaced the relatively peaceful co-existence which, with occasional trading contacts and client relationships, had prevailed in earlier times. The contrast is well illustrated

Fig. 92 Rock painting of cattle raid at Ventershoek, Cape (after Sampson, 1974)

by comparing the pottery recovered from Wilton sites with that which has been found associated with 'Smithfield' industries. The former was, as shown above, probably the work of Iron Age potters that had been obtained by trade: the latter is much coarser, mostly consisting of bowls decorated with massed comb-stamped designs, quite distinct from contemporary Iron Age wares, and may be interpreted as the handiwork of the 'Smithfield' people themselves. Smaller items, such as beads and iron arrow-heads, continued to be obtained from the neighbouring Iron Age societies; while more exotic objects, notably glass which was sometimes flaked into scrapers, attest for the first time contact with European settlers who were then steadily penetrating northwards from the Cape Colony. It was here that Europeans and Iron Age Bantu-speakers found themselves, perhaps for the last time in South Africa, fighting together against a common enemy – the 'Smithfield' stock raiders. By early in the nineteenth century the last of the 'Smithfield' folk had been destroyed or forced to settle as serfs on the European-owned farms which now covered their own former homeland.

This chapter has emphasized the contrast between the final stone-tool-users of the regions which were settled by Iron Age Bantu-speakers and those further to the south. It is argued that in most of the former regions the stone-tool-using hunter/gatherers continued to practise their traditional life-style and mode 5 technology, but were gradually drawn into dependence upon the incoming farming peoples, with whom a client relationship was probably in many cases established. In a few areas, Early Iron Age settlement was sufficiently dense to bring about the rapid disappearance, through displacement or assimilation, of the earlier population. Elsewhere, this continued to flourish alongside the immigrants until well into the present millennium, long after the advent of the later Iron Age.

To the south of the Bantu-speakers' territory a markedly contrasting situation prevailed. Here, many of the stone-tool-using hunter/gatherers adopted, presumably from their western stream Early Iron Age neighbours to the north, techniques of pottery manufacture and the herding of domestic animals. The impact of these herds on the diverse economies of the coastal regions is not yet clear, nor do we understand the extent to which fishing, shellfish-gathering, hunting, gathering and herding were adopted by different populations or at alternating seasons of the year. In the interior of South Africa, the stone-tool-users were gradually drawn into conflict with the expansion first of the later Iron Age settlers and then of the European colonists, the advent of whom they did not long survive.

XI

The prehistoric rock art of
eastern and southern Africa

There remains one class of evidence which may be used for elucidating
the later prehistoric past of eastern and southern Africa, and which has
so far received only cursory consideration in this book. This is the
paintings and petroglyphs which are found on the walls of caves and
rockshelters and occasionally on more exposed rock surfaces in almost
all regions where suitable surfaces occur. In previous chapters the
evidence obtained from study of the subject matter of this art has often
been cited and used in the reconstruction of prehistoric events and
economies. It has not, however, been found appropriate to present in
the general narrative a detailed discussion of the date, attribution and
meaning of the rock art. These topics are, by the very nature of the
evidence, matters for speculation as much as for scientific reasoning:
until the important questions of the periods to which the various art
styles belong and of the artists' identities have been supplied with
plausible and acceptable answers, any consideration of the significance
which the art had in the lives of those responsible for its execution
will necessarily lack a firm basis. For these reasons it has been felt
appropriate to present the main discussion of the rock art in a separate
chapter. Particular emphasis will be placed on an attempt to ascertain
the authorship of the various art styles in the light of the prehistoric
successions which have been discussed above.

It is only rarely that physical evidence is available for the absolute
age of the paintings or petroglyphs, although in several areas study of
superimpositions, or of relative states of preservation, has resulted in
the elucidation of a stylistic sequence (e.g. C. K. Cooke, 1963b; D. W.
Phillipson, 1976a). With the exception of rare situations where
paintings or petroglyphs have been found on stone slabs buried in
stratified archaeological deposits or on shelter walls which were
subsequently covered by such deposits, it is difficult to make correlations between the sequence of art styles to be seen on the wall of
a rockshelter and the datable archaeological succession which may
have accumulated on its floor. Another method of dating rock paintings
involves the chemical analysis of the paints themselves. Such studies
are still in their infancy, but pioneer research in Namibia by Edgar
Denninger (1971) indicates that the albuminous binders that were
often used in paint manufacture incorporate traces of several amino
acids which persist for differing lengths of time – as long as two
thousand years in some cases. Analyses based on these observations
have enabled absolute ages to be proposed for several paintings; and
the results obtained are in broad agreement with the relative stylistic
sequence which had been established previously (Willcox, 1971b).

These researches offer exciting possibilities for future development, although their application is at present restricted to the more recent paintings.

Further indications of the age of African rock art may be found in its subject matter. Representations of such things as domestic animals or metal tools must presumably be contemporary with, or later than, the first appearance of the corresponding objects in the local archaeological record. Sometimes the rock art of relatively recent periods includes motifs which may be identified in terms of the beliefs or practices of modern societies – with symbols used in religious ceremonies, for example, or with the ownership marks which are branded on livestock to facilitate identification of herds belonging to a particular individual or clan.

Study of subject matter clearly invites consideration of the significance and meaning of the rock art to those who were responsible for its execution. Except in the case of the more recent societies, where it is sometimes possible to employ modern parallels to suggest plausible interpretations, this is a field of study where rigorous scientific argument is only just beginning to replace subjective speculation. Such studies, pioneered so far as Africa is concerned by Patricia Vinnicombe (1972a; 1976), involve detailed quantitative analysis of the subject matter to discover patterns in the representation of individual figures and in the inter-relationship of the figures to one another. These investigations are of great value to the prehistorian because of the light which they can throw on aspects of past societies which are not otherwise represented in the archaeological record.

REGIONAL SURVEY

The known distribution of the rock art depends on several factors, not all of which are connected with the culture of the prehistoric populations. This is particularly true of the paintings. The main factor controlling their distribution is the occurrence of suitable rock surfaces on which people could paint. It is only where these surfaces are reasonably well protected from sun and rain, and also where the rock does not flake away rapidly, that paintings will survive for any appreciable period of time. Petroglyphs of course are more permanent and can remain visible for many centuries even when executed on completely exposed boulders or cliffs. Nevertheless, it must be remembered that many African petroglyphs are pecked rather than incised, and involve little more than the removal of the surface patina of the rock. Weathering, staining and the growth of lichen can succeed in obliterating such designs in a remarkably short time. These factors should be borne in mind, together with the very incomplete coverage of research, when considering the distribution of the rock art. The apparent absence of examples from much of Ethiopia, for example, may be due to the lack of adequate search; while the lacunae in the distribution map (Fig. 93) covering much of western Zambia and the greater part of the Congo basin are due to the nature of the local surface geology (see p. 286).

The Horn, Ethiopia and East Africa

The rock art which will be considered here is found principally in Eritrea, in the Harar region, in northern Somalia, in highland Kenya

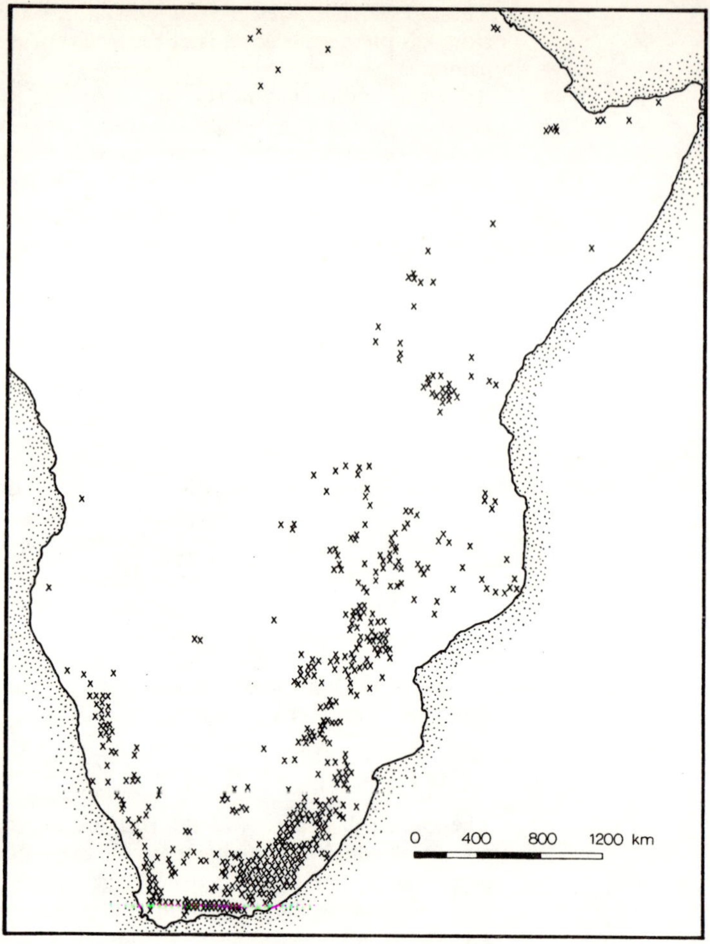

Fig. 93   Distribution of rock paintings in eastern and southern Africa

and the Lake Victoria basin, and in central Tanzania. In other areas rock art is rare and often of very late date. Throughout this region paintings are much more common than petroglyphs.

In Somalia and in northern and eastern Ethiopia a fairly uniform stylistic succession may be demonstrated (Breuil, 1934, J. D. Clark, 1954; Graziosi, 1964). The earliest paintings are simple naturalistic representations of animals, with occasional human figures. At the majority of sites the animals most frequently depicted are long-horned humpless cattle, and the human figures appear to be herdsmen rather than hunters. In the pictures of cattle, particular emphasis is placed on the horns which are often shown in twisted perspective, and on the udders, as at Genda Biftu, sixty kilometres west of Dire Dawa (Fig. 94). Wild animals are also shown in this series of paintings. At some sites, such as Porc Epic near Dire Dawa, the animals depicted seem to be exclusively wild; but it is not yet clear whether this is due to chance or whether there is a distinct group of earlier paintings which dates from a time prior to the advent of pastoralism. These naturalistic

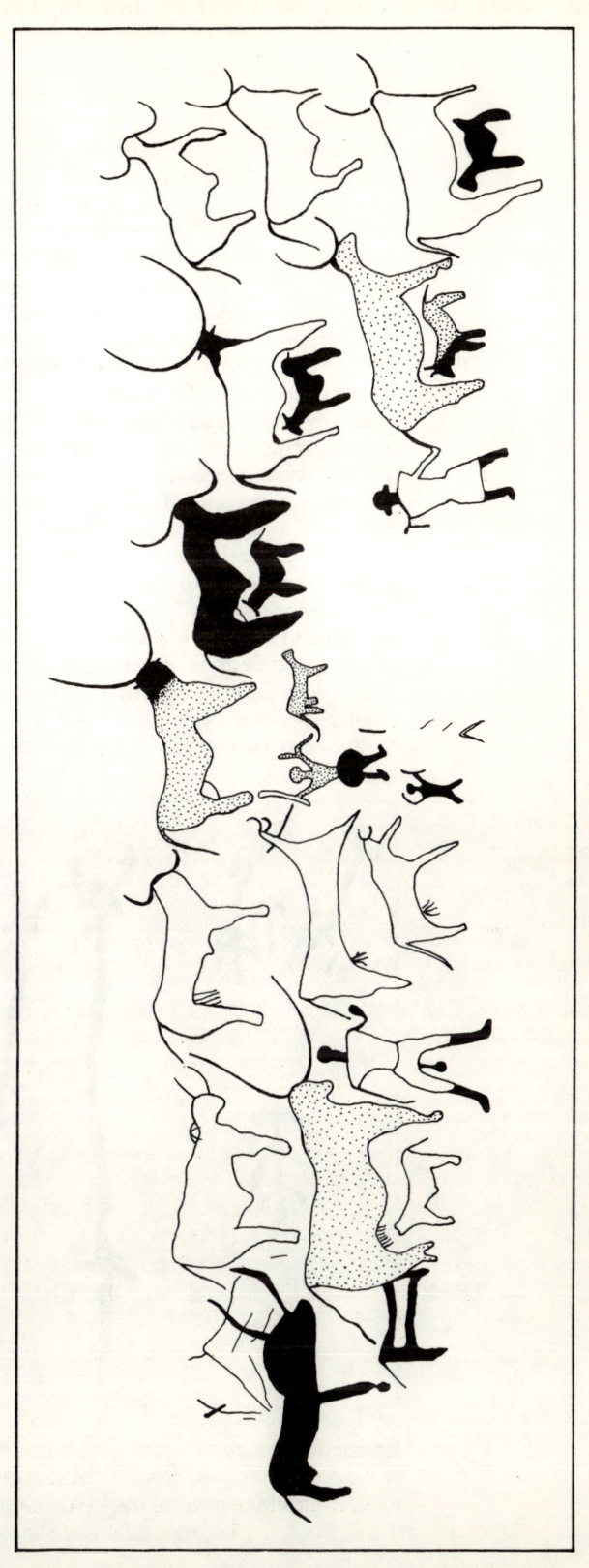

Fig. 94 Rock paintings at Genda Biftu, Ethiopia (after J. D. Clark, 1954)

paintings are followed by ones which display increasing schematiza-
tion. The subjects are now almost exclusively domestic animals,
mainly cattle but with some camels and, possibly, horses making their
first appearance. On some of the cattle may be distinguished ownership brands similar to those which are still used in the region today
(e.g. J. D. Clark, 1954: plate 50). The most recent paintings are highly
schematized figures of animals, mostly cattle and camels, and of human
figures, together with some completely schematic designs of which the
significance remains unknown. This last series has a wider distribution
than the others, and the majority of the known petroglyphs may also
be correlated with it.

Several areas around the shores of Lake Victoria have revealed paintings, all of a stylized or schematic type (Chaplin, 1974). Particularly on
the western shore of the lake, as at Bugombe and Bwanja near the
mouth of the Kagera river, highly stylized red representations of
horned cattle, shown as seen from above, are the dominant type (Fig.
95). Particular interest attaches to a few designs, such as those at Nyero
in Teso, which appear to show canoes (Posnansky and Nelson, 1968).
Also in red, and apparently broadly contemporary with the other
paintings, is a varied series of schematic designs, the affinities of which
are with the regions to the south and south-east, with central Tanzania
and – more especially – with Zambia and Malawi. To the east,
in highland Kenya, the known paintings consist almost exclusively
of schematic designs, in white or red, and appear to be very recent.
They occur most commonly in the territory occupied by the Eastern
Nilotic-speaking pastoralists; and in many cases the painted rockshelters may be identified with the meat-feasting places of the warriors

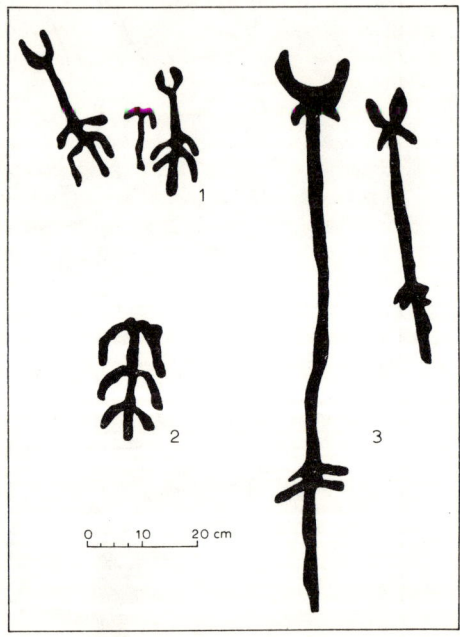

*Fig. 95 Stylized rock paintings of cattle from the Lake Victoria region of
Tanzania (after Chaplin, 1974): 1, at Bugombe; 2, at Kyegamo; 3, at
Ruasina*

(Gramly, 1975*b*). Shields are frequently represented in these paintings, while other designs are best interpreted as examples of ownership marks such as are branded on livestock. The apparently much earlier paintings of long-horned cattle on Mount Elgon, noted above in chapter IV, are at present without parallel in East Africa.

By far the greatest concentration of rock art in East Africa occurs in the northern half of the Central Plateau of Tanzania, notably in the Kondoa and Singida areas (Fosbrooke *et al.*, 1950; Masao, 1976). Here, the long and varied series of paintings is in marked stylistic contrast with those described above from regions further to the north; and the closest parallels which may be proposed are with the rock art of Zambia and southern Africa. The earliest Tanzanian paintings are fully naturalistic and display a greater degree of realism than any of the more northerly examples noted above. Animals, exclusively wild, are the most frequent subjects. They are depicted in outline, generally but not invariably filled in with either a flat colour-wash or a mass of fine lines. Human figures also occur, although less common and more stylized. Most of the humans and animals are depicted in isolation, but there are occasional group compositions or scenes: hunting and dancing appear to be the most common human activities recorded by the artists (Fig. 96). It seems clear that these naturalistic paintings were executed over a long period. Several attempts have been made to demonstrate a homotaxial stylistic sequence based upon the study of superimpositions, but it has not yet proved possible to produce a scheme which holds good for the whole area, probably because the individual styles which have been recognized have been too narrowly defined, and the resultant successions too complicated.

The most recent of the central Tanzanian paintings are schematic motifs, sometimes in red but more commonly in a thick greasy white paint, associated with highly stylized anthropomorphic figures and representations of cattle, including humped varieties (Culwick, 1931). Some of the red designs, which appear to pre-date those in white, may be paralleled in the Lake Victoria basin and, with greater confidence, in Zambia and Malawi further to the south. Since in the latter area the schematic art has been studied in greater detail than elsewhere, it is well to postpone discussion of it to the following section.

Before proceeding to a consideration of the rock art from further to the south, it is necessary to discuss the date of the extant examples in eastern Africa. The paintings in Ethiopia and Somalia clearly belong, in the main, to the period subsequent to the inception of pastoralism which, on the evidence cited in chapter III, may be regarded as covering approximately the last four millennia. It is possible, but perhaps unlikely, that some of the paintings which depict exclusively wild animals may be slightly older than this. The later stylized paintings and petroglyphs, which include representations of camels (Plate XXXII, p. 291), cannot exceed two thousand years in age and are probably in most cases considerably more recent. The same time-span may be attributed to the paintings of the Lake Victoria basin, at least to those (apparently an integral part of the series as a whole) which represent cattle, which were probably not present in that region prior to the Early Iron Age. In highland Kenya it is only the Mount Elgon paintings, which may be as old as the first millennium BC, that can be shown to precede the arrival of Eastern Nilotic-speaking peoples within the last four or five centuries. It is more difficult to suggest reasonable limits for the central Tanzanian paintings. Evidence will be cited below which

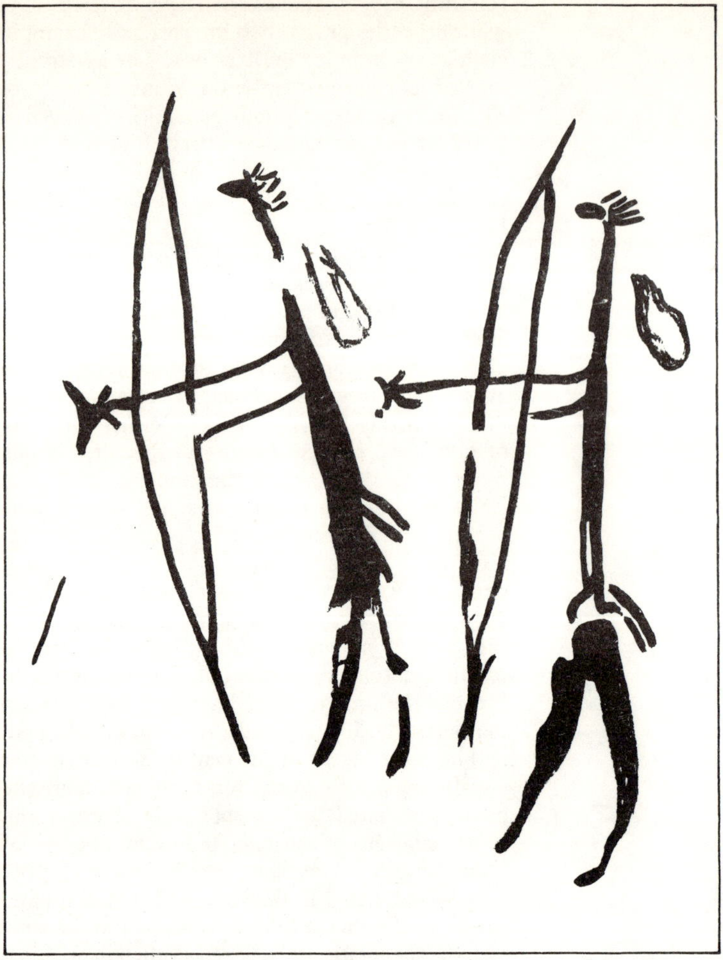

Fig. 96   Rock painting of bowmen at Masange, central Tanzania (after Sassoon, 1967b)

suggests that the schematic series belongs to the Iron Age. In the naturalistic series the animals depicted are exclusively wild, and the few items of material culture shown in use by the human figures are all concordant with an attribution to the stone-tool-using hunter/ gatherers. Clearly, as shown in chapter X, these people continued to occupy the region long after the inception of the Early Iron Age, probably until less than a thousand years ago. Ray Inskeep (1962a) was able to demonstrate at Kisese II that some of the red paintings belong to the period when both mode 5 stone artefacts and Iron Age pottery were being deposited on the floor of the shelter. How far back the dates of the older extant paintings extend it is not possible, on present evidence, to estimate.

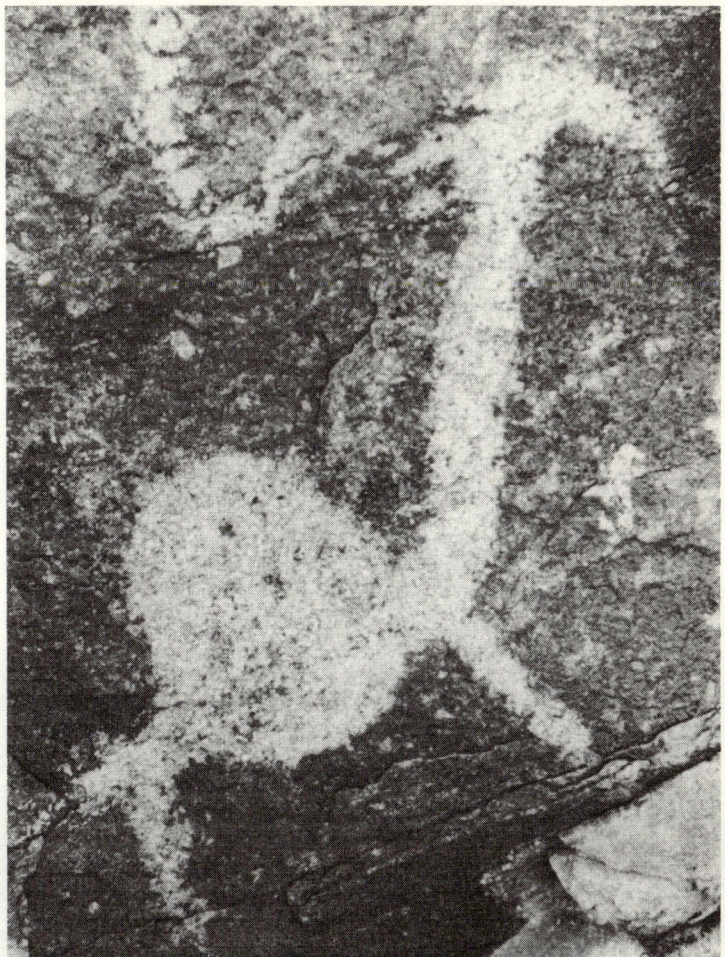

Plate XXXII   Petroglyph of a camel, Loiengelani, Kenya. Height: c. 20 cm

South-central Africa

In this section it will be convenient to discuss first the rock art of the areas north of the Zambezi in the modern Zambia and Malawi, and then that of Rhodesia and adjacent parts of Mozambique. The Zambian examples occur mainly in the northern and eastern parts of the country, with a few outlying paintings on the Copperbelt (D. W. Phillipson, 1972*b*; 1972*c*). Although paintings are widespread in Malawi, their distribution is most dense in the central region (Cole-King, 1973*a*). As in Tanzania, two basic stylistic categories may be recognized: naturalistic representations and schematic designs. Generally, but not invariably, the naturalistic art is earlier than the schematic.

Naturalistic paintings are most common in northern Zambia, especially in the Kasama area. Flat monochrome silhouettes are the rule, usually in red but with occasional black examples. Single wild animals are the subjects most frequently chosen: at Nachikufu there are also human figures armed with a bow or a spear. Two group compositions at Mwela and Somena Rocks, Kasama, are unique in the corpus of Zambian rock art which is currently known; and one of these (Plate XXXIII) is of particular interest as apparently representing a man armed with a spear attempting to drive a lion away from an injured cow. These naturalistic paintings are frequently overlain by later schematic designs in red paint, including grid-like designs and elaborate arrangements of finger-dots. At a few sites is represented a third, still more recent, series of paintings in thick greasy white pigment. This last series is marked by a return to a certain crude naturalism: stylized anthropomorphic and zoomorphic designs are typical, as are representations of metal tools. The Copperbelt may be regarded as an extension of this northern region, where the same general sequence is attested, but without the final phase which elsewhere is marked by the white paintings. Both the naturalistic and the schematic motifs, especially the latter, show regional differences from those seen further to the north.

Plate XXXIII   Rock painting of a lioness and cow(?), Somena Rocks, Zambia. Height of Lioness: 39 cm

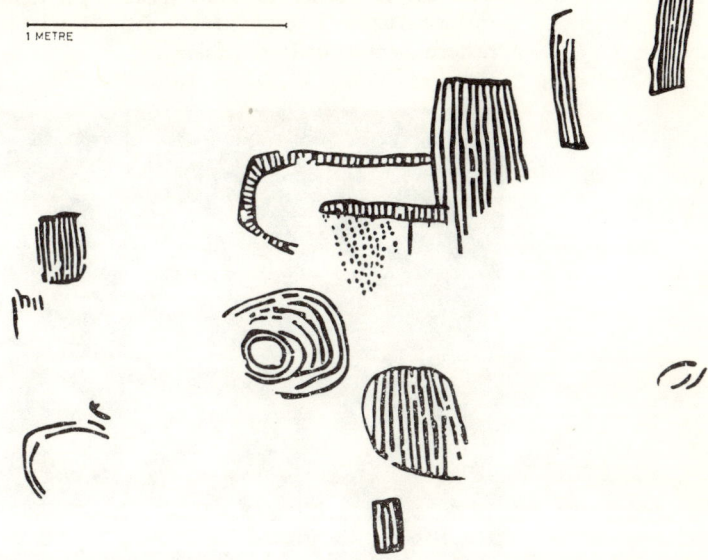

1 METRE

Fig. 97   Red schematic paintings at Katolola, eastern Zambia (after D. W. Phillipson, 1972b)

The rock-painting sequence of eastern Zambia and Malawi is essentially similar to that described above. The rare naturalistic paintings are exclusively of single animals, predominantly eland. The red schematics (Fig. 97) are both more common and more varied, with elaborate angular grids and patterns of concentric circles replacing the finger-dot designs of the north. At Katolola near Chipata a large figure of an eland overlies a schematic grid, demonstrating that the schematic art is not invariably later than the naturalistic, but that there was some chronological overlap between the two styles. In this region the red schematic art was followed by a series of red and white bichromes which has been shown to provide a continuous stylistic link with the latest white paintings. The latter show a great variety of motifs, both schematic and stylized: they evidently continued to be executed into the early decades of the present century, and were connected with the ceremonies of the Chewa *nyau* brotherhood (D. W. Phillipson, 1976a).

Petroglyphs in Zambia generally show a more westerly distribution than do the paintings; and many of them are of recent date. Particular interest attaches to a group of engravings in the Zambezi/Congo watershed country west of the modern Copperbelt. These petroglyphs are exclusively schematic, with the possible exception of one which may represent a hafted metal gad. Not only were some of these engravings painted, but at one site, Chifubwa Stream near Solwezi, they were found to be partly buried beneath accumulated deposits on the rockshelter's floor (Plate XXXIV), thus offering possibilities for establishing their age by archaeological means. On the Munwa Stream in the Luapula valley are further petroglyphs of elaborate circular schematic designs pecked into the top of flat rock outcrops unprotected by any overhang (Plate XXXV). Traditions have been recorded which connect these petroglyphs with the later Iron Age Butwa cult (Chaplin, 1959).

The closest parallels come from the upper Zambezi region of north-eastern Angola (Redinha, 1948). No petroglyphs are yet known from eastern Zambia or from Malawi.

Plate XXXIV   The schematic petroglyphs at Chifubwa Stream, Zambia. Area photographed: c. 1.3 × 1.0 m

Plate XXXV   Petroglyphs at Munwa Stream, Zambia (photograph by the late J. H. Chaplin). Area photographed: c. 1.0 m²

In Rhodesia, although petroglyphs are very rare, over 1500 painted sites have been recorded. They are widely distributed through the broad band of granite terrain which extends across the country from the east to the south-west. Detailed study of superimpositions has enabled a six-stage stylistic sequence to be worked out (C. K. Cooke, 1963*b*; 1969). Wild animals and human figures are the principal subjects in the first two styles, which in fact form an apparently continuous progression from simple monochrome silhouettes similar to some of the Zambian naturalistic paintings to finer, more lifelike pictures, giving a good impression of movement, which were usually carefully outlined before filling in with one or more coats of paint (Plate XXXVI). After an apparently long process of slow development marked by large numbers of paintings, there is a relatively abrupt change to style 3, in which the figures are shown only in outline. Cooke has presented convincing arguments that several of the style 3 human figures depict people whose physical appearance and activities differ from those shown in the earlier paintings. These representations of newcomers become even more clear in style 4, most notably at Silozwane Cave (Plate XXXVII) in the Matopo Hills (C. K. Cooke, 1959). Style 4 is marked by a return to silhouette, by the first appearance of bichrome and polychrome paintings, and by a substantial increase in the frequency of group compositions. The latter are sometimes elaborated, especially in Mashonaland (Goodall, 1959), by the inclusion of landscape features such as trees and rocks. Domestic animals, in the form of sheep, are represented for the first time: cattle are noticeably absent. Human figures are sometimes shown clothed or elaborately decorated. A fine example of a style 4 painting is that at Diana's Vow near Rusape (Plate XXXVIII), where a large supine figure, masked and elaborately decorated, is associated with a complex scene of people and animals engaged in various activities: it has been interpreted, perhaps a trifle fancifully, as representing a ceremonial burial.

Plate XXXVI Style 2 painting of a kudu bull at Nswatugi Cave, Matopo Hills. Length: c. 50 cm

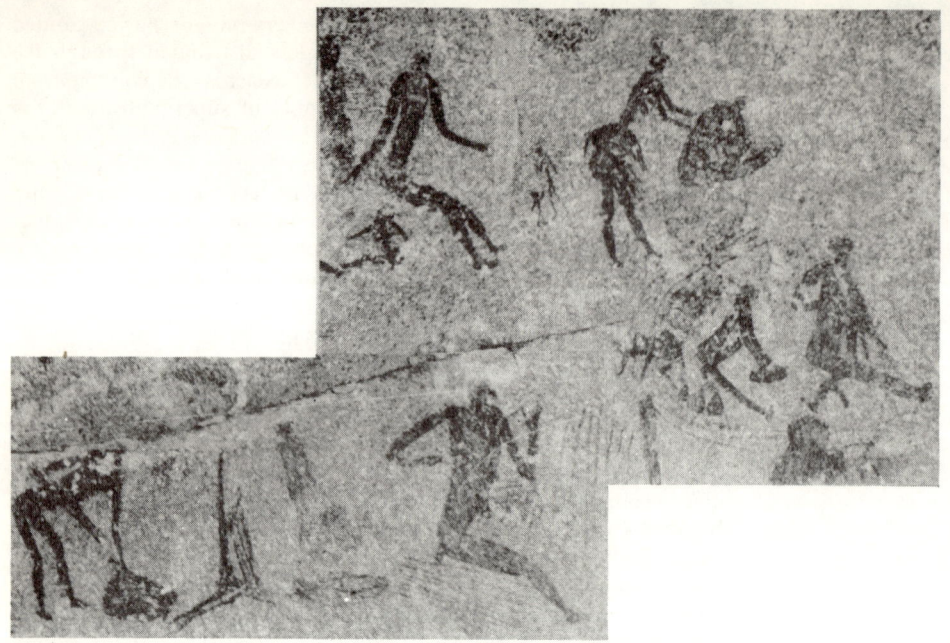

Plate XXXVII Style 4 paintings, apparently depicting strangers, at Silozwane Cave, Matopo Hills. Width of photographed area: c. 3.5 m

At this point there is a pronounced break in the Rhodesian rock painting sequence. Style 5 consists of schematic designs and rough zoomorphic figures so crude that the species shown cannot be identified. The final style, 6, is a development of this, characterized by large figures, usually of elephant, in a thick, white, plaster-like paint. The re-plastering of such figures has continued into very recent times, in connexion with rain-making ceremonies (C. K. Cooke, 1964*b*).

Despite the apparent dissimilarity of the Zambian and Rhodesian rock art, the two series share a number of points in common, and evidently follow broadly parallel and synchronous stylistic sequences. There is a strong similarity between the simple naturalistic silhouettes which mark the earliest stage of the painting sequence in each area, while the latest schematic and crudely stylized designs also have much in common. It is the middle phases, marked in Rhodesia by the superb naturalistic figures and scenes of styles 3 and 4, and in Zambia by the red schematic motifs, that are so strikingly different. I have argued elsewhere (D. W. Phillipson, 1972*b*) that, in Zambia, the early naturalistic paintings were – like their counterparts in Tanzania – the work of stone-tool-using hunter/gatherers, and that the schematic art was done by Iron Age people. The evidence for some degree of chronological overlap between the two series may be paralleled by the survival, demonstrated in chapter X, of the stone-tool-users long after the arrival of the Early Iron Age settlers. Regional styles within the red schematic painting series correlate closely with the different streams and groups that are recognized in the archaeological record of the Early Iron Age. In eastern Zambia and Malawi the schematic art follows a continuous process of development leading to very recent paintings which are demonstrably connected with later Iron Age religious practices. In

Plate XXXVIII   Style 4 painting at Diana's Vow, Rusape, Rhodesia. Width of illustrated area: c. 1.1 m

Rhodesia, styles 3 and 4 are also to be linked with an early stage of the Iron Age settlement (C. K. Cooke, 1969), but here the old naturalistic style continued, and the newcomers are seen as the artists' subjects rather than as artists themselves. It is only later that the schematic paintings, which are relatively poorly developed south of the Zambezi, replace the naturalistic ones. Here again, the most recent paintings may be connected with later Iron Age ceremonies. In both regions the tradition of rock painting can be shown to have survived into the colonial period.

Such evidence as we have for the date of the petroglyphs is in no way contradictory to that presented above. The schematic petroglyphs may be regarded as broadly contemporary with the schematic paintings: it has been argued that the painted engravings at Chifubwa Stream date to the fifth millennium bc or earlier, or even that they are contemporary with the use of the shelter by the makers of a 'Nachikufan I' industry; but closer examination of the stratigraphic evidence shows this to be inconclusive (J. D. Clark, 1958, 1959*b*; Willcox, 1963). For most of the later petroglyphs, such as those from Munwa Stream, a later Iron Age date (equivalent to that of the latest white paintings) is strongly indicated.

From the correlations proposed above it is possible to devise a reasonably precise absolute chronology. The tradition of naturalistic painting began, both north and south of the Zambezi, at an unknown date well before the advent of the Early Iron Age. It would be reasonable to suggest that the extant examples of styles 1 and 2 in Rhodesia were executed during the last millennium bc and first few centuries ad. There is no reason to believe that the paintings which survive were the first to be executed, and it may well be that the results of several thousands of years of rock painting endeavour have been lost to us. Style 3, marked by the appearance of strangers, would have begun soon after the arrival of the first Early Iron Age folk in the fourth century ad; and was probably not of long duration, soon giving way to style 4. There, the absence of pictures of cattle is strongly indicative of a date prior to the beginning of the later Iron Age in the eleventh century ad, for it is on sites of the later Iron Age that cattle bones and figurines are first found in large numbers. It was also, as argued above in chapter X, the substantial increase in population attained by the later Iron Age folk that resulted in the final eclipse of the stone-tool-using hunter/gatherers, by whom the paintings of styles 1 to 4 were clearly executed. Occasional red schematic paintings, which were probably executed by Early Iron Age artists, may thus be broadly contemporary with style 4. North of the Zambezi, the Early Iron Age folk were responsible for most of the art, whether painted or engraved, which was executed during the period from the fourth to the eleventh century; and this was predominantly schematic. There was relatively little naturalistic painting done either before or after the Early Iron Age advent; and only one example is known (that from Somena Rocks, noted above) where the incoming cattle herders were depicted in a scene reminiscent of those of the Rhodesian style 4. Finally, after the eclipse of the stone-tool-using hunter/gatherers, there are found through nearly all regions of south-central Africa schematic and stylized paintings and petroglyphs – known in Rhodesia as styles 5 and 6 – which may confidently be attributed to the later Iron Age.

Southern Africa

Southern Africa holds a greater wealth of rock art than any other region considered in this book; and it is here also that the investigation of the art has its longest history. Of particular interest is a series of paintings found on cobbles or detached slabs of rock which were used as gravestones in human burials at cave sites along the southern Cape coast (Rudner, 1971). Since in several cases these gravestones have been recovered from stratified archaeological contexts, they provide a unique opportunity for dating paintings which are in many ways similar to those found on rockshelter walls. In southern Namibia, W. E. Wendt (1972) has recovered small painted rock slabs, which do not appear to have been used as gravestones, from an Oakhurst Complex deposit at 'Apollo II Cave' dated to between the twelfth and the ninth millennia bc. Three of these paintings are recognizable naturalistic figures: a human figure and the outline of a rhinoceros, both in black, and part of a black and white striped creature which may be either a zebra or a giraffe, according to the excavator. These remarkable objects, which do not appear to be exfoliations from a painted wall, are by far the oldest definite evidence we have for the practice of painting on rock from any part of eastern or southern Africa. They invite speculation as to the wealth of mural art, older than any which still survives, which has been lost to us through weathering. A substantially later date seems probable for all the painted gravestones from the south Cape coast: although most of these come from old excavations and their associations are by no means clear, it seems that they may all be attributed to the Wilton Complex. At Klasies River Mouth, Ronald Singer and John Wymer (1969) recovered three

Plate XXXIX Painted stone from Coldstream Cave, Cape (after Rudner and Rudner, 1970). Size of original: 30 × 23 cm

painted burial stones from a dated sequence of deposits. One, depicting a man and four dolphins swimming, is firmly placed between the fifth and the third centuries bc. More problematical is a stone with a painted grid design, which appears to belong to a slightly earlier period. Probably the finest of these painted burial stones is that illustrated in Plate XXXIX, from Coldstream shelter in the Humansdorp District, depicting three polychrome human figures.

The rock art of the northern and eastern Transvaal includes naturalistic, schematic and stylized paintings, and shows many points in common with the Rhodesian material described above. Most of the naturalistic representations are single silhouettes of animals or humans, comparable with those of the Rhodesian style 2; but there are also some group compositions, bichromes and polychromes which closely resemble the style 4 paintings from north of the Zambezi. Stylized and schematic motifs in red and in white frequently overlie the earlier naturalistic paintings, as is also the case in Rhodesia: such designs are more common in the Transvaal than in other regions of southern Africa.

In the south-western Transvaal is the northern limit of a widespread zone where the surviving rock art consists almost exclusively of petroglyphs. The zone extends southwards through the western half of the Orange Free State into the central Cape Province (Willcox, 1963: 6), and shows hardly any overlap with the distribution of the paintings. The petroglyphs are found on unprotected rock surfaces in the open: they include naturalistic and schematic examples both pecked and incised. Some of the pictures of animals, such as those from Sweitzer Reneke in the Transvaal, portrayed by a simple incised outline or by fine overall pecking, show a mastery of technique and economy of line which, in the present writer's opinion, surpasses that of any of the extant paintings (Fig. 98). It has been claimed on several occasions that some of the petroglyphs show species of animals which are now extinct (e.g. Fock, 1972), and a very high antiquity has been postulated in consequence. None of these claims has been substantiated, however, and dates for the petroglyphs within the last few millennia at the most seem more probable, in line with those of the surviving paintings. Because most of the petroglyphs are on small isolated boulders which rarely have room for more than one figure, superpositions have only very rarely been found, and it has proved correspondingly difficult to demonstrate a stylistic sequence. Such sequences as have been postulated (e.g. Goodwin, 1936) have almost

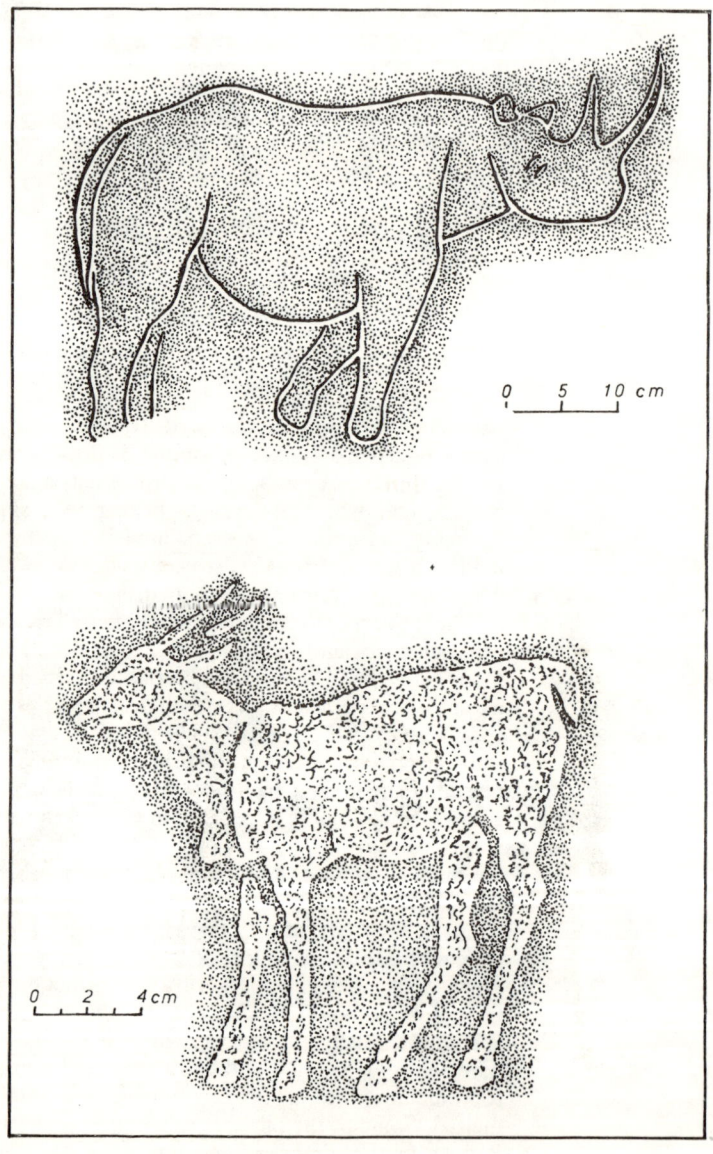

Fig. 98 Petroglyphs from the Transvaal (after Willcox, 1963): top, from Doornkloof; bottom, from Sweitzer Reneke

certainly been far too complex. There may be a tendency for incised petroglyphs to be older than those executed by pecking, but even this is far from certain. The schematic examples, best known from the site of Driekops Eiland some 60 kilometres south-west of Kimberley, are generally pecked (Slack, 1962). Pecked representations of fat-tailed sheep at Vryburg and Klerksdorp (Willcox, 1965) presumably date from some period within the last two millennia.

Far to the west, in Namibia, is one of the few regions where paintings and petroglyphs both occur in substantial numbers. This is in the highlands which mark the eastern edge of the Namib Desert; and the greatest concentrations of sites are in the Brandberg and the Erongo mountains in the northern part of the territory. The paintings are predominantly naturalistic and show considerable stylistic variation, although no overall sequence of styles has yet been conclusively demonstrated. Probably, as in Rhodesia, the earliest extant paintings are simple monochrome figures. At many sites, especially in the Brandberg (Breuil, 1955; 1959), these are followed by more elaborate figures, generally in groups or scenes, which are often bichrome or polychrome. Human figures are shown more frequently than animals; and they are commonly adorned either with simple clothing or with beads (Fig. 99). Fat-tailed sheep are sometimes depicted in paintings of this type, which bear quite a strong resemblance to those of the Rhodesian style 4. White schematic and stylized designs, usually crudely executed with the fingers dipped in paint, are the most recent paintings.

The petroglyphs of Namibia also show several different styles which are most clearly represented at the extremely rich site of Twyfelfontein, some 60 kilometres north of the Brandberg (Viereck and Rudner, 1957). Interestingly, it seems that the earliest petroglyphs here are pecked schematic motifs, which were followed by incised outlines of

Fig. 99   Rock painting in the Tsisab ravine, Brandberg (after Rudner and Rudner, 1970)

animals in fine naturalistic style, the surface within the outline being sometimes pecked away. In contrast with the paintings, the Namibian petroglyphs only rarely depict human figures. Also at Twyfelfontein, and perhaps occupying a fairly late stage in the stylistic sequence, are pecked representations of footprints, both animal and human. This is a remarkably widespread motif, being found from southern Angola to the southern Kalahari of Botswana, and northwards to the Wankie area of north-western Rhodesia (Rudner and Rudner, 1970). Unfortunately, nowhere can the footprints' chronological position relative to other art styles be adequately determined.

To the south, in the south-western Cape, petroglyphs do not occur. The paintings continue many features of the Namibian ones, although lacking counterparts for some of the scenes and elaborately decorated human figures of the latter area. There are several representations of fat-tailed sheep among the naturalistic paintings, but recognizable cattle only appear in the latest stylized art. A further feature of the rock paintings of this region, not found further to the north, is the representation of European-style ships – which can hardly be older than the end of the fifteenth century AD – and of settlers and their ox-waggons (Fig. 100). The style of the latter, and of the clothing worn by some of the figures, suggest a date of the late eighteenth or early nineteenth century. Such paintings are mainly found in the Cold Bokkeveld, north of the Cedarberg, and also belong to the late stylized series. There are also occasional red schematic paintings in this region, but they have received little attention from investigators and their place in the local stylistic sequence is not clearly understood.

Further inland, the rock art of the Cape Thirstland is quite distinct from that of the surrounding areas, being almost exclusively stylized or schematic (Rudner and Rudner, 1968). Both paintings and petroglyphs are found; and these show clear resemblances to those of the

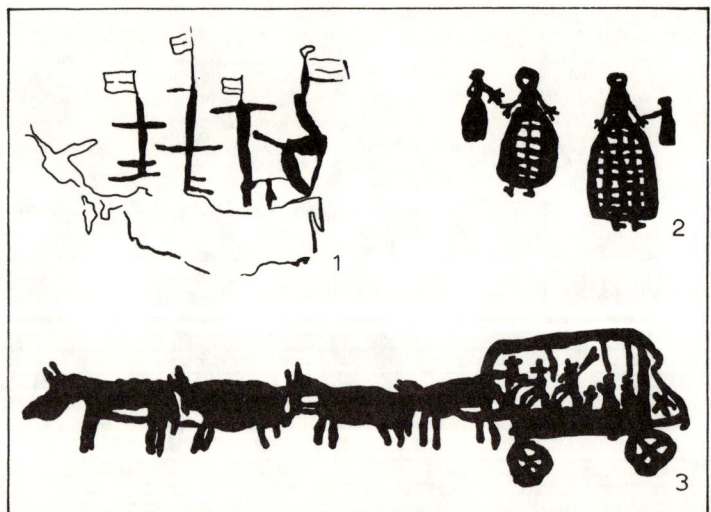

Fig. 100   *Rock paintings in the south-western Cape: 1, galleon at Noordbron (after Johnson, 1960); 2, 3, women in European dress and horse-drawn waggon at Katbakkies, Cold Bokkeveld (after Johnson, Rabinowitz and Sieff, 1959)*

later phases of the Namibian sequence. Fine naturalistic work is markedly absent, except among the petroglyphs in the north-east, adjacent to the main centre of such art noted above in the western Orange Free State and neighbouring areas. Comparison of the patination of the prehistoric petroglyphs with that of dated European *graffiti* at the same sites suggests that not all of the former are as recent as has sometimes been claimed (e.g. van Riet Lowe, 1952*b*). The only reliable dating evidence for the paintings comes from Glen Elliott in the Middle Orange area, where Garth Sampson (1967*b*) was able to demonstrate a connexion between crude white paintings of domestic cattle and of schematic grids and the final 'Smithfield' stone industry of the seventeenth and eighteenth centuries ad.

To the east, in the Drakensberg and adjacent mountain regions of Lesotho and Natal, the majority of the rock art is likewise of late date, but it provides a remarkable contrast with that described above. Petroglyphs are virtually unknown; and the paintings, which are almost exclusively naturalistic, display a greater variety of form and technique than is known from any other part of southern Africa. The earliest figures may be compared with those of the south-western Cape. The animals depicted are exclusively wild, and the human figures show no features which would suggest that they – and, presumably, the artists – were other than stone-tool-using hunter/gatherers. Subsequently, shaded bichromes and polychromes appear, accompanied by an increase in the number and complexity of group compositions. As in earlier times, eland are the animals most often depicted (Plate XL, p. 306). The subject-matter now includes clear representations of Iron Age people, recognizable both by their distinctive physique and by their belongings, notably spears and shields. Some of these figures are shown wearing voluminous skin cloaks or karosses similar to those of the recent Bantu-speaking folk of the mountains. For some time it has been believed that Iron Age people did not penetrate this mountainous region until the sixteenth century AD, and that all these paintings could therefore be attributed to the last four hundred years or so. Although relevant archaeological data from Lesotho and highland Natal are not yet available, the general picture of later Iron Age settlement presented in chapter VII suggests that this region may have been penetrated somewhat earlier than was formerly thought, thus allowing a greater time-span for the execution of the rock paintings. At some time subsequent to the appearance of Iron Age people, domestic cattle begin to be depicted in some numbers, in a style which is at first indistinguishable from that used for representations of eland and other wild species. It is at this late stage in the local rock painting sequence that are found scenes of cattle raids and of battles between the hunter/gatherer artists and the Iron Age cattle herders, such as that reproduced in Fig. 92 (p. 266, above). In the most recent paintings, the Iron Age people are joined by soldiers armed with rifles, wearing European-style clothing, and often mounted on horseback. These scenes must date from the time of the raids and punitive expeditions which took place through the greater part of the nineteenth century, resulting in the final extermination of the hunter/gatherers in this region in about 1890 (Willcox, 1956; Pager, 1971).

The earlier rock paintings of southern Africa show a much greater inter-regional homogeneity than do their successors. They also show more features in common with broadly contemporaneous paintings

Plate XL Paintings at Mpongweni near Underberg in the Natal Drakensberg (by courtesy of A. R. Willcox). The scale is in inches

from regions to the north, especially Rhodesia. At one time it was possible to regard the southern African paintings as derived from the apparently earlier Rhodesian art tradition, but such a belief can no longer be upheld in view of the very early dates now indicated for painting in southern Africa itself, notably at the 'Apollo 11 Cave'. The most acceptable hypothesis would take account of the facts that, probably in all regions, the earliest mural rock paintings have long since been lost, and that it is only the rare discoveries of buried gravestones or other painted pieces of rock that can provide us with an indication of the true antiquity of the tradition. It seems likely, indeed, that a tradition of naturalistic rock painting was formerly widespread through much of eastern and southern Africa, at least as far to the north as the modern Tanzania. (Interestingly, this broadly coincides with the zone where there is evidence that the stone-tool-using hunter/ gatherers may have spoken a Khoisan-related language.) Such a tradition appears, on the basis of the earliest extant paintings from each region, to have been relatively uniform, even though the later art shows much local differentiation. In origin, the art tradition clearly goes back, at least in southern Namibia, to a time before the local inception of the mode 5 industries. It would be premature to attempt to trace the origin of the tradition to any particular area, within or without the region of its eventual distribution.

The later developments of the rock painting tradition in southern Africa indicate the presence of several regional styles, the principal features of which have been outlined above. In Namibia and the south-western Cape the appearance of representations of fat-tailed sheep provides the earliest point in the sequence to which it is possible on archaeological grounds to attribute an absolute date – in this case one not earlier than about the beginning of the Christian era. Probably, therefore, the main series of group compositions in Namibia, those incorporating elaborately decorated human figures, are broadly contemporary with their closest Rhodesian counterparts, style 4. Clearly, the practice of painting continued into the nineteenth century, at least in parts of the south-western Cape and in the Drakensberg. Indeed, in the latter region there are good reasons for believing that the main florescence of the art occurred at a somewhat later date than it did elsewhere. In some areas, notably the Transvaal, Namibia and the thirstlands of the Cape interior, there are stylized and schematic paintings which may well have been the work of Iron Age people or other pastoralists, by analogy with the better-known schematic art of Zambia and Malawi. Petroglyphs, present in southern Africa mainly in Namibia, parts of the Transvaal, western Free State and central and western Cape, appear to follow developmental stages comparable with those of the paintings, although group compositions are extremely rare, and animals are portrayed far more frequently than humans. It is possible, although it cannot yet be demonstrated, that some of the petroglyphs have an antiquity greater than that of any of the surviving parietal paintings.

THE MEANING OF THE ART

In the foregoing section, attention has been concentrated on the evidence for determining local sequences within the rock art of eastern and southern Africa, and for establishing links with dated archaeological successions which enable us to postulate approximate ages for the various art-styles of each region. In the present writer's opinion, it is only when plausible suggestions can be made as to the authorship of the art that inquiry as to its original meaning and significance becomes either useful or practicable. There are three main areas where such inquiries have so far yielded acceptable results.

In East Africa, many of the most recent, predominantly white, paintings are clearly representations of livestock ownership brands. They may confidently be connected with the meat-feasts of the warriors in Nilotic-speaking pastoral societies.

The schematic and stylized art centred on Zambia and Malawi, but extending also northwards through Tanzania as far as Lake Victoria and southwards to most regions of Rhodesia and on into the Transvaal, may be attributed to the Bantu-speaking Iron Age folk. There are good reasons for regarding the earlier red schematic paintings as the work of Early Iron Age people, while the later bichrome and white designs, which include highly stylized pictures, seem to belong to the later Iron Age (D. W. Phillipson, 1972b; 1976a). In several cases the more recent paintings can be linked with religious ceremonies, most notably those connected with initiations and with rainmaking. It is reasonable to suggest that the red schematic paintings had a similar significance to the Early Iron Age artists.

The third art-group of which we are beginning to understand the meaning comprises the naturalistic paintings of southern Africa. Research has concentrated on a statistical investigation of the subject-matter (Maggs, 1967; Vinnicombe, 1972b). It has been shown that, in most areas, the animal most frequently depicted is the eland, a creature which is known to have occupied an important place in the creation myths of several southern African hunter/gatherer groups. Wildebeest, shown in the myths to have been associated with bad luck in hunting, are very rarely shown. Certainly, the choice of animals depicted in the rock art shows no correlation with the dietary preferences of the hunters, as indicated by the faunal remains preserved in the archaeological deposits. This effectively precludes the possibility that 'sympathetic magic' to aid the hunter could have been a primary motivating factor behind the naturalistic art. Similarly, although the painters must have taken considerable pride in the quality of their work, the creation of a thing of beauty cannot have been their sole aim, in view of the frequency of instances where paintings overlie others in an almost meaningless jumble, or are sited in inaccessible places. Seemingly, it was the act of painting, rather than the finished product, which was really significant; and we are now beginning to understand why this may have been so.

This chapter has concentrated upon an outline description of the rock art of eastern and southern Africa, upon the establishment of local sequences, and upon the attribution of the various art styles and groups to particular prehistoric communities. It is argued that very little of the surviving parietal art has an age in excess of a few millennia, although there is some evidence that the art tradition itself has a considerably greater antiquity. The earliest paintings of the region from Tanzania southwards, representing wild animals and occasional human figures, show a certain stylistic homogeneity and are attributed to the stone-tool-using hunter/gatherers. The later art of this region is more diverse and includes styles which are attributed to Early and later Iron Age peoples as well as to their stone-tool-using contemporaries. To the north, most of the surviving art appears to have been the work of pastoral peoples. These attributions are used as the basis for a brief consideration of the meaning and significance of the art – a study which is only now beginning to yield meaningful results. The construction of a realistic cultural and chronological framework for the rock art is a prerequisite to its proper understanding. Its absence has held up studies of the art for many years. Now that at least the broad design for such a framework is available, and methods are being devised for the scientific study of the art itself, whole new vistas of comprehension are opening for the Africanist prehistorian.

Epilogue

A synthesis such as has been presented in this book is clearly only a preliminary stage in developing a detailed view of the later pre-historic societies of eastern and southern Africa. I have tried to give a balanced account of the developmental processes which have taken place during the past twenty thousand years, and to show how these have contributed to the variety of recent African cultures. If I have paid great attention to matters of chronology, it is because I believe that this is an essential basis for an understanding of human develop-ment, as well as for confirming the validity of inter-regional corre-lations and overall trends. Rather than as a definitive statement, this book must be seen as a progress report on an ever-continuing study.

The topics which I have discussed have been primarily those illus-trated by archaeology. Details of material culture and economy un-doubtedly occupy a larger place in the narrative than they will in future studies. Archaeology is but one of many disciplines which are at the disposal of the prehistorian; but it cannot be emphasized too strongly that it occupies a pre-eminent place both because of the primary nature of much of its evidence and in view of its unique ability to provide an absolute chronology. The data which may be obtained from studies of, for example, historical linguistics, ethnography, oral tradition, or mythology are all floating in a historiographical vacuum until they can be anchored to a sequence and chronology based on archaeology. The same is true of several recently developed archaeological tech-niques and emphases, such as the study of prehistoric man's exploita-tion of the resources provided by his natural environment, of territorial groupings and the resultant inferences which may be made about social and political organization. Studies such as these assume a far greater relevance to the prehistorian when their results can be seen in their correct position in an overall sequence. The 'new' archaeology is marked by no great change of emphasis: it is a logical development from the old, which retains its importance as providing the foundations for the prehistorian's edifice.

If the archaeologist is to take maximum advantage of his discipline's pre-eminent position in African prehistoric studies, it is important that he should seek ways in which his discoveries can be related to those obtained by researchers in other fields. This is particularly desirable with regard to later periods of prehistory, where the con-tributions of non-archaeological prehistorical disciplines are relatively numerous. Examples from the preceding chapters showing how this correlation may be achieved include the tie-in of linguistic data with the archaeological sequence, notably that illustrating the development of Iron Age societies in the Bantu-speaking regions, and the suggested absolute chronology for the stylistic sequence of the southern and eastern African rock art.

In future studies the part played by linguistics will almost certainly increase; and language, as a diachronic cultural phenomenon which is relatively resistant to total eclipse, provides a valuable connecting thread between prehistoric societies and their successors. Linguistic development is a continuous process, however, and one must beware of projecting backwards the existence of individual modern languages far into the preliterate past. It is with the processes of linguistic development, divergence and interaction that the prehistorian should be primarily concerned.

Likewise, the individual names of modern societies or 'tribes' are of little relevance to the prehistorian, or even – it is now widely recognized – to the historian who is dealing with events of more than a very few centuries ago. The concept of 'tribe' springs from an individual's sense of identity or, on occasion, from a classification imposed upon a heterogeneous population by outsiders. Even at the present time, an individual's view of his own identity may vary according to the circumstances in which he finds himself. Beyond the range of fairly detailed oral tradition, 'tribal' identity is an intangible aspect of culture about which the prehistorian cannot expect to learn. Even oral traditions, having passed through the filter of human memories which have been exposed to more recent events and circumstances, cannot always be reliable sources in such matters.

As will have been apparent from even a cursory reading of the foregoing pages, there is still much to learn. Not only are there vast gaps in the geographical and chronological distribution of our knowledge, but the obtaining of a coherent overview is also hampered by the differing emphases of the studies which have been undertaken. This is a particularly unfortunate handicap when we come to consider the relationship between the literate cultures of north-eastern Africa, such as Meroe and Axum, and their preliterate neighbours. Investigations of the former have concentrated on studies of inscriptions, monumental architecture and the like, to the neglect of such topics as domestic economy and the more plebeian items of material culture such as could be expected better to illustrate the place of these cultures in the web of African prehistory.

It is not my intention to point out directions for future research: indeed, I hope that many of the major gaps in our present knowledge have been indicated in the preceding narrative. If this book has provided a lower storey on which future investigations may be based, it will have served its purpose. New directions and emphases are needed, as well as more basic exploration and field-work: to a large extent it may be expected that this will be achieved through the involvement of many more African scholars in the study of African prehistory.

References

ABBREVIATIONS

A.C.P.M.	*Annals of the Cape Provincial Museums*
A.E.	*Annales d'Ethiopie*
A.J.P.A.	*American Journal of Physical Anthropology*
A.N.M.	*Annals of the Natal Museum*
A.P.C.I.A.A.	*Actes du Premier Colloque International d'Archéologie Africaine*, ed. J. P. Lebeuf, Fort Lamy, 1969
A.S.	*African Studies*
A.S.A.M.	*Annals of the South African Museum*
C.A.	*Current Anthropology*
D.S.H.C.E.	*Documents pour Servir à l'Histoire des Civilisations Ethiopiennes*
G.J.	*Geographical Journal*
G.S.	*Goodwin Series* (South African Archaeological Society)
I.J.A.H.S.	*International Journal of African Historical Studies*
J.A.H.	*Journal of African History*
J.E.A.U.N.H.S.	*Journal of the East Africa and Uganda Natural History Society*
J.R.A.I.	*Journal of the Royal Anthropological Institute*
J.S.A.I.M.M.	*Journal of the South African Institute of Mining and Metallurgy*
M.A.D.P.	*Malawi Antiquities Department Publications*
M.N.M.B.	*Memoirs of the National Museum, Bloemfontein*
N.C.	*Numismatic Chronicle*
O.P.A.R.U.	*Occasional Papers, Archaeological Research Unit*, University of the Witwatersrand
O.P.N.M.S.R.	*Occasional Papers of the National Museum of Southern Rhodesia*
P.A.	*Palaeoecology of Africa*, ed. E. M. van Zinderen Bakker, Cape Town, from 1966
P.A.C.	*Proceedings of the Panafrican Congress on Prehistory*
P.P.S.	*Proceedings of the Prehistoric Society*
P.T.R.S.A.	*Proceedings and Transactions of the Rhodesia Scientific Association*
R.N.M.B.	*Researches of the National Museum, Bloemfontein*
S.A.A.B.	*South African Archaeological Bulletin*
S.A.J.S.	*South African Journal of Science*
S.N.R.	*Sudan Notes and Records*
T.J.H.	*Transafrican Journal of History*
T.N.R.	*Tanganyika (Tanzania) Notes and Records*
T.R.S.S.A.	*Transactions of the Royal Society of South Africa*
U.J.	*Uganda Journal*
W.A.	*World Archaeology*
Z.M.J.	*Zambia Museums Journal*

WORKS CITED

D. P. Abraham, 1962. 'The early political history of the empire of Mwene Mutapa, 850–1589', 61–91 in *Historians in Tropical Africa*, Salisbury.

D. P. Abraham, 1966. Review of Summers, 1963, *Africa* 36: 101–3.

D. Adamson, J. D. Clark and M. A. J. Williams, 1974. 'Barbed bone points from central Sudan and the age of the Early Khartoum tradition', *Nature* 249: 120–3.

F. Addison, 1949. *Jebel Moya*, London.

W. Allan, 1965. *The African Husbandman*, Edinburgh.

A. de Almeida and J. Camarate Fraca, 1960. 'Recintos muralhados de Angola', *Memorias da Junta de Investigaçoes do Ultramar* 16: 107–24.

F. Anfray, 1963a. 'Une compagne de fouilles à Yeha (février–mars 1960)', *A.E.* 5: 171–232.

F. Anfray, 1963b. 'Première compagne de fouilles à Matara', *A.E.* 5: 87–166.

F. Anfray, 1965. 'Matara – deuxième, troisième et quatrième compagnes de fouilles', *A.E.* 6: 49–85.

F. Anfray, 1967a. 'Les sculptures rupestres de Chabbé dans le Sidamo', *A.E.* 7: 19–32.

F. Anfray, 1967b. 'Matara', *A.E.* 7: 33–88.

F. Anfray, 1968. 'Aspects d'archéologie Ethiopienne', *J.A.H.* 9: 345–66.

F. Anfray, 1975. 'Sites et monuments du Soddo', *D.S.H.C.E.* 6: 35–48.

B. W. Anthony, 1967. 'Excavation near Elmenteita, Kenya', *P.A.* 2: 47–8.

C. Arambourg, P. Lester and J. Roger, 1943. 'Mission scientifique de l'Omo, 1932–3: géologie et archéologie', *Bulletin du Musée d'Histoire Naturelle* 1: 61–230.

A. J. Arkell, 1945. 'Iron in the Meroitic ages', *Antiquity* 19: 213–14.

A. J. Arkell, 1949. *Early Khartoum*, Oxford.

A. J. Arkell, 1953. *Shaheinab*, Oxford.

A. J. Arkell, 1954. 'Four occupation sites at Agordat', *Kush* 2: 33–62.

A. J. Arkell, 1961. *A History of the Sudan*, London.

A. J. Arkell, 1962. 'The distribution in central Africa of one early Neolithic ware (dotted wavy-line pottery) and its possible connection with the beginning of pottery', *P.A.C.* 4: 283–7.

A. J. Arkell, 1964. *Wanyanga*, Oxford.

A. J. Arkell, 1966. 'The Iron Age in the Sudan', *C.A.* 7: 451–2.

A. J. Arkell, 1969. Review of Wendorf, 1968, *J.A.H.* 10: 487–9.

A. J. Arkell, 1972. 'Dotted wavy-line pottery in African prehistory', *Antiquity* 46: 221–2.

A. J. Arkell and P. J. Ucko, 1965. 'Review of pre-dynastic development in the Nile Valley', *C.A.* 6: 145–66.

A. L. Armstrong, 1931. 'Excavations at Bambata Cave and researches on prehistoric sites in Southern Rhodesia', *J.R.A.I.* 61: 239–76.

G. Avery, 1974. 'Open station shell midden sites and associated features from the Pearly Beach area, south-western Cape', *S.A.A.B.* 29: 104–14.

G. Avery, 1975. 'Discussion on the age and use of tidal fish-traps (visvywers)', *S.A.A.B.* 30: 105–13.

E. Axelson, 1940. *South-East Africa 1488–1530*, London.

R. P. Azais and R. Chambard, 1931. *Cinq Années de Recherches Archéologiques en Ethiopie*, Paris.

G. Bailloud, 1959. 'La préhistoire de l'Ethiopie', *Cahiers de l'Afrique et de l'Asie* 5: 15–43.

G. Bailloud, 1969. 'L'évolution des styles céramiques en Ennedi (République du Tchad)', *A.P.C.I.A.A.*: 31–45.

J. Barthelme, 1977. 'Holocene sites north-east of Lake Turkana', *Azania* 12: in press.

D. Bate, 1953. Faunal report in Arkell, 1953.

H. Baumann, 1919. 'Ancient tin mines of the Transvaal', *Journal of Chemical Society of South Africa* 29: 120–32.

H. Baumann, 1935. *Lunda: bei Bauern und Jägern in Inner-Angola*, Berlin.

R. de Bayle des Hermens, 1975. *Recherches Préhistoriques en République Centrafricaine*, Paris.

L. C. Beadle, 1974. *The Inland Waters of Tropical Africa*, London.

P. B. Beaumont and J. C. Vogel, 1972. 'On a new radiocarbon chronology for Africa south of the Equator', *A.S.* 31: 67–89, 155–82.

G. van Beek, 1967. 'Monuments of Axum in the light of South Arabian archaeology', *Journal of the American Oriental Society* 87.

G. van Beek, 1969. *Hajar bin Humeid*, Baltimore.

J. T. Bent, 1893. 'The ancient trade route across Ethiopia', *G.J.* 2: 140–6.

F. O. Bernhard, 1961. 'The Ziwa ware of Inyanga', *Native Affairs Dept. Annual* (Rhodesia), 38: 84–92.

F. O. Bernhard, 1963. 'A Bambata-type pot from Inyanga', *S.A.A.B.* 18: 72.

F. O. Bernhard, 1964. 'Notes on the pre-ruin Ziwa culture of Inyanga', *Rhodesiana* 12.

I. Bidder, 1959. *Lalibela*, Cologne.

W. W. Bishop and J. D. Clark (eds.), 1967. *Background to Evolution in Africa*, Chicago.

M. S. Bisson, 1975. 'Copper currency in central Africa: the archaeological evidence', *W.A.* 6: 276–92.

R. H. Blackburn, 1974. 'The Okiek and their history', *Azania* 9: 139–57.

W. Blohm, 1931–3. *Die Nyamwezi*, Bamburg.

J. R. F. Bower, 1973a. 'Seronera: excavations at a stone bowl site in the Serengeti National Park, Tanzania', *Azania* 8: 71–104.

J. R. F. Bower, 1973b. 'Early pottery and other finds from Kisii district, western Kenya', *Azania* 8: 131–40.

J. R. F. Bower, C. M. Nelson, A. F. Waibel and S. Wandibba, 1977. 'The University of Massachusetts later Stone Age Pastoral "Neolithic" comparative study in central Kenya', *Anzania* 12: in press.

J. H. Breasted, 1906. *Ancient Records of Egypt*, Chicago.

H. Breuil, 1934. 'Peintures rupestres préhistoriques du Harar, Abyssinie', *L'Anthropologie* 44: 437–83.

H. Breuil, 1955. *The White Lady of the Brandberg*, London.

H. Breuil, 1959. *The Tsisab Ravine and other Brandberg sites*, London.

D. R. Brothwell, 1971. 'The skeletal remains from Gwisho B and C' in Fagan and van Noten, 1971.

D. R. Brothwell and T. Shaw, 1971. 'A late Upper Pleistocene proto-West African Negro from Nigeria', *Man* (*N.S.*) 6: 221–7.

F. H. Brown, 1975. 'Barbed bone points from the lower Omo Valley, Ethiopia', *Azania* 10: 144–8.

J. Brown, 1966. 'The excavation of a group of burial mounds at Ilkek near Gilgil, Kenya', *Azania* 1: 59–77.

J. Brown, 1969. 'Some polished axes from East Africa', *Azania* 4: 160–6.

J. Bruce, 1790. *Travels to Discover the Source of the Nile*, Edinburgh.

K. W. Butzer, G. Ll. Isaac, J. L. Richardson and C. Washbourn-Kamau, 1972. 'Radiocarbon dating of East African lake levels', *Science* 175: 1069–76.

D. Buxton, 1970. *The Abyssinians*, London.

D. Buxton, 1971. 'The rock-hewn and other medieval churches of Tigre Province, Ethiopia', *Archaeologia* 103: 33–100.

A. de Calonne-Beaufaict, 1921. *Azande*, Brussels.

J. Campbell, 1822. *Travels in the Interior of Southern Africa*, London.

G. Camps, 1974. *Les Civilisations Préhistoriques de l'Afrique du Nord et du Sahara*, Paris.

P. L. Carter, 1969. 'Moshebi's Shelter: excavation and exploitation in eastern Lesotho', *Lesotho* 8: 13–23.

P. L. Carter, 1970. 'Late Stone Age exploitation patterns in southern Natal', *S.A.A.B.* 25: 55–8.

P. L. Carter and J. C. Vogel, 1974. 'The dating of industrial assemblages from stratified sites in eastern Lesotho', *Man* (*N.S.*) 9: 557–70.

G. Caton-Thompson, 1931. *The Zimbabwe Culture*, Oxford.

G. Caton-Thompson, 1971. New introduction to *The Zimbabwe Culture* (second edition), London.

G. Caton-Thompson and E. W. Gardner, 1934. *The Desert Fayum*, London.

E. Cerulli, 1934. 'Gruppi etnici negri nella Somalia', *Archivo per l'Antropologia e la Etnologia* 64.

E. Cerulli, 1956. *Peoples of South-West Ethiopia and its Borderland*, London.

P. Červíček and U. Braukämper, 1975. 'Rock paintings of Laga Gafra, Ethiopia', *Paideuma* 21: 47–60.

M. C. Chamla, 1968. *Les Populations Anciennes du Sahara et des Régions Limitrophes*, Paris.

J. H. Chaplin, 1959. 'The Munwa Stream rock engravings', *S.A.A.B.* 14: 28–34.

J. H. Chaplin, 1961. 'Notes on traditional smelting in Northern Rhodesia', *S.A.A.B.* 16: 53–60.

J. H. Chaplin, 1974. 'The prehistoric rock art of the Lake Victoria region', *Azania* 9: 1–50.

S. Chapman, 1967. 'Kantsyore Island', *Azania* 2: 165–91.

H. N. Chittick, 1965. 'The "Shirazi" colonization of East Africa', *J.A.H.* 6: 275–94.

H. N. Chittick, 1966. 'Kilwa: a preliminary report', *Azania* 1: 1–36.

H. N. Chittick, 1967. 'Discoveries in the Lamu archipelago', *Azania* 2: 37–67.

H. N. Chittick, 1969. 'An archaeological reconnaissance of the southern Somali coast', *Azania* 4: 115–30.

H. N. Chittick, 1974a. *Kilwa: an Islamic Trading City on the East African Coast*, Nairobi.

H. N. Chittick, 1974b. 'Excavations at Aksum: a preliminary report', *Azania* 9: 159–205.

J. D. Clark, 1942. 'Further excavations (1939) at Mumbwa Caves, Northern Rhodesia', *T.R.S.S.A.* 29: 133–201.

J. D. Clark, 1944. 'The use of the bored stone in Abyssinia', *Man* 44: article 25.

J. D. Clark, 1945. 'Short notes on Stone Age sites at Yavello, S. Abyssinia', *T.R.S.S.A.* 31: 29–37.

J. D. Clark, 1950a. 'The newly discovered Nachikufu Culture of Northern Rhodesia', *S.A.A.B.* 5: 86–98.

J. D. Clark, 1950b. *The Stone Age Cultures of Northern Rhodesia*, Cape Town.

J. D. Clark, 1950c. 'A note on the pre-Bantu inhabitants of Northern Rhodesia and Nyasaland', *S.A.J.S.* 47: 80–5.

J. D. Clark, 1954. *The Prehistoric Cultures of the Horn of Africa*, Cambridge.

J. D. Clark, 1958. 'The Chifubwa Stream rockshelter, Solwezi, Northern Rhodesia', *S.A.A.B.* 13: 21–4.

J. D. Clark, 1959a. *The Prehistory of Southern Africa*, Harmondsworth.

J. D. Clark, 1959b. 'The rock paintings of Northern Rhodesia and Nyasaland', pp. 163–220 in Summers, 1959.

J. D. Clark, 1966. *The Distribution of Prehistoric Culture in Angola*, Lisbon.

J. D. Clark, 1967. 'The problem of neolithic culture in sub-Saharan Africa', pp. 601–27 in Bishop and Clark, 1967.

J. D. Clark, 1968. 'Some early Iron Age pottery from Lunda', pp. 189–205 in J. D. Clark, *Further Palaeo-Anthropological Studies in Northern Lunda*, Lisbon.

J. D. Clark, 1970. *The Prehistory of Africa*, London.

J. D. Clark, 1971a. 'An archaeological survey of northern Aïr and Ténéré', *G.J.* 137: 455–7.

J. D. Clark, 1971b. 'A re-examination of the evidence for agricultural origins in the Nile Valley', *P.P.S.* 37(2): 34–79.

J. D. Clark, 1972. 'Mobility and settlement patterns in sub-Saharan Africa: a comparison of late prehistoric hunter/gatherers and early agricultural occupation units', pp. 127–48 in P. J. Ucko, R. Tringham and G. W. Dimbleby (eds.), *Man, Settlement and Urbanism*, London.

J. D. Clark, 1974. *Kalambo Falls Prehistoric Site, II*, Cambridge.

J. D. Clark and B. M. Fagan, 1965. 'Charcoals, sands, and channel-decorated pottery from Northern Rhodesia', *American Anthropologist* 67: 354–71.

J. D. Clark and A. Stemler, 1975. 'Early domesticated sorghum from central Sudan', *Nature* 254: 588–91.

J. D. Clark and J. Walton, 1962. 'A Late Stone Age site in the Erongo mountains, South West Africa', *P.P.S.* 28: 1–16.

J. G. D. Clark, 1969. *World Prehistory: a New Outline*, Cambridge.

H. H. Coghlan, 1956. *Notes on Prehistoric and Early Iron in the Old World*, Oxford.

M. Cohen, 1970. 'A re-assessment of the Stone Bowl Cultures of the Rift Valley, Kenya', *Azania* 5: 27–38.

M. Cohen, 1972. 'Deloraine Farm: a new type of pottery', *Azania* 7: 161–7.

G. Cole, 1967. 'A re-investigation of Magosi and the Magosian', *Quaternaria* 9: 153–68.

S. Cole, 1963. *The Prehistory of East Africa*, London.

P. A. Cole-King, 1973a. *Kukumba Mbiri mu Malawi*, M.A.D.P. 15.

P. A. Cole-King, 1973b. 'Zomba Range – an Early Iron Age site', *M.A.D.P.* 14: 51–70.

C. K. Cooke, 1959. 'Rock art in Matabeleland', pp. 112–62 in Summers, 1959.

C. K. Cooke, 1963a. 'Report on excavations at Pomongwe and Tshangula caves, Matopo Hills, Southern Rhodesia', *S.A.A.B.* 18: 73–151.

C. K. Cooke, 1963b. 'The painting sequence in the rock art of Southern Rhodesia', *S.A.A.B.* 18: 172–5.

C. K. Cooke, 1964a. 'Iron Age influences in the rock art of Southern Rhodesia', *Arnoldia* 1: no. 12.

C. K. Cooke, 1964b. 'An unusual burial in the Gwanda district of Southern Rhodesia', *S.A.A.B.* 18: 41–2.

C. K. Cooke, 1965. 'Evidence of human migration from the rock art of Southern Rhodesia', *Africa* 35: 263–85.

C. K. Cooke, 1966. 'The archaeology of the Mafungabusi area, Gokwe, Rhodesia', *P.T.R.S.A.* 51: 51–78.

C. K. Cooke, 1969. *Rock Art of Southern Africa*, Cape Town.

C. K. Cooke, 1970. 'Shelters for Late Stone Age man shown in the paintings of Rhodesia', *S.A.A.B.* 25: 65–6.

C. K. Cooke, 1971a. 'The rock art of Rhodesia', *S.A.J.S.* special issue 2: 7–10.

C. K. Cooke, 1971b. 'Excavation in Zombepata Cave, Sipolilo District, Mashonaland, Rhodesia', *S.A.A.B.* 25: 104–27.

C. K. Cooke and K. R. Robinson, 1954. 'Excavation at Amadzimba Cave, Matopo Hills', *O.P.N.M.S.R.* 19: 699–728.

C. K. Cooke and H. A. B. Simons, 1969. 'Mpato shelter, Sentinel Ranch, Limpopo River, Beitbridge, Rhodesia: excavation results', *Arnoldia* 4: no. 18.

C. K. Cooke, R. Summers and K. R. Robinson, 1966. 'Rhodesian prehistory re-examined, part II – Iron Age', *Arnoldia* 2: no. 17.

H. J. Cooke, 1975. 'The palaeoclimatic significance of caves and adjacent land forms in western Ngamiland, Botswana', *G.J.* 141: 430–44.

C. S. Coon, 1963. *The Origin of Races*, London.

Y. Coppens, 1969. 'Les cultures protohistoriques et historiques du Djourab', *A.P.C.I.A.A.*: 129–46.

J. Courtain, 1969. 'Le néolithique du Bourkou (nord-Tchad)', *A.P.C.I.A.A.*: 147–59.

J. R. Crawford, 1967. 'The Monks Kop ossuary', *J.A.H.* 8: 373–82.

O. G. S. Crawford, 1951. *The Fung Kingdom of Sennar*, Gloucester.

A. T. Culwick, 1931. 'Ritual use of rock paintings at Bahi, Tanganyika Territory', *Man* 31: article 41.

D. Dalby, 1975. 'The prehistorical implications of Guthrie's *Comparative Bantu*: I – problems of internal relationship', *J.A.H.* 16: 481–501.

D. Dalby, 1976. 'The prehistorical implications of Guthrie's *Comparative Bantu*: II – interpretation of cultural vocabulary', *J.A.H.* 17: 1–27.

S. G. H. Daniels, 1967. 'A note on Iron Age material from Kamusongolwa Kopje, Zambia', *S.A.A.B.* 22: 142–50.

S. G. H. Daniels and D. W. Phillipson, 1969. 'The Early Iron Age site at Dambwa near Livingstone', pp. 1–54 in Fagan, Phillipson and Daniels, 1969.

C. D. Darlington, 1969. 'The silent millennia in the origin of agriculture', pp. 67–72 in P. J. Ucko and G. W. Dimbleby (eds.), *The Domestication and Exploitation of Plants and Animals*, London.

R. A. Dart and P. B. Beaumont, 1968. 'Ratification and retrocession of earlier Swaziland iron ore mining radiocarbon datings', *S.A.J.S.* 64: 241–6.

B. A. Datoo, 1970. 'Rhapta: the location and importance of East Africa's first port', *Azania* 5: 65–75.

O. Davies, 1971. 'Excavations at Blackburn', *S.A.A.B.* 26: 165–78.

O. Davies, 1974. 'Excavations at the walled early Iron Age site in Moor Park, near Estcourt, Natal', *A.N.M.* 22: 289–323.

O. Davies, 1975. 'Excavations at Shongweni South Cave: the oldest evidence to date for cultigens in southern Africa', *A.N.M.* 22: 627–62.

H. J. Deacon, 1966. 'Note on the X-ray of two mounted implements from South Africa', *Man* (*N.S.*) 1: 87–90.

H. J. Deacon, 1969. 'Melkhoutboom Cave, Alexandra District, Cape Province: a report on the 1967 investigation', *A.C.P.M.* 6: 141–69.

H. J. Deacon, 1972. 'A review of the post-Pleistocene in South Africa', *G.S.* 1: 26–45.

H. J. Deacon, 1976. *Where Hunters Gathered*, Cape Town.

J. Deacon, 1972. 'Wilton: an assessment after fifty years', *S.A.A.B.* 27: 10–48.

J. Deacon, 1974. 'Patterning in the radiocarbon dates for the Wilton/Smithfield complex in southern Africa', *S.A.A.B.* 29: 3–18.

O. Dempwolff, 1916. *Die Sandawe*, Hamburg.

E. Denninger, 1971. 'The use of paper chromatography to determine the age of albuminous binders, and its application to rock paintings', *S.A.J.S.* special issue 2: 80–4.

R. M. Derricourt, 1972. 'Archaeological survey of the Transkei and Ciskei: interim report for 1972', *Fort Hare Papers* 5: 449–55.

R. M. Derricourt and T. M. Evers, 1973. 'Robertsdrift, an Iron Age site and settlement on the banks of the Vaal and Klip rivers near Standerton, south-eastern Transvaal', *A.S.* 32: 183–96.

R. M. Derricourt and R. J. Papstein, 1976. 'Lukolwe and the Mbwela of north-western Zambia', *Azania* 11: 169–76.

D. E. Derry, 1949. Report on human remains in Arkell, 1949: 31–3.

B. Doe, 1971. *Southern Arabia*, London.

J. Dombrowski, 1970. 'Preliminary report on excavations in Lalibela and Natchabiet Caves, Begemeder', *A.E.* 8: 21–9.

J. Dombrowski, 1971. *Excavations in Ethiopia: Lalibela and Natchabiet Caves, Begemeder Province*, Ph.D. thesis, Boston University.

J. H. Driberg, 1923. *The Lango*, London.

D. Drost, 1967. *Töpferei in Afrika*, Berlin.

D. Dunham, 1950. *The Royal Cemeteries of Kush, I – El Kurru*, Boston.

D. Dunham, 1955. *The Royal Cemeteries of Kush, II – Nuri*, Boston.

D. Dunham, 1957. *The Royal Cemeteries of Kush, IV – Royal Tombs at Meroe and Barkal*, Boston.

D. Dunham, 1963. *The Royal Cemeteries of Kush, V – The West and South Cemeteries at Meroe*, Boston.

D. S. Dyson and V. E. Fuchs, 1937. 'The Elmolo', *J.R.A.I.* 67: 327–38.

C. Ehret, 1967. 'Cattle keeping and milking in eastern and southern African history: the linguistic evidence', *J.A.H.* 8: 1–17.

C. Ehret, 1968a. 'Cushites and the Highlands and Plains Nilotes', pp. 158–76 in B. A. Ogot and J. A. Kieran (eds.), *Zamani*, Nairobi.

C. Ehret, 1968b. 'Sheep and Central Sudanic peoples in southern Africa', *J.A.H.* 9: 213–21.

C. Ehret, 1971. *Southern Nilotic History*, Evanston.

C. Ehret, 1972. 'Bantu origins and history: critique and interpretation', *T.J.H.* 2: 1–19.

C. Ehret, 1973. 'Patterns of Bantu and Central Sudanic settlement in central and southern Africa', *T.J.H.* 3: 1–71.

C. Ehret, 1974a. *Ethiopians and East Africans*, Nairobi.

C. Ehret, 1974b. 'Agricultural history in central and southern Africa c. 1000 BC to AD 500', *T.J.H.* 4: 1–25.

C. Ehret *et al.*, 1972. 'Outlining southern African history: a re-evaluation AD 100–1500', *Ufahamu* 3: 9–27.

C. Ehret, 1976. 'Linguistic evidence and its correlation with archaeology', *W.A.* 8: 5–18.

W. B. Emery and L. P. Kirwan, 1935. *The Excavations and Survey between Wadi es-Sebua and Adindan 1929–31*, Cairo.

H. Epstein, 1969. *The Origin of the Domestic Animals of Africa*, New York.

E. E. Evans-Pritchard, 1940. *The Nuer*, Oxford.

E. E. Evans-Pritchard, 1971. *The Azande: History and Political Institutions*, Oxford.

T. M. Evers, 1973. 'Three Early Iron Age sites in the N.E. Transvaal lowveld', *S.A.J.S.* 69: 325.

T. M. Evers, 1975. 'Recent Iron Age research in the eastern Transvaal, South Africa', *S.A.A.B.* 30: 71–83.

T. M. Evers and R. P. van den Berg, 1974. 'Ancient mining in southern Africa, with reference to a copper mine in the Harmony Block, north-eastern Transvaal', *J.S.A.I.M.M.* 74: 217–26.

B. M. Fagan, 1960. 'The Glentyre shelter and Oakhurst re-examined', *S.A.A.B.* 15: 80–94.

B. M. Fagan, 1964. 'The Greefswald sequence: Mapungubwe and Bambandyanalo', *J.A.H.* 5: 337–61.

B. M. Fagan, 1965a. 'Radiocarbon dates for sub-Saharan Africa – III', *J.A.H.* 6: 107–16.

B. M. Fagan, 1965b. *Southern Africa in the Iron Age*, London.

B. M. Fagan, 1966. 'Radiocarbon dates for sub-Saharan Africa – IV', *J.A.H.* 7: 495–506.

B. M. Fagan, 1967a. 'Radiocarbon dates for sub-Saharan Africa – V', *J.A.H.* 8: 513–27.

B. M. Fagan, 1967b. *Iron Age Cultures in Zambia, I*, London.

B. M. Fagan, 1967a. 'Radiocarbon dates for sub-Saharan Africa – V', *J.A.H.* 8: 513–27.

B. M. Fagan, 1969b. 'Excavations at Ingombe Ilede 1960–2', pp. 55–161 in Fagan, Phillipson and Daniels, 1969.

B. M. Fagan and F. van Noten, 1964. 'Two channel-decorated pottery sites from northern Rhodesia', *Man* 64: article 8.

B. M. Fagan and F. van Noten, 1971. *The Hunter-Gatherers of Gwisho*, Tervuren.

B. M. Fagan and D. W. Phillipson, 1965. 'Sebanzi, the Iron Age sequence at Lochinvar, and the Tonga', *J.R.A.I.* 95: 253–94.

B. M. Fagan, D. W. Phillipson and S. G. H. Daniels, 1969. *Iron Age Cultures in Zambia, II*, London.

B. M. Fagan and J. E. Yellen, 1968. 'Ivuna: ancient salt-working in southern Tanzania', *Azania* 3: 1–43.

B. Fagg, 1969. 'Recent work in West Africa: new light on the Nok culture', *W.A.* 1: 41–50.

T. H. G. Farnden, 1965. 'Notes on two Late Stone Age sites at Muden, Natal', *S.A.A.B.* 20: 19–23.

P. M. Faugust and J. E. G. Sutton, 1966. 'The Egerton Cave on the Njoro river', *Azania* 1: 149–53.

H. Faure, 1966. 'Evolution des grands lacs sahariens à l'Holocène', *Quaternaria* 8: 167–75.

H. Faure, E. Manguin and R. Nydal, 1963. 'Formations lacustres du Quaternaire supérieur du Niger oriental: diatomites et âges absolus', *Bulletin du Bureau de Recherches Géologiques et Minières* 3: 41–63.

H. Fleming, 1964. 'Baiso and Rendille: Somali outliers', *Rassegna di studi Etiopici* 20: 35–96.

H. Fleming, 1969. 'Asa and Aramanik: Cushitic hunters in Masai-land', *Ethnology* 8: 1–35.

G. J. Fock, 1972. 'Extinct bovine on rock engraving', *R.N.M.B.* 2: 349–53.

J. Forbes-Munro, 1967. 'Migrations of the Bantu-speaking people of the eastern Kenya highlands: a re-appraisal', *J.A.H.* 8: 25–8.

H. A. Fosbrooke *et al.*, 1950. 'Tanganyika rock paintings', *T.N.R.* 29: 1–61.

L. Fouché, 1937. *Mapungubwe, I*, Cambridge.

G. S. P. Freeman-Grenville, 1957. 'Coinage in East Africa before Portuguese times', *N.C.* (6) 17: 151–79.

G. S. P. Freeman-Grenville, 1962. *The East African Coast: Select Documents from the First to the earlier Nineteenth Century*, Oxford.

C. Gabel, 1965. *Stone Age Hunters of the Kafue*, Boston.

C. Gabel, 1969. 'Six rockshelters on the northern Kavirondo shore of Lake Victoria', *I.J.A.H.S.* 2: 205–54.

A. Galloway, 1959. *The Skeletal Remains from Bambandyanalo*, Johannesburg

G. A. Gardner, 1963. *Mapungubwe, II*, Pretoria.

T. Gardner, L. H. Wells and J. F. Schofield, 1940. 'The recent archaeology of Gokomere, Southern Rhodesia', *T.R.S.S.A.* 18: 215–53.

P. S. Garlake, 1966a. *The Early Islamic Architecture of the East African Coast*, Nairobi.

P. S. Garlake, 1966b. 'Iron Age archaeology', pp. 19–22 in *Rhodesian Schools' Exploration Society Shashi Expedition*, Bulawayo.

P. S. Garlake, 1967a. 'Excavations at Maxton Farm, near Shamva Hill, Rhodesia', *Arnoldia* 3: no. 9.

P. S. Garlake, 1967b. 'Iron Age burials at Mount Hampden near Salisbury, Rhodesia', *Arnoldia* 3: no. 10.

P. S. Garlake, 1968a. 'The value of imported ceramics in the dating and interpretation of the Rhodesian Iron Age', *J.A.H.* 9: 13–33.

P. S. Garlake, 1968b. 'Test excavations at Mapela Hill, near the Shashi River, Rhodesia', *Arnoldia* 3: no. 34.

P. S. Garlake, 1969a. 'Chitope: an Early Iron Age village in northern Mashonaland', *Arnoldia* 4: no. 19.

P. S. Garlake, 1969b. 'Excavations at the seventeenth-century Portuguese site of Dambarare, Rhodesia', *P.T.R.S.A.* 54: 23–61.

P. S. Garlake, 1970. 'Iron Age sites in the Urungwe District of Rhodesia', *S.A.A.B.* 25: 25–44.

P. S. Garlake, 1973a. *Great Zimbabwe*, London.

P. S. Garlake, 1973b. 'Excavations at the Mhunguza and Ruanga Ruins in northern Mashonaland', *S.A.A.B.* 27: 107–43.

P. S. Garlake, 1974. *The Ruins of Zimbabwe*, Lusaka.

P. S. Garlake, 1976. 'An investigation of Manekweni, Mozambique', *Azania* 11: 25–47.

J. Garstang, 1912. 'Second interim report on the excavations at Meroe in Ethiopia', *Liverpool Annals of Archaeology and Anthropology* 4: 45–52.

G. Gerster, 1970. *Churches in Rock*, London.

H. A. Gibb, 1961. *The Travels of Ibn Battuta, II*, Cambridge.

J. L. Gibbs (ed.), 1965. *Peoples of Africa*, New York.

M. Gluckman, 1961. 'The Lozi of Barotseland in North-Western Rhodesia', pp. 1–93 in E. Colson and M. Gluckman (eds.), *Seven Tribes of British Central Africa*, Manchester.

E. Goodall, 1959. 'Rock paintings of Mashonaland', pp. 3–111 in Summers, 1959.

E. Goodall, 1962. 'Report on an ancient burial ground, Salisbury', *P.A.C.* 4: 315–22.

A. J. H. Goodwin, 1930. 'A new variation of the Smithfield culture from Natal', *T.R.S.S.A.* 19: 7–14.

A. J. H. Goodwin, 1936. *Vosburg: its Petroglyphs*, Cape Town.

A. J. H. Goodwin, 1938. 'The archaeology of the Oakhurst shelter, George', *T.R.S.S.A.* 25: 229–324.

A. J. H. Goodwin, 1946. 'Prehistoric fishing methods in South Africa', *Antiquity* 20: 134–9.

A. J. H. Goodwin, 1952. 'Jan van Riebeeck and the Hottentots 1652–62', *S.A.A.B.* 7: 1–53.

A. J. H. Goodwin and C. van Riet Lowe, 1929. 'The Stone Age cultures of South Africa', *A.S.A.M.* 28: 151–234.

C. Gouldsbury and H. Sheane, 1911. *The Great Plateau of Northern Rhodesia*, London.

R. M. Gramly, 1974. 'Analysis of faunal remains from Narosura', *Azania* 9: 219–22.

R. M. Gramly, 1975a. *Pastoralists and Hunters: Recent Prehistory in southern Kenya and Northern Tanzania*, Ph.D. thesis, Harvard University.

R. M. Gramly, 1975b. 'Meat-feasting sites and cattle brands: patterns of rock-shelter utilization in East Africa', *Azania* 10: 107–21.

R. M. Gramly, 1976. 'Upper Pleistocene archaeological occurrences at site GvJM/22, Lukenya Hill, Kenya', *Man (N.S.)* 11: 319–44.

R. M. Gramly and G. P. Rightmire, 1973. 'A fragmentary cranium and dated later Stone Age assemblage from Lukenya Hill, Kenya', *Man (N.S.)* 8: 571–3.

P. Graziosi, 1964. 'New discoveries of rock paintings in Ethiopia', *Antiquity* 38: 91–8, 187–90.

J. H. Greenberg, 1963a. *The Languages of Africa*, The Hague.

J. H. Greenberg, 1963b. 'Mogogodo: a forgotten Cushitic people', *Journal of African Languages* 2: 29–43.

J. H. Greenberg, 1972. 'Linguistic evidence regarding Bantu origins', *J.A.H.* 13: 189–216.

J. H. Greenberg, 1974. 'Bantu and its closest relatives', pp. 115–19 in W. R. Leben (ed.), *Papers from the Fifth Annual Conference on African Linguistics*, Los Angeles.

J. R. Grindley, 1967. 'The Cape rock lobster *Jasus lalandii* from the Bonteberg excavation', *S.A.A.B.* 22: 94–102.

V. L. Grottanelli, 1975. 'The peopling of the Horn of Africa', pp. 44–75 in H. N. Chittick and R. I. Rotberg (eds.), *East Africa and the Orient*, New York.

A. T. Grove and A. S. Goudie, 1971. 'Late Quaternary lake levels in the Rift Valley of southern Ethiopia and elsewhere in tropical Africa', *Nature* 234: 403–5.

A. T. Grove, F. A. Street and A. S. Goudie, 1975. 'Former lake levels and climatic change in the Rift Valley of southern Ethiopia', *G.J.* 141: 177–202.

A. T. Grove and A. Warren, 1968. 'Quaternary land forms and climate on the south side of the Sahara', *G.J.* 134: 194–208.

P. H. Gulliver, 1955. *The Family Herds*, London.

M. Guthrie, 1962. 'Some developments in the prehistory of the Bantu languages', *J.A.H.* 3: 273–82.

M. Guthrie, 1967–71. *Comparative Bantu*, Farnborough.

W. D. Hambly, 1934. *The Ovimbundu of Angola*, Chicago.

W. D. Hammond-Tooke (ed.), 1974. *The Bantu-speaking Peoples of Southern Africa*, London.

J. R. Harding, 1961. 'Conus shell disc ornaments (vibangwa) in Africa', *J.R.A.I.* 91: 52–66.

G. Harinck, 1969. 'Interaction between Xhosa and Khoi', pp. 145–69 in L. Thompson (ed.), *African Societies in Southern Africa*, London.

J. R. Harlan, 1969. 'Ethiopia – a center of diversity', *Economic Botany* 23: 309–14.

J. R. Harlan, 1971. 'Agricultural origins: centers and non-centers', *Science* 174: 468–74.

J. R. Harlan and J. M. J. de Wet, 1973. 'On the quality of evidence for the origin and dispersal of cultivated plants', *C.A.* 14: 51–62.

T. R. Hays, 1974. 'Wavy-line pottery: an element of Nilotic diffusion', *S.A.A.B.* 29: 27–32.

T. R. Hays, 1975. 'Neolithic settlement of the Sahara as it relates to the Nile Valley', pp. 193–204 in F. Wendorf and A. E. Marks (eds.), *Problems in Prehistory: North Africa and the Levant*, Dallas.

B. Heine, 1973. 'Zur genetischen Gliederung der Bantu-sprachen', *Afrika und Übersee* 56: 164–85.

B. Heine, 1976. 'Notes on the Rendille language (Kenya)', *Afrika und Übersee* 59: 176–223.

J. de Heinzelin de Braucourt, 1957. *Les Fouilles d'Ishango*, Brussels.

D. P. Henige, 1974. *The Chronology of Oral Tradition*, Oxford.

A. Henrici, 1973. 'Numerical classification of Bantu languages', *African Language Studies* 14: 82–104.

M. d'Hertefelt, 1965. 'The Rwanda of Rwanda', pp. 405–40 in Gibbs, 1965.

J. Hiernaux, 1962. 'Le début de l'âge des métaux dans la région des grands lacs africains', *P.A.C.* 4: 381–9.

J. Hiernaux, 1974. *The People of Africa*, London.

J. Hiernaux, E. de Longrée and J. de Buyst, 1971. *Fouilles Archéologiques dans la Vallée du Haut-Lualaba, I Sanga*, Tervuren.

J. Hiernaux and E. Maquet, 1954. 'Un haut-fourneau préhistorique au Buhunde, Kivu, Congo belge', *Zaire*: 615–19.

J. Hiernaux and E. Maquet, 1960. 'Cultures préhistoriques de l'âge des métaux au Ruanda-Urundi et au Kivu, Congo belge, II', *Mémoires de l'Académie royale des Sciences d'Outre-Mer* 10: 5–88.

J. Hiernaux and E. Maquet, 1968. *L'âge du fer à Kibiro, Uganda*, Tervuren.

J. Hiernaux, E. Maquet and J. de Buyst, 1968. 'Excavations at Sanga, 1958: a first millennium civilization on the Upper Lualaba', *S.A.J.S.* 64: 113–17.

J. Hiernaux, E. Maquet and J. de Buyst, 1973. 'Le cimetière protohistorique de Katoto, vallée du Lualaba, Congo-Kinshasa', *P.A.C.* 6: 148–58.

E. S. Higgs and M. R. Jarman, 1972. 'The origins of animal and plant husbandry', pp. 3–13 in E. S. Higgs (ed.), *Papers in Economic Prehistory*, Cambridge.

F. Hintze, 1962. 'Preliminary report on the excavations at Musawwarat', *Kush* 10: 170–202.

F. Hintze, 1968. 'Musawwarat es Sufra: Vorbericht über Ausgrabungen 1963 bis 1966', *Wissenschaftliche Zeitschrift der Humboldt-Universität zu Berlin* 17: 667–84.

F. Hintze and U. Hintze, 1966. *Alte Kulturen im Sudan*, Leipzig.

F. Hivernel-Guerre, 1970. 'Introduction à l'étude du Late Stone Age de Kella, Melka Kontouré, Ethiopie', *D.S.H.C.E.* 1: 39–43.

E. C. N. van Hoepen, 1939. 'Pre-European Bantu culture in the Lydenburg District', *R.N.M.B.* 2: 47–74.

A. C. Hollis, 1909. *The Nandi*, Oxford.

P. M. Holt, 1963. 'Funj origins: a critique and new evidence', *J.A.H.* 4: 39–55.

L. Holý, 1974. *Neighbours and Kinsmen*, London.

P. Huard, 1966. 'Introduction et diffusion du fer au Tchad', *J.A.H.* 7: 377–404.

P. Huard and J. M. Massip, 1964. 'Harpons en os et céramique à décor en vague au Sahara tchadien', *Bulletin de la Société Préhistorique Française* 61: 105–23.

T. N. Huffman, 1970. 'The Early Iron Age and the spread of the Bantu', *S.A.A.B.* 25: 3–21.

T. N. Huffman, 1971a. 'A guide to the Iron Age of Mashonaland', *O.P.N.M.S.R.* 4(1): 20–44.

T. N. Huffman, 1971b. 'Excavations at Leopard's Kopje main kraal: a preliminary report', *S.A.A.B.* 26: 85–9.

T. N. Huffman, 1971c. 'Cloth from the Iron Age in Rhodesia', *Arnoldia* 5: no. 14.

T. N. Huffman, 1972. 'The rise and fall of Zimbabwe', *J.A.H.* 13: 353–66.

T. N. Huffman, 1973. 'Test excavations at Makuru, Rhodesia', *Arnoldia* 5: no. 39.

T. N. Huffman, 1974a. *The Leopard's Kopje Tradition*, Salisbury.

T. N. Huffman, 1974b. 'The linguistic affinities of the Iron Age in Rhodesia', *Arnoldia* 7: no. 7.

T. N. Huffman, 1975. 'Cattle from Mabveni', *S.A.A.B.* 30: 23–4.

H. J. Hugot, 1962. *Missions Berliet, Ténéré–Tchad*, Paris.

H. H. Hugot, 1968. 'The origins of agriculture–Sahara', *C.A.* 9: 483–9.

A. J. B. Humphreys, 1969. 'Four bifacial tanged and barbed arrowheads from Vosburg', *S.A.A.B.* 24: 72–4.

A. J. B. Humphreys, 1972. 'Comments on aspects of raw material usage in the later Stone Age of the middle Orange River area', *G.S.* 1: 46–53.

A. J. B. Humphreys, 1973. 'A report on excavations carried out on a Type R settlement unit (Khartoum I) in the Jacobsdal District, O.F.S.', *A.C.P.M.* 9: 123–57.

A. J. B. Humphreys, 1974. 'Preliminary report on test excavations at Dikbosch Shelter I, Herbert District, Northern Cape', *S.A.A.B.* 29: 115–19.

A. J. B. Humphreys and T. M. O'C. Maggs, 1970. 'Further graces and cultural material from the banks of the Riet river', *S.A.A.B.* 25: 116–26.

G. W. B. Huntingford, 1929. 'Modern hunters: some account of the Kamelilo–Kapchepkendi Dorobo (Okiek) of Kenya Colony', *J.R.A.I.* 59: 333–78.

G. W. B. Huntingford, 1953. *The Southern Nilo-Hamites*, London.

G. W. B. Huntingford, 1955. *The Galla of Ethiopia*, London.

R. R. Inskeep, 1959. 'A Late Stone Age camping site in the upper Zambezi valley', *S.A.A.B.* 14: 91-6.

R. R. Inskeep, 1961. Review of Louw, 1960, *S.A.A.B.* 16: 30–1.

R. R. Inskeep, 1962a. 'Some Iron Age sites from Northern Rhodesia', *S.A.A.B.* 17: 136–80.

R. R. Inskeep, 1962b. 'The age of the Kondoa rock paintings in the light of recent excavations at Kisese II rock shelter', *P.A.C.* 4: 249–56.

R. R. Inskeep, 1965. Review of Arkell, 1964. *S.A.A.B.* 20: 41.

R. R. Inskeep, 1967. 'The Late Stone Age in southern Africa', pp. 557–82 in Bishop and Clark, 1967.

R. R. Inskeep, 1969. 'The archaeological background', pp. 1–39 in Wilson and Thompson, 1969.

R. R. Inskeep, 1971. Letter to the editor. *S.A.J.S.* 67: 492–3.

R. R. Inskeep and K. L. von Bezing, 1966. 'Modelled terracotta head from Lydenburg, South Africa', *Man (N.S.)* 1: 103.

R. R. Inskeep and T. M. O'C. Maggs, 1975. 'Unique art objects in the Iron Age of the Transvaal, South Africa', *S.A.A.B.* 30: 114–38.

G. Ll. Isaac, H. V. Merrick and C. M. Nelson, 1972. 'Stratigraphic and archaeological studies in the Lake Nakuru basin, Kenya', *P.A.* 6: 225–32.

J. Irle, 1906. *Die Herero*, Gütersloh.

A. H. Jacobs, 1972. 'The discovery and oral history of the Narosura site', *Azania* 7: 79–87.

A. H. Jacobs, 1975. 'Maasai pastoralism in historical perspective', pp. 406–25 in Monod, 1975.

A. J. E. Jaffey, 1966. 'A re-appraisal of the Rhodesian Iron Age up to the fifteenth century', *J.A.H.* 7: 189–95.

T. Johnson, 1960. 'Rock-paintings of ships', *S.A.A.B.* 15: 111–13.

T. Johnson, H. Rabinowitz and P. Sieff, 1959. 'Rock-paintings at Katbakkies, Koue Bokkeveld, Cape', *S.A.A.B.* 14: 99–103.

K. Jolly, 1947. 'Preliminary note on a new excavation at Skildergat, Fish Hoek', *S.A.A.B.* 2: 11–12.

K. Jolly, 1948. 'The development of the Cape Middle Stone Age in the Skildergat Cave', *S.A.A.B.* 3: 106–7.

A. M. Jones, 1964. *Africa and Indonesia*, Leiden.

A. M. Jones, 1969. 'The influence of Indonesia: the musicological evidence reconsidered', *Azania* 4: 131–45.

N. Jones, 1933. 'Excavations at Nswatugi and Madiliyangwa', *O.P.N.M.S.R.* 1(2): 1–44.

R. Joussaume, 1971. 'Les monuments mégalithiques du Harrar, Ethiopie', *L'Anthropologie* 75: 177–99.

R. Joussaume, 1975. 'Les monuments funéraires protohistoriques du Harar, Ethiopie, 2me mission', *D.S.H.C.E.* 6: 19–34.

H. A. Junod, 1927. *The Life of a South African Tribe*, London.

C. M. Keller, 1970. 'Montagu Cave: a preliminary report', *Quaternaria* 13: 187–204.

C. M. Keller, 1973. *Montagu Cave in Prehistory: a Descriptive Analysis*, Berkeley.

J. Kenyatta, 1938. *Facing Mount Kenya*, London.

P. R. Kirby, 1956. 'The building in stone of a new kraal for the Paramount Chief of the Venda', *S.A.J.S.* 52: 167.

J. S. Kirkman, 1954. *The Arab City of Gedi*, Oxford.

J. S. Kirkman, 1964. *Men and Monuments on the East African Coast*, London.

J. S. Kirkman, 1966. *Ungwana on the Tana*, The Hague.

L. P. Kirwan, 1972a. 'The Christian Topography and the Kingdom of Axum', *G.J.* 138: 166–77.

L. P. Kirwan, 1972b. 'An Ethiopian-Sudanese frontier zone in ancient history', *G.J.* 138: 457–65.

L. P. Kirwan, 1974. 'Nuba and Nubian origins', *G.J.* 140: 43–51.

M. Klapwijk, 1973. 'An Early Iron Age site near Tzaneen, N.E. Transvaal', *S.A.J.S.* 69: 324.

M. Klapwijk, 1974. 'A preliminary report on pottery from the north-eastern Transvaal', *S.A.A.B.* 29: 19–23.

R. G. Klein, 1974. 'Environment and subsistence of prehistoric man in the southern Cape Province, South Africa', *W.A.* 5: 249–84.

R. G. Klein and K. Scott, 1974. 'The fauna of Scott's Cave, Gamtoos Valley, south-eastern Cape', *S.A.J.S.* 70: 186–7.

L. Kohl-Larsen, 1943. *Auf den Spuren des Vormenschen*, Stuttgart.

L. Krzyzaniak, 1976. Note on Kadero, *Nyame Akuma* 9: 41.

H. Kuper, 1955. *The Shona*, London.

H. Kurashina, 1973. 'Archaeological investigations along the Nanyangu', *M.A.D.P.* 14: 71–89.

L. Laman, 1953, 1957. *The Kongo*, Stockholm.

C. S. Lancaster and A. Pohorilenko, 1976. 'Ingombe Ilede and the Zimbabwe culture', *I.J.A.H.S.* 9.

H. W. Langworthy, 1972. *Zambia before 1890*, London.

E. C. Lanning, 1970. 'Ntusi: an ancient capital site in western Uganda', *Azania* 5: 39–54.

L. S. B. Leakey, 1931. *The Stone Age Cultures of Kenya Colony*, Cambridge.

L. S. B. Leakey, 1935. *The Stone Age Races of Kenya*, Oxford.

L. S. B. Leakey, 1936. *Stone Age Africa*, Oxford.

L. S. B. Leakey, 1943. 'Industries of the Gorgora rockshelter, Lake Tana', *J.E.A.U.N.H.S.* 17: 199–203.

L. S. B. Leakey, 1952. 'Capsian or Aurignacian? Which term should be used in Africa?', *P.A.C.* 1: 205–6.

M. D. Leakey, 1943. 'Notes on the ground and polished stone axes of East Africa', *J.E.A.U.N.H.S.* 17: 182–95.

M. D. Leakey, 1945. 'Report on the excavations at Hyrax Hill, Nakuru, Kenya Colony', *T.R.S.S.A.* 30: 271–409.

M. D. Leakey, 1966. 'Excavation of burial mounds in Ngorongoro Crater', *T.N.R.* 66: 1–13.

M. D. Leakey, R. L. Hay, D. L. Thurber, R. Protsch and R. Berger, 1972. 'Stratigraphy, archaeology and age of the Ndutu and Naisiusiu beds, Olduvai Gorge, Tanzania', *W.A.* 3: 328–41.

M. D. Leakey and L. S. B. Leakey, 1950. *Excavations at Njoro River Cave*, Oxford.

M. D. Leakey, W. E. Owen and L. S. B. Leakey, 1948. *Dimple-based pottery from central Kavirondo, Kenya Colony*, Nairobi.

V. Lebzelter, 1934. *Eingeborenenkulturen in Südwest und Südafrika*, Leipzig.

J. Leclant, 1956. 'Le fer à travers les âges', *Annales de l'Est* 16: 83–91.

R. B. Lee, 1968. 'What hunters do for a living', pp. 30–48 in Lee and DeVore, 1968.

R. B. Lee and I. DeVore (eds.), 1968. *Man the Hunter*, Chicago.

H. S. Lewis, 1966. 'The origins of the Galla and Somali', *J.A.H.* 7: 27–46.

I. M. Lewis, 1960. 'The Somali conquest of the Horn of Africa', *J.A.H.* 1: 213–29.

I. M. Lewis, 1961. *A Pastoral Democracy*, London.

I. M. Lewis, 1965. 'The northern pastoral Somali of the Horn', pp. 319–60 in Gibbs, 1965.

H. Lhote, 1953. 'Le cheval et le chameau dans les peintures et gravures du Sahara', *Bulletin de l'I.F.A.N.* 15: 1140 ff.

G. Liesegang, 1975. 'Some Iron Age wares from central Tanzania', *Azania* 10: 93–105.

G. Lindblom, 1916. *The Akamba*, Uppsala.

E. Littmann, 1913. *Deutsche Aksum Expedition*, Berlin.

L. Lofgren, 1967. 'Stone structures of South Nyanza, Kenya', *Azania* 2: 75–88.

M. H. Logan, 1918. 'The Biers', *S.N.R.* 1: 238–48.

J. T. Louw, 1960. *Prehistory of the Matjes River Rockshelter*, *M.N.M.B.* I.

A. Lucas, 1962. *Ancient Egyptian Building Materials and Industries*, London.

M. Lucas, 1935. 'Renseignements ethnographiques et linguistiques sur les Danakils de Tadjourah', *Journal de la Société des Africanistes* 5: 181–202.

H. R. MacCalman, 1965. 'Carbon-14 dates from South West Africa', *S.A.A.B.* 20: 215.

H. R. MacCalman and B. J. Grobbelaar, 1965. 'Preliminary report of the stone-working OvaTjimba groups in the northern Kaokoveld of South West Africa', *Cimbebasia* 13: 1–39.

R. MacIver, 1906. *Mediaeval Rhodesia*, London.

T. M. O'C. Maggs, 1967. 'A quantative [*sic*] analysis of the rock art from a sample area in the western Cape', *S.A.J.S.* 63: 100–4.

T. M. O'C. Maggs, 1971*a*. 'Some observations on the size of human groups during the Late Stone Age', *S.A.J.S.* special issue 2: 49–53.

T. M. O'C. Maggs, 1971*b*. 'Pastoral settlements on the Riet river', *S.A.A.B.* 26: 37–63.

T. M. O'C. Maggs, 1972. 'Bilobial dwellings: a persistent feature of southern Tswana settlements', *G.S.* 1: 54–64.

T. M. O'C. Maggs, 1973*a*. 'The NC3 Iron Age tradition', *S.A.J.S.* 69: 326.

T. M. O'C. Maggs, 1973*b*. 'The Iron Age of the Orange Free State', *P.A.C.* 6: 175–81.

T. M. O'C. Maggs, 1975. 'Faunal remains and hunting patterns from the Iron Age of the southern Highveld', *A.N.M.* 22: 449–54.

T. M. O'C. Maggs, 1976. 'Iron Age patterns and Sotho history on the southern Highveld, South Africa', *W.A.* 7: 318–32.

T. M. O'C. Maggs and M. A. Michael, 1975. 'Ntshekane: an Early Iron Age site in the Tugela basin, Natal', *A.N.M.* 22: 705–40.

T. M. O'C. Maggs and E. Speed, 1967. 'Bonteberg shelter', *S.A.A.B.* 22: 80–93.

M. Mainga, 1973. *Bulozi under the Luyana Kings*, London.

B. D. Malan and J. C. van Niekerk, 1955. 'Die Later Steentyd in Transvaal', *S.A.J.S.* 51: 231–5.

P. de Maret, 1975. 'A carbon-14 date from Zaire', *Antiquity* 49: 133–7.

H. Martin and R. J. Mason, 1954. 'The test trench in the Phillip Cave, Ameib, Erongo Mountains, South West Africa', *S.A.A.B.* 9: 148–51.

A. Martin del Malino, 1965. 'Secuencia cultural en el neolitico de Fernando Poo', *Trab. Prehist. Inst. Espan.* 17.

F. T. Masao, 1976. 'Some common aspects of the rock paintings of Kondoa and Singida', *T.N.R.* 77/8: 51–64.

R. J. Mason, 1962. *Prehistory of the Transvaal*, Johannesburg.

R. J. Mason, 1965. 'The origin of South African society', *S.A.J.S.* 61: 255–67.

R. J. Mason, 1967. *Prehistory as a Science of Change: new research in the South African interior*, *O.P.A.R.U.* 1.

R. J. Mason, 1968*a*. 'Transvaal and Natal Iron Age settlement revealed by aerial photography and excavation', *A.S.* 27: 1–14.

R. J. Mason, 1968*b*. 'Southern African Iron Age and present-day Venda architecture and pottery from the northern Transvaal, South Africa', *A.S.* 27: 15–22.

R. J. Mason (ed.), 1971. *Prehistoric Man at Melville Koppies, Johannesburg*, *O.P.A.R.U.* 6.

R. J. Mason, 1973. 'First Early Iron Age settlement in South Africa: Broederstroom 24/73, Brits District, Transvaal', *S.A.J.S.* 69: 324–5.

R. J. Mason, 1974. 'Background to the Transvaal Iron Age – discoveries at Olifantspoort and Broederstroom', *J.S.A.I.M.M.* 74: 211–16.

D. H. Matthews and A. Mordini, 1959. 'The monastery of Debra Damo, Ethiopia', *Archaeologia* 97.

R. Mauny, 1967. 'L'Afrique et les origines de la domestication', pp. 583–99 in Bishop and Clark, 1967.

R. Mauny, 1971. 'The western Sudan', pp. 66–87 in Shinnie, 1971*c*.

A. J. D. Meiring, 1953. 'The Matjes River shelter: evidence in regard to the introduction of rock painting into South Africa', *R.N.M.B.* 1: 77–84.

F. Melland, 1923. *In Witch-bound Africa*, London.

M. Merker, 1911. *Die Maasai*, Berlin.

H. V. Merrick, 1973. 'Aspects of the size and shape variation of the East African stone bowls', *Azania* 8: 115–30.

N. J. van der Merwe, 1968. 'Radiocarbon chronology of the Iron Age in sub-Saharan Africa', *C.A.* 9: 54–8.

N. J. van der Merwe and R. T. K. Scully, 1971. 'The Phalaborwa story: archaeological and ethnographic investigation of a South African Iron Age group', *W.A.* 3: 178–96.

K. Michalowski, 1962. *Faras - Fouilles Polonaises, 1961*, Warsaw.

K. Michalowski, 1964. 'Polish excavations at Faras, 1962–63', *Kush* 12: 195–207.

J. Middleton, 1953. *The Kikuyu and Kamba of Kenya*, London.

J. C. Miller, 1972. 'The Imbangala and the chronology of early Central African history', *J.A.H.* 13: 549–74.

S. F. Miller, 1969a. *The Nachikufan Industries of the Zambian Later Stone Age*. Ph.D. thesis, University of California, Berkeley.

S. F. Miller, 1969b. 'Contacts between the later Stone Age and the Early Iron Age in southern central Africa', *Azania* 4: 81–90.

S. F. Miller, 1971. 'The age of the Nachikufan industries in Zambia', *S.A.A.B.* 26: 143–6.

S. F. Miller, 1973. 'The archaeological sequence of the Zambian later Stone Age', *P.A.C.* 6: 565–72.

E. A. C. Mills and N. T. Filmer, 1972. 'Chondwe Iron Age site, Ndola, Zambia', *Azania* 7: 129–47.

R. Moffat, 1842. *Missionary Labours and Scenes in Southern Africa*, London.

U. Monneret de Villard, 1938. *Storia della Nubia Cristiana*, Rome.

T. Monod (ed.), 1975. *Pastoralism in Africa*, London.

T. Monod and R. Mauny, 1957. 'Découverte de nouveaux instruments en os dans l'Ouest Africain', *P.A.C.* 3: 242–7.

F. Mori, 1964. 'Some aspects of the rock art of the Acacus (Fezzan Sahara) and dating regarding it', pp. 247–59 in L. Pericot-Garcia and E. Ripoll-Perello (eds.), *Prehistoric Art of the Western Mediterranean and the Sahara*, New York.

F. Mori, 1965. *Tadrart Acacus: Arte Rupestre e Culture del Sahara Preistorico*, Turin.

G. Mortelmans, 1962a. 'Archéologie des grottes Dimba et Ngovo', *P.A.C.* 4: 407–25.

G. Mortelmans, 1962b. 'Vue d'ensemble sur la préhistoire du Congo occidental', *P.A.C.* 4: 129–64.

F. Moysey, 1943. 'Excavation of a rockshelter at Gorgora, Lake Tana', *J.E.A.U.N.H.S.* 17: 196–8.

S. F. Nadel, 1947. *The Nuba*, London.

E. Naville, 1898. *The Temple of Deir el Bahari*, London.

C. M. Nelson and M. Posnansky, 1970. 'The stone tools from the re-excavation of Nsongezi rock shelter', *Azania* 5: 119–72.

J. Nenquin, 1959. 'Dimple-based pots from Kasai, Belgian Congo', *Man* 59: article 242.

J. Nenquin, 1963. *Excavations at Sanga, 1957*, Tervuren.

J. Nenquin, 1967. *Contributions to the Study of the Prehistoric Cultures of Rwanda and Burundi*, Tervuren.

M. D. D. Newitt and P. S. Garlake, 1967. 'The "aringa" at Massangano', *J.A.H.* 8: 133–56.

F. van Noten, 1971. 'Excavations at Munyama cave', *Antiquity* 45: 56–8.

F. van Noten, 1972. *Les Tombes du Roi Cyirima Rujugira et de la Reine-Mère Nyirayuhi Kanjogera*, Tervuren.

F. van Noten, 1974. 'Excavations at the Gordon's Bay shell midden, south-western Cape', *S.A.A.B.* 29: 122–42.

H. A. Nordström, 1972. *Neolithic and A-Group Sites*, Stockholm.

C. A. S. Northcote, 1907. 'The Nilotic Kavirondo', *J.R.A.I.* 37: 58–66.

K. P. Oakley, 1961. 'A bone harpoon from Gamble's Cave, Kenya', *Antiquaries' Journal* 41: 86–7.

T. P. O'Brien, 1939. *The Prehistory of Uganda Protectorate*, Cambridge.

K. Odner, 1971a. 'An archaeological survey of Iramba, Tanzania', *Azania* 6: 151–98.

K. Odner, 1971b. 'Usangi Hospital and other archaeological sites in the North Pare mountains, north-eastern Tanzania', *Azania* 6: 89–130.

K. Odner, 1971c. 'A preliminary report on an archaeological survey on the slopes of Kilimanjaro', *Azania* 6: 131–50.

K. Odner, 1972. 'Excavations at Narosura, a stone bowl site in the southern Kenya highlands', *Azania* 7: 25–92.

B. A. Ogot, 1967. *History of the Southern Luo*, Nairobi.

R. Oliver, 1963. 'Discernible developments in the interior, c. 1500–1840', pp. 169–211 in R. Oliver and G. Mathew (eds.), *The Oxford History of East Africa*, I, Oxford.

R. Oliver, 1966. 'The problem of the Bantu expansion', *J.A.H.* 6: 361–76.

R. Oliver and B. M. Fagan, 1975. *Africa in the Iron Age*, Cambridge.

J. D. Omer-Cooper, 1966. *The Zulu Aftermath*, London.

J. C. Onyango-Abuje, 1977. 'Crescent Island: a preliminary report on excavations at an East African Neolithic site', *Azania* 12: in press.

B. Ottaway, 1973a. 'Dispersion diagrams: a new approach to the display of carbon-14 dates', *Archaeometry* 15: 5–12.

B. Ottaway, 1973b. 'Estimating the duration of cultures', *Antiquity* 47: 231–3.

K. H. Otto, 1963. 'Shaqudud', *Kush* 11: 108–15.

H. Pager, 1971. *Ndedema*, Graz.

R. Pankhurst, 1961. *An Introduction to the Economic History of Ethiopia*, London.

R. Paribeni, 1908. *Richerche nel Luogo dell'antica Adulis*, Rome.

J. E. Parkington, 1972. 'Seasonal mobility in the later Stone Age', *A.S.* 31: 223–43.

J. E. Parkington and C. Poggenpoel, 1971. 'Excavations at de Hangen, 1968', *S.A.A.B.* 26: 3–36.

W. J. A. Payne, 1964. 'The origin of domestic cattle in Africa', *Empire Journal of Experimental Agriculture*, 32: 97–113.

S. Pearce and M. Posnansky, 1963. 'The re-excavation of Nsongezi rockshelter, Ankole', *U.J.* 27: 85–94.

L. Peringuey, 1911. *The Stone Ages of South Africa*, A.S.A.M. 8.

J. G. Peristiany, 1939. *The Social Institutions of the Kipsigis*, London.

W. M. F. Petrie, 1886. *Naukratis*, I, London.

D. W. Phillipson, 1968a. 'The Early Iron Age in Zambia – regional variants and some tentative conclusions', *J.A.H.* 9: 191–211.

D. W. Phillipson, 1968b. 'The Early Iron Age site at Kapwirimbwe, Lusaka', *Azania* 3: 87–105.

D. W. Phillipson, 1968c. 'Finds from Kapwirimbwe', *Inventaria Archaeologica Africana* Z5.

D. W. Phillipson, 1968d. 'Cewa, Leya and Lala iron smelting furnaces', *S.A.A.B.* 23: 102–13.

D. W. Phillipson, 1969. 'The prehistoric sequence at Nakapapula rockshelter, Zambia', *P.P.S.* 35: 172–202.

D. W. Phillipson, 1970a. 'Excavations at Twickenham Road, Lusaka', *Azania* 5: 77–118.

D. W. Phillipson, 1970b. 'Notes on the later prehistoric radiocarbon chronology of eastern and southern Africa', *J.A.H.* 11: 1–15.

D. W. Phillipson, 1971. 'An Early Iron Age site on the Lubusi River, Kaoma District, Zambia', *Z.M.J.* 2: 51–7.

D. W. Phillipson, 1972a. 'Early Iron Age sites on the Zambian Copperbelt', *Azania* 7: 93–128.

D. W. Phillipson, 1972b. 'Zambian rock paintings', *W.A.* 3: 313–27.

D. W. Phillipson, 1972c. *Prehistoric Rock Paintings and Rock Engravings of Zambia*, Livingstone.

D. W. Phillipson, 1973. 'The prehistoric succession in eastern Zambia: a preliminary report', *Azania* 8: 3–24.

D. W. Phillipson, 1974. 'Iron Age history and archaeology in Zambia', *J.A.H.* 15: 1–25.

D. W. Phillipson, 1975. 'The chronology of the Iron Age in Bantu Africa', *J.A.H.* 16: 321–42.

D. W. Phillipson, 1976a. *The Prehistory of Eastern Zambia*, Nairobi.

D. W. Phillipson, 1976b. 'Archaeology and Bantu linguistics', *W.A.* 8: 65–82.

D. W. Phillipson, 1977a. 'The excavation of Gobedra rock-shelter, Axum: an early occurrence of cultivated finger millet in northern Ethiopia', *Azania* 12.

D. W. Phillipson, 1977b. 'Lowasera', *Azania* 12.

D. W. Phillipson and B. M. Fagan, 1969. 'The date of the Ingombe Ilede burials', *J.A.H.* 10: 199–204.

L. Phillipson, 1975. *A Survey of Upper Pleistocene and Holocene Industries in the upper Zambezi Valley, Zambia*, Ph.D. thesis, University of California, Berkeley.

L. Phillipson, 1976. 'Survey of the Stone Age archaeology of the upper Zambezi valley, II – excavations at Kandanda', *Azania* 11: 49–81.

L. Phillipson and D. W. Phillipson, 1970. 'Patterns of edge damage on the Late Stone Age industry from Chiwemupula, Zambia', *Z.M.J.* 1: 40–75.

J. Pirenne, 1975. 'L'imbroglio de trois siècles de chronologie aksumite: IV–VI siècles', *D.S.H.C.E.* 6: 49–58.

M. Posnansky, 1961. 'Dimple-based pottery from Uganda', *Man* 61: article 168.

M. Posnansky, 1966. 'Kingship, archaeology and historical myth', *U.J.* 30: 1–12.

M. Posnansky, 1967a. 'The Iron Age in East Africa', pp. 629–49 in Bishop and Clark, 1967.

M. Posnansky, 1967b. 'Excavations at Lanet, Kenya, 1957', *Azania* 2: 89–114.

M. Posnansky, 1968a. 'The excavation of an Ankole capital site at Bweyorere', *U.J.* 32: 165–82.

M. Posnansky, 1968b. 'Cairns in the southern part of the Kenya Rift Valley', *Azania* 3: 181–7.

M. Posnansky, 1968c. 'Bantu genesis: archaeological reflexions', *J.A.H.* 9: 1–11.

M. Posnansky, 1969. 'Bigo bya Mugenyi', *U.J.* 33: 125–50.

M. Posnansky, 1973. 'Terminology in the Early Iron Age of eastern Africa, with particular reference to the dimple-based wares of Lolui Island, Uganda', *P.A.C.* 6: 577–9.

M. Posnansky and R. McIntosh, 1976. 'New radiocarbon dates for northern and western Africa', *J.A.H.* 17: 161–95.

M. Posnansky and C. M. Nelson, 1968. 'Rock paintings and excavations at Nyero, Uganda', *Azania* 3: 147–66.

M. Posnansky and J. W. Sekibengo, 1959. 'Ground stone axes and bored stones from Uganda', *U.J.* 23: 179–81.

A. H. J. Prins, 1952. *The Coastal Tribes of the North-East Bantu*, London.

A. H. J. Prins, 1967. *The Swahili-Speaking Peoples*, London.

H. P. Prinsloo, 1974. 'Early Iron Age site at Klein Afrika', *S.A.J.S.* 70: 271–3.

S. Puglisi, 1946. 'Industria litica di Aksum nel Tigrai occidentale', *Rivista di Scienze Preistoriche* 1: 284–90.

M. E. L. Pumphrey, 1941. 'The Shilluk tribe', *S.N.R.* 24: 1–45.

W. H. J. Rangeley, 1963. 'The earliest inhabitants of Nyasaland', *Nyasaland Journal* 16: 38–42.

H. Reck, 1926. 'Prähistorische Grab-und Menschenfunde und ihre Beziehungen zur Pluvialzeit in Ostafrika', *Mitteilungen aus den deutschen Schutzgebieten* 34: 50–86.

J. Redinha, 1948. *As Gravuras Rupestres do Alto-Zambeze*, Lisbon.

A. I. Richards, 1939. *Land, Labour and Diet in Northern Rhodesia*, London.

C. van Riet Lowe, 1952a. *The Pleistocene Geology and Prehistory of Uganda, II*, Entebbe.

C. van Riet Lowe, 1952b. *The Distribution of Prehistoric Rock Engravings and Paintings in South Africa*, Johannesburg.

P. Rigby, 1969. *Cattle and Kinship among the Gogo*, New York.

G. P. Rightmire, 1970. 'Iron Age skulls from southern Africa re-assessed by multiple discriminant analysis', *A.J.P.A.* 23: 147–68.

G. P. Rightmire, 1974. 'Problems in the study of later Pleistocene man in Africa', *American Anthropologist*, 77: 28–52.

G. P. Rightmire, 1975. 'New studies of post-Pleistocene human skeletal remains from the Rift Valley, Kenya', *A.J.P.A.* 42: 351–70.

L. H. Robbins, 1972. 'Archaeology in Turkana District, Kenya', *Science* 176: 359–66.

L. H. Robbins, 1974. *The Lothagam Site*, East Lansing.

P. A. Robins and A. Whitty, 1966. 'Excavations at Harleigh Farm, near Rusape, Rhodesia', *S.A.A.B.* 21: 61–80.

K. R. Robinson, 1952. 'Excavations in two rockshelters near the Rusawi river, central Mashonaland', *S.A.A.B.* 7: 108–29.

K. R. Robinson, 1959. *Khami Ruins*, Cambridge.

K. R. Robinson, 1961a. 'An Early Iron Age site from the Chibi District, Southern Rhodesia', *S.A.A.B.* 16: 75–102.

K. R. Robinson, 1961b. Archaeological report in *Rhodesian Schoolboys' Exploration Society Expedition to Buffalo Bend*, Salisbury.

K. R. Robinson, 1963. 'Further excavations in the Iron Age deposits at the Tunnel site, Gokomere Hill, Southern Rhodesia', *S.A.A.B.* 18: 155–71.

K. R. Robinson, 1964. 'Dombozanga rockshelter, Mtetengwe river, Beit Bridge, Southern Rhodesia: excavation results', *Arnoldia* 1: no. 7.

K. R. Robinson, 1965. 'A note on Iron Age sites in the Zambezi Valley and on the escarpment in the Sipolilo District, Southern Rhodesia', *Arnoldia* 1: no. 27.

K. R. Robinson, 1966a. 'A preliminary report on the recent archaeology of Ngonde, northern Malawi', *J.A.H.* 7: 169–88.

K. R. Robinson, 1966b. 'The Leopard's Kopje culture: its position in the Iron Age in Southern Rhodesia', *S.A.A.B.* 21: 5–51.

K. R. Robinson, 1966c. 'Bambata ware: its position in the Rhodesian Iron Age in the light of recent research', *S.A.A.B.* 21: 81–5.

K. R. Robinson, 1966d. 'The Iron Age site in Kapula Vlei, Wankie Game Reserve, Rhodesia', *Arnoldia* 2: no. 39.

K. R. Robinson, 1966e. 'The Sinoia Caves, Lomagundi District, Rhodesia', *P.T.R.S.A.* 51: 131–55.

K. R. Robinson, 1966f. 'The archaeology of the Rozwi', pp. 3–27 in E. Stokes and R. Brown (eds.), *The Zambesian Past*, Manchester.

K. R. Robinson, 1967. 'Further work on Iron Age sites in the Chibi District, Southern Rhodesia', *Arnoldia* 3: no. 1.

K. R. Robinson, 1970. *The Iron Age in the Southern Lake Area of Malawi*, M.A.D.P. 8.

K. R. Robinson, 1973a. *The Iron Age of the Upper and Lower Shire, Malawi*, M.A.D.P. 13.

K. R. Robinson, 1973b. 'The pottery sequence of Malawi briefly compared with that already established south of the Zambezi', *Arnoldia* 6: no. 18.

K. R. Robinson, 1975. *Iron Age Sites in the Dedza District of Malawi*, M.A.D.P. 16.

K. R. Robinson and B. Sandelowsky, 1968. 'The Iron Age in northern Malawi: recent work', *Azania* 3: 107–46.

J. Roscoe, 1911. *The Baganda*, London.

S. Rudd, 1969. 'Preliminary report of excavations 1963–6 at Lekkerwater Ruins, Tsindi Hill, Theydon, Rhodesia', *P.T.R.S.A.* 52: 38–50.

J. Rudner, 1957. 'The Brandberg and its archaeological remains', *Journal of the South West Africa Scientific Society* 12: 7–44.

J. Rudner, 1968. 'Strandloper pottery from South and South West Africa', *A.S.A.M.* 49: 441–663.

J. Rudner, 1971. 'Painted burial stones from the Cape', *S.A.J.S.* special issue 2: 54–61.

J. Rudner, 1973. 'Radiocarbon dates from the Brandberg in South West Africa', *S.A.A.B.* 27: 164–5.

J. Rudner and I. Rudner, 1968. 'Rock art in the thirstland areas', *S.A.A.B.* 23: 75–89.

J. Rudner and I. Rudner, 1970. *The Hunter and his Art*, Cape Town.

C. G. Sampson, 1967a. 'Excavations at Zaayfontein shelter, Narvalspont, Northern Cape', *R.N.M.B.* 2: 41–119.

C. G. Sampson, 1967b. 'Excavations at Glen Elliott shelter, Colesberg District, Northern Cape', *R.N.M.B.* 2: 125–209.

C. G. Sampson, 1967c. 'Zeekoegat 13: a later Stone Age open site near Venterstad, Cape', *R.N.M.B.* 2: 211–37.

C. G. Sampson, 1970. *The Smithfield Industrial Complex: further field results*, *M.N.M.B.* 5.

C. G. Sampson, 1972. *The Stone Age Industries of the Orange River Scheme and South Africa*, *M.N.M.B.* 6.

C. G. Sampson, 1974. *The Stone Age Archaeology of Southern Africa*, New York.

C. G. Sampson and M. E. Sampson, 1967. *Riversmead shelter: excavation and analysis*, *M.N.M.B.* 3.

B. Sandelowsky, 1973. 'Kapako, an Early Iron Age site on the Okavango River, South West Africa', *S.A.J.S.* 69: 325.

J. R. dos Santos Junior and C. M. N. Everdosa, 1970. 'A estacao arqueologica de Benfica, Luanda', *Rivista da Faculdade de Çiençias da Universidade de Luanda* 5: 33–51.

H. Sassoon, 1966. 'Engaruka: excavations during 1964', *Azania* 1: 79–99.

H. Sassoon, 1967a. 'New views on Engaruka, northern Tanzania', *J.A.H.* 8: 201–17.

H. Sassoon, 1967b. 'The Masange bowmen', *Azania* 2: 193–4.

H. Sassoon, 1968. 'Excavation of a burial mound in Ngorongoro Crater', *T.N.R.* 49: 15–32.

H. Sassoon, 1971. 'Excavations at Engaruka, northern Tanzania', *National Geographic Society Research Reports for 1965*: 221–30.

I. Schapera, 1930. *The Khoisan Peoples of South Africa*, London.

I. Schapera, 1933. *The Early Cape Hottentots*, Cape Town.

P. R. Schmidt, 1975. 'A new look at interpretations of the Early Iron Age in East Africa', *History in Africa* 2: 127–36.

W. H. Schoff, 1912. *The Periplus of the Erythraean Sea*, New York.

M. Schoffeleers, 1973. 'Towards the identification of a proto-Chewa culture: a preliminary contribution', *Malawi Journal of Social Science* 2: 47–60.

J. F. Schofield, 1935. 'Natal coastal pottery from the Durban District: a preliminary survey', *S.A.J.S.* 32: 508–27.

J. F. Schofield, 1936. 'Natal coastal pottery from the Durban District, part II', *S.A.J.S.* 33: 993–1009.

J. F. Schofield, 1938. 'The pottery', pp. 295–301 in Goodwin, 1938.

J. F. Schofield, 1940. 'Report on the pottery from Bambata Cave', *S.A.J.S.* 37: 361–72.

J. F. Schofield, 1948. *Primitive Pottery*, Cape Town.

M. Schoonraad and P. B. Beaumont, 1968. 'The North Brabant shelter, north-western Transvaal', *S.A.J.S.* 64: 319–31.

C. A. Schoute-Vanneck and R. C. Walsh, 1959. 'The shell middens at the Ingane River Mouth', *S.A.A.B.* 14: 43–55.

C. Schrire, 1962. Oakhurst: a re-examination and vindication', *S.A.A.B.* 17: 181–95.

G. Schweinfurth, 1874. *The Heart of Africa*, London.

F. R. Schweitzer, 1970. 'A preliminary report of excavations of a cave at Die Kelders', *S.A.A.B.* 25: 136–8.

F. R. Schweitzer, 1974. 'Archaeological evidence for sheep at the Cape', *S.A.A.B.* 29: 75–82.

F. R. Schweitzer and K. J. Scott, 1973. 'Early appearance of domestic sheep in sub-Saharan Africa', *Nature* 241: 547–8.

T. Scudder, 1962. *The Ecology of the Gwembe Tonga*, Manchester.

H. S. Sergew, 1972. *Ancient and Medieval Ethiopian History*, Addis Ababa.

W. A. Shack, 1966. *The Gurage: a People of the Ensete Culture*, London.

W. A. Shack, 1974. *The Central Ethiopians*, London.

N. J. Shackleton, 1973. 'Oxygen isotope analysis as a means of determining season of occupation of prehistoric midden sites', *Archaeometry* 15: 133–41.

J. C. Sharman, 1974. 'Meroitic: its ancestors and descendants – some relationships', *Azania* 9: 207–18.

T. Shaw, 1969. 'On radiocarbon chronology of the Iron Age in sub-Saharan Africa', *C.A.* 10: 226–8.

T. Shaw, 1972. 'Early agriculture in Africa', *Journal of the Historical Society of Nigeria* 6: 142–90.

T. Shaw, 1976. 'Hunters, gatherers and first farmers in West Africa', in J. V. S. Megaw (ed.), *Hunters, Gatherers and First Farmers Outside Europe*, London.

J. L. Shiner, 1968. 'The Khartoum variant industry', pp. 768–90 in Wendorf, 1968.

P. L. Shinnie, 1960. 'Excavations at Bigo, 1957', *U.J.* 24: 16–29.

P. L. Shinnie, 1963. 'The University of Ghana excavation at Debeira West, 1962', *Kush* 11: 257–63.

P. L. Shinnie, 1964. 'The University of Ghana excavation at Debeira West, 1963', *Kush* 12: 208–15.

P. L. Shinnie, 1967. *Meroe*, London.

P. L. Shinnie, 1969. 'On radiocarbon chronology of the Iron Age in sub-Saharan Africa', *C.A.* 10: 229–30.

P. L. Shinnie, 1971a. 'The Sudan', pp. 89–107 in Shinnie, 1971c.

P. L. Shinnie, 1971b. 'The legacy to Africa', pp. 434–55 in J. R. Harris (ed.), *The Legacy of Egypt*, Oxford.

P. L. Shinnie, 1971c. *The African Iron Age*, Oxford.

P. L. Shinnie and M. Shinnie, 1965. 'New light on medieval Nubia', *J.A.H.* 6: 263–73.

A. Siiriäinen, 1971. 'The Iron Age site at Gatung'ang'a, central Kenya', *Azania* 6: 199–232.

G. B. Silberbauer, 1965. *Bushman Survey Report*, Gaberones.

F. J. Simoons, 1960. *North-West Ethiopia – Peoples and Economy*, Madison.

F. J. Simoons, 1965. 'Some questions on the economic prehistory of Ethiopia', *J.A.H.* 6: 1–13.

R. Singer and J. Wymer, 1969. 'Radiocarbon date for two painted stones from a coastal cave in South Africa', *Nature* 224: 508–10.

L. M. Slack, 1962. *Rock Engravings from Driekops Eiland*, London.

E. W. Smith, 1956. 'Sebetuane and the Makololo', *A.S.* 15: 49–74.

E. W. Smith and A. Dale, 1920. *The Ila-Speaking Peoples of Northern Rhodesia*, London.

P. E. L. Smith, 1968. 'Problems and possibilities of the prehistoric rock art of northern Africa', *I.J.A.H.S.* 1: 1–39.

G. Smolla, 1956. 'Prähistorische Keramik aus Ostafrika', *Tribus* 6: 35–64.

R. C. Soper, 1967a. 'Kwale: an early Iron Age site in south-eastern Kenya', *Azania* 2: 1–17.

R. C. Soper, 1967b. 'Iron Age sites in north-eastern Tanzania', *Azania* 2: 19–36.

R. C. Soper, 1969. 'Radiocarbon dating of "dimple-based ware" in western Kenya', *Azania* 4: 148–53.

R. C. Soper, 1971a. 'A general review of the Early Iron Age in the southern half of Africa', *Azania* 6: 5–37.

R. C. Soper, 1971b. 'Iron Age archaeological sites in the Chobi sector of Murchison Falls National Park, Uganda', *Azania* 6: 53–87.

R. C. Soper, 1971c. 'Resemblances between East African Early Iron Age pottery and recent vessels from the north-eastern Congo', *Azania* 6: 233–41.

R. C. Soper, 1974. 'New radiocarbon dates for eastern and southern Africa', *J.A.H.* 15: 175–92.

R. C. Soper and B. Golden, 1969. 'An archaeological survey of Mwanza region, Tanzania', *Azania* 4: 15–79.

A. Southall, 1956. *Alur Society*, Cambridge.

P. Spencer, 1965. *The Samburu*, London.

M. G. Spratling, 1970. 'Interim report on the archaeological finds (Blue Nile Expedition, 1968), *G.J.* 136: 59–60.

G. Steindorff, 1935–7. *Aniba*, Gluckstadt.

D. W. Stirke, n.d. *Eight Years among the Barotse*, London.

R. Summers, 1958. *Inyanga*, Cambridge.

R. Summers (ed.), 1959. *Prehistoric Rock Art of the Federation of Rhodesia and Nyasaland*, London.

R. Summers, 1963. *Zimbabwe: a Rhodesian Mystery*, Johannesburg.

R. Summers, 1967. 'Iron Age industries of southern Africa, with notes on their chronology, terminology and economic status', pp. 687–700 in Bishop and Clark, 1967.

R. Summers, 1969. *Ancient Mining in Rhodesia*, Salisbury.

R. Summers, 1970. 'Forty years' progress in Iron Age studies in Rhodesia', *S.A.A.B.* 25: 95–103.

R. Summers, K. R. Robinson and A. Whitty, 1961. *Zimbabwe Excavations*, *O.P.N.M.S.R.* III: 23a.

J. E. G. Sutton, 1964. 'A review of pottery from the Kenya highlands', *S.A.A.B.* 19: 27–35.

J. E. G. Sutton, 1966. 'The archaeology and early peoples of the highlands of Kenya and northern Tanzania', *Azania* 1: 37–57.

J. E. G. Sutton, 1968. 'Archaeological sites in Usandawe', *Azania* 3: 167–74.

J. E. G. Sutton, 1969. 'Ancient civilisations and modern agricultural systems in the Southern Highlands of Tanzania', *Azania* 4: 1–13.

J. E. G. Sutton, 1972. 'New radiocarbon dates for eastern and southern Africa', *J.A.H.* 13: 1–24.

J. E. G. Sutton, 1973a. *The Archaeology of the Western Highlands of Kenya*, Nairobi.

J. E. G. Sutton, 1973b. *Early Trade in Eastern Africa*, Nairobi.

J. E. G. Sutton, 1973c. 'Ilula: excavations of Late Iron Age "brick" sites in the Southern Highlands of Tanzania', *Azania* 8: 141–50.

J. E. G. Sutton, 1973d. 'The East African "Neolithic"', *P.A.C.* 6: 88–90.

J. E. G. Sutton, 1974. 'The aquatic civilization of middle Africa', *J.A.H.* 15: 527–46.

J. E. G. Sutton and A. D. Roberts, 1968. 'Uvinza and its salt industry', *Azania* 3: 45–86.

R. D. F. Taylor, 1966. 'The Gumba and "Gumba pits" of the Fort Hall District, Kenya', *Azania* 1: 111–17.

H. B. Thom (ed.), 1952. *The Journal of Jan van Riebeeck*, Cape Town.

M. Titherington, 1923. 'City mounds in the Bahr el Ghazal Province', *S.N.R.* 6: 111–12.

J. Tixier, 1967. 'Procédés d'analyse et questions de terminologie concernant l'étude des ensembles industriels du Paléolithique récent et de l'Epipaléo-lithique dans l'Afrique du Nord-Ouest', pp. 771–820 in Bishop and Clark, 1967.

P. V. Tobias, 1958. 'Skeletal remains from Inyanga', pp. 159–72 in Summers, 1958.

T. G. Trevor, 1912. 'Some observations on ancient mine workings in the Transvaal', *Journal of the Chemical Society of South Africa* 12: 267–75.

B. G. Trigger, 1966. 'The languages of the northern Sudan: an historical perspective', *J.A.H.* 7: 19–25.

B. G. Trigger, 1969. 'The myth of Meroe and the African Iron Age', *I.J.A.H.S.* 2: 23–50.

B. G. Trigger, 1976. *Nubia*, London.

J. S. Trimingham, 1952. *Islam in Ethiopia*, Oxford.

M. Trowell and K. P. Wachsmann, 1953. *Tribal Crafts of Uganda*, Oxford.

C. M. Turnbull, 1961. *The Forest People*, New York.

C. M. Turnbull, 1965. *Wayward Servants*, London.

C. M. Turnbull, 1972. *The Mountain People*, New York.

E. R. Turton, 1975. 'Bantu, Galla and Somali migrations in the Horn of Africa: a re-assessment of the Juba/Tana area', *J.A.H.* 16: 519–37.

J. B. de Vaal, 1943. ''N Soutpansbergse Zimbabwe', *S.A.J.S.* 40: 303–18.

J. Vansina, 1965. *Oral Tradition*, London.

J. Vansina, 1966. *Kingdoms of the Savanna*, Madison.

J. Vansina, 1969. 'The bells of kings', *J.A.H.* 10: 187–97.

R. Vaufrey and G. Joubert, 1946. 'Le néolithique du Ténéré', *L'Anthropologie* 50: 325–30.

N. Vavilov, 1951. 'The origin, variation, immunity and breeding of cultivated plants', *Chronica Botanica*, 13: 1–364.

P. M. Vérin, 1966. 'Les recherches archéologiques à Madagascar', *Azania* 1: 119–37.

A. Viereck and J. Rudner, 1957. 'Twyfelfontein, a centre of prehistoric art in South West Africa', *S.A.A.B.* 12: 15–26.

H. de Villiers, 1970. 'Die Skelettreste der Ziwa: Kultur und die Frage des frühesten Auftretens von Negriden in Südafrika', *Homo* 21: 17–28.

H. de Villiers, 1976. Reports on skeletal remains in D. W. Phillipson, 1976a.

P. Vinnicombe, 1972a. 'Myth, motive and selection in southern African rock art', *Africa* 42: 192–204.

P. Vinnicombe, 1972b. 'Motivation in African rock art', *Antiquity* 46: 124–33.

P. Vinnicombe, 1976. *People of the Eland*, Pietermaritzburg.

J. O. Vogel, 1969. 'On early evidence of agriculture in southern Zambia', *C.A.* 10: 524.

J. O. Vogel, 1970. 'The Kalomo Culture of southern Zambia: some notes toward a reassessment', *Z.M.J.* 1: 77–88.

J. O. Vogel, 1971a. 'Early Iron Age metallurgy in south-central Africa', *Z.M.J.* 2: 39–49.

J. O. Vogel, 1971b. *Kamangoza*, Lusaka.

J. O. Vogel, 1971c. *Kumadzulo*, Lusaka.

J. O. Vogel, 1972a. 'The Shongwe tradition', *Z.M.J.* 3: 27–34.

J. O. Vogel, 1972b. 'On Early Iron Age funerary practise [*sic*] in southern Zambia', *C.A.* 13: 583–6.

J. O. Vogel, 1973a. 'Some Early Iron Age sites in southern and western Zambia', *Azania* 8: 25–54.

J. O. Vogel, 1973b. 'The Early Iron Age site at Sioma Mission, western Zambia', *Z.M.J.* 4: 153–69.

J. O. Vogel, 1975a. 'The Iron Age archaeology of the Victoria Falls region', pp. 48–58 in D. W. Phillipson (ed.), *Mosi-oa-Tunya*, London.

J. O. Vogel, 1975b. *Simbusenga*, Lusaka.

J. O. Vogel and N. M. Katanekwa, 1976. 'Early Iron Age pottery from western Zambia', *Azania* 11: 160–7.

G. Wagner, 1956. *The Bantu of North Kavirondo*, London.

G. A. Wainwright, 1945. 'Iron in the Napatan and Meroitic Ages', *S.N.R.* 26: 5–36.

J. Walker and G. S. P. Freeman-Grenville, 1956. 'The history and coinage of the sultans of Kilwa', *T.N.R.* 45: 33–65.

J. Walsh and P. G. Powys, 1970. 'Obsidian flakes from Laikipia District, Kenya', *Azania* 5: 178–9.

J. Walton, 1951. 'Corbelled stone huts in southern Africa', *Man* 51: article 82.

J. Walton, 1965. *Early Ghoya Settlement in the Orange Free State*, *M.N.M.B.* 2.

N. J. van Warmelo, 1940. *The Copper-Miners of Musina and the Early History of the Zoutpansberg*, Pretoria.

C. K. Washbourn-Kamau, 1971. 'Late Quaternary lakes in the Nakuru-Elmenteita basin, Kenya', *G.J.* 137: 522–35.

R. G. Welbourne, 1973. 'Identification of animal remains from the Broederstroom 24/73 Early Iron Age site', *S.A.J.S.* 69: 325.

L. H. Wells, 1957. 'Late Stone Age human types in central Africa', *P.A.C.* 3: 183–5.

F. Wendorf (ed.), 1968. *The Prehistory of Nubia*, Dallas.

F. Wendorf, R. Said and R. Schild, 1970. 'Egyptian prehistory: some new concepts', *Science* 169: 1161–71.

W. E. Wendt, 1966. 'Two prehistoric archaeological sites in Egyptian Nubia', *Postilla* 102: 1–46.

W. E. Wendt, 1972. 'Preliminary report on an archaeological research programme in South West Africa', *Cimbebasia* B 2: 1–61.

A. Werner, 1915. 'The Bantu coast tribes of the East Africa Protectorate', *J.R.A.I.* 45: 326–54.

D. Whitehouse, 1970. 'Siraf: a mediaeval port on the Persian Gulf', *W.A.* 2: 141–58.

W. H. Whiteley, 1969. *Swahili: the Rise of a National Language*, London.

A. Whitty, 1957. 'The origins of the stone architecture of Zimbabwe', *P.A.C.* 3: 366–77.

A. Whitty, 1958a. 'An Iron Age site at Coronation Park near Salisbury', *S.A.A.B.* 13: 10–20.

A. Whitty, 1958b. 'An Iron Age cemetery near Salisbury Kopje', *O.P.N.M.S.R.* 2: 141–7.

T. Whitworth, 1965. 'Artefacts from Turkana', *S.A.A.B.* 20: 75–8.

H. A. Wieschoff, 1941. *The Zimbabwe-Monomotapa Culture in South-East Africa*, Menasha.

A. R. Willcox, 1956. *Rock Paintings of the Drakensberg*, London.

A. R. Willcox, 1957. 'A cave at Giant's Castle Game Reserve', *S.A.A.B.* 12: 87–97.

A. R. Willcox, 1963. *The Rock Art of South Africa*, Johannesburg.

A. R. Willcox, 1965. 'Petroglyphs of domestic animals', *S.A.A.B.* 20: 214.

A. R. Willcox, 1971a. 'Domestic cattle in Africa, and a rock-art mystery', *S.A.J.S.* special issue 2: 44–8.

A. R. Willcox, 1971b. 'Summary of Dr Edgar Denninger's reports on the ages of paint samples taken from rock paintings in South and South West Africa', *S.A.J.S.* special issue 2: 84–5.

M. A. J. Williams, 1971. 'Geomorphology and Quaternary geology of Adrar Bous', *G.J.* 137: 450–5.

M. A. J. Williams and D. A. Adamson, 1973. 'The physiography of the central Sudan', *G.J.* 139: 498–508.

J. Wilson, 1972. 'The use of stone hammers in the alteration of horn profile and the postulated origin of this and other customs in Ancient Egypt', *U.J.* 36: 57–65.

M. Wilson, 1969*a*. 'The hunters and herders', pp. 40–74 in Wilson and Thompson, 1969.

M. Wilson, 1969*b*. 'The Nguni people', pp. 75–130 in Wilson and Thompson, 1969.

M. Wilson, 1969*c*. 'The Sotho, Venda and Tsonga', pp. 131–82 in Wilson and Thompson, 1969.

M. Wilson, 1969*d*. 'Changes in social structure in southern Africa: the relevance of kinship studies to the historian', pp. 71–85 in L. Thompson (ed.), *African Societies in Southern Africa*, London.

M. Wilson and L. Thompson (eds.), 1969. *The Oxford History of South Africa, I*, Oxford.

W. Wolska-Conus, 1968. *Cosmas Indicopleustés, Topographie Chrétienne*, Paris.

J. Woodburn, 1968*a*. 'An introduction to Hadza ecology', pp. 49–55 in Lee and DeVore, 1968.

J. Woodburn, 1968*b*. 'Stability and flexibility in Hadza residential groupings', pp. 103–10 in Lee and DeVore, 1968.

R. Wright, 1961. 'A painted rockshelter on Mount Elgon', *P.P.S.* 27: 28–34.

C. C. Wrigley, 1958. 'Some thoughts on the Bacwezi', *U.J.* 22: 15–17.

J. Yellen and H. Harpending, 1972. 'Hunter-gatherer populations and archaeological inference', *W.A.* 4: 244–53.

E. M. van Zinderen Bakker, 1972. 'Late Quaternary lacustrine phases in the southern Sahara and East Africa', *P.A.* 6: 15–27.

E. M. van Zinderen Bakker and J. A. Coetzee, 1972. 'A re-appraisal of late Quaternary climatic evidence from tropical Africa', *P.A.* 7: 151–81.

Index